Becoming Agile

Becoming Agile

... IN AN IMPERFECT WORLD

GREG SMITH
AHMED SIDKY

MANNING

Greenwich
(74° w. long.)

For online information and ordering of this and other Manning books, please visit www.manning.com. The publisher offers discounts on this book when ordered in quantity. For more information, please contact

Special Sales Department
Manning Publications Co.
Sound View Court 3B   fax: (609) 877-8256
Greenwich, CT 06830   email: orders@manning.com

Manning Publications Co.   Development Editor: Nermina Miller
Sound View Court 3B   Copyeditor: Tiffany Taylor
Greenwich, CT 06830   Typesetter: Gordan Salinovic
                                      Cover designer: Leslie Haimes

ISBN 978-1-933988-25-2
Printed in the United States of America
1 2 3 4 5 6 7 8 9 10 – MAL – 14 13 12 11 10 09

brief contents

v

contents

foreword

Over the years I have seen a lot of software development organizations try to become agile. Some have succeeded beyond their wildest dreams and continue to improve to this day. But those are the exceptions. In a more typical scenario, agile development shows some initial success, but once the low-hanging fruit has been picked, it doesn't seem to deliver that much sustained value over time. The question is, why does sustained success from agile development seem to be so elusive?

I observe three reasons why agile initiatives seem to plateau:

First, agile development is frequently initiated as a grassroots movement to develop better software—it is seen as a "developer thing." Consequently, development managers and customer organizations are often not on board. This is a mistake, because dramatic improvements from agile development require a different mindset on the part of both development managers and the organizations for which the software is being developed.

Second, some companies have made serious missteps in applying agile—perhaps by developing an unmaintainable code base or creating an unsupportable set of expectations in the minds of development teams or customers. Sometimes an agile implementation follows a simple recipe that is a bad fit to the company needs; sometimes the implementation is perfect for some people in the company (developers, for instance), but it doesn't take into account the needs of others (testers, for example).

Finally, agile development might be considered a silver bullet—a quick and easy fix to problems that plague software development. In this case, the hard work required to make agile successful is ignored, and when companies come to the realization that agile is not going to be as easy as they anticipated, all too often commitment dissipates.

Initiating and sustaining an effective agile development program is a challenging journey. First, implementation should involve far more than the development team. A broad array of cross-functional impacts should be considered, not to mention the fact that agile might well require a different management approach. Second, the technical practices that agile brings to the table—short iterations, test-first development, continuous integration—are not optional. Ignore them or leave them until later at your own risk. Finally, nothing, not even agile development, will remove the inherent complexity of software development or its nonlinear escalation with size.

In *Becoming Agile*, Greg Smith and Ahmed Sidky lay out a path to agile software development that addresses the typical failure modes. First, they understand that no environment is perfect, and it is practically impossible to roll out a perfect agile process. To compensate for this reality, Greg and Ahmed suggest numerous ways of pursuing the agile principles within the constraints of your business. The book does not ask you to discard processes that have been successful for you; the authors realize your existing processes may have many positive aspects. They show you how to convene a cross-functional steering committee to guide the agile implementation so that it fits into your organization.

Second, since part of being agile is learning and adapting, Greg and Ahmed show you how to pilot the new approach. They explain how to select a pilot project and how to try out the new ideas and adapt them so they work in your context. Through an extended case study, they show what actually happened in agile deployments they have led. The case study also introduces real personas so you can see how different personality types react to a move to agile.

Finally, Greg and Ahmed dispel the notion that agile is a simple recipe that anyone can learn in a day with guaranteed success. Instead of offering a simple, foolproof formula, this book shows how to thoughtfully introduce agile into a company. After leading you through a readiness assessment to determine the most logical areas to introduce agile, Greg and Ahmed take you through assembling a cross-functional leadership team, identifying the best aspects of your current process, designing more adaptive processes, carefully choosing a pilot, trying and adapting the process, and gradually improving and expanding agile processes over time. This strikes me as a more likely approach to successfully evolve a new development process that fits the company.

The book is full of simple tools that will help people think clearly; it is about readiness, chartering, specifying, estimating, assuring quality, product demonstrations, retrospectives, and so on. By using an extended case study, Greg and Ahmed show you one example of a migration to agile, all the while pointing out other ways to accomplish the same objectives. Their book is neither a recipe nor a set of principles. It is a thoughtful, practical set of steps, presented with commentary and alternatives, about how to become agile. It will help you put together an agile development approach that matches your company needs and has a high likelihood of delivering sustained value over time.

MARY POPPENDIECK
PRESIDENT, POPPENDIECK, LLC

preface

In 2005 I began teaching an Agile Project Management course at Bellevue Community College. Although my students noted I was a bit "wordy," they appreciated the real-world case study I used for the course, based on my own agile experiences. I told the students I had created the course because most available agile training was based on perfect world explanations of agile practices and the creation of a pure agile environment. The case study used in the course showed what it was like to start *transitioning* to agile versus what it looked like *after* a team had been using agile for many years.

Positive student feedback made me wonder if a book on transitioning to agile would be of value to the software community. I began searching through the shelves of Barnes & Noble and through the inventory available on Amazon.com. I was surprised to see that very few books addressed agile migration, and I could not find any books that demonstrated what the process looked like from day one through the completion of a pilot project. Maybe it was time to find out if I had any writing skills!

Needless to say, Manning saw the value in the idea and helped me refine the concept. Manning also sought out experts in the agile community who provided unfiltered feedback on the first chapters of the book (reviewers, you were anonymous to us, but we want you to know we appreciate all of your feedback and we worked quite a bit of it into the book).

As I started writing the book I kept receiving feedback that I needed to discuss agility levels within an organization. Reviewers wanted a tool for assessing their ability to use agile and also for measuring their agility at the organization level, similar to the Capability Maturity Model Integration (CMMI). I was not an authority in the assessment field, so I sought out an expert and came across Ahmed Sidky, creator of the Sidky Agile Measurement Index (SAMI).

At first I just wanted permission to use Ahmed's assessment materials, but as we spoke more on the phone it felt like we were two lost agile brothers who had spent a lifetime apart. Although our software experiences were completely different, Ahmed and I were in synch with our core agile beliefs. So much so that Ahmed signed on to not only provide the assessment content, but also to coauthor and refine the book with me. He suggested great ways to organize the content and also provided insight into agile practices where my experience was light. His contribution was invaluable and helped take the book to another level.

I am proud of our final product and I hope our experiences do help others *become agile.*

GREG SMITH

acknowledgments

Writing this book has been an exciting journey that brought several incredible people into my life. I want to thank the entire team who helped with the book's structure, content, and presentation. First, thank you to Ahmed Sidky for your superb ideas on how to organize the book and for the superb content you provided. Your insights on agile adoption are groundbreaking, and I am honored to work with you. You are a great partner.

I also want to thank Michael Stephens of Manning for spending weeks working with me to convert a raw idea into a real book. Your guidance and feedback had a huge impact on the final product.

We also had a first-class review team for this book. Craig Smith provided solid technical proofreading and helped us enrich the content for different perspectives. Nermina Miller was the main editor and provided great guidance for connecting with the reader. You are the best, Nermina!

The final edit team also put the book through several reviews to improve continuity, wording, grammar, and flow. Tiffany Taylor, Linda Recktenwald, and Katie Tennant may need a vacation after correcting all of our typos. Director of Production, Mary Piergies, did an excellent job of coordinating all of our work and getting the book into print.

And of course, thank you to Publisher Marjan Bace for taking on this book and sticking with it as it went down various paths and side roads on the way to final copy.

I would also like to thank all of the people who have shaped my ideas about software development throughout my career. Joe Woodmancy, thank you for my first commercial software job. You were a great mentor and provided sound guidance on application development. Jim Highsmith, you have influenced me more than any other person. The first class I took from you opened my eyes and allowed me to start enjoying software projects again. Thank you for the great training and inspiration you have provided to me. Mary Poppendieck, thank you for providing the foreword and for pioneering new discoveries and insights in the agile community. I am always learning something new from your work.

Thank you also to all the reviewers who took time out of their busy schedules to read our manuscript in different stages during its development. Your feedback was invaluable. Thanks to John C. Tyler, Robi Sen, Randy Miller, Andrew Siemer, Tariq Ahmed, Bernard Farrell, Bruno Lowagie, Carlo Bottiglieri, Paul King, Mike Tian-Jian Jiang, Federico Tomassetti, Robert Dempsey, Patrick Debois, Doug Warren, Horaci Mcias, Daniel Alford, Amr Elssamadisy, Dave Corun, Bas Vodde, Vincent Yin, Valentin Crettaz, Marco Ughetti, Darren Neimke, Hannu Terävä, Eric Raymond, Jason Kolter, Christopher Haupt, Robert Hanson, Dusty Jewett, and Christian Siegers.

Lastly, I thank my family. Thanks to my parents, Darrell and Eva, for providing unconditional support for whatever endeavor I have pursued. Thanks to my wife, Peggy, who continued to provide support even after we discovered what it really means to write a book. And finally, a thank you to my daughter, Lauren, for listening to me go on and on about agile for years. Although only 10 years old, Lauren now has the skills necessary to lead any company in its move to agile.

GREG SMITH

First and foremost, I am grateful and thankful to Allah, who blessed me with guidance, health, family, and friends who supported me and helped me through the writing of this book. I am especially forever grateful to my sisters and beloved parents, Samy and Hoda, who supported me and encouraged me through every step of my life to reach where I am today. I am very fortunate to have been blessed with an amazing and supportive wife, Noura, who has felt both the pain and joy of this book. Thank you, Noura, for your love and enthusiasm, and I hope you are ready for my next book.

This book could not have happened without the hard work and dedication of my dear friend and coauthor Greg Smith. I really enjoyed working with him and thank him for his patience and perseverance.

AHMED SIDKY

about this book

You may be wondering if there is a need for another book on agile. We have dozens of books on Extreme Programming and Scrum. Areas such as retrospectives, Test Driven Development, and estimating have been covered well. It seems every subject has been thoroughly discussed. However, one area that still does not have a lot of coverage is the actual process of adopting agile. You may find all of the information you need related to agile practices, but you may have a hard time finding information on how to go from your existing process to an agile one.

The authors have created this book in the hope of providing more information on what it takes to move to a more agile process. We have taken all of our migration experiences and rolled them into this book to help you with your own agile adoption. To make the adoption steps even more tangible, we have created a case study that is an amalgamation of our experiences. As you follow the case study, you will be reviewing actual situations that we encountered during migrations and how the companies we worked with dealt with constraints and cultural change. Real company names are not used, but the events are real.

Our case study also helps you envision working with different personality types and experience levels during a migration to agile. We will introduce several personas at the start of the pilot project, and you will see how the personas react to the process and cultural changes of an agile environment.

The approach we outline in this book is based on five key observations we have made:

- Moving to agile is not a straightforward process. Every organization has unique constraints it must address.
- Adopting agile can be risky and even harmful if done incorrectly.
- Many teams try to use popular agile practices before they are ready for them. They believe they "are not agile" if they are not using techniques such as Test Driven Development or Pair Programming.
- Many teams rush to adopt agile practices without properly embracing the agile values and principles. They assume "that's how we become agile."
- Many teams start from scratch when moving to agile, discarding legacy practices that may have been effective and valuable in their environment.

We address these five discoveries with the following approach.

First, we understand the realities of constraints within a company. We have witnessed agile constraints such as

- Distributed teams
- The need to support production operations in parallel with projects
- Compliance and regulatory constraints
- Limited employee experience
- Limited customer availability
- And many more

To support these realities we will walk you through a process of reviewing your existing process and performing an assessment/survey of your company culture and maturity. This process will allow you to identify many barriers before you begin your migration, and you can make an informed decision about which constraints to accept and which ones to challenge as you move to agile.

Second, we have witnessed the risks associated with moving to agile. We have seen product delivery jeopardized, and we have seen employees become upset with a change to the development process.

To minimize these risks we will guide you through a process that involves the development team in the migration. Any concerns the team has with the new process will be taken into account because the team will be involved in creating the new agile process for your company. Involving the team will also help you create an agile lifecycle that should flourish in your environment. Your team is closest to the work, and they will know how things work today and in which areas a change could introduce high risk.

Related to the third observation and the desire to use popular practices, the assessment tool we provide will help you determine which practices the team, company, and customer can support. We will not encourage you to pursue the most trendy or popular practices. Instead we will ask you to select practices that add value for your situation.

Concerning the fourth item and the desire to become agile overnight, we have seen many companies try to shotgun agile in, attempting to get through the pain as quickly as possible. While there are situations where this makes sense, it can be a risky approach. Instead we will walk you through an iterative process for bringing agile into your organization. We will guide you through developing and piloting an agile process that meets your needs, and we will provide a system for maintaining, improving, and sustaining the lifecycle over time.

Lastly, concerning starting from scratch, if you are a startup, or if your company is very dysfunctional, it may make sense to start from scratch and throw away everything you currently do. However, if you have significant experience with your company, you probably have some practices that add value, and these practices may continue to add value as you move to agile. In many cases it will not make sense to discard everything you do today.

Our hope is that we can show you how to make your team and organization become as agile as possible within your current constraints.

Roadmap

- Chapter 1 discusses why agile is a better development process. The chapter also ties agile to the two most important factors for most companies: increasing revenue and lowering costs.

- Chapter 2 introduces our case study and the circumstances that have added urgency to its projects. The chapter also provides an example of a company going from no agility, to medium-level agility, to high agility.

- Chapter 3 discusses the ability for any company to increase its agility and how you can become agile within your constraints.

- Chapter 4 kicks off our approach for becoming agile. We will walk you through a process of assessing your ability to use each agile practice.

- Chapter 5 builds on the assessment from chapter 4. Now that you have an understanding of your ability to become agile, you will pursue executive support within your company. You will also follow along as our case study pursues executive support and obtains an executive sponsor.

- Chapter 6 discusses the selection of the "core team." This core team is made up of project team members and includes agile supporters, agile detractors, and people on the fence. Working with their coach, the core team will determine which agile practices to pilot.

- Chapter 7 talks about the agile mindset and how managers need to shift to more of a coaching role as the team matures.

- Chapter 8 focuses on designing a development process that works for a specific environment. Acme Media's core team will document their existing process and compare it to an agile process. The core team will then document modifications to the existing process to make it more agile. This new process will be piloted on a test project.

- Chapter 9 walks you through the process of identifying a pilot project to test your new, more agile process. We will provide guidelines for how to select a pilot project based on size, scope, and priority.

- Chapter 10 starts the pilot project. Acme Media will analyze the pilot to verify it is feasible. The feasibility work answers two questions: (1) is the project technically possible? and (2) is there truly a market/need for this project?

- Chapter 11 shows the selection of the project team members who will perform the pilot. The pilot team will go through an exercise of chartering and alignment to reach a clear understanding on the project benefits and objectives. Chartering will also expose the main features of the pilot.

- Chapter 12 explains feature cards and how Acme Media learns to create the correct level of requirements throughout the project. Historically Acme Media has created detailed specifications before work begins. Feature cards will require a change in mindset.

- Chapter 13 follows Acme Media as it more clearly defines and prioritizes features for the project. The features are prioritized by business value and risk.

- Chapter 14 introduces Acme Media to a new approach on early estimation: estimating for relative size versus identifying tasks and trying to map out the project hour by hour. The work in this chapter is based on the story-point process that Mike Cohn promotes in his book *Agile Estimating and Planning*.

- Chapter 15 leads Acme Media through the process of creating an overall release/project schedule. Iterations are identified, and the team compares capacity to estimates to determine what features will be initially targeted for each iteration.

- Chapter 16 follows Acme Media through detailed iteration planning. The team will identify the tasks for each feature in iteration 1 and verify that they can commit to the features that were assigned during release planning. The team will also create a burndown chart to support daily meetings and transparency of iteration status.

- Chapter 17 covers iteration 0, the time needed to get foundational pieces of the project in place before development begins. This includes environment preparation, finalization of funding, and negotiation of contracts with vendors or partners that may be needed for the project.

- Chapter 18 follows Acme Media through the first iteration of development. The team will begin designing, coding, refining, testing, and delivering features in the 10 working days allocated for the iteration. The team will focus on early testing and integration of features to identify requirement gaps or technical issues as soon as possible.

- Chapter 19 covers the different types of testing in an agile environment. These include unit, integration functional, exploratory, and usability testing. We also focus on identifying tests that can be automated to speed up the build process.

- Chapter 20 is about adapting during and after an iteration. This chapter, more than any other, demonstrates what it is like to work in an agile environment and respond successfully to discoveries during a project. The chapter also discusses customer demonstrations and validating status via the measurement of working code.

- Chapter 21 focuses on aggregating iterations and releasing them to a production environment. We discuss important areas such as determining when quality is good enough for releasing and validation of nonfunctional requirements.
- Chapter 22 is about project retrospectives. We identify the common issues with retrospectives and walk you through a process that optimizes the use of everyone's time. We also follow Acme Media through a retrospective and provide templates and guides that you can use during your retrospectives.
- Chapter 23 is about "what's next?" We review what Acme Media learned from its pilot and discuss what it takes to go from project-level agile adoption to enterprise-level adoption. We also introduce the Sidky Agile Measurement Index (SAMI). The SAMI highlights five agile value levels or steps and guides organizations in introducing the practices that satisfy each step.

About the graphics

Most of the photos and illustrations in this book were created by the authors or obtained via stock photos, unless otherwise noted. Several graphics and photos have been reduced to fit the format of this book. You can view and download many of the graphics in full size from the publisher's website: www.manning.com/BecomingAgile.

Author Online

The purchase of *Becoming Agile* includes free access to a private forum run by Manning Publications where you can make comments about the book, ask technical questions, and receive help from the authors and other users. To access and subscribe to the forum, point your browser to www.manning.com/BecomingAgile or www.manning.com/smith. This page provides information on how to get on the forum once you are registered, what kind of help is available, and the rules of conduct in the forum.

Manning's commitment to our readers is to provide a venue where a meaningful dialogue between individual readers and between readers and the authors can take place. It's not a commitment to any specific amount of participation on the part of the authors, whose contribution to the book's forum remains voluntary (and unpaid). We suggest you try asking them some challenging questions, lest their interest stray!

The Author Online forum and the archives of previous discussions will be accessible from the publisher's website as long as the book is in print.

about the cover illustration

The figure on the cover of *Becoming Agile* is "un Fauconnier" or a falconer, taken from a compendium of French dress customs published in Paris between 1835 and 1839. The four-volume collection is entitled *Costumes Français depuis Clovis jusqu'a nos jours* and consists of hand-colored engraved plates, many heightened with gilt.

The lithographs from this collection, like the other illustrations that appear on our covers, bring to life the richness and variety of dress customs of two centuries ago. Dress codes have changed since then and the diversity by region, so rich at the time, has faded away. It is now often hard to tell the inhabitant of one continent from another, not to mention a country or region. Perhaps, trying to view it optimistically, we have traded a cultural and visual diversity for a more varied personal life. Or a more varied and interesting intellectual and technical life.

We at Manning celebrate the inventiveness, the initiative, and, yes, the fun of the computer business with book covers based on the rich diversity of regional life of long ago—brought back to life by the pictures from collections such as this one.

Part 1

Agile fundamentals and a supporting case study

The following two chapters will provide a foundation for understanding what agile is and introduce a case study that we will use throughout the book. Chapter one will discuss the origins of agile and contrast agile to traditional software development practices. Chapter one also focuses on correlating agile to the two most important goals for many companies: making money and holding down costs.

Chapter two will introduce you to our case study, Acme Media. Acme Media has business needs that are driving it to become more agile. They have not delivered software very well in the past, and there has not been urgency surrounding their projects. This has all changed with the rise of online advertising. The team needs to learn how to deliver valuable software quickly, else their customers will shift to their competitors.

Moving to agile

The tragedy started when the crew accidentally bored into an adjacent, abandoned mine that was flooded with water. The miners' map told them, incorrectly, that the abandoned mine was hundreds of yards away. The men scrambled to reach the exit, but the rising water blocked the way out. Their only option was to seek out the highest point in the mine.

Word of the accident spread above ground and a rescue team was formed. The rescue team estimated where the crew was located in the mine and picked a spot to drill. Maps revealed a gas line that ran close to the target drilling point; and if their coordinates were incorrect, they might rupture the line and create an explosion. Being careful to avoid the gas line, the team began drilling a small, exploratory hole. After 90 minutes the drill broke through the wall of the tunnel, and the rescuers listened anxiously for any sounds from the miners. After minutes of sobering silence, the rescuers could hear the trapped men pounding on the drill bit with their hammers. The miners had been located. Now the challenge was to get them out of the mine before hypothermia set in.

The rescue team outlined a two-part plan. First, they would drill additional holes to help pump water from the mine. Second, they would use a "super drill" to create a 2-foot-wide escape tunnel for the miners. The drilling work began without a hitch, but then the super drill bit broke 105 feet below the surface. A special "fishing" tool was needed to extract the bit. In the past it had taken 3 days to build such a tool. The rescuers knew they did not have 3 days to get to the miners out.

Rescue workers contacted Frank Stockdale, the plant manager at Star Iron Works, and asked him to build the tool they needed. They faxed engineering prints to Stockdale and explained the dire situation to him. Using his 95-member machine shop, Stockdale was able to reduce a 3-day job to 3 hours. The rescue team then removed the broken bit and resumed drilling the rescue tunnel.

Finally, 78 hours after the tragedy began, the drill penetrated the shaft and the drill operator shouted with joy. The last miner was pulled to safety 5 hours later from the Quecreek Mine in Somerset County, Pennsylvania on July 28, 2002. After being trapped 240 feet below the surface, and with body temperatures as low as 92.5 Fahrenheit, they would all make full recoveries (see figure 1.1).

You may wonder why a software development book starts with a story about a mining rescue. If you've performed agile software development previously, you've probably identified the parallels. Let's look at a few.

All software projects have constraints. Similar to the situation during the Quecreek rescue, the number-one constraint is frequently *time*. The Quecreek rescue team had a few days to reach the miners. Software projects are often limited to a few days, weeks,

Figure 1.1   A Quecreek miner is rescued from the flooded mine after spending 3 days crouched in waist-deep water. (Photo courtesy of the U.S. Department of Labor.)

or months, after which they're of no value. Like a Sunday newspaper delivered on Monday, all the quality work and effort invested in the project are worthless if you don't meet your most critical priority.

The rescue project also had a clear vision of the primary project priority: to reach the miners while they were still alive. A secondary priority was to reach them before they got hypothermia, and a third priority was to reach them before they started losing consciousness due to hunger. The team focused on delivering the number-one priority first.

When you perform software projects, you can lose track of your priorities, things can get muddy, and low-value work can hold up project delivery. Agile software development asks you to follow the Quecreek model by identifying what is critical and focusing on delivering to meet the critical need as soon as possible.

Quecreek also reinforces another agile tenet: you should expect change, you should embrace change, and you should be ready to plan and adapt frequently. The Quecreek rescuers adapted to broken drill bits, gas lines blocking their path, and the need to reduce the time required to create a fishing device. In software development, you encounter similar situations. You discover a missing requirement, you identify a technical constraint that prevents you from following your initial design, or a third party delivers their part of the project later than expected. These types of issues happen on every software project; and to ensure success, agile asks you not to be surprised but to continue to perform by adapting to the reality of the situation.

Finally, the Quecreek rescue demonstrated goodwill and collaborative team work. Ideas came from all team members, such as the suggestion to try positive air pressure to keep the water at bay. Goodwill and collaboration were also demonstrated when the rescue team approached Frank Stockdale and asked if he could create the fishing tool. Stockdale didn't ask the rescuers to spend days creating a contract and going through legal papers; instead, he trusted the rescue team and quickly delivered the fishing device.

Agile development depends on this type of relationship with customers and vendors. You want a vendor who is a partner, not a vendor who is considered the enemy because you spend more time talking about contracts than ensuring the delivery of value.

In this chapter, we'll help you understand the need for agile practices, what agile really is, and how agile contrasts to plan-driven development practices. We'll conclude the chapter by discussing the most important consideration when pursuing a development process: how does agile correlate to the most common corporate goal of increasing revenue and reducing expenses?

1.1 Is Agile just another process?

Many people may think that agile is just another software development process. Although that is true to a degree, there is a lot more to agile than just a process or just a set of practices. Agile (or agility) is more of a mindset—a way of thinking about software development. This agile mindset can be applied to any process using any set of practices. The best way to illustrate our understanding of agile is through figure 1.2.

Today the market is moving quickly, and as a result, the software development lifecycle needs to be flexible enough to enable organizations to seize new and emerging market opportunities before their competitors do. To reach the desired ability to respond to constant change, your software process needs to focus on what is truly important.

Similar to the way you pack light when you're going to backpack around Europe, your process needs to be light. You need to increase everything in the process that adds value to the end goal and decrease everything that doesn't add value. Agile values attempt to highlight what adds value in a software development process.

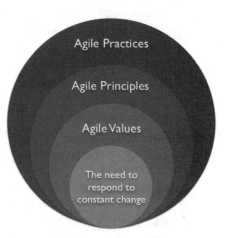

Figure 1.2   The relationship between agile values, principles, and practices

1.1.1   *The Agile Manifesto and related values*

In 2001, a group of authors wrote a document called the *Manifesto for Agile Software Development,* with a goal of identifying the values that yield the most benefit to a software development process. Let's look at the manifesto, which is available online at http://agilemanifesto.org/:

> *We are uncovering better ways of developing software by doing it and helping others do it. Through this work we have come to value:*
>
> - *Individuals and interactions over processes and tools*
> - *Working software over comprehensive documentation*
> - *Customer collaboration over contract negotiation*
> - *Responding to change over following a plan*
>
> *That is, while there is value in the items on the right, we value the items on the left more.*

When people first read the manifesto they immediately agree with the stated values or they hesitate. The hesitation usually comes from the perception that an agile methodology throws away the items on the right (processes, tools, documentation, contracts, and planning). This is completely false. The manifesto is saying that the items on the right do add value to the development process but the items on the left (interaction between individuals, developing working software, and so on) provide *more* value to the process. The manifesto is trying to point out that organizations traditionally put a huge emphasis on the items on the right, such as processes and tools, and neglect the items on the left, such as the interaction between individuals. An agile mindset promotes the items on the left while maintaining the level required for the items on the right. Let us re-emphasize that an agile process can and sometime should contain some of the items on the right; but you need to make sure that each of those items adds indispensible value to the project.

1.1.2   *The agile principles*

Moving to the layer that surrounds agile values in figure 1.2, let's consider the agile principles. The *Manifesto for Agile Software Development* defines a set of 12 principles that represent the characteristics or inherent traits of an agile process:

1   *Our highest priority is to satisfy the customer through early and continuous delivery of valuable software.*   As obvious as this principle may seem, it's often violated in traditional software development. It's important to remember that customers are asking you to deliver working software that adds value; they don't want a prototype or a set of documents. The earlier you can start delivering working software, the earlier you can begin satisfying your customer.

2   *Welcome changing requirements, even late in development.*   Agile processes harness change for the customer's competitive advantage. Your customers are competing in a dynamic market, and therefore they may have to change the requirements for their software in order to gain a competitive advantage. It is important to note that you should welcome changing requirements, but no one said this change is free.

3   *Deliver working software frequently, from a couple of weeks to a couple of months, with a preference to the shorter timescale.*   Have you ever shown your customer software for the first time and received no feedback? In most cases, you receive feedback—sometimes minor, but usually major. The trick is to deliver software early so that you can get feedback early. This early feedback can save you re-work down the road.

4   *Business people and developers must work together daily throughout the project.*   This principle is careful to say *business people* and not the *customer.* In most cases, it would be impractical to work with the customer on a daily basis; but generally there are multiple business proxies. These proxies may not know everything about the customer's wants and needs, but they usually know more about the business needs than the developers do. These proxies may be analysts, product managers, or program managers. The key is to maintain constant communication between the developers and the business people to ensure that the project never goes off track—not even for a day.

5   *Build projects around motivated individuals.*   Give them the environment and support they need, and trust them to get the job done. Remember, people aren't resources. Software development is different from manufacturing. Software development is more of an art. Project teams need to be motivated and trusted. If you have motivated team members they will find a way to give you their best; and that's what an agile process needs—everyone's best.

6 *The most efficient and effective method of conveying information to and within a development team is face-to-face conversation.* Instant messaging or the telephone should never replace face-to-face communication. A lot of context is lost in communication over email and instant messaging—not to mention the fact that ambiguity increases with nonverbal communication. Face-to-face communication also lets you run with less formal documentation.

7 *Working software is the primary measure of progress.* If you recall, the customer is primarily interested in working software. So why would you measure progress in terms of anything else? Today, the progress of most software development efforts is measured in terms of their plan. When requirements are complete, the managers say the project is 30 percent complete. In a plan-driven world, this may be correct; but in a value-driven world, where the value is the working software, the project is 30 percent complete when 30 percent of the required functionality is coded, integrated, tested, and deployed. This is a fundamental difference between the agile value-driven world and the traditional plan-driven world.

8 *Agile processes promote sustainable development.* The sponsors, developers, and users should be able to maintain a constant pace indefinitely. In traditional development, the team often has to work late toward the end of a project, although at the beginning of the project they may have taken 2-hour lunch breaks. This is primarily due to the way project activities are distributed across the project's lifecycle. There isn't much for developers to do at the beginning of the project, but at the end everything is put on their shoulders because of tight delivery schedules. With agile development, you deliver every two weeks or so, and development begins with the first iteration. Efforts are distributed more consistently throughout the project lifecycle, which leads to a constant development pace for the team.

9 *Continuous attention to technical excellence and good design enhances agility.* A successful gymnast needs strong muscles. Similarly, technical excellence is an essential enabler for a truly agile software development process. For example, extensible designs and architectures make it much easier to build the product in an evolutionary manner. Automated testing frameworks are needed to ensure that refactoring one part of the system doesn't affect other parts. Continuous integration is essential if you want assurance that your software is working after every change.

10 *Simplicity—the art of maximizing the amount of work not done—is essential.* No code means no bugs. The more code you write, the more bugs your code may have. If something isn't essential to the product, then don't build it. Some developers tend to develop massive underlying frameworks and infrastructures in the system under the assumption that those elements may be needed in the future. The key is simplicity: try not to develop anything that isn't essential to the features you're developing now. Remember, the more time you invest in anything, the more you get attached to it. This attachment makes it harder to accept the fact that you don't need a piece of code or that you need to change it.

11 *The best architectures, requirements, and designs emerge from self-organizing teams.* In traditional software development, analysts write requirements, and architects lay out the architecture of the system. Then the requirements and architectures are communicated to the team in a document. In the agile world, we encourage teams to self-organize. True self-organization involves giving the whole team the task and asking them, as a team, to complete the task without specifying who should do what—they're left to self-organize. It will naturally occur that architects will lead the discussion when it comes to architecture, but now everyone is free to challenge them and suggest new ideas that may enhance the architecture the architects would have come up with on their own. This form of collaboration also increases the knowledge transfer within the team.

12 *At regular intervals, the team reflects on how to become more effective, then tunes and adjusts its behavior accordingly.* We believe this is probably the most important principle of agility. The idea of always reflecting on what you're doing and trying to figure out better ways to do things is the essence of continuous improvement. Without continuous improvement, people and organizations remain at a status quo. If you adopt only one thing that will make your process better, regularly reflect on your process as a team. You need to identify what you're doing well and continue doing it, and you need to identify what you're doing poorly and improve it.

1.1.3 *The agile practices*

The last layer in figure 1.2 represents the agile practices. These are activities that are used to manifest or implement the agile principles and values. There are numerous agile practices, such as user stories, test-driven development, pair programming, daily stand-up meetings, and so forth. But no specific set of agile practices is defined—it's anti-agile to say that there is a defined set of practices and that no new practices can be created. Organizations create different agile practices or tailor existing agile practices to address specific organizational or team needs. Teams may also need to be creative and come up with new agile practices to achieve agility while adhering to organizational constraints.

Known agile development methodologies like Extreme Programming (XP), Scrum, Lean, and Feature Driven Development (FDD) consist of a set of agile practices that have a certain synergy. Some methodologies, like Scrum, focus more on agile practices related to project management; others, like XP, focus more on technical agile practices. *No methodology is better than the other; it all depends which works best in your environment and within your constraints.* Better yet, in this book, we won't talk about a certain methodology: we'll talk about a generic set of agile practices and then show how you can customize the practices to fit your organization.

1.2   *A paradigm shift from a plan-driven mentality*

Traditionally, once a project starts, a requirements package is created and then is "signed off." The project manager assumes that this sign-off results in a fixed set of requirements and that now planning can begin. The project manager estimates how long it will take to complete the requirements and creates the project plan. The plan predicts that the project will be finished by a certain date, and that date is communicated back to the customer.

The fundamental flaw in this approach is that the plan, which drives everything, is based on an assumption that the requirements are fixed and won't change. Experience has shown us that this is never the case; requirements are never fixed—they always change. When the requirements change, the plan is affected; and as a result, the completion date needs to change too. Unfortunately, in many cases, that is impossible, and the team *has* to deliver by the date they committed to. This is when a major crisis occurs and the project starts to go out of control.

The value-driven agile approach switches the whole mindset. It assumes from the start that whatever requirements exist up front are *not* fixed and that they *will* change. The agile mindset also assumes that you have to deliver by a certain date. This approach fixes the time and resources and leaves the requirements undetermined. To us, this approach more closely resembles the reality of creating software. Now the whole notion of *value-driven* makes perfect sense. When you have a fixed amount of time in which you aren't sure whether you can deliver all the requirements (because they will change and hence the time needed to finish them will change), the natural reaction is to prioritize the requirements and finish first those that add the most value to the customer.

You may be thinking, "What about the requirements that aren't finished by the delivery date?" That is the reason you use the value-driven approach. You acknowledge the fact that not all of the requirements will be completed by the delivery date. The important question to ask is whether you have delivered enough features to support a system that provides value to the customer.

Figure 1.3 shows an interesting finding from a study by the Standish Group. Only 20 percent of the features in a system are often or always used; 45 percent of the features are never used. Another study showed that when a new system was installed at DuPont, only 25 percent of the system's features were really needed. The important point we're trying to emphasize is that if you can deliver, say, 35 percent of the features by the delivery date, you may be giving the customer all the value they're looking to attain from the system.

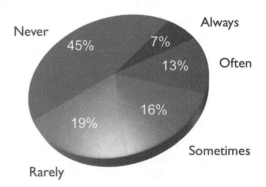

Figure 1.3 A study by the Standish Group indicates how often features are used in a typical application.

The traditional plan-based approach isn't flawed in and of itself; it just isn't suitable for today's software industry. The plan-based approach was originally based on traditional project management concepts, which originated from the construction industry. In the construction industry, the plan-based approach is suitable: the blueprints, which are the requirements, are fixed and probably won't change while the building is being built. You can estimate how long it will take to build the steel pillars, pour the concrete, and so forth.

The reason why the traditional plan-based approach is suitable for the construction industry but not for the software industry comes back to the difference in the way we control empirical systems (like software development) and the way we control defined systems (like construction or manufacturing). Table 1.1 shows the differences between the characteristics of a defined process and those of an empirical process.

Table 1.1   Comparison between a defined process and an empirical process

Predictable manufacturing (defined process)	New product development (empirical process)
It's possible to first complete specifications and then build.	It's rarely possible to create up-front, unchanging, detailed specs.
Near the beginning, you can reliably estimate effort and cost.	Near the beginning, it isn't possible to reliably estimate effort and cost. As empirical data emerge, it becomes increasingly possible to plan and estimate.
It's possible to identify, define, schedule, and order all the detailed activities at the start of the project.	Near the beginning, it isn't possible to identify, define, schedule, and order activities. Adaptive steps driven by build-feedback cycles are required.
Adaptation to unpredictable change isn't the norm, and change rates are relatively low.	Creative adaptation to unpredictable change is the norm. Change rates are high.

After reading the table, it's easy to see that software development is definitely an empirical process, not a defined process. The problem is that we've been approaching software development for years as a defined process—and that approach doesn't work.

1.3   Agile and the bottom line

If you're an executive, you may wonder whether agile can provide any value for what matters: the company's bottom line. If agile can't help you make money and reduce costs, is it worth pursuing? Most companies would say, "no, we don't need agile if it doesn't help us make money." Thankfully, agile does tie directly to the bottom line. To see the financial correlation, let's start by looking at statistics related to agile adoption.

In 2007, VersionOne, a leading provider of agile management tools, surveyed 1,700 people in 71 countries. All the participants were using agile to some extent in their companies. VersionOne asked the participants to identify specific improvements they had realized from implementing agile practices; see figure 1.4.

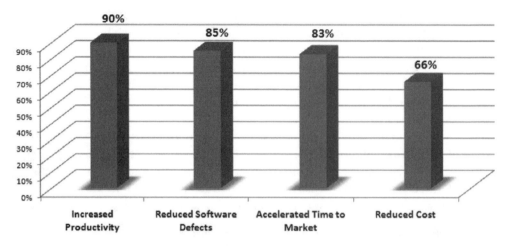

Figure 1.4   Teams that use agile attest to the benefits.

VersionOne's data shows that agile does help in key areas related to software development, with increased productivity, fewer defects, quicker time to market, and reduced costs. We have witnessed similar results with the companies we've helped move to agile.

The VersionOne survey provides proof that agile worked for most of the companies interviewed, but the main question for most people remains: "Will agile help my specific company with my specific situation?" Agile will help your company if you have changing requirements and a need to deliver functioning software frequently. If your requirements rarely change and you have the luxury of delivering when you feel the product is satisfactory, then you may not obtain the full benefits recorded in VersionOne's survey. (Note that we've never worked for any companies where this was true.)

It's valuable to see how well agile has worked for others, but the most important thing is how agile correlates to the bottom line. How does agile help you to increase revenue and/or reduce costs?

To increase revenue and profits indefinitely, your company must identify the key objectives that ensure success within your business environment. These objectives will vary depending on your customers, your competition, and your product market. But almost all companies list the following five items among their key objectives:

1   *Customer retention*—Retaining customers is key for almost all businesses. An existing customer provides continuous revenue and spreads the word to other potential customers, leading to increased revenues.

2   *Accurate delivery*—To be successful, you need to understand the needs of your market. You must deliver what the customer needs, or satisfaction will decline and revenues will go down.

3 *Innovation*—Not only must you help customers address their known needs, you must also anticipate their future needs. Innovative companies solve problems that their customers don't realize they have.

4 *Timely delivery*—Similar to the Sunday newspaper analogy at the start of the chapter, you must deliver while the need still exists.

5 *Motivated workforce*—As the poet Hebbel noted, "Nothing great in the world has ever been accomplished without passion." Executives know their development teams need to be passionate about their projects; otherwise, the projects and the company will remain mediocre.

If these are the strategic objectives, then what principles do companies follow to obtain these objectives? We believe the following agile principles should be pursued:

1 *Embrace change.*   The world is volatile, and many discoveries occur during any development project. You'll discover missing requirements, business needs may change, or you may encounter a technical constraint. The goal is to succeed, not to make excuses. A good development team adapts and delivers in the face of adversity.

2 *Plan and deliver software frequently.*   To ensure customer satisfaction and timely delivery, you must work with customers and prioritize their needs. After the needs are prioritized, the team works to deliver the functionality iteratively, starting with the minimal features necessary to deploy a working system.

3 *Use human-centric methods.*   Don't abandon practices and disciplines, but put more focus on individuals and interactions. Your focus should be on collaboration and communication. Productive teams have frequent face-to-face interaction, minimizing delays due to email chains or the need to formally schedule meetings.

4 *Achieve technical excellence.* You want processes that enhance quality during development. Solid development processes ensure delivery of a quality product and do wonders for team morale and pride.

5 *Engage in customer collaboration.*   To ensure timely delivery, you must be as efficient as possible when you develop. To be efficient, you require frequent feedback and customer interaction to validate that you're delivering to the need. Real-time customer collaboration also minimizes the effort required to adjust your work. You can't wait for testing: you need feedback on your understanding of the requirements, on your design thoughts, on your prototypes, and on your code as you iteratively deliver it.

We believe these five principles are the foundation for successfully moving to agile. Figure 1.5 illustrates the relationship between agile principles, company strategies, and the ultimate goal.

We'll reference and use these principles as we work through a case study that follows a company called Acme Media during its migration to agile. (We'll introduce this

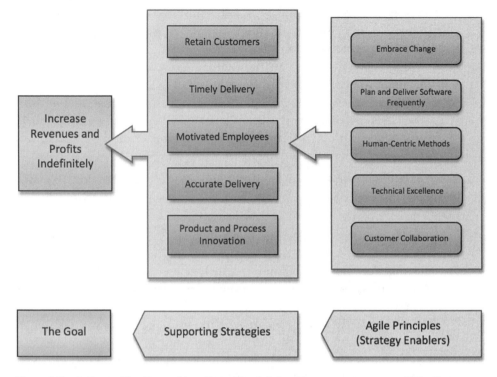

Figure 1.5   Agile provides the enablers that ultimately lead to company success. (This diagram was inspired by the Strategic Intermediate Objectives Map H. William Dettmer discusses in *The Logical Thinking Process*, American Society for Quality, *2nd Edition 2007*.)

case study in chapter 2.) Before we delve into the details, let's spend a moment discussing how this book can help you with your own move to agile.

1.4   *How this book will help you become more agile*

We've helped several companies become more agile. Greg has been in the United States helping the companies he worked for and the students who take his course at Bellevue Community College. Ahmed has been helping companies all over the world, some as an employee and others as an agile coach/consultant. We have nothing in common in terms of personal experiences, but amazingly we agree on the best way to bring agile into an organization. We believe that using a single flavor or approach to migrate to agile doesn't make sense—each company needs to approach its migration uniquely.

We believe the following five steps can ensure your success in your own unique move to agile:

  1 *Assess your potential for becoming agile.*   We'll provide an assessment tool that will help you identify potential risks. The assessment will also help you determine which agile practices you are ready for.

2 *Ensure company buy-in.*   We'll walk you through the steps for obtaining executive management, line management, and team support, ultimately leading the team to ownership of the process.

3 *Understand your current process.*   We'll walk you through reviewing your existing process and making sure it's clearly understood before you try to change it. We'll help you identify your constraints and become agile within them.

4 *Pilot a more agile process.*   We'll walk you through the process of selecting, conducting, and evaluating an agile pilot project.

5 *Perform a retrospective.*   We'll show you a solid approach for reviewing, maintaining, enhancing, and scaling a more agile process across your company.

In effect, we're trying to put all of our migration experience into this book and provide a virtual consultant to help you along the way.

The need for agile today: a story from Greg

A few years ago, I worked for a major financial institution. Interest rates were low, and business was booming. We spent a lot of money on extravagant meetings, everyone was paid well, and almost everyone had a Blackberry. We planned projects for the long term, looking to package in as much functionality as we could. Projects could run 2 or 3 years.

We also went overboard on ensuring that we were compliant with a formal project-management lifecycle. Huge groups were dedicated to making sure we followed the process, even if the process overhead marginalized project benefits. Project managers were located in a project-management office and received one-off assignments. A good portion of project time was devoted to project-team members acclimating to each other.

In 2007, my company was hit by the subprime mortgage crisis. Suddenly the Blackberries started disappearing. A group was formed to simplify our project-management process. The goal was to remove bureaucracy and make the process more agile and lean. The company also disbanded many of the project-management offices and put the project managers directly into the business teams so they could be closer to the customer.

A large project I was helping with was restructured. Instead of trying to deliver mega-benefits 2 years down the road, we outlined an iterative plan to deliver critical, minimal functionality within a few months.

My company lacked a sense of urgency when I started working there, but suddenly we were similar to a dotcom. We were fighting for survival, and we began to follow practices that supported the urgency. Looking back, I wish my company had pursued an agile mentality to prevent the issues in the first place as opposed to trying to use agile to save the ship.

1.5   Key points to remember

Here are the key points to remember from this chapter:

- Agile provides solid business values for almost every company.
- Agile isn't a trend. After 9 years and proven results, agile is here to stay.
- You must understand the principles behind the agile practices first, and then apply the practices accordingly.
- Software product development is unpredictable and requires creative adaptation to be successful.
- Agile methods tie directly to the key objectives of most companies: increasing revenue/market share while lowering costs.
- Migrating to agile is unique for each company. This book will help you approach your migration in a way that provides the best possible chance for long-term success.

1.6   Looking ahead

In this chapter, we discussed what agile development really means and the value it provides. As this book continues, our goal will be to demonstrate what moving to agile looks like. We'll do this via a case study that is representative of our years of helping teams become agile within their constraints. The case study, *Acme Media*, is introduced in chapter 2.

The story of Acme Media

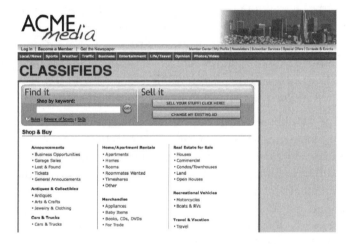

To make it easier to follow the practices discussed throughout this book, we've created a case study to demonstrate the practices in action. The case study will allow you to reflect on the issues and constraints encountered by real companies as they move to agile.

The Acme Media case study is a blend of our experiences with various companies as they migrated to a more agile process. These companies have ranged from tiny internet startups to Fortune 500 companies. The products have included commercial software, internal applications, and online services. The existing development methods have ranged from formal to no defined processes at all. The cultures have ranged from open and collaborative to closed and bureaucratic. The products have ranged from ultrasound equipment to beef jerky.

We don't use actual company names in order to protect their privacy, but the scenarios discussed are based on real events. Our case study follows Acme Media as the company moves to a custom agile methodology and learns how to deliver maximum value from its software projects.

Let's look at the details of the Acme Media case study.

2.1   *Case study background and circumstances*

Acme Corporation is a media company that engages in television broadcasting and interactive media operations. The interactive media operations consist of three product websites. Our case study is tied to the interactive media group and its following three sites:

- The first website focuses on delivering the news. If the television station is covering a breaking story, the news site needs to have the story online during the TV coverage or a few minutes afterward. The news website also provides enriched coverage about news articles, such as blogs, opinion surveys, and deeper analysis.
- The second website is focused on classified advertising for the local metropolitan area. The classifieds are for real estate, autos, and merchandise. The case study's pilot project will deliver an application for the classifieds site.
- The third website is responsible for travel and outdoors. This site contains content related to tourism, hiking, getaways, and lodging.

All three websites sell online advertising space to national and local businesses.

The three sites are supported by a group of 20 people. The skill sets in this group include product management, development, design, database analysis, business analysis, architecture, implementation, support, testing, and project management. Several team members wear various hats depending on the state of the project. For example, developers may do their own DBA work, or a product manager may end up doing the requirements documentation. The development group is also the maintenance and support group for the production environment.

The Acme Media websites have always been a secondary priority for the company. They don't make much money and exist only as a supplementary presence to the television station. Until about a year ago, working in the web group was laid-back and easy; there was rarely any pressure, and projects were completed on a loose schedule. All of that has changed now.

With the popularity of online advertising on the rise, Acme Media's web division found itself overwhelmed with advertising requests and a significant increase in site traffic. In addition, advertisers were asking Acme to publish more television content on the websites to attract a younger crowd. Suddenly, web projects had urgency, and revenue was on the line.

The heat was on the three product teams. The lack of reliable schedules and the teams' frequent need to push out promise dates were motivating advertisers and readers to go to competitive websites. Projects needed to be delivered on time to retain the customers.

In the following chapters, we'll help Acme Media migrate to a methodology that is more in tune with the urgency of its environment.

2.2 About the Acme Media teams

Acme Media started down its road to more agility when the company's project manager, Wendy Johnson, began investigating ways to deliver products sooner. Wendy conducted research and discussed her issue with a number of friends and colleagues. One friend Wendy spoke with, Jim Moore, happened to be an agile coach. Jim told Wendy about several companies he had helped move to agile and the benefits these companies had achieved. After Wendy was convinced, she set about selling Acme's CIO on the idea that Acme's development team needed to give agile a try. Wendy will get approval from the executive team to pilot agile.

Acme will create two teams as the company completes its pilot project and evaluates how agile it can become. First, the company will create a *core team*. The core team will be trained and mentored by the agile coach, Jim Moore. The core team will be in charge of reviewing the existing development process at Acme Media to see where agile practices can be injected. This team will consist of actual project team members. After the core team outlines a new process to test, a *pilot project team* will be selected to actually complete the pilot project.

The pilot project team will include a few core team members, but most of the pilot team members selected will be getting their first look at the new process. The pilot team will receive training on agile principles and basic practices, and then they will perform the pilot and provide feedback to the core team. The core team will use the feedback to refine the process and then continue to scale the new process throughout the company.

2.3 About the individuals

You'll learn more about the individual team members in chapter 6, when we establish the core team, and in chapter 11, when we select team members for the pilot project. Acme Media's development team has various experiences, backgrounds, and opinions about how software development should be completed (see figure 2.1). Some team members have experience in formal, plan-driven environments; many team members have worked in environments where the development process was homegrown; and a few team members have experience in agile environments.

As Acme Media pursues its new process, some team members will be energetic, some will be neutral, and some will be skeptics. In our experience, a variety of responses is common in most companies. Acme will use all three perspectives to help roll out the best possible new process.

Some of the energetic team members will help in documenting the existing process. The team members on the fence will be part of the core team and the pilot team. Skeptics will also be included on both teams, and their input will be welcome as the new process is created and critiqued.

Figure 2.1   Acme Media's development team is composed of a variety of personality types and personal experiences. Regardless of background, you want everyone to learn the value of moving to agile; and over time you want the team to buy in to the new process.

2.4   What does it look like when a team "becomes agile"?

Before we take off with the story of Acme Media, you may wonder what it looks like when a team moves to a more agile process. Let's take a look at a real-world example.

2.4.1   The existing process

One company we worked with, which we'll call Archway Software, had a development-release process that is depicted in figure 2.2.

As you can see, Archway's development process was traditional and for the most part reflective of a waterfall lifecycle. Archway released software somewhat effectively every four months. This company was comfortable with the development process and didn't have any incentives to change it.

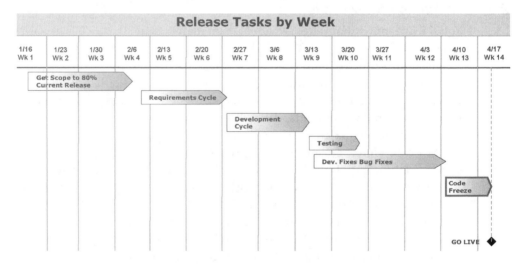

Figure 2.2   A development-release process with little flexibility. Discoveries are certain to delay the project or jeopardize the quality level of the release.

But over the years issues began to evolve. First, every software release supported up to 20 existing customers. The customers competed with each other to get the features they desired into a release. If a request didn't make the release list, customers became upset.

The second issue related to discovering missing functionality during a release. The project plan didn't allow for changes. Discoveries went into a backlog and were reviewed when Archway was planning the subsequent release for delivery four months later. Deferring these findings lowered the value of the current software release and led to challenging discussions with customers after the release. Requirements that were discovered midstream were often as valuable as the requirements identified during the requirements phase.

2.4.2 A process with more agility

Archway Software decided to visit another company—an insurance company—that had encountered similar issues when creating software for its online sales website. The insurance company walked Archway through the changes it had made to deal with those issues. The main changes the insurance company made were as follows:

- Reduced the release cycle from 12 weeks to 8 weeks so that customers weren't as upset if their request didn't make a release. The customers always knew another release was just around the corner.
- Broke the development cycle into two feature sets, with the first cycle focused on the most critical features. If issues were encountered during the first cycle, work on the critical features continued into the second cycle.
- Modified the work area to enhance information sharing and support quicker turn times. This included
  - Co-locating all team members.
  - Cutting the cubicle walls in half so team members could see and communicate with each other freely.
  - Providing tools for quick discussions, including rolling whiteboards and always-available open areas for collaboration.
  - Working hard to keep the tribe together. The insurance company learned that the longer teams stayed together, the more knowledge they had about the software and customers, which led to quicker development.

Archway Software was impressed with what the insurance company had done to address its issues. Back in the workplace, Archway designed the development process outlined in figure 2.3.

Archway Software tried the new process on several releases and was pleased with the results. Customers were more patient if their features didn't make a release, and the team had a few days to recover if a discovery was made when they were working on the features in development cycle 1. The team also implemented an informal process to let customers preview features before official user-acceptance testing.

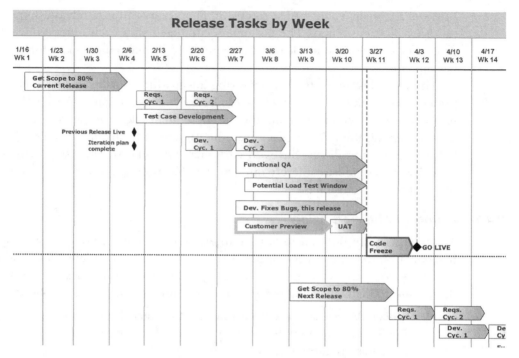

Figure 2.3   A process with more agility and the opportunity to adapt to discoveries. Note how the subsequent release gets started as the current release is wrapping up.

2.4.3   *The ultimate process*

After several releases, Archway Software discovered some interesting things about the new process. First, the company had always completed functional specifications before passing the work to the developers to start coding. But in reality, the analysts needed to meet with the developers while creating the specifications. The analysts worked with the developers to begin envisioning a design and also to take technical constraints into account.

Archway Software also learned that after the initial discussions, the developers started working on technical designs and coding features while the functional specifications were being completed by the analysts.

The last thing Archway learned was that even though there were two development cycles, the team still didn't have time to recover from customer discoveries exposed during user-acceptance testing. If a customer discovered an issue, the team had to rush to fix and test the issue before the looming code-freeze date.

Taking these findings into account, Archway Software revised its development process again; see figure 2.4.

The company modified its process to reflect the realities it saw during releases. Archway realized that requirements, design, and coding weren't performed serially but more frequently happened in parallel. Therefore, the iterations weren't split into

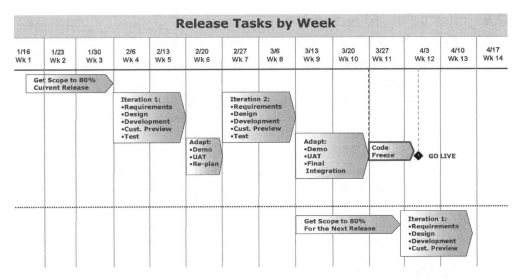

Figure 2.4   As a team addresses its issues, a process becomes more agile with early customer demonstrations and dedicated time to adapt, re-plan, and adjust. True iterative development takes place, and requirements, design, and coding frequently happen concurrently.

types of work—rather, all the work required to deliver a feature could happen simultaneously. Business requirements initiated feature development, but functional specification, design, and coding usually happened in parallel.

Archway also realized that discoveries were made during every iteration and that the company should quit pretending that re-planning was an exception; instead, it was a reality. Based on this finding, Archway outlined a 5-day window in which to demonstrate to the customer at the end of each iteration; then the company adjusted the plan for the subsequent iteration based on the demonstration findings and the throughput the team was achieving.

At this point, Archway Software had revisited its development process twice. The company revisited and reviewed the process frequently, adjusting it for the realities of the company, its customers, and the constraints of the business.

> In this chapter, we demonstrate how a process becomes more agile. What we don't discuss is how a company changes its culture and mindset in parallel with process changes. In our example, we discuss how an insurance company reached a high level of workflow agility. To do this, their organization had to mature and embrace an agile mindset; otherwise, the team wouldn't buy into the changes. (The agile mindset is discussed in chapter 7.)

This is one example of how a team became agile. Turn to chapter 3, and you can follow along as this book's case study, Acme Media, moves to a more agile process.

2.5   *Key points to remember*

Here are the key points to remember from this chapter:

- We'll use a case study to illustrate what a migration to a more agile process can look like.
- We'll discuss common constraints that limit how agile you can become. In some cases, we'll show how to resolve the constraint; in other cases, we'll explain why you should accept the constraint.
- Our case study represents a company that needs to improve delivery speed and accuracy. The web development team didn't have a sense of urgency because it was a small part of the business model. Now that web traffic has increased, Acme Media needs to learn how to deliver quickly in a volatile environment.
- Our case study team contains a variety of personality types. We'll discuss how the migration affects different personalities as the case study proceeds.

2.6   *Looking ahead*

In this chapter, we provided an example of how a real company followed the process outlined in this book to iteratively add agility to their development lifecycle. This should help you envision what your own migration will look like and how your lifecycle will constantly evolve and improve.

You've also met our case study. In subsequent chapters, Acme Media will develop its own custom development process and test that process on a pilot project. In chapter 3, we'll discuss whether your team is ready to attempt a move to a more agile process, and we'll also discuss the common constraints that teams encounter when moving to agile.

Part 2

Getting started

When we start an agile project, we frequently have an iteration 0. Iteration 0 is the time to put the project foundation in place before construction begins. This includes tasks such as establishing development environments, finalizing contracts with third parties, and assembling the project team.

You'll have the equivalent of an iteration 0 when you begin your migration to a more agile process. You'll need to put the foundation pieces in place that support an environment conducive to the migration. The following chapters will help you put a process in place to support adding agility to your existing methodology.

We'll lead you through an assessment that will let you understand your potential for improving your existing development lifecycle. Afterward, we'll explain the importance of buy-in across the company and provide a blueprint you can use to obtain executive and team-member support. We'll conclude this part of the book by rejoining our case study and watching the team at Acme Media document their existing process and identify ways to make it more agile. Acme will then select a pilot project on which to test the new process.

These pages reflect our personal experiences, trials and errors, and beliefs for bringing agility into an organization. We believe this foundational work will prepare you for long-term success and give you the best opportunity to become and *stay* agile.

Are you ready for agile? 3

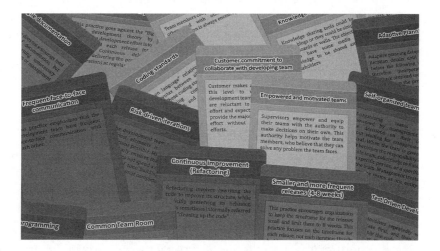

Yes, you're ready for agile. The real questions are as follows:

- How much agility are you ready for *today*?
- How much agility can you add *tomorrow*?
- How can you continuously adapt to your ever-changing business climate?

We're confident you can improve your current development process and obtain a level of agility. If your environment is conducive to it, you may be able to reach the level of agility that Archway Software reached in our discussion in chapter 2.

We'll start this chapter by providing information that helps you understand the goals of an agile process and how these goals relate to packaged agile methods such as Extreme Programming (XP) and Scrum. The chapter will conclude by discussing our approach for bringing agile into your workplace. We'll start your migration by providing a tool that will let you assess your potential for bringing in agile practices and cultural changes.

3.1 What areas will you become more agile in?

When people think of becoming agile, they often envision the practices and not the goals of an agile process. We often hear people say that they can't become agile because their developers don't want to do pair programming, or they have limitations with co-locating their project team members. Although these types of practices may help you become agile, they aren't the only practices that support the *goals* of an agile process. Let's take a moment to look at some of the key agile goals you'll be able to accomplish on some level.

3.1.1 Increasing customer involvement

A traditional process has the customer involved mainly at the beginning and the end of the project. In agile, you seek customer feedback and input throughout the project. The customer or product owner is involved in planning, tradeoff decisions, prioritization, and demonstrations. Increased customer involvement leads to several benefits such as quicker feedback, accurate delivery, increased customer satisfaction, and rapid decisions. A great indirect benefit of customer involvement is the customer's new-found appreciation for the work needed to deliver on requests.

3.1.2 Improving prioritization of features

Agile processes improve prioritization and deliver higher-value features first. This is accomplished by creating feature cards or user stories and evaluating features before requirements are detailed. You'll evaluate features for their customer value, level of risk, frequency of use, and dependencies. This allows you to do the following:

- Estimate work and evaluate risks early in the process.
- Prioritize features in terms of customer value early in the process.
- Deliver features in usable subsets.

In effect, the agile prioritization process lets your team run leaner and create deep requirements only for work that passes the prioritization test.

3.1.3 Increasing team buy-in and involvement

The majority of people on an agile project team are involved in planning, estimating, and sequencing. The team is also involved in adapting to discoveries between iterations. Over time, the team begins suggesting features for the product or platform. Increasing team involvement ensures that everyone understands the value of the project before work begins and also increases team satisfaction.

3.1.4 Clarifying priorities and reminding everyone of the consequences of changing them

An agile team works with the customer and/or sponsor to determine the most critical category for the project. Is schedule the number-one priority, or is staying within budget? Additional categories may include quality, feature richness, and compliance. The project team learns the priorities and uses this knowledge to make tradeoff decisions along the way.

Many projects wait for a fire before identifying their priorities. An agile team knows the project priorities in advance of an emergency and can react quickly to keep the focus on the main objective.

3.1.5 *Adapting to change during development*

A more agile and iterative methodology provides an opportunity to reassess and redirect the project while it's in motion. You perform development in iterations and offer demonstrations at the end of each. The customer has an opportunity to request changes based on the demonstrations, even though this may affect other features or potentially the project timeline. Team members learn to expect and embrace change.

3.1.6 *Better understanding the project's status*

Agile development is time-boxed. You evaluate status by demonstrating functioning code. Supporting tasks are also measured in binary terms (done or not done) to eliminate possible confusion related to expressing status as "percent complete." An agile process also involves team members reporting their status themselves versus through a manager or other intermediary. This improves tracking accuracy and personal accountability.

3.1.7 *More efficient planning and estimating*

Many companies try to plan all of a project's details at the start. The planning may be at a detailed level even though the amount of uncertainty at this point is extremely high. An agile team performs a level of planning that correlates to the current level of uncertainty in the project.

As you learn more about desired features you'll do more detailed planning, but you won't waste time trying to guess intricate details early in the project. Figure 3.1 illustrates this point.

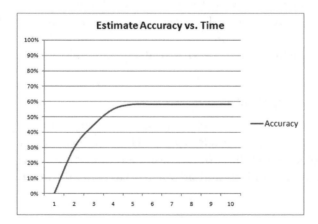

Figure 3.1 The accuracy of initial feature estimates improves dramatically during the first few hours of estimation but levels out over time. In this example, the effort and time spent after five hours of estimating doesn't improve accuracy and is wasted project time.

3.1.8   Continuous risk management

A secondary definition of *agile* could be *continuous risk management*. The processes are all intended to make the team alert and responsive to new information and changes as the project progresses. The following are a few examples of how agile manages risk:

- Features are evaluated for requirements uncertainty and technical uncertainty. These attributes help determine whether a feature goes into an iteration and what iteration it should go into, to mitigate risk. For example, a feature with high business value and high technical risk, such as an interface, would go into an early iteration to allow more time for uncertainty. On the other hand, a feature with low business value and high technical uncertainty might be moved to the last iteration or removed from the project all together.

- Risk is managed via demonstrations throughout the project. The customer gets a feel for how requirements are translated into an application before the project is complete. This provides a window for adapting and hitting the final target.

- Risk is managed on a daily basis by building and integrating the latest code. This process allows the team and the customer to validate the status of the latest build.

- Deployment risk is also managed by gathering maintenance and deployment concerns as early as possible. This starts early in the planning phase and continues throughout development.

- Risk is managed via team review of potential features. During the feature-card exercise, representatives from all areas can raise risks and concerns with proposed features. These concerns are noted with the feature information and sometimes can lead to a feature not being pursued.

3.1.9   Delivering the project needed at the end

Jim Highsmith, one of the founding members of the Agile Alliance, taught Adaptive Software Development a few years before the Agile Manifesto was created. One of Jim's adaptive principles is, "Deliver the project needed at the end, not the one requested at the beginning."

This idea is a foundational piece of agile software development. Jim knew the world wasn't static during the project lifecycle; therefore the lifecycle should support changes that happen during the project. This includes identifying new requirements, discovering technical risks, and identifying potential changes in the business environment.

3.1.10   Achieving the right level of project structure

Many companies have created a formal Project Management or Software Development Lifecycle (PMLC/SDLC) to support their projects. These lifecycles are collections of processes that every project must follow. By establishing required processes, companies eliminate variation between projects and provided a safety net for inexperienced project teams and project managers. If you don't know what to do next, you just look at the lifecycle documentation to determine your next step.

This approach is beneficial when you have inexperienced employees. A standardized process defines roles, provides common tools, and offers gateways to evaluate status.

If your employees are more experienced, this formal methodology has drawbacks. The team will notice that every step or process isn't needed for their specific project. They will frequently find themselves doing compliance work that adds no value, except to be in compliance.

The agile process described in this book approaches the issue differently. We suggest a standardized methodology, but the required processes are minimal and are of value to every project. Your team chooses the majority of the processes to use at the start of the project. The team also revisits their process and documentation options as the project proceeds, to see if they need to add or remove a process or document.

To illustrate this idea, let's look at an example from Acme Media *after* the company has outlined a new, more agile process (see table 3.1).

Acme Media has projects that last from 1 week to 6 months. The company doesn't require the teams for one-week projects to create iteration plans or to do a cost-benefit analysis every time.

Table 3.1   Required and optional processes and documentation

Required for all projects	Optional processes and documents
Project worksheet	Elevator statement
Operational worksheet	Documented answers to feasibility discussion guide questions
Feature-card exercise (cards optional)	Feature-card document (possibly created using only index cards)
Retrospective discussion	User scenarios
	Prototypes and/or mockups
	Iteration plan
	Maintenance plan
	Evolutionary requirements
	Additional documentation as required by the team/project
	Test plan
	Detailed schedule
	Launch plan
	Action items from project retrospective
	Test Driven Development (TDD)
	Agile estimating
	Daily stand-up meeting
	Demonstrations

These one-week projects are frequently driven by a need to increase readership or to provide support in the aftermath of a major news event such as an election. Executive approval is almost immediate, and the projects use team members already assigned to the website. These teams only need the processes and documents outlined in the first column of table 3.1.

Conversely, Acme Media pursues some major projects that require funding, synchronization with third parties, and identification of milestones. In these instances, the project teams review the items in the second column of table 3.1 and decide which ones to use in addition to the required ones in the first column.

In this way, agile provides the correct amount of structure for the project. Time isn't wasted on processes that don't add value, and teams can scale their processes mid-project if needed.

Now that you understand the goals of an agile process, you need to know the best way to obtain them. You can do this by selecting a prepackaged agile process, creating a process from scratch, or a combination of the two. Let's evaluate each option.

3.2   The different flavors of agile

Many packaged methods are available for agile. For our purposes, *packaged* will mean a framework with a common set of practices. In this section, we'll discuss two of the most popular packages in use today: Scrum and XP. According to VersionOne's 2008 "State of Agile Development" survey, 77 percent of the respondents said they use Scrum, XP, or a Scrum/XP hybrid. Each of these packages has its own unique characteristics, strengths, and weaknesses. Let's examine each package.

3.2.1   Scrum

The Scrum process begins by reviewing a product backlog with the product owner. You identify the highest-priority features and then estimate how many will fit into a sprint. These features then compose the sprint backlog. A *sprint* is a predefined period of time, usually 2 to 4 weeks, during which the team analyzes, designs, constructs, tests, and documents the selected features. Figure 3.2 shows an overview of the process.

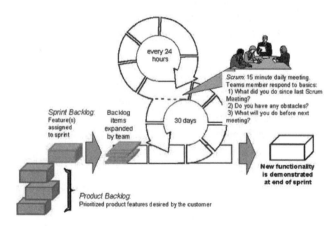

Figure 3.2 A high-level overview of the Scrum process (graphic provided courtesy of Ken Schwaber and Control Chaos)

The team holds a daily status meeting, referred to as the daily *Scrum*, to review feature status. Individual team members answer these three questions:

- What have you accomplished since our last meeting?
- What will you work on today?
- Are you encountering any impediments or roadblocks in completing your work?

When a sprint is completed, the features are demonstrated to the customer, and the team and the customer decide whether additional work is needed or if the sprint work is approved to be released to a beta or production environment. Each sprint is followed by a retrospective during which the team lists items that went well or poorly; action plans are documented to keep the successes going and to improve the areas that performed poorly.

Some of the characteristics of Scrum are as follows:

- *Discipline*—Scrum is strict about time-boxing activities, compiling code daily, and team members being punctual and responsible.
- *Three major roles*—Scrum teams have a ScrumMaster, a product owner, and team members.
- *Quality*—Features are expected to be totally complete and deployable at the end of a sprint.

Scrum has a number of strengths:

- *Prioritized delivery*—Features are delivered in a sequence that ties to business value.
- *Non-prescriptive on practices performed during a sprint*—This is demonstrated by the fact that a Scrum/XP hybrid is the second most popular agile methodology in use. Many teams pull their detailed practices from XP while using the Scrum framework.
- *Demonstrated success across the software industry*—Scrum has been successful in multiple environments.
- *Status transparency*—The daily meetings expose the project status.
- *Team accountability*—Everyone signs off on the work that will be pursued during the sprint.
- *Continuous delivery*—Scrum delivers product features (commercial software or web portals) continuously.

Scrum also has some weaknesses:

- Scrum doesn't want specialists. It may be difficult to quickly convert an existing team from a group of specialists to a group where anyone can perform any task.
- A Scrum team can't be successful without a strong ScrumMaster, which makes the process highly dependent on one individual.
- Because Scrum is mainly a framework, the team still needs to identify the practices and methods to use within the framework.

Scrum is incredibly popular today—it's almost become synonymous with the term *agile development*. Scrum provides a great, repeatable process that is well suited for product development and steady-state release management. In addition, a plethora of books, consultants, and other resources are available for those who pursue Scrum.

Scrum may be more difficult to use with teams that do one-off projects versus steady-state releases, or if a team has highly specialized resources and skill sets. In addition, the Scrum framework still needs agile practices inserted to support a complete development lifecycle.

3.2.2 *Extreme Programming*

Similar to Scrum, XP starts the process by creating a backlog of work to perform during a sprint/iteration. XP creates the backlog by working with customers and creating user stories. In parallel with this work, the team performs an architectural *spike*, during which they experiment with the features to envision the initial architecture. XP classifies this work as the *exploration phase.*

The *planning phase* follows exploration. This phase focuses on identifying the most critical user stories and estimating when they can be implemented. Tasks are defined for each feature, to aid with estimating complexity. The team outlines an overall release schedule, with an understanding that a high level of uncertainty exists until the work begins. A release will have one to many iterations, which are typically 2- to 4-week construction windows.

When an iteration begins, the specific plan for the iteration is revisited. The team adds any new user stories and tasks that have been discovered since the overall release was outlined.

XP integrates customer testing into the development iteration. The customer is asked to identify the acceptance tests, and the team works to automate these tests so they can be run throughout the iteration.

The planning phase is followed by the *productionizing phase*, during which the code is certified for release. *Certified* means the code passes all customer tests plus nonfunctional requirements such as load testing, service-level requirements, and response-time requirements. You can see an overview of XP in figure 3.3.

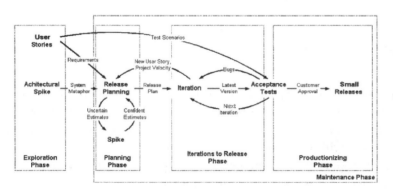

Figure 3.3 The Extreme Programming (XP) lifecycle (graphic provided with permission from Scott Ambler, based on the writings of Don Wells and the first edition of Kent Beck's XP Explained)

Some of the characteristics of XP are as follows:

- *Specific practice*—Unlike Scrum, XP is specific about the practices that should be used during a software project. These practices include pair programming, TDD, continuous integration, refactoring, and collective code ownership.
- *Modeling*—XP teams frequently use modeling to better understand the tasks and architecture needed to support a user story.
- *Simplicity*—Teams perform the minimum work needed to meet requirements.
- *Automation*—Unit and functional tests are automated.
- *Quality through testing*—Features are tested constantly, and developers check each other's code via pair programming.

These are some of XP's strengths :

- Customer-focused (it's all about user stories)
- Quality via frequent testing
- Constant focus on identifying and delivering the critical user stories
- High visibility on project status
- Great support for volatile requirements

It also has weaknesses:

- *Need for team maturity*—Practices such as pair programming and TDD require responsible developers, and they aren't always easy to obtain.
- *Dependency on testing*—If developers know that significant testing will take place downstream, they may be less than diligent when they're creating designs.
- *Scalability*—XP may not work well for large projects.
- *Dependency on team member co-location*—The team usually has a team room.

XP supports many of the critical goals of an agile process, such as dealing with volatile requirements and delivering prioritized, working software as soon as possible. XP also supports the principle of *just enough*, keeping with the lean philosophy of minimizing waste.

XP has sometimes been criticized for its lack of formality in system documentation and system design. In recent years this has changed, and XP teams now create the documentation needed to support a project's customers.

3.3 Create your own flavor to become agile within your constraints

As we discussed in chapter 1, VersionOne's 2007 "State of Agile Development" survey validated the benefits of using agile. If the survey is accurate, then should every company migrate to agile methods tomorrow?

We're huge proponents of agile, but we need to tell you a few things that the surveys don't reveal. Here are some questions that would bring additional perspective to VersionOne's findings.

- How difficult was it to convert to an agile development process?
- How was your conversion initiated? Did the idea originate with executive management or from within the development team?
- Have your employees bought into the process, or was it forced on them?
- What are you doing to ensure that your development process is viable for the future?
- What did you do to make agile work within the realities of your environment?

We believe 100 percent of the survey respondents would say that moving to agile was a lot of work. We think they would tell you that to be successful, you need your project team to buy into the process; and that management requires time to learn how to provide value in an agile environment.

This discussion reminds us of a popular commercial from our childhood. When we were kids, we ate Jiffy Pop popcorn. Jiffy Pop ran a commercial for many years that stated, "Jiffy Pop: it's as much fun to make as it is to eat!"

After you establish an agile culture and lifecycle, it's "fun to eat" (as illustrated in figure 3.4), and you'll do a better job of delivering projects. But creating an agile environment is work. Many companies implement an agile methodology and then fade back into their previous process because they didn't cover all the delicate areas needed to ensure long-term support for agile.

We've spent a lot of time with companies that have made it to the other side and stayed there. As this book continues, we'll show you how companies got to be agile with the least amount of pain and sustainable benefits.

Now let's take a moment to look at the importance of creating an agile process that supports the unique characteristics of your environment.

Figure 3.4 Is agile development like Jiffy Pop popcorn—as much fun to make as it is to eat? Not during the migration phase. Managers need to learn when to manage (or not), and team members need to experiment with their new freedoms. These cultural changes take work and time.

3.3.1   *Your goal: reach the right level of agility for your organization*

Many companies try to "shotgun" agile into their organization. They think, "Let's get through the migration pain quickly and start obtaining the benefits as soon as possible." We've seen a few cases where this approach makes sense: for example, a project team that has become so dysfunctional that they're delivering practically no functionality or business value. This approach also works well for a start-up company that hasn't yet established its development process. But for most companies, you should allow time for the process to "bake."

This is why we suggest an iterative approach for bringing agile into an organization. An iterative approach allows you to see how well your employees are adapting to the change. It also lets you learn what works and what doesn't in your environment. In effect, it allows you to reach the right level of agility for your organization.

Part of your iterative approach will include a process for maintaining the methodology. We suggest establishing a core team to support this maintenance. A core team is composed of employees from all aspects of the development process. They play a huge part in establishing your custom methodology and then settle into a maintenance mode with the goal of constantly adapting to your environment. The core team is covered in detail in chapter 6.

Next, you need to choose the best way to iteratively create a methodology at your company. Should you select a packaged method, such as Scrum or XP? Or should you create a custom or hybrid process?

CUSTOM PROCESS OR PACKAGED METHOD?

In order to be successful, you should customize your agile process. For many years, consultants and others have said that you must embrace agile completely or not at all.

In 2006, we witnessed a shift in this attitude. Highly respected folks such as Kent Beck (the founder of XP) and Steve McConnell (the writer of *Code Complete*) now endorse customization. Kent Beck noted the following in an interview with InfoQ (InfoQ.com is an independent online community focused on change and innovation in enterprise software development) in 2006:

> *Failure at an organizational level seems to come from the inability to customize processes and make them their own. Trying to apply someone else's template to your organization directly doesn't work well. It leaves out too many important details of the previous successes and ignores your company's specific situation. Rubber-stamping agile processes isn't agile. The value of having a principle-based process is that you can apply the principles for an individualized process for your situation and, as an extra bonus, one that has been designed to adapt from your learning as you adopt changes into your organization. It's always "custom."*

Kent's quote is comforting to us because it supports our personal experiences. *Custom* means picking and choosing the agile practices that best support your environment. *Custom* means you shouldn't use a pure packaged methodology off the shelf, such as Scrum or XP. You can start with one of these methods as a basis for your process, but you should modify it to obtain the best results for your company.

If we revisit VersionOne's 2008 survey, we see that 14 percent of the people who responded are using a hybrid process based on Scrum and XP. The hybrid model is closer to what we'll suggest for you. To be specific, here are the steps we'll walk you through as the book continues:

1 Assess your organization to determine where you should begin adding agility.
2 Obtain executive support for the move to a more agile process. You can use the readiness assessment in chapter 4 to quantify the value of bringing in agile and identify the risks you must manage during migration.
3 Get the development team involved in the migration process to ensure buy-in. You do this by establishing a core team.

4   Identify a coach or consultant to help you with your migration. They will train the core team on agile and help you with other adoption aspects.

5   Develop a clear understanding of your current processes by documenting them.

6   Review your current process, and look for areas that can be shifted to more agile methods. Focus on areas with the most potential for improvement and the most value to the customer and your organization. The readiness assessment will also help with this task.

7   Outline a custom process based on the findings in step 6.

8   Try the new process on a pilot project.

9   Review the findings after the pilot, make changes, and continue to scale out your new methodology.

As this book continues, our case study, Acme Media, will represent your company. We'll take Acme through these nine steps and show you how the company iteratively creates and tests a custom process. We'll also show you how Acme Media takes its own constraints into account with the new methodology.

Before we jump into the case study, let's spend a moment looking at the characteristics that make it easier to adopt agile and the characteristics that make agile adoption more challenging.

3.3.2   *Characteristics that make agile easier to adopt*

As we stated earlier in this chapter, agile principles can be applied in any environment, but some environmental characteristics influence how easy the principles are to adopt. Let's look at these characteristics.

URGENCY TO DELIVER

Agile works best in an urgent environment. It provides tools to prioritize features quickly and determine how much scope to pursue within the constraints of a critical timeline. If you have urgency due to a competitive market, compliance deadlines, or a large backlog of project requests, agile provides methods for quicker delivery.

EVOLVING OR VOLATILE REQUIREMENTS

One descriptor of agile could be *just enough.* "Give me just enough requirements to start a design." "Give me just enough design to start my code." "Give me just enough code to demonstrate some level of value to the customer." If you don't have all the requirements, you can still get started with an agile project. If you complete an iteration and the customer wants to change the requirements, you can adapt and still meet the objectives. Managing changing requirements still takes effort in an agile environment, but you don't have to fight the project framework. The framework is designed to support uncertainty.

CUSTOMER AVAILABILITY

One Agile Manifesto principle states, "Business people and developers must work together daily throughout the project." In our experience, these groups don't have to work together every day throughout a project cycle, but there are definite times when the customer must be available. In theory, a project must not be urgent if the customer can't make time to clarify requirements or review functionality. The customer can have a proxy, such as a product manager; but someone needs to be available every day to represent the customer's vision.

CONSISTENT RESOURCES

Part of the power of agile is a level of familiarity within the team and a consistent understanding of the processes they use. Agile teams and processes get better over time. If project team members are new to each other, they must learn processes together while at the same time trying to complete the project. Agile works best with a core group of people who work together on continuous projects. Agile isn't a good methodology to use with a team that has never worked together before, unless you have long-term plans to keep them together.

CO-LOCATED RESOURCES

Agile promotes face-to-face communication and common understanding. One of the best ways to support this principle is to put your team members face to face. Co-location is an amazing tool. Your team can get out of *email hell,* and their mutual understanding of the project will increase.

One of the best setups we have seen is at a Fortune 500 company we visited. All 10 of the project team members are in an area approximately 25 feet by 25 feet. The cubicles have half-walls that provided a level of privacy when people are sitting but let them easily see the rest of the team and communicate when they stand up. This setup provides the privacy the developers enjoy when they're deep into a coding session but also lets team members stand up to converse with each other at any time without having to go to each others' cubicles. Team members can also walk a few feet and reach common areas where they can whiteboard a design or have a quick caucus.

THE TEAM IS A TEAM

In larger companies, a project team may be constructed of team members from a shared resource pool. For example, the QA (Quality Assurance) lead for a project may be from the QA shared resources pool. If such team members view themselves as resources on loan, and not as team members dedicated to the project, the result can be functional silos.

When silos exist, team members are more concerned about the welfare of their team or area than they are with the livelihood of the project. This mentality doesn't bode well for agile development and leads to customer neglect. The team needs to bond as a unified group toward the goals of the project. Roles are assigned, but one of the objectives of agile is for the team to working collectively.

Working collectively can also be applied to team member roles. A tester can point out a possible code improvement. A developer can suggest a feature enhancement. In general, team members *speak out*—they don't limit their roles to their titles.

Management should ensure that individual goals include how well employees support the common good of the project.

3.3.3   *Roadblocks that others have overcome*

Now that you know the characteristics that make agile easier to implement, let's look at a few that make agile more difficult to move to.

LACK OF AGILE KNOWLEDGE

Your first challenge will be finding expertise to help you with your migration. If you're fortunate, you'll have some level of agile experience within your company; but this probably won't be true to the point that you can coach yourself through an agile migration.

We'll help you with this issue by showing you how often Acme Media requested assistance, from initial training to issues encountered along the way.

LARGE PROJECT TEAMS

Agile is compromised as team size increases. Major principles such as face-to-face communication and common understanding require additional effort to maintain their effectiveness as a team grows.

Larger teams require additional overhead to ensure that information is shared consistently across all groups. Scrum teams frequently use the term *scrum of scrums*, meaning a representative from each team Scrum attends a master Scrum meeting to share information with other groups.

Jeff Bezos of Amazon.com believes that the most productive and innovative teams can be "fed with two pizzas." Jeff shared this thought with his senior managers at an offsite retreat. He envisioned a company culture of small teams that could work independently, which would lead to more innovative products. Since that time, the Amazon "pizza teams" have created some of the most popular features on the site (Fast Company, 2004).

If your team has an average appetite, you can convert Jeff's concept into a team of five to seven people. This is a nice-size group for communication and agility. If five to seven is perfect, then what is the maximum size for a team to remain agile? On the high side, we believe you can have a team of 15 people without major impact on your agility. When you have more than 15, communication needs to become more formal, which slows the team.

There are ways to make agile work with larger or distributed teams, but you'll sacrifice some level of agility.

DISTRIBUTED DEVELOPMENT

Related to large teams, many companies use distributed development. Frequently, the distributed development is performed by offshore resources.

Distributed development implies that the team is large in size and that communication methods must be scaled to get information to all involved. In addition, you may have issues with time zone differences, language, and code integration into a common environment. Some offshore companies support and advertise the use of agile methodologies, but their location may make it challenging to support the core principles.

We've seen agile teams successfully use offshore resources for commodity or repeatable-type work, such as regression testing, smoke testing, and cookie-cutter development (for example, providing an offshore group with standardized tools to create automated workflows).

FIXED-BID CONTRACT WORK

Fixed-bid contract work goes against most of the agile principles. The customer isn't a partner, evolving requirements are a no-no, and adapting is usually called *scope creep*. We used to believe that fixed-bid work couldn't be performed using an agile process, but recently we've met several managers who have customized their process to allow the inner workings to be agile while customer interaction remained contract oriented.

AN IMMATURE OR ONE-TIME TEAM

If you have a team that will work together for only one project, they're usually better served by using a plan-driven methodology unless they have previous exposure to agile. If the team will work through multiple projects or releases, you can introduce agile techniques, and the team can migrate to a full agile methodology as their knowledge matures.

GOING TOO FAST

"Hey, it's agile. We don't need to do any planning to convert to it, just start thinking agile!" A lot of folks take this approach when migrating to agile. But if you go too fast, you don't give your company enough time to digest the concepts. When this happens, you may experience issues with common understanding and terminology.

Don't let this happen to you. You need to plan before migrating to agile, and this book will show you how to do it with an *awareness, buy-in, ownership* approach. If you take your time, the methodology will stick, and you'll minimize the risk of failure. You'll learn more about ownership in chapter 5.

TEAM WITH SPECIALIZED SKILL SETS

An organization's structure can create artificial barriers between teams, and so can skill sets. If your team has specialized skill sets, it's hard to be agile when the work mix doesn't correlate well to the available resource types. Some tasks always have to be done by certain individuals, which doesn't help the team bond or unite when pursuing the completion of a feature.

Specialized skill sets also place an additional constraint on team capacity. Imagine that your team has only one person who can perform user-interface design, and the work assigned to an iteration is 80 percent user-interface work. Other team members can look for work to do outside of the iteration, but delivery will be slow due to the one-person constraint.

Teams that are just becoming agile usually have members with specialized roles. You can overcome this constraint by cross training over time and rewarding employees for obtaining and using additional skills.

AVOIDING CUSTOMIZATION

Many people get hung up on the questions, "Are we doing it right? Are we doing it in an agile fashion? Are we following a pure agile process?"

When teams ask us these questions, we tell them the answers aren't important. All we want to know is this: Have you created a development process that provides the most benefit to your company?

This same mentality has managers trying to find a perfect agile methodology and insert it directly into their company. As we discussed earlier, you can start with a packaged agile process, but you need to look at the realities of your company and adjust accordingly. Acme Media will look at a generic agile process and see how it applies to their realities; then, they'll modify the process to fit their environment.

3.4   Key points to remember

The key points to remember from this chapter are as follows:

- Moving to agile isn't a one-time event. You can and will add agility over time.
- The goals of an agile process tie directly to company success.
- You can start with a prepackaged agile process such as Scrum and then modify and enrich the process to support the realities of your environment.
- Some of your existing company characteristics will make it easier to move to agile. This is especially true if you have volatile requirements or urgency to deliver frequently.
- Every migration to agile encounters roadblocks. We'll identify the most common roadblocks and show you how others have addressed them.
- Every migration to agile is unique, but we believe our nine-step framework will work for most companies and provide the best chance of moving to and sustaining an agile process.

3.5   Looking ahead

In this chapter, you've learned that the question isn't whether you're ready to become agile, but rather what level of agility you're ready for today. In chapter 4, we'll help you answer this question by discussing the use of assessment tools to determine which agile practices you can initially adopt with minimum risk. Assessing your current potential is also important for gaining executive support, which we'll cover in chapter 5.

The fitness test:
all about
readiness assessments

Imagine the average Joe hears about a marathon that is being run for a great cause. He gets motivated and decides to participate. Joe thinks that running a marathon is no big deal and does absolutely no preparation. He starts the marathon and gets off to a great start. But after half an hour or so, Joe's body can't take it. He doesn't have what it takes to run the marathon.

Similarly, organizations may hear about agile and its benefits and get motivated to adopt agile practices. Although becoming agile is about adopting a new mindset toward software development, many organizations think that adopting agile is only about embracing some new practices, and that's it. Hence, those organizations do no preparation for the transition to agile. The danger is that those organizations and/or teams may not have what it takes to adopt certain agile practices.

Just as people have to go through fitness training before they can run a marathon, organizations and teams need to go through an agile-readiness test before they begin their journey to agile. This assessment shows organizations if they have what it takes for the transition and which areas they need to improve to prepare for the transition.

In this chapter, we'll talk about the importance of readiness assessments and show how you can conduct a quick agile-readiness assessment for your team or organization.

4.1   *The importance of readiness assessments*

The idea of conducting an assessment before the adoption process begins isn't new. In an article titled "Management challenges to implementing agile processes in traditional development organizations," the first suggestion Barry Boehm and Richard Turner have for organizations is to incorporate preparation up front. They urge organizations to spend time and effort conducting a significant up-front analysis to identify any mismatches between the organization and the set of agile practices it wants to adopt. Also, Ceschi et al point out in another journal article titled "Project Management in Plan-Based and Agile Companies" that one of the biggest challenges to introducing agile methods in an organization is the lack of a detailed preliminary evaluation of the challenges this introduction may cause.

Although it's important to know whether an organization is ready to handle the adoption of certain agile practices *before* it starts adopting them, all too often the adoption efforts overlook this pre-adoption assessment phase or don't spend enough time and effort on it. Many organizations and teams start the transformation initiative to agile without knowing whether they're ready. Challenges begin to emerge, and hardships follow. Unfortunately, the most common reaction is to try harder to adopt the practice (which translates to additional cost and effort), to abandon the practice and deem it unsuitable, or, worse, to declare agility unsuitable.

4.2   *Reducing the risks of agile adoption using assessments*

Conducting readiness assessments can help identify and reduce the risks associated with the adoption process, because you have better insight into whether adopting the practice will succeed or fail before you begin the transition phase.

For example, collaborative planning is a commonly adopted agile practice. It calls for all stakeholders to be involved with the planning process, not only the project manager. This seems like a pretty simple practice, so it's common for organizations to mandate it without any readiness assessment. But in reality, successfully adopting this practice relies on four organizational characteristics:

- *Management style*—Before you begin using collaborative planning, you need to find out whether a collaborative or a command-control relationship exists between managers and the employees. The management style is an indication of whether management trusts the developers and vice versa. If management doesn't trust the employees' opinions, then collaborative planning may result in many arguments.

- *Manager buy-in*—It's great to know whether management supports collaborative planning. Many managers prefer to maintain control over the planning process and hence are apprehensive during collaborative planning sessions.
- *Power distance*—Power distance is a characteristic related to organizational and national cultures. By measuring power distance, you can find out whether people are intimidated by their managers and afraid to participate and be honest in their presence. If a big power distance exists between managers and employees, then having everyone sit around a table to plan together may not be as effective as you'd wish.
- *Developer buy-in*—To reap the benefits of collaborative planning, the entire team (including the developers) should be willing to be part of a collaborative planning environment. As obvious as this may seem, many developers don't see any benefit in being part of the planning process, and therefore even if collaborative planning is mandated, they won't be active participants.

These are some of the organizational characteristics that you should assess before you attempt to adopt an agile practice like collaborative planning. The absence of some or all of these characteristics may result in a failed attempt to adopt the practice.

The problem is that when a change initiative fails for any reason, a number of dangerous, negative consequences may result:

- Decreased team productivity
- Unmotivated team
- Increased team resistance to future change initiatives
- Jeopardizing of management's credibility (if the change was mandated from management)

If you conduct a readiness assessment, you'll recognize whether the organization lacks some of the essential characteristics needed to support the agile practice you're considering. For example, the assessment results outlined in table 4.1 indicate that the current management style is a risk if this organization tried to adopt collaborative planning. Note that this result came from an online assessment tool.

Table 4.1 The results of a sample agile-readiness assessment. The results show the suitability of each of the characteristics needed to successfully adopt collaborative planning.

Characteristic	Suitability result
Management style Whether a collaborative or a command-control relation exists between managers and subordinates. The management style indicates whether management trusts the developers and vice versa.	Partially suitable (30.5%)
Manager buy-in Whether management supports or resists having a collaborative environment.	Largely suitable (72.5%)

Table 4.1   The results of a sample agile-readiness assessment. The results show the suitability of each of the characteristics needed to successfully adopt collaborative planning. *(continued)*

Characteristic	Suitability result
Power distance Whether people are intimidated by / afraid to participate and be honest in the presence of their managers.	Largely suitable (60.5%)
Developer buy-in Whether the developers are willing to plan in a collaborative environment.	Fully suitable (92.5%)

In the case of this example, now that you know the risk up front, you can attempt to mitigate that risk by conducting training related to collaborative management style versus command-and-control management styles. Your goal is to ensure, before you begin the transition, that the team possesses the necessary characteristics to successfully adopt the practice.

4.3   *Increasing productivity during transitions*

The Virginia Satir change curve (figure 4.1) illustrates how change initiatives cause organizations to go through an intense period of resistance and chaos and how these

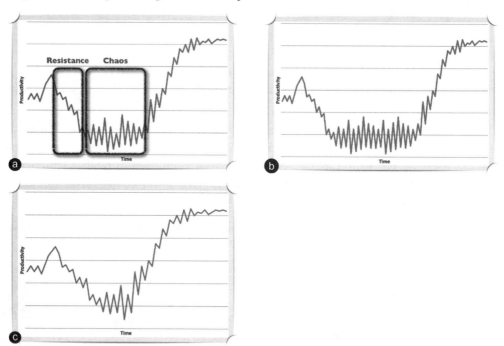

Figure 4.1   The Virginia Satir change curve depicted in figure 4.1a shows the relationship between productivity and time during a transition. The curve suggests that after an initial gain, productivity usually decreases during the resistance and chaos phases of a transition. Figure 4.1b shows how the curve looks if the chaos phase is prolonged, and figure 4.1c shows how the curve looks with a shortened chaos phase.

periods cause a drop in performance. (Virginia Satir is a family therapist who created a change model to help families understand and deal with change.) No wonder executives are concerned about the risks associated with any change initiative. They want to ensure that the transition goes as smoothly as possible. They also want to find ways to shorten or eliminate the resistance and chaos phase (figure 4.1c). Financial and productivity losses are usually incurred when the period of resistance and chaos is prolonged (figure 4.1b).

It's important to realize that if the organization isn't ready to successfully adopt an agile practice, it will have to go through some preparation efforts one way or another. This preparation should take place before the transition starts; but if for some reason that doesn't happen, the preparation must occur sometime during the actual transition—you can't just skip it.

Change models like Virginia Satir's show that once you start a change initiative, a drop in productivity is highly probable due to the period of resistance and chaos. Your objective is to shorten this phase by completing all your preparation efforts before the transition starts, not during the transition.

Figure 4.2 shows two curves overlaid on each other. The lower curve shows how an adoption would look if you didn't conduct a readiness assessment—you'd start right away, but the resistance and chaos phase would be much longer because no preparation took place up front. The downside of this model is that the organization spends a long, intense time with reduced productivity; not many organizations can handle this. On the other hand, the upper curve illustrates a transition that included a readiness assessment. The transition didn't start right away; the assessment identified some shortcomings that were fixed before the transition began. After the transition started, the resistance and chaos phase was dramatically shorter, and the organization spent the least time possible with decreased productivity.

You can increase productivity during the transition to agile by conducting a comprehensive readiness assessment before you start. This way, all preparation efforts can be identified early on, before the transition into resistance and chaos.

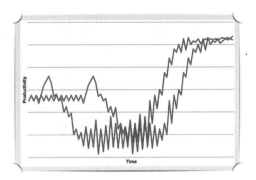

Figure 4.2   A Virginia Satir change curve with a shortened chaos phase overlaid on a change curve with a prolonged chaos phase

4.4   Getting executive buy-in for agile adoption using readiness assessments

Many managers hesitate to begin major change initiatives like becoming agile because they must objectively identify the risks involved with the transition. By conducting a comprehensive readiness assessment, you can prove to management that the organization possesses the necessary characteristics for a successful transition to agile. If your organization isn't ready for certain agile practices, the assessment will help pinpoint exactly which characteristics need to be enhanced. This information will help management make a more informed decision about whether the organization should start the agile initiative.

Figure 4.3 shows part of a complete readiness assessment report from an online readiness assessment tool, created by Ahmed, named Dr. Agile (www.dragile.com). As you can see, the first column lists different agile practices. To the right of each practice are the organizational characteristics that are assessed; the final columns show the assessment results. A report like this is beneficial and insightful to executives because it shows them the amount of effort needed to adopt agile in the organization. Many times, executives are reluctant to start an agile adoption initiative because there are too many unknowns. One of these important unknowns is whether the organization is ready. Readiness assessments give executives visibility into the amount of effort (which they translate into cost) required for the adoption process.

When executives looks at this report and sees that their organization has all the necessary characteristics for a successful adoption, they're more inclined to support and even champion the initiative. If the organization needs to enhance some of the characteristics required for the adoption of agile practices, then executives have the option to either undertake the necessary steps to improve these characteristics or go ahead with the adoption of those practices the organization is currently ready for.

We believe that readiness assessments provide executives with the right amount of information, visibility, and insights to make them support the agile transition initiative. Executive support is covered in more detail in chapter 5.

Agile Practice	Assessment Area	Assessment Characteristics	Not Achieved 0% - 30%	Partially Achieved 30% - 60%	Largely Achieved 60%-85%	Fully Achieved 85% - 100%
Retrospectives	Managers	Willingness to participate in retrospectives				92
	Adaptability of Process	Ability to change and improve the software process in the middle of a project				92
Collaborative Planning	Project Planning	Willingness to plan with others	29			
	Management Style	Collaboration		50		
	Management Transparency	Openness with developers		48		
	Power Distance	Intimidation to give honest feedback			79	
Collaborative Teams	Interaction	Existence of interaction between developers		33		
	Culture	Willingness to work in collaborative teams				92
		Belief in group work			71	
Coding Standards	Standards	Existence of coding standards				100
	Discipline	Willingness to abide to coding standards			71	
...	...	...	...	...	...	...

Figure 4.3 Part of a readiness-assessment report generated by Dr. Agile (www.dragile.com). The report shows each agile practice (far-left column) and the degree to which its supporting characteristics are achieved in the organization (far-right columns).

4.5 Conducting readiness assessments

Now that we've highlighted the importance of conducting agile readiness assessments, the next question is, how do you conduct such an assessment? You can set up an assessment many ways, but our goal has been to create one that is flexible and extensible.

We identified a set of 20 or so common agile practices. Then we created a readiness-assessment table for each of these practices. By creating a separate readiness-assessment table for each practice, we've given people the flexibility to assess their team/organization for one particular practice without having to go through the assessment questions for all the other practices; and we've made the assessment extensible, because new practices can easily be added to the assessment by creating readiness-assessment tables for them. The next section will show you the readiness-assessment table for an agile practice and take you through a step-by-step description of how to use the table to determine whether your team or organization is ready to adopt this practice.

Whether someone suggests a practice for you to adopt or you read a book (like this one) that encourages you to adopt certain practices, you can look for the readiness-assessment tables for those practices and find out whether you possess the necessary characteristics to successfully adopt them.

4.5.1 Readiness-assessment tables

Let's imagine that Mike works for a company that uses some agile development methods. His friend Jay works for Acme Media, which uses traditional development methods. Mike and Jay meet one day, and Mike starts talking about this new way of working called *agile.* Jay is skeptical, but one practice Mike mentions catches his attention: collaborative planning. Jay is intrigued by the idea that the whole team is involved in the planning process. Jay tells Mike that he wants to try this new practice with his team. Mike is happy that Jay is taking a small step toward agility and tells him to first go buy a book named *Becoming Agile.* Mike emphasizes that Jay should do a readiness assessment for his team before discussing agile with his boss. Jay buys the book and goes straight to the readiness-assessment table for collaborative planning (see figure 4.4).

Before we continue the story, let's dissect the readiness-assessment table and understand its layout. The assessment uses two main components: organizational characteristics and assessment indicators.

Organizational characteristics are the various attributes you need to assess to determine whether a team or organization is ready to adopt a certain agile practice. These characteristics may be related to a number of different aspects of the organization, most commonly the following:

- *Customers*—The project's customers and clients
- *Builders*—The technical staff involved with the development of the project
- *Managers*—The managers or executives overseeing the project and involved with decision making

COP	**Collaborative Planning**				
	All stakeholders of the project, developers, managers and business people come together during the planning activities of the project				
Various characteristics to be assessed to determine the team's readiness for this practices					**Indicators**
Management Style:					COP_M1, COP_M2
Whether or not a collaborative or a command-control relation exists between managers and subordinates.					
The management style is an indication of whether or not management trusts the developers and vice-versa.					COP_D1, COP_D2
Manager's Buy-In					COP_M3
Whether or not management is supportive of or resistive to having a collaborative environment					
Power Distance:					COP_D3, COP_D4
Whether or not people are intimidated/afraid to participate and be honest in the presence of their managers					
Developer's Buy-in					COP_D5
Whether or not the developers are willing to plan in a collaborative environment					
Indicators (questions) to be answered by the project manager(s)					
COP_M1	**Irrelevant of your personal preferences, as a manager you actively encourage team work over individual work**				
	Strongly Disagree	Tend to Disagree	Neither Agree or Disagree	Tend to Agree	Strongly Agree
COP_M2	**You frequently brainstorm with the people you are managing**				
	Strongly Disagree	Tend to Disagree	Neither Agree or Disagree	Tend to Agree	Strongly Agree
COP_M3	**It is beneficial to have developers and business people take part in creating the project plan**				
	Strongly Disagree	Tend to Disagree	Neither Agree or Disagree	Tend to Agree	Strongly Agree
Indicators (questions) to be answered by the developers					
COP_D1	**Your manager encourages you to be creative and does not dictate what to do exactly**				
	Strongly Disagree	Tend to Disagree	Neither Agree or Disagree	Tend to Agree	Strongly Agree
COP_D2	**Your manager gives you the authority to make some decisions without referring back to him/her**				
	Strongly Disagree	Tend to Disagree	Neither Agree or Disagree	Tend to Agree	Strongly Agree
COP_D3	**It is acceptable for you to express disagreement with your manager(s) without fear of their retribution**				
	Strongly Disagree	Tend to Disagree	Neither Agree or Disagree	Tend to Agree	Strongly Agree
COP_D4	**People's titles and positions are not a great cause of intimidation in the organization**				
	Strongly Disagree	Tend to Disagree	Neither Agree or Disagree	Tend to Agree	Strongly Agree
COP_D5	**You would like to participate in the planning process of the project you work on**				
	Strongly Disagree	Tend to Disagree	Neither Agree or Disagree	Tend to Agree	Strongly Agree

Figure 4.4   The readiness-assessment table for the agile practice of collaborative planning

- *Tools*—The software tools used within the organization or for a certain project
- *Culture*—The overall culture of the people within an organization or the project team
- *Project management*—The procedures and practices related to managing projects in the organization
- *Software process*—The activities and artifacts related to the software-development process in the organization
- *Physical environment*—The physical layout of the organization and the geographical and spatial distribution of its employees

Indicators are the questions you use to assess each organizational characteristic. Indicators can be targeted at four different groups in the organizations:

- *Developers*—Team members who are involved in building the actual system. They usually include developers/coders, architects, and testers.
- *Managers*—Any team members involved with management of the project. This role is suitable for project managers, team leaders, and any other management positions in direct relation with the project.

- *Product owners*—Team members who are involved with the product's business direction. This role is suitable for any team member who is in direct contact with the customer. Some of the common positions that fall under this role are business analyst, product manager, product leader, engagement manager, and project manager (if they're in contact with the client).

- *Assessors*—People outside the team. Their main role is to observe whether certain process activities and artifacts exist. Common positions that fall under this role are agile coaches, quality-assurance personnel, process-improvement personnel, and independent observers outside the team.

Figure 4.5 shows where the organizational characteristics and indicators are laid out in the readiness-assessment table for collaborative planning.

The top part of the table names the agile practice and briefly describes it. Section A lists the organizational characteristics. In this example, four characteristics should

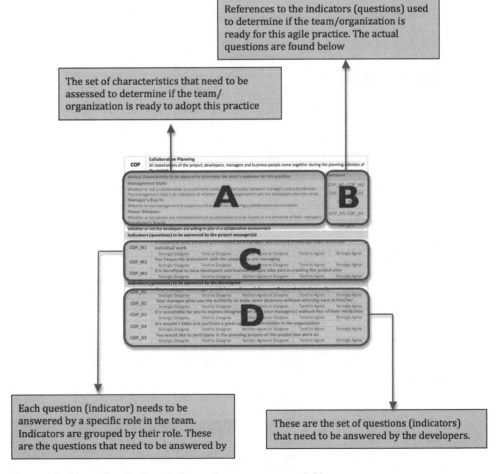

Figure 4.5   Dissecting the layout of a readiness-assessment table

be assessed for collaborative planning (management style, manager buy-in, power distance, and developer buy-in). Each characteristic is accompanied by a brief explanation of what you want to discover by assessing it. For example, as mentioned earlier, you assess power distance to determine whether people are intimidated by their managers and afraid to participate and be honest in the presence of those managers.

In front of each characteristic (section B) are reference codes. These codes refer to the indicators that are used to assess the organizational characteristic. The first letter after the underscore in the code denotes whom the indicator is targeted at. If the letter is an *M*, then a manager should answer the indicator. The letter *D* refers to a developer, *C* to a customer or product owner, and *A* to an assessor. The indicators are grouped depending on this letter. In this example, we have only three indicators for managers and five for developers; indicators targeted at managers are grouped together (section C), and indicators targeted at developers are also grouped together (section D). If we were analyzing an agile practice that had more indicators targeted at assessors, then we would have a section E (beneath D) that contained those indicators.

Now, back to our story about Mike and Jay. The next section will show you how Jay uses the readiness-assessment table to determine the areas in which his team is ready and those in which it isn't.

4.5.2   *Finding out the results*

Jay looks at the readiness assessment table for collaborative planning. He reads the organizational characteristics, picks a project team, and sends the three questions that are directed toward the project manager to Wendy. Jay sends the five questions directed toward developers to Matt (a developer on the team) and Vijay (the team's tester).

Wendy asks Jay what the questions are about, and Jay replies that he wants to try something new and needs her honest opinion. Wendy answers the questions in no time and sends them back to Jay. Her answers are in table 4.2.

Table 4.2   Wendy's answers to the questions for the project manager as part of the agile-readiness assessment

COP_M1	*Regardless of your personal preferences, as a manager you actively encourage team work over individual work*				
	Strongly Disagree	Tend to Disagree	Neither Agree nor Disagree	Tend to Agree	Strongly Agree
COP_M2	*You frequently brainstorm with the people you're managing*				
	Strongly Disagree	Tend to Disagree	Neither Agree nor Disagree	Tend to Agree	Strongly Agree
COP_M3	*It's beneficial to have developers and business people take part in creating the project plan*				
	Strongly Disagree	Tend to Disagree	Neither Agree nor Disagree	Tend to Agree	Strongly Agree

Vijay and Matt also send back their surveys. Vijay's answers are shown in table 4.3.

Table 4.3 Vijay's answers to the questions for developers as part of the agile-readiness assessment

COP_D1	Your manager encourages you to be creative and doesn't dictate what to do exactly				
	Strongly Disagree	Tend to Disagree	Neither Agree nor Disagree	Tend to Agree	Strongly Agree
COP_D2	Your manager gives you the authority to make some decisions without referring back to him/her				
	Strongly Disagree	Tend to Disagree	Neither Agree nor Disagree	Tend to Agree	Strongly Agree
COP_D3	It's acceptable for you to express disagreement with your manager(s) without fear of their retribution				
	Strongly Disagree	Tend to Disagree	Neither Agree nor Disagree	Tend to Agree	Strongly Agree
COP_D4	People's titles and positions aren't a great cause of intimidation in the organization				
	Strongly Disagree	Tend to Disagree	Neither Agree nor Disagree	Tend to Agree	Strongly Agree
COP_D5	You would like to participate in the planning process of the project you work on				
	Strongly Disagree	Tend to Disagree	Neither Agree nor Disagree	Tend to Agree	Strongly Agree

Matt's answers are shown in table 4.4.

Table 4.4 Matt's answers to the questions for developers as part of the agile-readiness assessment

COP_D1	Your manager encourages you to be creative and doesn't dictate what to do exactly				
	Strongly Disagree	Tend to Disagree	Neither Agree nor Disagree	Tend to Agree	Strongly Agree
COP_D2	Your manager gives you the authority to make some decisions without referring back to him/her				
	Strongly Disagree	Tend to Disagree	Neither Agree nor Disagree	Tend to Agree	Strongly Agree
COP_D3	It's acceptable for you to express disagreement with your manager(s) without fear of their retribution				
	Strongly Disagree	Tend to Disagree	Neither Agree nor Disagree	Tend to Agree	Strongly Agree
COP_D4	People's titles and positions aren't a great cause of intimidation in the organization				
	Strongly Disagree	Tend to Disagree	Neither Agree nor Disagree	Tend to Agree	Strongly Agree
COP_D5	You would like to participate in the planning process of the project you work on				
	Strongly Disagree	Tend to Disagree	Neither Agree nor Disagree	Tend to Agree	Strongly Agree

Jay takes these answers and begins to compute the results of the readiness assessment. He needs to complete four calculations to determine the final results.

STEP 1: COMPUTE A WEIGHT FOR EACH INDICATOR

The first step is to assign a weight to each indicator. A *weight* is a fractional value between 0 and 1 that expresses the indicator's level of influence on the characteristic being assessed. The weights of all the indicators belonging to the same characteristic must sum to 1. Jay assumes that all the indicators have an equal weight, but some indicators can be weighted higher than others.

Jay looks at the first characteristic to be assessed for collaborative planning: management style. As shown earlier in figure 4.4, this characteristic has a total of four indicators: two answered by managers and two answered by developers. At this point, Jay doesn't care which indicators are answered by whom—all he is interested in is the total number of indicators required to assess the team's management style. Jay computes the weights as follows (assuming all indicators have an equal influence on the parent factor):

1 (sum of all weights) / 4 (number of indicators, including developers and managers)
= 0.25 (weight per indicator)

STEP 2: COMPUTE WEIGHED INTERVALS

After Jay computes the weight for each indicator, the next step is to compute the *weighted intervals* for each of the indicators. To achieve more accurate assessment results, each answer represents a range of values, not a fixed number. Table 4.5 shows the lists of ranges assigned to each answer in the readiness assessment.

Answer	Value range
Strongly Disagree	0–15%
Tend to Disagree	15–40%
Neither Agree nor Disagree	40–60%
Tend to Agree	60–85%
Strongly Agree	85–100%

Table 4.5   The range of values assigned to each answer option in the readiness-assessment survey

These ranges can change, depending on the threshold and the answer values the assessor uses. Table 4.6 shows another set of answers with different value ranges.

Answer	Value range
Never	0–20%
Rare	20–50%
Seldom	50–80%
Frequently / Usually	80–100%
Always	85–100%

Table 4.6   A set of numeric values assigned to different answer options in the readiness-assessment survey

What's important is to ensure that you have a suitable range for each of the answer values in the assessment.

Jay starts to compute the weighted intervals for management style. Table 4.7 shows the answers given to the sample indicators.

Table 4.7   Answers provided during the readiness assessment for the Management style characteristic

	Strongly Disagree	Tend to Disagree	Neither Agree nor Disagree	Tend to Agree	Strongly Agree
Indicator	0%-15%	15%-40%	40%-60%	60%-85%	85%-100%
COP_M1		1 (Wendy)			
COP_M2		1 (Wendy)			
COP_D1		1 (Vijay)		1 (Matt)	
COP_D2	1 (Vijay)	1 (Matt)			

Once you have the answers from the sample indicators, the next step is to multiply the weight of the indicator by the high and low end of the interval range selected for the indicator. Because Jay sent the survey to Vijay and Matt, there are two intervals for each of the developers' indicators. So, before he multiples the indicator's weight by the low and high interval values, Jay adds the low end of Vijay's interval to the low end of Matt's interval and then divides the total by 2. He does the same thing with the high ends of the intervals. When Jay has the resulting new interval, he multiplies it by the weights computed in step 1. Table 4.8 shows the answers converted into their range values and multiplied by the weight.

Table 4.8   All the answers provided during the readiness assessment are converted into number ranges and then multiplied by the weight of each assessment indicator.

Reference number	Computed weight	Interval low end	Interval high end	Interval low end × weight	Interval high end × weight
COP_M1	0.25	15	40	15 x 0.25 = 3.75	40 x 0.25 = 10
COP_M2	0.25	15	40	15 x 0.25 = 3.75	40 x 0.25 = 10
COP_D1	0.25	(15 + 60)/2 = 37.5	(40 + 85)/2 = 62.5	37.5 x 0.25 = 9.4	62.5 x 0.25 = 15.6
COP_D2	0.25	(0 + 15)/2 = 7.5	(15 + 40)/2 = 27.5	7.25 x 0.25 = 1.8	27.5 x 0.25 = 6.8

STEP 3: CALCULATE THE RESULT RANGE

The next step is to compute the result range by calculating the *optimistic* and *pessimistic* *range* for each characteristic. You do this by summing up all the weighed intervals you obtained from the previous step. The following shows some of Jay's calculations:

Pessimistic result = Sum of all the weighted low-end results from step 2
Pessimistic result: 3.7 + 3.7 + 9.4 + 1.8 = 18.6

Optimistic result = Sum of all the weighted high-end results from step 2
Optimistic result: 10 + 10 + 15.6 + 6.8 = 42.4

Result in terms of an interval = 18.6–42.4
Result as a single number = (18.6 + 42.4) / 2 = 30.5

STEP 4: TRANSLATE TO A NOMINAL SCORE

Now Jay has the result range for the management style characteristic: 18.6–42.4. He also has the result as a single number: 30.5. The last step is to map the result range to a *nominal value.*

Table 4.9 shows a list of the nominal values used for Acme Media's readiness assessment. Although this step is optional, people will be able to read your report more easily if the results are translated to a nominal value. These nominal values are used to evaluate the suitability of the characteristic to support the successful adoption of the agile practice. If the result range from step 3 fits within one of these nominal value intervals, then that suffices; if it doesn't, then you need to obtain an average and see where that number lies in the nominal-value intervals.

Jay's calculated result for management style falls between the *Not suitable* and *Partially suitable* values. So he uses the single-number result and finds that management style barely makes it into the *Partially suitable* range.

Nominal value	Value range
Not suitable	0–30%
Partially suitable	30–60%
Largely suitable	60–75%
Fully suitable	75–100%

Table 4.9   A set of nominal values and the ranges associated with each

Jay goes on and calculates the results for the rest of the organizational characteristics. Table 4.10 shows the results of his readiness assessment for collaborative planning. Looking at the results, it seems that it may be risky to try to adopt the practice right now; but after some training on collaborative management, the team may be ready.

Characteristic	Suitability result
Management style	Partially suitable (30.5%)
Manager buy-in	Largely suitable (72.5%)
Power distance	Largely suitable (60.5%)
Developer buy-in	Fully suitable (92.5%)

Table 4.10   Results illustrating the suitability of each characteristic needed for the successful adoption of the agile practice collaborative planning

Just as Jay did a quick assessment to see if his team was ready for collaborative planning, we encourage you to do a readiness assessment to determine which practices your team is ready for before you begin your transition to agile. Appendix A contains the readiness-assessment tables for more than 20 different agile practices.

TIP   If you like the idea of readiness assessments but feel that they're too much work to do, a free agile-readiness assessment tool is available online. The tool is called Dr. Agile, and you can find it at www.dragile.com. Dr. Agile consists of more than 300 different assessment indicators that are used to determine your team's readiness for 40 different agile practices.

4.6   *Key points*

The key points from this chapter are as follows:

- Readiness assessments are crucial *before* agile adoption.
- Conducting readiness assessments can help you identify and reduce the risks associated with agile adoption.
- You can use assessments as tools to help gain more executive buy-in.
- By conducting readiness assessments, you can shorten the period of time during which a drop in productivity usually occurs with a major change initiative.
- Readiness assessment tables for more than 20 different agile practices are included in appendix A of this book. Feel free to add organizational characteristics or questions to the readiness-assessment tables; the assessment is designed to be flexible and extensible.
- Dr. Agile (www.dragile.com) is an online agile readiness assessment tool that can help determine your readiness for 40 different practices.

4.7   *Looking ahead*

In this chapter, we discussed how to assess your ability to adopt agile practices and how to assess your organization's overall readiness. This work will help your team prepare for the migration and also provide valuable data points for your executive team. Management will have early information related to areas where you should be able to pursue agile practices and also where agile could be risky.

Preparing executives for a migration to agile involves more than taking an assessment. Your executive team also needs to understand the value of moving to agile and what their role will be in the migration. We'll cover these areas in chapter 5.

The importance of obtaining executive support

Ralph Waldo Emerson said, "Nothing great was ever achieved without enthusiasm." Those of you with significant business experience know that nothing great was ever achieved without executive support. This is not true because of executive team impact; rather, it's true because executives will stop any initiative they have not endorsed. They will want details, justification, meetings, and more meetings if they are caught by surprise on a major initiative—and a migration to agile would be considered a major initiative in most companies.

If you surprise the executive team, they may still let you go forward, but you'll lose energy and momentum if you get sidetracked by not involving them at the start.

Executives are just like everyone else. They have specific needs, and whenever a major initiative is suggested, they want to know what the benefits are for the company and for themselves. In this chapter, we'll show you how to obtain executive support for agile by addressing the specific needs of your company's executives.

A few things are guaranteed when you meet with your executive team. They will want answers to the following questions:

- Why are you pursuing this initiative?
- What is the value of this initiative?
- What are the costs?
- What are the risks?
- What will it do for me?

Let's look at some potential answers to these questions and determine which ones best fit your situation.

5.1 Why should we pursue agile?

There are a variety of reasons *why* you're pursuing agile and what the *value* is. Here are the ones that resonate with executives:

- *No methodology is in place today.* You don't have any process or framework in place, and you do projects differently every time with varying results. You're pursuing consistent, successful delivery of projects.
- *Your current methodology is struggling to keep up with the volume and volatility of your work.* You're looking for a way to deal with projects that need a quick turnaround but have minimal requirements defined.
- *Your customers aren't happy.* The customers feel disconnected from the process and feel their needs aren't being met. You're looking for a way to get customers more involved in the development process and improve their satisfaction.

These items are solid reasons for migrating to agile. But your executives may be concerned that the migration is inspired by something else, such as boredom or trying to become cutting edge. Perhaps team members are looking for a good resume bullet. There is nothing wrong with migrating to agile to get a resume bullet or to modernize your processes, but these should be secondary benefits. Migrating to agile isn't free, and it should be pursued only if it benefits the company and the bottom line.

As you saw in chapter 1, this book includes many statistics related to the value of agile: business satisfaction after migration, cost reduction, and improved quality. These statistics are good for appeasing employees in your company who try to measure everything in terms of probabilities. You can use these statistics to justify your migration to agile; and for lack of better words, your backside will be covered if the migration goes awry.

But there are several things statistics *can't* tell you:

- How much effort the companies put into their migration
- How passionate the employees were who brought agile into these companies
- How much executive support was obtained before the migration began
- How much training the employees received

In effect, the statistics only prove that agile isn't a fad, because enough people have used it that statistics are available about it.

A migration to agile involves so many intangibles that we would feel guilty if we recommended it based solely on statistics. We recommend agile because we've seen it work in several environments. We recommend agile because we have enough experience to know the common issues related to software development. We know agile principles address these issues and increase the *probability* of successfully delivering projects.

5.2   *The cost of migrating*

What will you say when the executives ask about cost? In the model proposed, your main expense will be obtaining a knowledgeable agile coach or consulting company to come in and train and mentor your team. This usually involves 2 to 10 days of training, with several phone calls and one-off consulting sessions post training. These services can run from US$2,000 to $50,000, depending on the length of the engagement and the level of agile expertise already present in your company.

The other expenses are less tangible. They're frequently labeled *soft* expenses because they don't add to company outlay but reallocate existing employees. This will be true of your core team. Over a 3-month period, the core team may spend 10 percent of their time working on the new agile methodology. Other costs are relatively minor, such as printing out materials to support training.

The last expense of note is slower delivery. You can expect the first few projects to be slower as the team gets comfortable with the new processes and each other. After an acclimation period, the team will gel around the process and you will start to deliver high-priority features sooner than before; but patience is required during the first few projects.

An analogy that comes to mind is automobile reviews. We subscribe to magazines such as *Motor Trend*, and we frequently read the road-test reviews for new vehicles. Almost every auto review laments the position of the shifter, the strange angle of the seats, or the lack of cup holders. The test driver may not feel comfortable in the car and may even prefer the previous model.

If you buy the same magazine six months later, it will contain the long-term road-test results for the same vehicle. Frequently, the extended review will say something like, "Although initially quirky, the position of the shifter becomes intuitive with long-term use and simplifies the shifting process. We also found the seating position to be excellent for long-distance road trips." Your migration to agile will be similar. After you get comfortable with how agile works, you'll find it "becomes intuitive with long-term use and simplifies the development process."

While we're discussing the cost of migrating to agile, we should also consider the cost of *not* migrating. Reflect on the reasons for pursuing agile listed in the previous section, and imagine what will happen if you *don't* address those issues:

- Declining customer satisfaction
- Loss of key employees
- Missed deadlines for compliance-related projects
- Lost sales
- Lost product opportunities

Dr. Phil frequently asks his guests a question that relates to migrating to agile: "How is your current process working for you?" This is Dr. Phil's subtle way of saying that if what you're doing today isn't working for you, you need to make a change.

5.3 *The risks in migrating*

If you migrate to agile correctly, we believe the risks are minimal. But we'll list some that can occur with poor management of the migration process:

- You can fail on a critical project if you use it to pilot your agile methodology. The first few agile projects shouldn't be mission critical. Begin with projects that have medium priority, and work your way up to critical ones.
- The migration can fail if it's executive driven and there is disregard for pursuing employee buy-in.
- Projects may be affected if employees hear about the work the core team is doing and decide to experiment without guidance. We've seen teams take one agile practice and try it with disregard for how it needs to dovetail into the upstream and downstream processes.
- The migration can lead to cowboy coding and insufficient documentation with improper training and coaching.
- The migration can fail if you obtain too much coaching. You can end up rolling out a process that the consultant likes versus one that provides value in your environment.
- The migration can fail if you obtain too little coaching. Many teams have labeled their lifecycle as agile after adding one or two agile practices. In these instances, the improvements are marginal, and a true migration doesn't occur.

You can also comfort your executives and mitigate risk by following the process outlined in this book:

- Completing an assessment to see your potential for adding agility
- Identifying people within your organization who are passionate about improving your process and involving them in the migration
- Reviewing your existing process to identify logical places to add agility
- Performing a pilot on a non-mission-critical project to identify potential issues before attempting to scale agile across the entire company

5.4   *Rewards for the executives*

Executives will wonder, "What will the agile migration do for me?" There is nothing wrong with this question. We all have career needs, and no one likes to undertake a venture that puts their career at risk. It's fair to ask "What will agile do for me?" on a personal level.

The answer to this question is usually unique. More than likely, the executives will never tell you the answer to this question directly. You must deduce the best way to make them look good. Here are a few ways we've seen an agile migration satisfy the personal needs of executives:

- Agile allows executives to acquire new skills and knowledge that enhance their value to the company and increase their chances for promotion.
- The move to agile provides an opportunity to demonstrate leadership skills by leading a major organizational change. The executive sponsor reaps this reward.
- The migration to agile leads to more wealth. Like most of us, executives care about their compensation. Migrating to agile lowers costs and increases revenues, which should also lead to an increase in stock value or, if you're a small company, survival.
- All managers dislike dealing with people issues. The agile work environment is more satisfying, and the executives will find themselves dealing with fewer employee issues. They will also be pleased to see employee retention rates increase.
- As we mentioned earlier, customer satisfaction increases with agile. A happier customer leads to more pleasant discussions with the executives.

Now, let's discuss the importance of keeping your executive team up to date during your migration to agile.

5.5   *Communicating frequently with your executive team*

You need to communicate frequently with the executive team and keep them abreast of the progress the core team is making. Although it may sound a bit anti-agile, you may want to publish a weekly status report that provides an overview of progress made, status related to the projected schedule, risks being managed, and issues encountered.

You should schedule a recurring meeting with the executive team to interact with them face to face. The meeting will allow you to add more depth to your status and continue with the executives' agile education. We believe you should meet with the executives weekly. This timeframe works well with their busy schedules and also allows you to spend more time managing the migration and less time reporting on it.

You should also encourage informal interaction with the executives. Some executives may like a one-on-one session with the core team. Welcome them with open arms.

You may have executives who like to drop in during core team meetings to listen. This is a positive, too; just make sure the presence of an executive doesn't intimidate the team so they can stay on course with the task at hand.

All of these are great ways to communicate with executives, but the best way is to have someone in their ranks directly tied to the migration. You need an executive sponsor.

5.6   *The role of the sponsor*

Your executive sponsor is the liaison to the executive team who helps clear hurdles for the team as they develop the new methodology. The most logical path is to find the executive most closely related to software development. Frequently, this is the VP of Development or the VP of Product Management.

If your desire to migrate to agile is being driven from the "doers"—that is, not at the executive management level—it's best to work your way up the ladder to obtain executive support. For example, if you're the project manager and you're proposing the change, you can discuss it with the director of software development. If they buy in, you can ask them to help you take it to their superior—perhaps the CIO. You can do a dual presentation to convince the CIO of the need. Chapter 1 of this book provides great information for such a presentation.

After you obtain your sponsor, you should expect him to play three major roles:

- *Keep the executive team up to speed on the migration outside of scheduled status meetings, and act as a champion for the migration*—The sponsor should help your team acquire funding for the migration and remove roadblocks at the executive level.
- *Represent the organization, ensuring that the agile migration is in line with the organization's goals and strategic objectives*—The sponsor helps the agile team ensure success and minimize risk to protect the organizations investment in the change.
- *Provide leadership for managing the organizational change that needs to occur with a shift to agile*—This includes working with the executive team to create a rewards structure that encourages agile behaviors.

These three roles can manifest themselves in many ways. Here are some typical activities of a project sponsor.

- Help the team define success for the migration.
- Help the team obtain outside help when needed.
- Ensure that the new methodology works within the organizational culture.
- Help with migration team morale, and recognize successes along the way.

Help your executive sponsor if he doesn't have a technical background. Train him to know how software development works and to understand the intricacies of agile. Be patient if he needs time to digest how it all comes together.

5.7   *Following Acme Media as the company obtains a sponsor*

Acme Media's move to agile was initiated by Wendy Johnson, the team project manager. Wendy was frustrated with the team's inability to deliver, and she began chatting with her friend, Jim Moore, who happened to be an agile coach.

Wendy explained that she and her boss, Steve (the CIO) had discussed agile but that for the most part she was doing methodology research on her own. The CIO knew that something needed to change to support the new urgency around their projects, and he empowered Wendy to do the research. Wendy suggested that Jim meet Steve and discuss the fundamentals of agile.

Steve was a well-seasoned IT executive, with most of his experience coming during his tenure as CIO at GE Information Services. He was well-read on the principles of Six Sigma, and he knew a little about developing lean processes.

Steve began: "Wendy tells me this agile stuff is a good fit for the projects we're starting to do. I know a little about it. Can you tell me why you think it would work well at Acme Media?"

Jim told Steve that agile wasn't radical or new and that agile involves the application of solid principles to a development environment with urgent timelines and volatile requirements. Jim went on to walk Steve through all of the principles outlined in chapter 1 of this book.

Steve asked, "What about all of agile's weaknesses? I've heard colleagues say that agile doesn't document requirements and that it leads to cowboy coding." "Not true," Jim assured him. "Agile says 'Don't document it if it doesn't add value to the process.' If you have legal, regulatory, or other business reasons to document, agile principles encourage you to do so." Jim went on to tell Steve that agile eliminates cowboy coding due to the short time-boxing of development. Developers are forced to demonstrate what they have quickly, which encourages developing to the minimal requirement.

Steve continued, "Well, I could try to do this in six months if I ask for midyear funding. I just completed budgeting for the coming year, and I don't have the money to do an agile project. I don't have funds for new project-management software or for several weeks of consulting."

Jim explained to Steve that Acme didn't need new tools and might find that it could dispense some of its current tools. Companies can support agile with spreadsheets or even hard-copy plans and features taped to a wall. A lot of teams get by with a large whiteboard.

Jim also told Steve that heavy consulting wasn't required and, to a point, could be a hindrance. "You want the team to develop a deep understanding of the agile principles, but you don't want someone to create the methodology for them." In Jim's opinion, a migration to agile has better staying power if it comes from within, over time. Jim suggested a 2- to 3-day session to teach the main principles to the core team and show them examples of how agile has been deployed at other companies. Then the core team could be turned loose on modifying Acme's methodology, with Jim coaching along the way. Steve agreed that he could probably fund a few days of training and coaching.

"OK," Steve said. "I might be up for piloting agile. But as you know, I have a Six Sigma and quality background. I believe a whole lot in measurement. I need some way to quantify the improvement if we go to agile." Jim told Steve, "In my limited experience with Six Sigma, I remember the main objective being the delivery of value to the end customer. Why don't we measure customer satisfaction and value delivered after every project?" Steve smiled. "If we can do that, I'll be very pleased." And thus began the migration of Acme Media to agile.

5.8   Key points

The key points from this chapter are as follows:

- If you don't involve your executives in the move to agile, there is a good chance that they will stop the move as soon as they learn of any issues with the migration.
- You and your executive team need to understand the benefits and costs associated with a migration.
- Your first few agile projects may be slower than your historical projects. You must prepare your executives for this reality and schedule a buffer to account for the learning experience.
- Numerous solid business reasons exist for moving to a more agile process. Make sure your migration ties to a solid reason, or you won't be able to get executives or team members to buy into the new process.
- Beyond value to the company, it's helpful for executives to understand the personal benefits that an agile process will provide to them.
- You need to establish a process that will provide frequent feedback to your executive team during your migration.
- An executive sponsor helps you communicate with the executive team and also helps remove roadblocks during your migration.

5.9   Looking forward

In this chapter, we looked at the importance of executive support when migrating to agile. As we mentioned in the introduction, executive support is important not so much because of the deliverables executives provide, but more so because executives will block a move to agile if they aren't involved. In chapter 6, we'll shift to the *doers*: the people who bring agile into your organization. This group is composed of your own team members, some level of management, and your agile coach. We will call this group the *core team*.

Improving buy-in
by creating a core team

If you want your migration to agile to last beyond a few projects, you need the change to be driven from within by key players throughout the company. You need to establish a team based on the people who build and deliver your software today.

The role of this group, which we call the *core team*, is to learn as much as they can about agile and to use this knowledge to add agility to your existing process with the help of an agile coach. The team collaborates and reaches consensus on new processes; then they mentor project teams as they use agile techniques.

This core team is powerful and influential for three reasons:

- *They aren't a part of line management.* A few members may come from the management ranks, but the majority of the team are *doers*: people who design, build, create, and test code. This adds to the team's credibility as you roll out the methodology to the company. Agile isn't a management initiative being forced on everyone; it's coming from real people who will be a part of the project teams.

- *Because the team is composed of doers, they know the ins and outs of developing in your environment.* This is different than when consultants come in, suggest standard practices, and disregard the realities of a specific company. The core team has experience with your company, and as they develop a methodology they know what to keep and what to discard from existing practices.
- *Having team members from all areas initializes awareness across the company.* Imagine a tester going back to the testing team and excitedly telling them what is going on with the new methodology, or a developer doing the same with the development team.

Many companies use outside consulting to get their methodology going. We've seen several companies choose to go with agile methods such as Scrum and then have a third party come in to train employees and design and deploy the methodology. In our opinion, this approach isn't as effective as growing the methodology from within. Creating it from within the organization addresses all the issues with ownership. It's hard to get a team to buy into a process that was forced on them. (Note that in rare cases, an organization is so dysfunctional that it needs to have a methodology forced on it—but this should be the exception, not the norm.)

We support using an agile coach along the way, but we prefer coaches who use a Socratic approach. This type of coach asks you questions that lead you to your own answers.

6.1   Who should be in the core team?

After you obtain executive support, you can begin to create the core team. Your sponsor will probably suggest several managers for the team, but you need to remind them that the core team gains part of their power and influence from their status as doers. You may also find yourself pursuing the best and brightest people from each area: people with a positive attitude and a pro-agile mentality; people who are open minded to change. These would be excellent attributes to list for a job opening, but do they reflect your current employee mix, the people you want to embrace the new methodology? Probably not.

If your company is like most, you probably have some blend of the following:

- Brilliant and collaborative people
- People who are brilliant but difficult to work with
- People who challenge every initiative
- People who loathe change and avoid it at all costs

You want the makeup of the core team to be similar to the makeup of the company as a whole. This will help you obtain buy-in from all employee types when you begin rollout.

After you determine the types of people for the team, you need to decide on the team size. You want a group that's large enough to capture a diverse set of perspectives but small enough to be, yes, *agile*. We suggest a number somewhere between 5 and 10 people. Note that if the team is larger, you can still make progress when a team member is pulled for a production issue or is out due to vacation or illness.

6.2   *Choosing the core team at Acme Media*

To give you a feel for creating your own team, let's return to Acme Media. Wendy Johnson has convinced the CIO, Steve Winters, to sign on as the executive sponsor for the agile migration.

> ### Do you really need a core team?
>
> The core-team concept may seem like a lot of work. To some extent, it is; but the return on the investment is worth it.
>
> We've seen other models work, especially in smaller companies. Acme Media is modeled as a medium-size company, with team members having managers and a decent-size executive team. In smaller companies, the managers are often doers, too. In some companies we've worked with, the company owner also writes code.
>
> If you're in a smaller company, you won't need this ceremony. You'll probably have most of your company involved in the migration due to your small size.
>
> Those of you in medium to large companies should appreciate the core-team approach. Change is difficult to drive through larger organizations, and having a core team makes the road a little easier to travel.

Wendy and Steve have identified their core team members and have received approval from those people's managers. Wendy and Steve worked hard to get a diverse group of people on the team, to allow many perspectives to be considered. Table 6.1 shows the list of team members. Notice that members are from various functional areas and that they all have different points of view about what a methodology should do—just like your team will.

Table 6.1   Acme Media's core team. Core teams are composed of cross-functional team members with various levels of agile knowledge. The diversity of the team works well for scrutinizing the new process.

Functional area/Role	Name	Background
Sponsor/CIO	Steve Winters	Six Sigma enthusiast. Doesn't believe in change for the sake of change. Willing to pilot agile and see if the benefits are realized.
Project management	Wendy Johnson	Frustrated with the status quo. Wants a methodology that supports the urgency that Acme Media is now seeing around its projects.

Table 6.1   Acme Media's core team. Core teams are composed of cross-functional team members with various levels of agile knowledge. The diversity of the team works well for scrutinizing the new process. *(continued)*

Functional area/Role	Name	Background
Development	Roy Williams	Familiar with Extreme Programming (XP) development techniques but comfortable with the waterfall/homegrown process that Acme Media has used for the last few years.
Quality assurance	Vijay Kumar	Concerned that agile will bypass or minimize the need for testing. Experience working in an ISO 9000 environment. Frequently says "document what you do, do what you document."
Operations	Matt Shiler	Exists in a stressful world of managing production issues and deploying new functionality. Worried that he won't have enough time to work with the core team.
Requirements	Wes Hunter	An agile zealot. Has been looking forward to this day for a long time. Dedicated to making agile work at Acme. Works with Product Management to refine feature design for customers.
Architecture	Keith Gastaneau	Wants to make sure that an agile methodology doesn't bypass good architectural practices and that there is enough time to build the infrastructure needed for projects.
Product management	Peggy Romani	Unfamiliar with agile but excited about the promise to embrace the customer and changing requirements. Identifies target markets and strategic needs for Acme Media's products.

Just like Acme Media, you'll need to get manager approval for the employees you select for your team. The managers will probably want you to provide a time estimate. You can take two approaches to the work the core team performs:

- *Get the work done as quickly as possible.* This is the preferred approach. You make process work the number-one priority for the group for 1 to 3 weeks.
- *Have team members work part-time on the core team.* Many teams can't pull several team members away from their daily work for a solid 1 to 3 weeks. Greg experienced this constraint at the *Seattle Times.* To compensate, Greg's team worked on the new process three times a week for 2 hours at a time. Using this process, the duration for establishing a new process was 6 weeks. Greg's team enjoyed the slower process, though, because it gave them more time to think about what they were designing.

After you select your team, you need to meet with the core-team members and set expectations. Let's continue with an example at Acme Media.

6.3   *The kickoff meeting*

After your team has been named, you should schedule a kickoff meeting to set expectations and goals. Similar to meeting with your executive sponsor, you need to start the meeting by telling the team why the company is migrating to agile. The verbiage is slightly different with the core team, with less focus on financials and more focus on process.

As an example, let's look at the presentation Steve Winters is using at Acme Media's core-team kickoff meeting. Steve starts the meeting with the following bullets:

- Acme Media's web division is no longer a supplemental site to the television station. The websites have their own audiences and advertisers now.
- With the increase in popularity of the websites, the backlog of new features and application requests has increased by 70 percent.
- Many of the feature requests are time sensitive. If the requests can't be completed soon, Acme's competitive advantage will be lost.
- Acme's development processes, where they exist, aren't working well with the tight deadlines or with the evolving requirements.
- Acme needs to identify a better way of dealing with urgent projects.

As you can see, Steve's message is tailored more to the project team than to an executive group. He speaks indirectly to revenue by saying "lost advantage," and he mainly targets process improvement. The best thing Steve says is "the websites are no longer supplemental sites to the TV station" and "the websites have increased in popularity." *Steve is telling the team that their work is important.*

You should follow Steve's example during your migration, especially when it comes to emphasizing the importance of the work the team does and how valuable the methodology they develop can be.

6.3.1 *Tough questions*

Of course, everything won't be roses at your kickoff. You can expect difficult questions and perhaps *attitude* from some of the core-team members. Here are a few of the questions and comments you're likely to hear during your kickoff:

- We can't create the methodology. We don't know anything about agile.
- We need consultants to do this for us.
- We've tried to change before and failed.
- What is our role?
- What is the role of the executive sponsor?

The response to the first comment is easy. The team will be trained and soon will have a basic understanding of agile principles. If you're lucky, a few team members will already be versed in agile.

On the second question, they're half right. You'll bring in a consultant or an agile guru to train the team on the fundamentals and perhaps to discuss what other companies have done with their methodologies. But the consultant won't create the methodology for you: the team will create the methodology with mentoring along the way.

The third question is a warning sign to you if you don't know the details of a past failure. Was the failure due to a methodology being forced on the team? Was it due to waning executive support for the change? Do your homework if you learn of a past failure, and make sure your plan covers the lessons learned from previous attempts to change processes.

Assuming the issues related to a previous failure no longer exist, you can explain why the migration should be a success this time:

- The design will be created by experts who know the business well: them.
- The team won't be forced to remove a legacy process if it's proven and adds value. If this is true, there is a good chance the legacy process already supports an agile principle.
- The approach won't be shotgunned into the organization. The methodology will be built iteratively and will be deployed iteratively to mitigate risk. In addition, the new process will *not* be used on a mission-critical project until it has been piloted and vetted.

Answering the question about the team's role is simple. The team will learn about agile and use this information to create the agile methodology. In a quick summary form, they will do the following:

- Train
- Document the existing development process
- Determine what to keep and what to discard from the current process
- Compare the existing process to a generic agile lifecycle (we have provided a generic example in appendix B)
- Design a new methodology based on agile principles and the findings from the organizational assessment
- Get feedback on the design, and tweak it
- Take the design for a test run on a medium-priority project
- Learn from the test run
- Continue refining and testing until the methodology is solid enough to be used on all projects and the team is comfortable with the processes being used

As we mentioned earlier, the role of the executive sponsor is to clear roadblocks for the team and to be the liaison to the executive team at large.

6.3.2 *Your role in the migration*

Another question that isn't listed but that may be asked is, "What is your role?" Assuming you, the reader, are the leader of the core team, there will probably be questions about your role. If you're a manager, you should make it clear that all team members will be equals during team meetings. Titles and status—including yours—will be left at the door. As leader, you'll help organize the meetings and report status to the sponsor. You'll act as facilitator and help the team reach consensus on design ideas. You'll also keep the team cognizant of the schedule and time-box the re-engineering activities.

6.4   *Key points*

The key points from this chapter are as follows:

- Any organizational change requires awareness, buy-in, and eventually owner-ship. A core team will help you achieve buy-in.
- Initiatives driven strictly by management frequently fail or have marginal success.
- Your core team needs to include diverse team members so that the process out-lined can be critiqued from all perspectives.
- Your core team must understand why you're pursuing a more agile process.
- Core team members need to clearly understand what their role is in the process and the work they will be doing in the following weeks.

6.5   *Looking forward*

In this chapter, we discussed the creation of a core team and preparing them for the work ahead. In chapter 7, we'll continue with the foundational work for migration. We'll discuss the cultural aspects of creating an agile environment and how your com-pany mindset will need to change in parallel with your process changes.

The mindset of an agile leader

A few months ago, Greg was contacted by a friend with a problem. The friend had let a compliance project slip through the cracks. The compliance deadline was year-end, which was a mere five weeks away. Failure to comply could mean serious governmental repercussions. Greg's friend asked for help in creating an agile team and doing an agile project in the following 5 weeks.

This would be a great time for us to tout how agile came in and saved the day, but that would be a lie. Greg did help his friend prioritize his work and make the deadline, and they did follow some agile principles along the way, but they didn't put an agile team or process in place. Why? Because it takes time to establish an agile methodology. Teams need time to feel comfortable with agile processes, and they need time to learn how to interact with each other. Managers need time to learn how to lead in an agile environment. The team needs to use an agile process for several months, and *then* major benefits will begin to become apparent.

Migrating to agile means more than changing your process. It also requires a change in culture. For most companies, changing culture is the most difficult part. We believe this is true for several reasons:

- Regardless of whether it's successful, companies get comfortable with their existing development process.
- Many people still believe that requirements change because they're poorly managed. They can't comprehend a process that embraces changing requirements.
- Most managers have been trained to control events. Empowering the development team to deliver and co-own the project isn't intuitive for managers.
- In larger companies, whole groups are dedicated to regulating and overseeing projects. An agile team has less need for these services, so some employees may feel that their jobs are threatened.

There are numerous other reasons, but we believe these are at the center of the issue.

You should address these issues in two ways. First, you must address the culture needs of each group head-on. We'll show you how to do that in this book by laying out a game plan for obtaining support from line management, the team, the individual, and executive management.

Second, you must establish practices that foster an agile culture. Practices such as high customer involvement, testing early, and collaborative decision making promote an agile mentality throughout the company. You'll see these practices as we follow the case study through the pilot project.

The information in this chapter establishes the foundation that allows an agile process to thrive (see figure 7.1). Similar to software development, if you get a good foundation in place, everything else is easier to do. If you don't, you'll fight the foundation with every change you make. Let's start by looking at the skills required for a good agile coach.

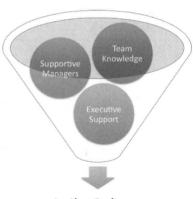

Agile Culture

Figure 7.1   An agile culture is established when three major groups come together within a company. Executive management endorses the agile principles, working managers learn to coach instead of direct, and the project team understands and supports agile principles and practices.

7.1   *The role of an agile coach*

The goal of this book is to convert you and your company into a self-reliant team that can design and maintain your own development process. But out of the gate, you'll have limited knowledge of agile, and you'll be looking for good leadership and guidance from an agile coach.

You use a coach to help you understand where you can become more agile, how to address your constraints, and to train your team on agile principles and practices. Let's start by discussing how to find an agile coach that meets your unique needs.

7.1.1   *Attributes of a good coach*

We've worked with several good coaches. Here are some of the areas to consider when you're looking for a coach:

- *Find a coach with proven results and references*—A good coach has experience in several industries with several flavors of agile. You should be able to speak to their references and validate that value was provided.

- *Don't hire a company, hire a person*—People often ask us for advice in selecting agile consulting companies. In our experience, the quality and experience of individuals within a company can vary greatly. When you need help, you can look at companies; but identify and assess the specific individual who will potentially be working with you.

- *Avoid a cookie-cutter approach*—Some individuals may tell you that one flavor of agile works for everyone. Some companies only support migration to Scrum. In our opinion, Scrum may work for you, but a consultant should evaluate your circumstances before committing to an approach. A good coach will help you evaluate your circumstances before committing to an approach.

- *What about certification?*—A certificate does not validate a coach's skills, but it shows their dedication to their occupation. For the most part, certification is lacking in the agile community today, but ScrumMaster certification and other credentials are available. Recently, the University of Washington opened an agile certificate program.

- *Is chemistry important?*—When you interview a potential coach, you'll get a feel for whether you click with them and whether their approach to migration makes sense to you. Regardless of credentials, you should be wary of selecting someone you aren't comfortable with.

- *Soft skills are critical for a coach*—You should select a coach who can motivate and inspire all the personality types on your team. They should have good interaction skills. Soft skills are discussed in detail in section 7.2.1.

- *Find someone you already know and trust*—As we've mentioned in previous chapters, Acme Media was lucky enough to have a connection to a good agile coach before the company began its search. If you don't know anyone personally, you may have friends at other companies who have moved to agile, and they may be able to provide recommendations.

Johanna Rothman, a well respected agile coach and consultant, recommends that a coaching engagement should always have a deadline so the team doesn't become reliant on the coach. This is a great recommendation, and we agree with it. We often see the coach and core-team leader working together initially; the coach becomes less involved as the team matures.

Now, let's discuss how an agile coach will help you.

7.1.2 *Training and mentoring the core team*

Your company will need some level of training to begin your move to agile. You may have enough experience in-house to lead your migration, but it's helpful to obtain a third party to coach your team and provide an outside perspective. By using a third party, you also demonstrate that management is neutral and open to new ideas.

Training should happen within a few days of the kickoff with the core team. Determining the level of training is tricky. You want to provide enough information so the team understands the agile principles and their value. But you don't want to train to the point that you hand them a methodology—especially somebody else's. The team should combine agile principles with their knowledge of your business to create a methodology that is effective for your company.

You and your coach must use your own judgment to decide how deeply to train your core team. The assessment in chapter 4 will help here, allowing your coach to understand the existing level of agile knowledge, practices, and culture within your company. Here is our suggested outline for training:

1 Begin training with the information in chapters 1 and 3. Explain to the team where agile came from, what makes it works, places where it's working, and why it hasn't faded away. This training should be focused around the agile principles and understanding how agile improves the process. This training should take 1 to 3 days. (Note that it would not be a bad idea for your team to review chapters 7 through 22 in this book. It will allow them to envision how to create and test a more agile lifecycle. It will also show them how agile practices tie to principles.)

2 Give the team a few days to absorb the principles, and then train them on the phases of agile detailed in appendix B. We've chosen phase names that map well to names used in traditional software development, which helps with the training process. This will help the team begin to connect principles to practices.

3 Use the case study in this book, along with your coach's knowledge, to quantify what agile looks like in practice. The example in chapters 9 through 22 shows Acme Media implementing its own online auction application and the inner details of the methodology the company creates. (In addition, appendix B provides a walkthrough of a project going through a basic agile lifecycle.)

After training is complete, the team will work with your coach and begin the design process by documenting the existing processes.

> ## Do you really need training and coaching?
>
> Many people believe they can do their own training on agile, using books or in-house knowledge. We've worked in environments where the team had good agile knowledge, but in most instances we recommend going with some level of agile coaching.
>
> When Greg worked for the *Seattle Times,* his team started a migration to agile with two team members who had worked on an agile migration at another company. These team members provided mentoring and guidance to other team members, but they still decided to bring Jim Highsmith in for basic agile training and to provide coaching as they created their custom process. This worked well because the team respected Jim, and the team tapped into his breadth of agile knowledge when considering practices and techniques.

A coach can be expensive, and you'll want to use your coaching hours effectively. In our experience, we've provided coaching during initial training and then returned one or two weeks later to answer team questions and do more detailed training related to agile practices. We've also provided a lot of coaching via telephone and email, which holds down travel-related charges.

Next, you need to prepare your line management team. Let's look at how things change for managers in an agile environment.

7.2 *Agile management: more shepherding, less directing*

Do you remember a commercial for a company named BASF a few years ago? Their slogan was, "We don't make a lot of the products you buy. We make a lot of the products you buy better." This is true of the agile manager.

An agile manager never writes a line of code, never documents any requirements, and never tests a feature. Instead, an agile manager does the following:

- Helps the development team track true status
- Encourages the automation of redundant, repeatable tests
- Mentors the team on agile processes and demonstrates their value
- Helps the team break their work into small chunks that can be delivered quickly
- Ensures that the work being delivered is in tune with the customer's needs
- Acts as a buffer for outside interruptions and limits team distractions

Jim Highsmith offers a good explanation of *light-touch leadership* in an agile environment:

> *While Light-Touch Leadership may be "light" in terms of decision making, it's heavy in articulating goals, facilitating interactions, improving team dynamics, supporting collaboration, and encouraging experimentation and innovation. These characteristics of a leader are more critical to success than delegation of decision-making authority, but decision making is still an important piece of the leader's role. When a good Light-Touch Leader is working, she or he is nearly invisible. Things seem to happen smoothly and the teams operate seemingly without a leader.*

An agile manager provides leadership without using formal power. Instead, the manager leverages the respect they earn from the team as they establish a history of working together to successfully deliver projects.

What does a manager need to do to establish a record of successful project delivery? Let's start with the soft skills.

7.2.1   Soft skills

If you look up *soft skills* on the United States Air Force website, you'll find, "A set of skills that influence how we interact with each other. It includes such abilities as effective communication, creativity, analytical thinking, diplomacy, flexibility, change-readiness, and problem solving, leadership, team building, and listening skills."

This definition is an excellent prescription for the behaviors an agile manager needs to subscribe to:

- Effective communication, to ensure that the team is synchronized on information
- Analytical thinking, to help the team brainstorm solutions when they encounter a challenge
- Diplomacy skills, to ensure tactful communications that don't offend or touch on sensitivities
- Great listening skills, to not only ensure accurate understanding but also enhance relationships with others

In summary, the manager should behave in a way that enhances human relations (see figure 7.2).

Diane Ehrlich, PhD, of the Human Resource Development program at the University of Illinois, defines soft skills as "[t]he skills needed to perform jobs where job requirements are defined in terms of expected outcomes, but the process(es) to achieve the outcomes may vary widely." This is a good description for agile development in general. You have a desired output (a project), and the way to achieve that output may vary wildly depending on the specific needs of the project.

Now, let's discuss how soft skills are used.

Figure 7.2   An agile leader brings their soft skills together to shepherd the team versus directing them.

7.2.2   Working with other managers

Let's look at team management from the perspective of the person who spends the most time with the team: a project manager or ScrumMaster. These individuals usually lead a group of people who are not their direct reports. In order to do this, the project manager or ScrumMaster must have the respect of the line managers who own the functional teams. The key is to ensure that the line managers buy into agile concepts before asking the project team to.

The line managers need some level of training before you pursue an agile migration. This training can come from any resource, internal or external; but during this training, managers need to normalize on their support of the principles. You don't want to ask the manager's team to buy into the process before the managers do.

You must also consider roles when working with other managers. Although everyone is flexible in the tasks they perform in an agile environment, everyone will have areas of responsibility.

Consider the development team. The development manager usually acts as a technical mentor and also assigns tasks to the development team. Historically, the development manager may have been in charge of reporting status for the team, too. This changes in an agile environment. Agile teams perform a 10-minute daily stand-up meeting that allows the entire team to discuss what they did, what they will do, and any roadblocks they have encountered. Team members speaks for themselves, and status isn't passed to a go-between manager. Traditional managers will need to learn how to provide value and interact in this open atmosphere.

7.2.3　*Working with stakeholders*

Stakeholders are also vital to your project success. *Stakeholders* are those who have interest in or influence on the project. Typical stakeholders include senior management along with indirect customers such as support teams, maintenance teams, help desks, third parties that integrate with the system, and other related product groups within the company.

All the soft skills mentioned earlier are useful when you're working with stakeholders. The stakeholders may not be the project's main customers, but you want them to feel valued. You should demonstrate good listening skills and make sure they know you understand their needs. You also need to demonstrate diplomacy and not upset the stakeholders by consciously providing information in a way that will inflame or incite them.

7.2.4　*Demonstrating value*

The most important role of the agile manager is to exemplify the agile principles and live them daily. If you want the team to follow you, you must provide a strong example. There are numerous principles to emulate and follow. Here are the ones that provide the most impact.

"JUST ENOUGH" PLANNING

In traditional project management, you identify features and then specify their requirements. Typically, an analyst wants to answer every question possible in the specification so the development process isn't impeded by a missing requirement.

In agile planning, you want to plan "just enough." Just enough planning to determine which features you want to build. Just enough coding to demonstrate the feature to the customer and verify that you're on track.

Old planning habits are among the hardest habits to break with a traditional team, and the agile manager needs to champion the just-enough mentality on a daily basis. You can also emulate this behavior by creating project plans the same way: a plan that has just enough information to get to the next level of the project, not a complete work breakdown structure before development has even begun.

ALWAYS READY TO STOP, DROP, AND DELIVER

Agile development is performed in iterations to enhance urgency and to support early delivery of the most valuable functionality. The project manager needs to infuse this mentality into the project team.

You need to get the team to inject the same urgency into an iteration that they do with a final deployment deadline.

UNRELENTING PURSUIT OF CUSTOMER VALUE

An agile manager is always thinking about the customer and their needs. *All other measurements of a project are meaningless if the product delivered is of no use to the customer.* Follow these three steps to ensure that you address the customer's needs:

1. *Clearly define the customer(s).* Many projects get underway with an incomplete understanding of who the customer is. Make sure your customers are clearly defined and their specific needs are clear.

2. *Develop a relationship with the customer.* Get to know the customer well, and integrate them into the project team. Use your soft skills to collaborate with the customer frequently and make sure they can be easily accessed by the team.

3. *Be an advocate for the customer at all times.* When features are being discussed and the customer isn't present, put your customer hat on and envision what their response would be to the discussion. Share those thoughts with the team.

ENSURE TECHNICAL EXCELLENCE

The technical skill sets of agile managers vary. A manager can come from a classic Project Management Institute (PMI) background, can be a former developer, or may have worked as a business analyst in the past. Regardless of technical knowledge, all agile managers can push the team to pursue technical processes that embody agile beliefs. Here are a few of the best practices for obtaining technical excellence:

- *Create a process for continuous code integration.* As functionality is completed, developers integrate their work into the existing code base. The key is to integrate as small pieces of functionality are completed, as opposed to waiting for a complete feature. This practice identifies code issues early and minimizes the complexity of tracking them down.

- *Automate testing wherever possible.* Work with the team to automate testing wherever possible. This is usually easiest to do with regression testing. You can also automate daily smoke tests to speed up testing.

- *Perform a daily build/smoke test.*   Related to automated testing, a daily build also helps mitigate risk by identifying code issues early. The daily test focuses on ensuring that the application's critical pieces are still functional.
- *Consider scalability.*   As an application is being developed, the team should consider future growth. What will happen if the application is extremely popular and usage exceeds expected volumes? The team can consider scalability as they design, keeping scalability in balance with simple design.
- *Follow the principle of simplicity in design.*   As we mentioned in chapter 1, you should avoid cowboy coding and deliver to the minimum requirement. You should also create the simplest design that will work.

When you've learned how to lead an agile team, you can begin teaching the team how to take part in ownership of the process.

7.2.5   *Leading the team to ownership*

In 1998, Arthur Andersen published a book titled *Best Practices: Building Your Business with Customer Focused Solutions*. One of the best practices outlined in the book is the ABO Continuum. This continuum identifies a vital element in introducing change to an organization: ensuring ownership of the change.

The continuum promotes the belief that organizational change goes through the following three steps:

- *Awareness*—In this phase, information about the change is shared early and informally. For example, during a team meeting, a manager can say, "The executives are discussing improvements for our development process." The manager can also indicate when they think they will hear more, and see what the team reaction is.

  The value isn't so much in what is said as in *when* it's said. Every individual has their own timeframe for evaluating a change. The earlier you can make a group aware of a potential change, the better your chances of getting them to buy into the change when you're ready to roll it out.
- *Buy-in*—This phase occurs when you roll out the change and begin implementing it. You created awareness earlier, and you're looking for the team to consider the change and to use it with your guidance.
- *Ownership*—The team has tried the change, begun to believe in it, and adopted it as a standard practice. They don't need management to encourage them to use it. They believe in it and will use it without being prodded.

The ABO Continuum is a great approach for rolling out an agile methodology.

Now that we've outlined the characteristics of an agile management group, let's discuss creating an agile mentality within your project teams.

The ScrumMaster

Scrum has become one of the most popular agile packaged methods. The Scrum-Master is at the heart of Scrum. This individual isn't a manager but more of a process facilitator and guide. A ScrumMaster does the following:

- Helps the team develop practices that support agile principles
- Acts as a guide in training the team on how to be agile and use Scrum
- Removes impediments that prevent the team from delivering software
- Shields the team from corporate bureaucracy and activities that don't add value to software development
- Champions engineering excellence and processes that support the creation of shippable software
- Ensures that the team has direct access to the customer

We believe Scrum is a good agile framework, especially when there is urgency to establish a development process quickly. But we worry that some teams can become too dependent on the ScrumMaster.

Our opinion is based on something we learned when we became certified as Scrum-Masters. Our instructor told us that ScrumMasters are the key to Scrum's ability to transform the organization. He also told us that ScrumMasters are responsible for team health. We understand that not everyone was taught this principle when they became ScrumMasters, but we are still concerned that many people believe the ScrumMaster is the sole owner of team health.

Over time, we've come to dislike the thought of one person with so much responsibility. In our experience, leads and managers have shared ownership when we migrated to agile. Our teams included definite agile experts and leaders, and we frequently asked those experts for guidance; but we never asked the experts to own the process or team health. We did this collaboratively as a leadership team. We've found this method to be successful because we do get expert opinion, but we don't relinquish ownership of team health or the development process to one person.

7.3   *Creating a team with an agile mindset*

An agile team comes across as poised and ready for wherever the project may lead them. Agile team members don't fear uncertainty; they look forward to the challenge and know they will succeed.

Where does this air of self-assurance come from? Does this attitude reflect the type of people who were hired? Or does it reflect the processes that are being used? Is the attitude a byproduct of executive support? Does confidence come from a history of successful deliveries?

The answer to all of these questions is *Yes*. Each of these items supports the effectiveness and self-reliance that is inherent in an agile team. In some ways, creating an agile team is like baking a cake. You can obtain the ingredients exactly as the recipe requests, bake at the suggested temperature, and let the cake cool the specified time before applying the icing. But what happens if you're at high altitude and you forget to make the necessary adjustments? The cake rises too quickly and then turns out too dry. Or what if someone jumps up and down in the kitchen while the cake is baking? The cake collapses and never rises.

In this section, we'll give you the ingredients for creating your agile team. In subsequent chapters, we'll walk you through "high-altitude baking" and how you should adjust your recipe accordingly.

7.3.1 Culture and roles

We find it hard to describe agile team culture in a sentence, but we can easily describe it with several words. The words that come to mind are *collaborative, open, passionate, courageous, honest, lighthearted, driven, synchronized, customer focused, funny, responsible, innovative,* and *successful.*

The culture is one of low politics and high transparency. Words are honest but not abrasive. Status is discussed in matter-of-fact terms. The team focuses on the situation, not the person.

Estimates are honest. There is no padding to make the work easier to do. There is no lying about how long it will take, in order to appease management.

Another nuance of an agile environment is the roles the team members play. Other than as suggested by Scrum, agile doesn't specify what team-member roles should be. In our experience, this hasn't been an issue. The teams we've worked with didn't change their roles after they migrated to agile. We still had developers, testers, project managers, product managers, customers, DBAs, and operations personnel.

What did change for those teams was attitude. After we migrated to agile, we rarely heard a team member saying something like "development isn't responsible for that" or "quality determines when the code is acceptable." We saw many more team decisions and much more collaboration around problem solving. A problem wasn't tied to one role that had to solve it. Instead, it was tied to the project, and *the team had to solve it.* An agile team focuses on the goal, not their job descriptions.

The last item related to culture is diversity. If you don't have a diverse team, your agile process can lead to *groupthink.* Groupthink happens when team members want to get along with each other so desperately that they won't voice their opinion when they disagree with an idea. This is a definite danger with agile. People assume collaboration means harmony and always getting along. They think that if they start agreeing with each other all the time, they're being collaborative. In fact, good collaboration often includes disagreement.

The reciprocal of groupthink is diverse opinion that is spoken freely. This is what you want in your agile environment. A good example of this occurred during the Apollo 13 space mission. In this instance, an explosion occurred aboard the spaceship while it was on its way to the Moon. The ship and crew were saved with a little luck and some spectacular collaboration.

> **A classic groupthink example: the space shuttle disaster of January 28, 1986**
>
> The space shuttle Challenger was preparing to launch on a cold day—the weather was colder than it had been for any other space shuttle launch. One of the engineers from a company that supplied parts to the space shuttle warned that there could be risk in launching. He was concerned that the O-ring seals his company provided might fail in the low temperatures because they had never been tested below 53 degrees Fahrenheit. The engineer shared this concern during a teleconference with NASA, and NASA urged him to reconsider his recommendation to not launch. The pressure from NASA persuaded the company to acquiesce to the request and overrule their engineer's warning. Subsequently, the O-rings failed just after launch, leading to the death of the entire Challenger crew (Griffin 1997).

As the Apollo 13 crew experienced various issues in trying to return to earth, the support team on the ground went through days of brainstorming and collaborating to solve the problems. No one team member had more influence than another in suggesting a solution, and "getting along" wasn't a requirement. When problems were discovered, ideas were discussed passionately until the group reached consensus.

Culture isn't an optional ingredient in your agile recipe. The majority of the team must embrace the agile culture or you won't be agile—you'll just be a team that calls itself agile and goes about business as before.

Let's take a moment to look at the building block of the team: the individual.

7.3.2 *Characteristics that influence individual performance*

Not everyone on your team needs to be competent and mature, but you should put a system in place that breeds competency and helps the entire team become competent over time. But just as in traditional development, competency alone doesn't guarantee team success. Several factors affect the productivity of an individual. Let's review a few of them.

MOTIVATION AND REWARD STRUCTURE

A talented, mature individual won't stick around to work on your agile projects if their efforts aren't rewarded. A person who is talented can frequently choose where they want to work. It's up to the company to create an environment that attracts and retains talented individuals.

In simplest terms, behavior reflects incentives. What incentives can you provide to attract talented individuals to your agile team?

Consider the following items related to motivating and rewarding the individual:

- Is the mission of your company clear? Has it been clearly communicated to each individual? Employees want to know where the company is going and how their projects tie to the vision.
- How is health of your company? Are you doing well financially? Are you a start-up fighting to survive? Company health can tie to motivation in two ways. First,

if you're healthy and growing, you can convey this message to employees and tell them that you offer stability, growth opportunity, raises, and potentially equity. If you're struggling to survive, the message is the importance of the project and how it affects the destiny of the company. *Everyone wants to work on projects that are important.*

■ The agile environment stresses the value of the employee beyond their job title. They make management decisions and are responsible for proactive communication. Talented individuals welcome this environment. Employee evaluations should recognize and evaluate collaboration skills.

Another factor related to employee motivation is career stage.

CAREER STAGE

As you migrate to agile, you must consider various approaches to moving your employees to an agile mindset. To help you determine the approach to use, consider where each employee is in regard to their career. Here are the main stages and suggested approaches:

■ *New employees*—Employees who are in a stage of rapid learning and trying to understand the company and processes around them. They're dependent on others to get things done, and they're working to become independent from support. Such employees enjoy learning agile because it levels the playing field for them. They're at ground zero, just like senior employees, and they're comforted by the fact that everyone is learning agile together. They should also do well using the methodology because they don't have a lot of previous experience to bias them.

You don't have to do anything special with these folks. Just be sure they get the same training as everyone else and that they're offered the same opportunities as other team members.

■ *Individual contributors*—The employees who make up the bulk of your teams. They aren't new, and they aren't supervisors or managers. They have a medium to large amount of experience, and they may have chosen not to become managers but instead to become an expert in their functional area.

These folks require the most management, and you must address their needs individually. Some general tips for motivating these employees are as follows:

– Give them an area to own and be responsible for in your migration.
– Give them an opportunity to use and share their expertise.
– Give them a chance to be innovative and unique.

A lot of these employees are looking for growth and embrace agile. Some of them are just getting comfortable with the way things have always been done and resent having to learn another new thing. Be patient with the "resenters" and remember them when the time comes to criticize the agile design: their feedback will be valuable.

- *Coaches*—Employees who are motivated by sharing their experience and mentoring others. They're also looking for an opportunity to renew and revitalize themselves. An agile migration project is just what the doctor ordered for these employees.

  Give these employees leadership opportunities during the migration, such as resolving design issues or leading the team to consensus. They can also be on the forefront of receiving agile training and can mentor novice employees on the process.

7.4   Key points

The key points from this chapter are as follows:

- Moving to agile requires a change in practices and culture.
- Moving to agile takes time. For optimum results, you need to allow time for your company to digest the change.
- An agile coach will help you move to a more agile process by mentoring and training your team.
- An agile coach will help you assess your team's ability to increase agility and also help you design a more agile process.
- Managers need to learn how to lead in an environment with empowered teams. Managers will earn their money by knowing when to lead, when to help, and when to let the team run on its own.
- Team members can maintain their existing roles, but a long-term goal for your team is to cross-train and to minimize dependency on specialized skills.
- You must consider the needs of individuals when you move to agile. Address the needs of the new employee, the individual contributor, and the coach.

7.5   Looking forward

In this chapter, we completed the organizational aspects of preparing for migrating to agile. Now we're ready to roll up our sleeves and start doing the work. In chapter 8, we'll join the Acme Media core team and watch as they review their existing process and look for ways to inject agility.

Injecting agility into your current process

8

Failure at an organizational level seems to come from the inability to customize processes and make them their own. Trying to apply someone else's template to your organization directly doesn't work well. It leaves out too many important details of the previous successes and ignores your company's specific situation. Rubber-stamping agile processes is not agile. The value of having a principle-based process is that you can apply the principles for an individualized process for your situation and, as an extra bonus, one that has been designed to adapt from your learning as you adopt changes into your organization. It is always "custom."

—Kent Beck in a 2006 interview with InfoQ.com

Custom means that you start with a waterfall process, Scrum, or a homegrown methodology, but you modify and enhance the process to obtain the best results for your company. You need to have a process that recognizes your unique challenges and constraints.

We've worked with many companies that have been successful with this approach. It brings agility into your organization iteratively, which reduces risk and provides time for employees to acclimate to an agile culture.

8.1 *Understanding your current process*

Many years ago, Greg's business professor looked around the classroom and said, "To pursue a solution, you must first clearly define the problem." Greg was a freshman in college and couldn't contain his laughter. This institute for higher learning was going to teach him something? This was the great insight he was going to absorb in the next four years? Everyone knows you have to define a problem before you can solve it.

Looking back now, Professor Poe may have been on to something. Greg has worked in business and technical environments for 22 years, and he'd be a rich man if he had a dollar for every time a group he worked with tried to solve a problem without defining it.

We're not sure why this happens. Maybe everyone is in a hurry to be the hero. Or perhaps everyone thinks they know what the problem is and assumes the others share the same thought. Whatever the reason, it happens a lot. We're dedicated to making sure it doesn't happen to you on your journey to agile.

A way to avoid this issue is to *reverse engineer* your existing practices and identify areas with the highest need for redesign. The first step is to document your existing development processes. If your company is like most, you probably have a few flowcharts around that illustrate how your process flows. Those diagrams are probably out of date and don't reflect how you really develop software. It's important to know how things work before you try to change them; so if you have doubts, err on the side of caution: go out and document your processes from scratch.

The tools you use can vary. You can use software like Visio or Acrobat to record your flow, or you can use index cards, butcher paper, and a lot of wall space. We suggest the index-card approach (see figure 8.1).

Butcher paper and index cards make it easy for the entire team to participate in the documentation exercise. This approach also makes the process easy to review and scrutinize: the flow is visible to everyone, and it's easier to comprehend than a flowchart on a computer screen. You can also use sticky notes in conjunction with the index cards to identify areas that could use improvement, as we'll discuss in section 8.2.1.

Figure 8.1 You need to document your current methodology before you try to tailor it. You may have existing documentation, but there is a good chance it's out of date and doesn't represent how you develop software today. You can use cards of various colors to differentiate your practices and improvement ideas.

8.1.1 *Documenting the existing process with Acme Media*

To illustrate, let's return to Acme Media and see how its reverse engineering work is going. As you may recall from chapter 2, Acme Media has three product groups: the news site, the classifieds site, and a travel/outdoors site. Each group has its own processes for development.

To minimize complexity and expedite the migration, the core team has decided to document only the classified's development process for now. The focus of this site is advertisements for real estate, autos, and merchandise.

Acme has assigned core-team members to various areas to document the phases. The assignments are based on experience. For example, Steve Winters (CIO) and Peggy Romani (product manager) are upstream, documenting how projects get started at Acme. They both spend a lot of time in that area, and their experience will help them document what happens during project initiation.

Roy Williams (developer) and Vijay Kumar (tester) have taken responsibility for documenting what happens on the development phase of projects at Acme. Other team members are likewise assigned to their areas of expertise.

The Acme team members have chosen to use butcher paper and index cards to document their methodology. They find this approach useful because they can see the progress that each mini-research team is making as they document their respective areas. It also lends itself to questions when the team meets daily to review progress on the documentation exercise.

Acme has time-boxed its reverse engineering work to ensure the process doesn't go on for months. One week is allotted for documenting the existing methodology. Most of the work will be performed offline from the core team meeting; then, the group will meet to review the findings gathered by subteams and individuals.

After a week, the Acme core team has recorded the information shown in table 8.1. Note that their findings are on index cards, but we've converted the cards to a table to make it easier for you to read.

Table 8.1   Acme Media's current development process. Documenting the existing methodology can be fun, and you'll discover things you didn't know. This exercise also helps the core team begin to bond.

Initiation phase	Description	Group(s)
Submit requirement documents (RDs) to request queue.	Documents that outline a request and known requirements.	Marketing, sales, product management
Review queue, and prioritize.	Review quarterly.	Executive team
Approve projects.	Approve quarterly.	Executive team
Assign a project sponsor and a project manager.	Assign project managers across the various projects for the quarter.	Executive team
Requirements & Analysis phase		
Obtain project-team members.	Work with line managers to identify team members.	Project manager
Create a project plan.	Interview team members to learn what they will do during the project.	Project manager

Table 8.1 Acme Media's current development process. Documenting the existing methodology can be fun, and you'll discover things you didn't know. This exercise also helps the core team begin to bond. *(continued)*

Requirements & Analysis phase	Description	Group(s)
Create functional specifications from RDs.	A project can have one to many functional specifications. The specs cover all known use cases.	Business analysts
Create storyboards, wireframes, and mockups.	Prototypes to aid design.	UI designer, product manager
Design phase		
Design the data model.	Identify data needs.	Development, DBA
Design the application.	Program design.	Development
Design the interface.	Designer and developer work together to ensure compatibility between front end and program.	UI design, development
Development phase		
Create code.	Programming and research.	Development
Unit-test the code.	Developer tests before releasing to QA.	Development
Create test cases.	Developer with tester.	Development, quality
Testing phase		
Smoke-test new functionality.	Verify that new programs run.	Quality
Build a verification test.	Regression test to verify new didn't break old.	Quality
Perform functional testing.	Validate requirements.	Quality
Identify bugs.	Record defects.	Quality
Repair bugs.	Fix and also determine if the code is functioning as designed.	Development, design
Perform load-testing.	After all code is complete, verify performance is still acceptable.	Quality
Obtain customer acceptance.	Meet with the customer to review functionality and obtain approval.	Requirements, quality
Deployment phase		
Integrate all features, and test.	System-integration testing of all features.	Development, quality
Create maintenance plans.	Background work needed to keep the application working.	Development

Table 8.1 Acme Media's current development process. Documenting the existing methodology can be fun, and you'll discover things you didn't know. This exercise also helps the core team begin to bond. *(continued)*

Deployment phase	Description	Group(s)
Create operation and support plans.	Information that support groups will need to support the application.	Development
Create documentation.	Other documentation as needed; marketing materials, release certification, customer approval.	Marketing, sales, quality
Train.	Train operations and customer service.	Training
Deploy code to production.	Deploy, usually off hours.	Implementation
Deploy code to disaster recovery.	Put new code on backup servers.	Implementation
Conditional tasks/as needed		
Change requests	Needed if the customer has a requirements change.	Business analysts
Create technical specifications	Some features are complex, and the design needs to be clearly understood.	Development
Architecture review	Some applications are complex and require an architecture review.	Development
Company bug stomp	Get the whole company involved with usability testing and final testing.	All departments
Create marketing plan	New, customer-facing features need to be publicized.	Marketing

As you can see, the core team has identified six phases in the existing process: Initiation, Requirements & Analysis, Design, Development, Testing, and Deployment. The team has also identified several processes that are conditional. Tasks such as *creating a change request* and *generating a technical specification* depend on the project's circumstances.

You'll discover similar phases when you document your processes. We believe most companies are doing similar tasks and labeling them slightly differently. For example, one company may call their first phase *feasibility*, whereas another one uses the word *initiate*. Don't worry about labels; worry about what happens within the labels.

8.1.2 Deciding what to keep: identifying existing valuable practices

Acme Media's core team is proud of the work they've put into documenting the company's methodology. They're also proud of what they've discovered. Their existing development processes aren't totally "throw-away." The documentation exercise has helped them recall the history behind some of the valuable steps in the process and why they exist.

For example, Acme used to require a technical specification for every feature regardless of complexity. Over time, the company found that the project manager was asking for approval to skip the technical specification for about 50 percent of features. This happened frequently for feature requests that were simple enhancements that used the existing infrastructure.

The team makes a list of all such processes that arose from trial and error. They feel these steps should be encapsulated in the new methodology (see table 8.2.)

Table 8.2   The core team lists the processes they feel are still valuable. They want to ensure that these processes are included in the new methodology. Many times, such "trial and error" processes are in line with agile principles and fit naturally into an agile lifecycle.

Existing process	Comments
Optional technical specifications	50% of the time, teams were creating them; but they didn't add value to the process.
Required interface design assignment	Almost all features need a UI designer to create the interface. In the past, developers created the interfaces on their own with resulting repercussions to usability and issues with browser compatibility.
Require unit testing	Acme has a long history of developers passing features to QA even when a program wouldn't run. Acme instituted unit testing as a requirement before system-integration testing.
Smoke testing	The QA team was burned many times by starting detailed functional testing before verifying that the basic program(s) ran and didn't blow up in the test environment. Now the QA team runs the basic scripts of the programs to look for "smoke" before initiating functional testing.
Load testing	The Acme project teams used to chat about whether a project needed load testing at the start of the testing phase. Several times, they assumed it wasn't needed, only to be surprised by performance issues after deployment. Acme decided to make load testing a requirement for all projects.
Company bug stomp	Although this is an optional step, most projects have a company-wide bug stomp. After QA is done with a release, employees are invited to spend their lunch hour testing features without instruction. This step has identified many issues and has also helped employees across the company understand what's being deployed.

Unless you're a start-up company, you should have an experience similar to Acme's when you start documenting your processes. You should see some keepers: processes that evolved after toiling with an issue for several projects. We'll speculate that a portion of your keeper processes can be labeled *agile*. Let's review Acme's keepers to see if this is true:

- *Making technical specifications optional* is definitely an agile thought. Agile encourages documenting at a level that supports the process and adds value. Acme realized this was not true for technical specifications and made them optional, at the developer's discretion. When the Acme team starts designing their new process, their coach will encourage them to consider this approach on all of their required documents. This will give the team the power to choose the right documentation level for each project.
- *Requiring the assignment of an interface designer* is agile because it brings the importance of the customer into the development process. This change was driven by a desire to improve usability for the customer and ensure that functionality worked regardless of the browser the customer chose. To make this a 100 percent agile process, the designer can review the UI with the customer during design.
- *Requiring unit testing* is compatible with the agile perspective of viewing status from a binary perspective. In the past, developers *thought* the code was finished, but they didn't know for sure. Now they execute unit tests before functional testing begins to ensure code completeness.
- *Smoke testing* also lends itself to viewing code status from a binary perspective. The program either passes the smoke test or fails.
- *Requiring load testing* for every release is an interesting step. In one sense, it doesn't seem agile because it takes the decision out of the team's hands. In another sense, it supports the agile principle of identifying and managing risk. When the Acme team designs their new process, their coach will ask them if they're able to load test with automated scripts; if so, we'll label this an agile process.
- The *company bug stomp* is a solid process, and it's highly agile. QA makes sure the code does what it's supposed to, and the company users make sure it doesn't do things it's not supposed to. This process adds to company-wide collaboration and leverages the knowledge of everyone who participates. This is a great process that Acme Media should use whenever possible.

Now that Acme has documented its existing processes, let's look at another tool that can help you improve your lifecycle: envisioning a pure agile process.

8.1.3 *Another potential tool: documenting a perfect process*

Acme Media has documented its existing process and now is looking for ways to add agility to it. Some teams we've worked with like to outline a perfect methodology before they begin redesigning their existing process. The thought is, "What would be an *ideal* process if I didn't have any constraints?"

This is a good exercise to perform because it lets the team envision agile principles in practice and motivates them to work around their constraints. It's also good to compare your existing process to one you consider perfect and then see what your current methodology can absorb.

This technique offers another benefit for start-ups and companies that don't have an existing process to change: you can document a perfect process and then review the assessment you undertook in chapter 4 to see where that perfect process will work and where it may have challenges.

Figure 8.2 shows an example of a team envisioning a perfect process.

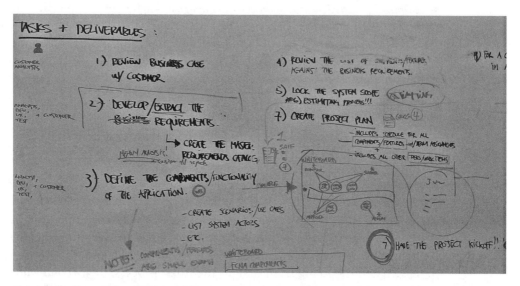

Figure 8.2   Some teams like to envision a perfect process before they modify their existing one.

In this example, a team has written their overall goal for a new process on the whiteboard and then outlined specific steps and the roles that will be involved in each. This team had an issue with trying to deliver features that were too large. Their goal was to break down work into features that could be completed in two weeks, so that miniteams could collaborate and deliver value quickly.

8.2   *Enhancing the existing process*

After achieving buy-in, the next most difficult step on your road to agile will be designing your new methodology. You've been trained on the principles and phases, you've reverse-engineered your existing process, and it's time for the rubber to meet the road.

If we were on your core team, we'd be hesitant. We've always learned from specific examples, and we'd be asking you to show us how another company created its methodology and what it looks like.

To remove the hesitancy and increase core team confidence, we suggest having the team read chapters 9 through 22 before you outline your design. These chapters take you through the design that Acme Media creates and how it works on a practice project. At a minimum, your team can copy the Acme methodology to get started. It's a sound agile methodology, and it's vanilla enough to support most business models. We also outline a phased, generic agile process in appendix B.

Now, let's rejoin Acme Media as the team reviews their existing process and decides what to change.

8.2.1 Deciding what to change at Acme Media

Just as you will, the Acme Media core team has reviewed the wall that outlines their existing process. While putting the wall together, the team made notes concerning things they want to change to be more agile. Earlier, we suggested using sticky notes to label processes for improvement. You should have quite a few of these at the conclusion of the documentation exercise. Let's review some of the sticky notes that the Acme Media team attached to its existing process; see, for example, figure 8.3.

Figure 8.3 Team members record comments about the existing process as they review it. Sticky "improvement" notes are reviewed after the documentation process is complete.

Table 8.3 summarizes the observations and improvement suggestions that Acme Media has identified for its existing process. The first few sticky notes are attached to the first two steps in the Initiation phase: "Submit requirement documents (RDs) to request queue" and "Review queue, and prioritize." The team likes these steps because they prove that feasibility is already being done, but the team also identifies shortcomings in the steps:

- The RDs are usually completed only by the submitter. If a submitter isn't familiar with an area, such as financials or technology, they guess at the information. Historically, the RDs have contained some pretty wild assumptions—for example, a request submitted for streaming live news to the web assumed that Acme would "leverage the existing infrastructure" and "not incur any additional expense" in pursuit of the request. This is an issue because the executive team bases approval decisions on the RDs.

- The executive team reviews the request queue once each quarter. On rare occasions, a request has been approved outside of the quarterly meeting, and that has required a special session of the executive group. The quarterly review process doesn't bode well with the new, urgent requests that are now coming in to Acme. Acme needs a quicker way to get projects started.

The Acme team reviews all the sticky notes before outlining their new process.

The Acme Media core team reviews the findings and then sits down to create their design. The team debates where to begin and decides to use the agile phases they were trained on as the framework for their design. They will build their steps around the Feasibility, Planning, Development, Adapt, and Deployment phases.

Table 8.3   A collection of sticky-note comments after a first review of the existing process. If you have numerous suggestions, they need to be prioritized. Understanding agile principles is imperative before you perform this exercise.

Initiation phase	Sticky-note improvement comment
Submit requirement documents (RDs) to request queue.	Requirement knowledge limited to submitters. Need better information on feasibility.
Review queue, and prioritize.	Needs to happen more frequently.
Approve projects.	Features in an idea or project aren't being prioritized. It's assumed the whole thing must be delivered.
Assign a project sponsor and a project manager.	
Requirements & Analysis phase	
Obtain project-team members.	
Create a project plan.	Hard to plan everything up front. We'll have many change requests, which leads to team guilt.
Create functional specifications from RDs.	Sometimes we create functional specifications for features that are later dropped.
Create storyboards, wireframes, and mockups.	
Design phase	
Design the data model.	
Design the application.	
Design the interface.	UI and dev work well together here.
Development phase	
Create code.	
Unit-test code.	
Create test cases.	Why can't we start creating these before development?
Testing phase	
Smoke-test new functionality.	
Build a verification test.	
Functional testing.	
Bug identification.	
Bug repair.	We compress the time available for bug repairs if the project is running late.
Load-testing.	
Customer acceptance.	Can we show the customer something earlier? We don't have time to recover if there are major discoveries.

Table 8.3   A collection of sticky-note comments after a first review of the existing process. If you have numerous suggestions, they need to be prioritized. Understanding agile principles is imperative before you perform this exercise. *(continued)*

Deployment phase	Sticky-note improvement comment
Integrate all features, and test.	The first time we integrate, we see lots of issues.
Create maintenance plans.	Can we start these earlier?
Create operation and support plans.	Can we start these earlier?
Create documentation.	Sometimes we're running late, and the documentation is compromised or delivered after the release.
Train.	
Deploy code to production.	On occasion, we have deployment issues and have to abort. This is a shame because we kick the users off of the system for a deployment.
Deploy code to disaster recovery.	We should do a retrospective at the end of a project.

The team begins to work for 2 hours at each of their core-team meetings. Team members also do research and design work between meetings. The work meetings are consumed by reviewing and debating design ideas and then reaching consensus about whether to use a given idea.

Here are some of the topics and questions Acme's core team discusses while developing their process:

- When does the methodology kick in? When is something a quick fix or an enhancement versus a project?
- What is the difference between a product, a project, a release, a feature, an enhancement, and a task?
- What are the minimum sets of processes and documents that need to be completed on a project? Related to that, what are all the process options and documents available to a project?
- How will we work with others? Will third parties and other departments need to support our methodology, or will we have to abort on using our new lifecycle when working with them?

After four core team meetings (elapsed time: 4 weeks), they've taken the design to a level that is ready for a test project. Let's review their phases. (Note that the total time elapsed is 5 weeks. One week was spent documenting the existing process, then 4 weeks were spent designing a new process to test.)

8.2.2   *Feasibility phase*

The Acme team previously started their project lifecycle with the Initiation phase. In the new design, they start with *Feasibility*. Table 8.4 outlines the processes for the Feasibility phase.

Table 8.4 Acme outlines a Feasibility phase for its new process. The new feasibility process accelerates evaluation and gets work started more quickly on urgent projects.

Step	Feasibility phase	Group(s)	Change notes
1	Submit idea to request site.	Any employee	In the past, ideas were only submitted by Marketing, Sales, or Product Management. Ideas don't need detailed requirements to be submitted now. The new online form requires minimal population of fields to be accepted.
2	Review queue, and assign features for investigation.	Product manager, line managers, or executive team	Ideas can be approved for more detailed investigation (feasibility) by managers at any time. Managers decide if a team is needed to help with the research.
3	Research ideas for feasibility.	Requestor, or feasibility team	In the past, we only used the requestor's information to determine if an idea was feasible. The team uses the *Feasibility Discussion Guide* to lead investigative work. (This guide is covered in chapter 10.) The team returns with information such as customer thoughts, information about what the competition is doing, cost/benefit analysis, key risks, time estimates, and main benefits to the customer. The feasibility team creates an elevator statement (covered in chapter 10).
4	Review findings to see if the idea should continue to the Planning phase.	Product manager, line managers, or executive team	Managers can send an idea on to planning. This is possible because 50% of the team's capacity is now reserved for unscheduled projects. The other 50% of the capacity is reserved to support projects that come out of the quarterly planning process. A manager can escalate the decision to the executive team if funds are needed or if the project will exceed the remaining capacity in the quarter.
5	Decide to approve, cancel, or defer the idea/project.	Product manager, line managers, or executive team	Make the call about whether to continue and assemble a project team.
6	Assign resources to the planning team.	Product manager, line managers, or executive team	We want the planning team to stay with the project throughout development.

Acme Media has redesigned its first phase to allow for quicker investigation of projects. Feasibility can now begin with approval from line or product managers. The team has also improved the accuracy of feasibility work by not limiting it to the person who submitted the idea. A feasibility team can be constructed quickly to help research areas where the requestor has limited knowledge.

The team likes the fact that the executive team does quarterly planning and is thinking about long-term strategy, so quarterly planning stays intact. What has changed is the fact that executives assign projects for only 50 percent of the capacity in the quarter. This allows 50 percent of the quarter's capacity to be available for the impromptu, urgent projects that are becoming more prevalent at Acme Media.

The next phase the team has outlined is the Planning phase.

8.2.3 *Planning phase*

The Acme core team has made the most changes around project planning; see table 8.5.

Acme Media has embraced the concept of "just enough" with the planning phase, which will let the team spend more time developing high-priority features.

Table 8.5 Acme Media's new planning process empowers the project team. The team determines the documents and processes to use from planning through development. Acme has also expedited the feature-evaluation process by not requiring full functional specifications until there is confidence that a feature will be pursued.

Step	Planning phase	Group(s)	Change notes
1	Determine documentation needs for the project.	Planning team	All projects must complete a few core processes and documents, but the team chooses (from a menu) a list of additional process and document requirements. This is a first pass at document needs. The team can make changes to the list as the project proceeds.
2	Hold a team envisioning meeting.	Planning team	Similar to a kickoff meeting, the assembled team reviews the output from the Feasibility phase. The team identifies the features of the project.
3	Prioritize feature cards.	Planning team and guests	This is a significant change for Acme Media. Historically, the requirements team created functional specifications for all features at the start of the project. The project team wasn't highly involved in prioritizing and fleshing out requirements with the requirements team. QA is involved in this process, and they begin envisioning and creating the test cases at this point.
4	Sequence feature cards.	Planning team and guests	This is another major change. Instead of the project manager creating the plan for feature development on her own, the whole team gets involved in specifying the sequence in which features will be built.
5	Plan iterations.	Planning team and guests	After sequencing, the team works together to assign the features to iterations.
6	Make a decision at the planning gateway.	Project manager with product manager or executives	The team makes a continue or stop decision. For the first time, Acme Media will have the option to cancel a project if the Planning phase identifies additional information that makes the project less feasible (technical discoveries, revision to work estimates, dependency issues).

The two biggest changes in this area are team involvement in planning and the assignment of features to iterations. In the past, most planning was completed by the project manager. They interviewed the team and documented the work-breakdown structure, and the team began immediately on the detailed requirements and designs for all the features.

In the new model, the team reviews candidate features together and determines their value and priority. Afterward, the team assigns features to iterations and only does design work for the items that are assigned.

Acme's core team worries about a large group working together on planning and notes that the planning team should have a maximum size of six to eight people. All groups will have at least one representative at the planning sessions.

The Planning phase also adds a new decision gateway for Acme Media. Because so much discovery takes place during the Planning phase, the team presents the information to a manager or the executive team to make the call about whether to proceed with development.

8.2.4   *Development phase*

The main change in the development area is that Acme Media will no longer use the *waterfall model* for development. In the past, the developer received a functional specification and started building from it. In the new model, the developer has the feature card, and all the information is recorded on it. The developer works with the requirements team and the product manager to build to the minimum specification so a demonstration and validation can be obtained quickly.

Another significant change is the daily stand-up meeting. The development team used to meet daily to discuss status during development; now, most of the project team (not just developers) is there to synchronize on information and quickly resolve roadblocks to keep development rolling. Table 8.6 outlines the Development phase.

Table 8.6   Acme Media's new Development phase is focused around delivering value early and early validation of customer requirements. Testing also occurs sooner so that issues are easier to trace and repair.

ID	Development phase	Group(s)	Change notes
1	Perform iteration 0: development initiation work.	Project team with potential executive assistance	In the past, Acme developers received a functional specification to build from at this point. This step is used to put foundation pieces in place, such as architecture, vendor contracts, and environment preparation.
2	Perform development iterations 1–*n*.	Project team	The team swarms on the features to clarify the design and build the functionality. Unit testing occurs at a minimum. Demonstrations are scheduled for the end of the iteration, but impromptu customer demonstrations can happen within the iteration.

Table 8.6 Acme Media's new Development phase is focused around delivering value early and early validation of customer requirements. Testing also occurs sooner so that issues are easier to trace and repair. *(continued)*

ID	Development phase	Group(s)	Change notes
3	Hold a daily stand-up meeting (part of the development iterations).	Project team	Acme Media had weekly status meetings in the past, but they were only attended by managers who reported status for their teams. The new daily stand-up meeting is limited to 15 minutes, and it's "standing." The team discusses what has been done, what will be done, and any roadblocks or issues. The team discusses the status of features and whether they're ready to be integrated.
4	Integrate-build.	Development-implementation	In the past, Acme waited until the end of development to integrate and build. Optimally, they would like to integrate every day, but for now they will settle for integrating three times a week.
5	Test.	Quality assurance	Acme hasn't made many changes to the testing process. The team considered test-driven development, but the assessment they completed indicated they aren't mature enough to pursue it at this time.
6	Repair bugs.	Development	Previously, Acme reserved a few weeks at the end of the project to do bug cleanup. In the new model, bugs identified during an iteration affect capacity for subsequent iterations. Acme reserves some time during the deployment phase to clean up bugs, but major bugs are treated as features.
7	Update maintenance and support plans.	Development	In the past, the team waited until deployment to create maintenance and support plans. Now they consider them part of feature delivery.
8	Complete the iteration.	Project team	This step indicates the end of the time allotted for the iteration.

Acme Media also needs to consider a new phase that was previously limited to the end of the project: the Adapt phase.

8.2.5 *Adapt phase*

In the past, *change* was a bad word at Acme. If you needed to change requirements, the schedule, the scope, or some other project attribute, you had to create a change request. Now, change is expected, and the Adapt phase is dedicated to reacting to change. See table 8.7.

Acme Media still requires change requests for some items, specifically those that require incremental cost; but most changes are embraced, and the team works to deliver what is needed at the end, not what was requested at the beginning.

Table 8.7 Acme Media's Adapt phase embraces change. The team focuses on learning as the project progresses and delivering what is needed at the end, not necessarily what was requested at the beginning.

Step	Adapt phase	Group(s)	Change notes
1	Perform customer acceptance.	Requirements and guests	In the past, Acme performed customer acceptance at the very end of development. The new process allows several reviews. The deliverables for the iteration are presented to the customer for review, testing, and ultimately acceptance. When the review is kicked off, stakeholders are invited to see the overall status of the iteration. In the past, the review was only for customers. This step helps prevent surprises. If features aren't accepted, the team reviews the issues and makes a decision on whether to continue work on the feature into the next iteration. In the past, rework time was limited to the bug-fix window.
2	Undertake discovery.	Project team	The team reviews new information that materializes during development: business-climate changes, competitor product changes, priority changes, and so on.
3	Evaluate the iteration pace.	Project manager	The project manager reviews development's actual velocity versus the forecast velocity and adjusts the features assigned to the next iteration accordingly.
4	Re-plan.	Project manager and team	The team modifies the plan for the next iteration based on all the information gleaned during the Adapt phase.

Adaptation occurs throughout Acme's development lifecycle, but it's stressed during the Adapt phase. Customer demonstrations provide the ultimate opportunity to validate whether the product is on track and, if not, what needs to be done to redirect.

This phase more than any other reveals what agile is all about. Change is unavoidable in a project, so the methodology should embrace change. The team will be busy enough reacting to the change; they don't need additional hassles from the process.

8.2.6 *Deployment phase*

Acme hasn't identified many functional changes for the Deployment phase, but they have found some cultural areas to work on; see table 8.8.

Table 8.8 Acme Media's Deployment phase finalizes work that has been in progress since the Feasibility phase. Items such as maintenance plans have been discussed and worked on throughout the project. The team has also added a step to stop and reflect on how well the process is working—a retrospective.

Step	Deployment phase	Group(s)	Change notes
1	Train support groups.	Implementation	This step is unchanged.
2	Finalize maintenance plans.	Development	In the past, the entire plan was created days before deployment; now it's tweaked and finalized. Work began back in the Planning phase.

Table 8.8 Acme Media's Deployment phase finalizes work that has been in progress since the Feasibility phase. Items such as maintenance plans have been discussed and worked on throughout the project. The team has also added a step to stop and reflect on how well the process is working—a retrospective. *(continued)*

Step	Deployment phase	Group(s)	Change notes
3	Finalize operation and support plans.	Implementation	The team finalizes these plans versus doing all the work at this point.
4	Finalize documentation.	Project Team	The team finalizes the documentation versus doing all the work at this point.
5	Deploy the code to disaster recovery.	Implementation	Acme has had issues deploying in the past. To mitigate risk, they will deploy to the disaster-recovery environment first to identify potential production deployment issues.
6	Deploy the code to production.	Implementation	This step is now performed after disaster-recovery deployment.
7	Hold a lessons-learned (retrospective) meeting.	Project team	Acme has never stopped to review its processes between releases.
8	Celebrate!	Project team and stakeholders	Things have been chaotic lately, and Acme has stopped celebrating. The company needs to return a sense of accomplishment to the team.

The team notes that they've never discussed the lessons learned after a project, and subsequently they've found themselves repeating the same mistakes. A retrospective will be part of the new process now.

When to skip this practice

Sometimes it doesn't make sense to reverse-engineer your existing process. If you're a start-up company, you probably don't have anything to reengineer. Likewise, if your existing process is atrocious and you want a separation from it, you may want to skip this exercise. In these cases, you may want to begin with a "perfect" process or a prepackaged method such as Scrum or Extreme Programming and then look at the realities of your environment and adjust accordingly. The readiness assessment in chapter 4 can help you make this decision.

The team also notes that they've quit celebrating at the end of projects. After many change requests, schedule slips, and chastisement from the executives, the team hasn't been in a celebratory mood lately. The team believes in the new process, and they believe that the future will warrant success, so celebrations have been added as an anticipated part of the delivery process.

8.3   *Key points*

The key points from this chapter are as follows:

- Your development process should focus on delivering as much value as possible within your constraints.
- Don't be afraid to design a development process that reflects the realities of your environment. Customizing and adapting is what agile is about.
- You can begin designing a new process immediately, but it's valuable to study your existing process. You'll identify practices that have been successful in your environment, and you don't want to throw them all away.
- Documenting your existing process is a fun exercise that will help the core team bond.
- You should time-box the time spent on creating your new process, or you could find yourself working on it for weeks. Take a first pass, and go try it with a pilot. You can refine your process as you learn.

8.4   *Looking forward*

In this chapter, we discussed how to add agility to your existing process. The goal is to add agility in an incremental fashion, focusing on areas where implementation isn't risky and the return can be great. Now that you have a process, we need to take it for a test drive to look for issues that can't be identified on a whiteboard. We'll show you how to test the new methodology on a pilot project in chapter 9.

Selecting a pilot project 9

Greg's wife kicked him out of bed, and he landed on the floor with a thud. His tropical-island dream was rudely interrupted. "Look!" she exclaimed. "Look at my bathroom. It's hideous. All that hard work to remodel it, and now it's ruined by a poor paint job!"

She was right. The new shower doors looked great, the tile floor could grace a palace, and the new sinks were sparkling. Unfortunately, the paint job had reduced the whole room to a cave. The paint was too dark and absorbed any and all light in the room. It was depressing.

How had they arrived here? They had done the whole project by the book. They hired a general contractor, they thoroughly identified all their requirements, and then they sat back to watch their perfect new bathroom take shape. For the most part, it had gone well. Of course, they hadn't anticipated that the new shower door wouldn't match the other fixtures. And they didn't get too upset when they realized that the new tile blocked their access to the bathtub plumbing. But the paint was the last straw for Greg's wife.

In hindsight, what should they have done differently? How could they have avoided this mistake? Greg walked through the process in his head.

Obviously, the biggest error was picking a color from the deck of paint chips and assuming it was exactly what they needed. In retrospect, Greg and his wife should have specified the paint color to the painter and told him the choice was *not* final. They should have asked him to paint a small part of the wall with the chosen color plus several similar colors. Then they would have seen that their choice was too dark and selected a lighter shade. They could have next asked the painter to try the lighter shade on one wall only. If it looked good on one wall, they would have turned the painter loose to paint the whole room.

And when they repainted the room, that is exactly the process they followed.

What does this have to do with adding agility? It would be ridiculous to assume that you know how well a new process is going to work across your organization without testing the process first. When you roll out your new development methodology, you'll pilot the process, gather feedback about it, refine it, and continue to scale it across your organization.

A pilot identifies hidden weaknesses, increases agile knowledge throughout the company, and acclimates the team to the new methodology. Similar to the bathroom-remodel analogy, you'll see what your company looks like when you apply a coat of agile paint. The pilot project demonstrates how effective your new process is and helps you prepare to scale agile across the organization.

In this chapter, we'll discuss how you select the correct pilot project (like the team shown in figure 9.1). We'll start by showing you the traits to look for and the traits to avoid. And We'll follow Acme Media as it uses the suggested guidelines to select a pilot.

Figure 9.1 A team evaluates potential pilot projects. The team looks for a project that can be completed relatively quickly with minimal risk to the company.

9.1 Characteristics of a good pilot

The pilot will be the first time the new lifecycle is exposed on a real project with a real team. In effect, it's a marketing event for the new process. If you choose the wrong type of pilot, you may end up aborting, which will be a poor advertisement for the new methodology.

With that thought in mind, you want to select a project that will push you through the test but not *shove* you. You want time to test the process in all areas such as requirements, design, development, testing, and implementation. You also want to give your pilot team time to acclimate to their new level of ownership. Agile is about methodology and culture. The team should understand the literal process, but they should also begin to understand *what it means to be agile*. You want them to start envisioning what it's like to own a project and be highly involved in decisions. Let's look at the traits of a good pilot project.

9.1.1 A project you can complete in 2 to 8 weeks

Your pilot project should have an overall completion estimate somewhere between a couple of weeks and a maximum of 8 weeks. If your project runs longer than this, you extend the time needed to record feedback on the process, which delays your ability to adjust your methodology. What is the right size for a pilot?

HOW LARGE IS TOO LARGE?

One of the easiest ways to complicate your migration is to test your new methodology on a large project. A large project requires training many people—and possible several third parties—on the new methodology. This will delay your ability to gather feedback about the new process and adjust it, which is the ultimate objective of the pilot.

Let us give you an example of a project that we consider large. We were upgrading a company's intranet platform, and the project was scheduled to run for 8 months. The project went through several gateways to obtain funding. It required high involvement from the software provider, and consultants were needed to train the team on the new software. Because the application affected the enterprise, we engaged several internal teams to help us with training, communication, and security. A project of this length and scope doesn't allow time for testing a new process.

You also don't want to work on a project that is too small. Such a project limits the areas and phases in which you can test the new process.

HOW SMALL IS TOO SMALL?

We recently worked on a project that allowed a company to change the appearance of its brand. All of the company's web pages needed to support new company colors, logos, and slogans. The project had to touch every page of every website, but most of the work was completed by changing one style sheet. The project required high involvement for the user interface (UI) team, but the development, implementation, and testing areas had minimal work to do.

The project was completed in a week. If you used such a project as an agile pilot, the UI team would learn more about agile, but the other teams would have limited exposure. The new process wouldn't be tested well because the areas outside UI wouldn't perform their typical project tasks.

USING A SUBSET OF A LARGE PROJECT

On occasion, we cross paths with folks who do nothing but large projects. They tell us that a short project for them lasts 6 months, and they don't know how they can do a pilot that meets our criteria. You can handle this issue by finding a subset that meets the criteria of a shorter project. The question you need to ask is, "What do you do during a project that can be completed within 8 weeks?" You need to identify a group of features to serve as a mini-project within the larger project.

For example, if you're building a website similar to eBay, the project may take 6 months to a year. To test your new methodology, you can grab a few features and test the new process on them. For example, you could do a mini-pilot project around seller feedback and its related features.

If you go the subset route you may have limitations on how far you can test the new process. Your subset of features may need to rejoin the other features and go through the legacy testing and deployment processes. If you experience this issue, you can try to pull the features completely out of the project in subsequent tests, running them all the way through to deployment.

9.1.2 *A medium-priority project*

Your pilot project needs to have some level of urgency to test the new process under pressure; but if the project is deemed critical, failure isn't a viable option. You may panic, abort, and revert to methods you're more comfortable with to complete the project. As we mentioned in section 9.1, the pilot project is a marketing effort as well as a test of the new methodology—you don't want to send a message to your company that the pilot was aborted.

A project is usually critical if your company or the customer can't survive without it. Here are some example projects that a business would consider critical:

- A project to ensure a revenue stream
- A project that supports meeting a regulatory or compliance deadline
- A project with expiring funds (budget tied to a time frame)
- A project that delivers functionality that is a foundation for the organization (such as service-oriented architecture [SOA])

From a customer perspective, these projects could be considered critical:

- A project tied to a fixed bid
- A project that the customer depends on for a marketing campaign
- A project that relates to a regulatory or compliance issue on the customer end

Your objective should be to find a medium-priority project. Such a project allows some flexibility as you feel out your new process and also provides a level of urgency. You're moving to agile to better support urgent projects, so you need to simulate this with your pilot.

Here are some examples of medium-priority projects:

- Adding the ability to book hotels on an existing travel site
- Delivering a maintenance release onto an existing platform
- Adding customizable stock quotes to a portal page
- Modifying your HR application to let employees view their vacation balance
- Adding advanced search capabilities to your existing simple search

Now that you understand the pilot's desired size and priority, let's look at the breadth of the project.

9.1.3   *A project that hits all phases and areas*

Your pilot project needs to touch all major areas related to projects at your company. You don't need to go deep, but you should go wide. It may be difficult to select a test project that utilizes all possible processes and departments, but you should select one that hits the majority of them.

Although your pilot will go wide, you don't want to test outside of your company. The reason is that you'll be busy watching the process within your company. Adding a third party into the mix may diminish your ability to record feedback and learn from the pilot. You can involve third parties in subsequent projects, when you have more bandwidth for their feedback.

It's tempting to try to test agile area by area, but doing so usually leads to poor results. Your new agile process will be designed to have practices integrate with each other. This integration is where a good portion of the value comes from. A segmented test may mask these benefits and also minimize your ability to identify issues with the process.

Here's an example. A few years ago, a prominent company implemented an agile development process. The company had created a core team to create the custom methodology. The core team was composed of employees from various departments such as Program Management, Development, QA, User Interface, Implementation, and Analytics. On occasion, core-team members demonstrated a proposed process on a live project. In one such instance, a program manager decided to test the agile feature-card process on a live project. The project was already following a traditional lifecycle.

The value of the feature-card meeting is that it lets you gather enough information to plan the project: it's a precursor to gathering detailed requirements. The project that was already in flight had complete functional specifications and a robust project plan.

To perform the feature-card meeting, the program manager had to pretend that all the information in the functional specifications didn't exist. She also had to determine what to do with the output from the feature-card meeting. In an agile process, the output feeds an iteration or sprint plan. The project in progress already had a detailed development plan, so no value was gained from the feature-card exercise.

This demo had a *negative* effect on the company's agile deployment. Because the feature-card meeting was used at the wrong time, it added no value. The employees who tested the process quickly spread their experience throughout the company, and other employees who were already against an agile methodology now had the ammo they needed to try to stop it: they had proof that agile didn't add any value to the development process.

In summary, you can use agile and traditional processes together, but you have to design interface points so the process flows logically. You'll see this in practice in subsequent chapters.

9.1.4 No external customers

At this point in the book, you should be surprised when you read the title of this section. Don't involve the customer? That sounds anti-agile.

You always want to show customers your good side. When you're piloting your new process, you're hoping to find issues with it. The mixing of issues and customers isn't necessarily a good thing.

There are exceptions to this rule. You may have a customer that is really a partner and with whom you can share almost anything. If this is true, you can keep them abreast of how things are going with development of the new process and include them in the pilot. A long-term goal of agile is to get your relationship to this point. But this is usually an exception for companies just starting to use agile techniques, where the customer may be viewed as an adversary.

We recommend that you have a customer advocate or proxy for the pilot. Typically, proxies come from product or program management; they can simulate external customer interaction during the project. You'll see this in practice during the pilot at Acme Media, where Acme's product manager will play the role of the customer.

Although you may not involve a customer in your pilot, you can still use the pilot to prepare for their involvement in the future. The pilot helps you more clearly define the customer role in the process.

9.2 Evaluating projects at Acme Media

To help you understand the selection criteria outlined in section 9.1, let's rejoin Acme Media and see how it selects it's pilot project.

9.2.1 Request backlog

Every company has a different way of populating their request/potential projects backlog (a.k.a. *project backlog*). Sometimes backlog evaluation is driven by an executive review process, sometimes it's driven by product marketing, and sometimes it's driven by a customer.

Acme Media populates its request backlog via a quarterly planning process. The executives review all known project requests once every three months, prioritize them, and loosely assign them to the quarter for completion.

As you may recall from chapter 2, Acme Media supports a website that includes news, classifieds, and travel/outdoors content. Executives from these three areas attend the quarterly planning process along with managers from support areas such as online advertising, user registration, and engineering. Acme's project backlog is pictured in table 9.1.

Table 9.1 Acme Media's project backlog. You'll review potential projects to identify the best one on which to test your new methodology.

Area	Potential projects	Priority H-M-L	Estimated duration	Request type	Detailed description
News	"My News" personalization	M	9 weeks	Customer	User can build their own page with content from AcmeNews.com along with other sites.
Classifieds	Free merchandise advertising	M	7 weeks	Customer	Compete with eBay and Craigslist for lost classified advertisements.
All	Investigate Flash for videos	H	2 weeks	Infrastructure	Many readers' videos are being blocked by firewalls. Investigate Flash as a solution.
Classifieds	Autos email alerts	L	1 weeks	Customer	User can enter criteria and be notified when a car they desire is posted for sale.
News	Wireless weather alerts	M	3 weeks	Customer	Deliver forecasts and alerts to customer phones.
Advertising	Behavioral targeting	H	10 weeks	Advertiser	Serve tailored ads to the reader based on their browsing habits.

When the Acme Media quarterly planning team sits down to identify their pilot project, they invite the project manager, Wendy Johnson, to assist. Wendy recently trained on the agile principles, and she has worked with the core team to outline the new methodology. Wendy also has a good feel for what a test project should do to exercise all the new processes. The team sits down and compares the projects in the backlog to the selection criteria outlined in section 9.1.

9.2.2 Selecting a pilot project: an example

Acme Media begins by screening projects by size. The team filters out the behavioral targeting and "My News" projects because they're estimated to run longer than 8 weeks.

Next, they filter by project breadth. The Macromedia investigation is only an investigation—it will hit few areas and won't have a code deliverable. It's also a high-priority project, which means there will be little patience for testing a new process.

The autos email alert item is closer to a feature than a project. It's a small enhancement to the existing autos site. This project doesn't require a feature-card meeting and will have only one iteration.

Wireless weather alerts is a niche project that requires a limited and specialized project team. It doesn't require team members from most of the departments.

That leaves Acme Media with the free merchandise advertising project. It's estimated to last less than 8 weeks, which will allow for timely feedback. It will hit all the phases of the new process and involve all the major functional areas of a project:

requirements, design, development, implementation, quality, and operations. It's a medium-priority project, so it will push the team along. It's also a good fit because third parties won't be involved.

The project is a product-management initiative, which means an internal product manager can play the role of the customer. This supports a pilot objective of not involving a real customer in the first test of the agile methodology.

Based on all these findings, Acme Media chooses the free merchandise advertising project as its pilot. Acme's next step will be to identify the team members needed to perform the pilot.

9.3 Key points

The key points from this chapter are as follows:

- A pilot project is needed to validate your agile process in the real world.

    The pilot must be brief, to allow for quick feedback on the process. It needs to be of medium priority so that it will push you but still allow time for scrutiny of the new methodology.

- The pilot should exercise as many processes as possible and involve as many areas as possible.

- You want to expose as many weaknesses as you can during the pilot so you can improve the process and prepare it for scaling across your organization.

- Avoid risks on your pilot. Don't select a mission-critical project.

- You can also invite risk if you involve your direct customer in the pilot. Work the major kinks out of your methodology before exposing it to the customer. The customer can participate after your team has matured around the process.

9.4 Looking forward

In this chapter, we identified a project that's a good test for the enhanced methodology Acme Media has created. In the next chapter, we'll join the case study as it starts the pilot project. In effect, you'll see agile in action.

The pilot project will start with an assessment of feasibility. Many projects are well into development before the team realizes the work isn't possible or the return on investment isn't there. Acme Media now does feasibility as a normal part of its process, and the team will find out whether the Free Merchandise Advertising concept is worth pursuing.

Part 3

Kicking off

We've worked on numerous projects where the team was expected to do the work but not necessarily understand the value of the project. Many repercussions can result if you don't orient the project team to the value of the idea.

First, if the team doesn't know why they're pursuing an idea, they won't be able to make decisions if they encounter issues. Development will slow while team members seek out management for redirection.

Second, your project team contains a large quantity of intellectual power. Team members may identify issues with an idea if they're consulted before work begins. The company can use this information to determine whether a project is feasible and, if necessary, cancel a project before time is wasted.

Third, it's demoralizing not to be consulted about a project you're going to work on. When you're told to do something, your underlying thought is, "Why should I do this?" We believe in treating team members respectfully. Asking the team for their input on a project before it begins shows respect and also helps with project buy-in.

In this part of the book, we'll address these three issues. You'll see how Acme Media gets the buy-in of its pilot team by involving them in the feasibility assessment and by going through an envisioning process that quantifies the value of the Free Merchandise Advertising idea.

Feasibility: is this project viable?

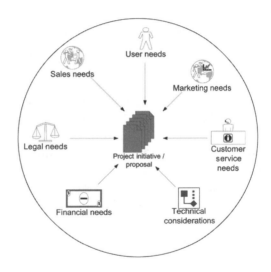

Our project backlogs are full of great ideas. In some cases, we get so excited about a great idea that we disregard all the challenges and jump right in to start development. Sometimes we succeed, and sometimes we have to abort.

Many companies struggle when trying to validate a project's value. Some companies initialize a project without knowing if it's viable; other companies scrutinize the value of a project for months before making a decision. There are issues with both approaches.

If you perform minimal validation, you'll frequently deliver projects that provide marginal value. You may also find that you're aborting on projects because you overlooked major risks at the outset. In both instances, you waste company time and resources and potentially lose the opportunity to deliver valuable projects.

Companies that perform too much validation have a different set of issues. These companies create so many hurdles and gateways that a considerable expense is associated with project justification. They also minimize their ability to achieve benefits from projects that need to deliver value early: time that could be spent performing the project is frequently lost to the justification cycle.

How do you know when you've done enough research? How can you tell if a project is feasible without overkill? We suggest using the feasibility process outlined in this chapter. This process works for two reasons:

- The feasibility effort is time-boxed.
- The team is empowered to question the viability of the project after the Feasibility phase.

Time-boxing the effort prevents a runaway train. A time limit adds urgency to the effort and prevents waste. Acme Media has a 3-day limit for feasibility work. We suggest you create a time limit for feasibility work within your company, too. A good rule of thumb is 2 to 5 days.

Some employees won't be happy with this time limit: they will say that each project is different and that larger projects require more time for feasibility work. They will also say that setting a fixed time for an activity is anti-agile. We agree with all these points. This is where our second point comes into play: the team can cancel the project at any time.

During the Feasibility phase, you'll make a quick call about whether to go forward. This will prevent you from missing an opportunity due to over-analysis. You'll use the Planning phase to learn more each individual feature; and as you do this, you'll continue to consider project feasibility. *You can still cancel the project if you encounter risks and issues during the Planning phase.*

10.1 *Feasibility in the big picture*

As Acme Media begins work on its pilot project, let's take a moment to discuss how feasibility fits into the overall agile lifecycle, depicted in figure 10.1. The agile process that Acme has created is represented by five virtual phases. We use the term *virtual* because in reality you may perform feasibility, planning, development, or adapting at any point in an agile project. The work is not performed in a serial fashion.

First is the Feasibility phase. You use this phase to determine if an idea has enough merit to justify going forward with more detailed requirements, planning, funding, and staffing. Why are you doing this project? What is the value of this request? What

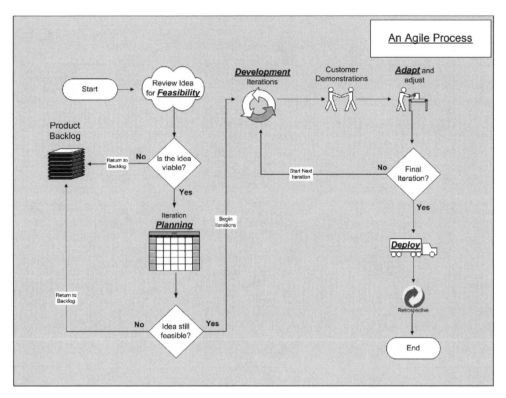

Figure 10.1   Overview of Acme Media's phases

are the risks in pursuing this project? The Feasibility phase provides answers to these questions quickly. You can see typical feasibility activities in figure 10.2.

The Planning phase gets started by reviewing the output of the Feasibility phase and going deeper into the information provided. You use the Planning phase to break the idea into discrete pieces of functionality called *features* or *user stories*. You then prioritize the features and loosely assign them to development iterations.

The release plan provides a first pass at the work that will be created, tested, and demonstrated during the Development phase. This work is completed in iterations and queued for later deployment. Each iteration is a deliverable subset of features; these features are demonstrated at the end of development iterations.

When the team reviews the features that are delivered, they adapt. The team gathers feedback from the customer during the Adapt phase to ensure their needs were satisfied by the features delivered. The team also reviews their velocity (pace) to see if their capacity estimates are correct. The team uses this information to adjust the plan for the forthcoming iteration.

The last phase is Deployment, which begins after the last iteration is complete. You use this phase to deliver code to the production environment. You also use the

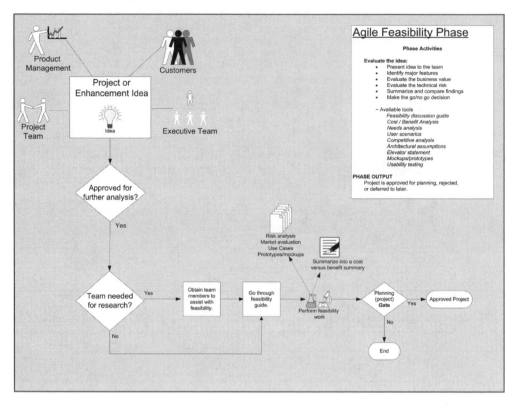

Figure 10.2   Acme's Feasibility phase. The team gathers just enough information to validate the value of the project and make the call about whether to go forward.

Deployment phase to prepare all of those affected by delivery of the project: you train customers, prepare support organizations, turn on marketing plans, and complete the phase with a project retrospective.

Acme Media's pilot project, free merchandise advertising (FMA), has been approved for feasibility research. Chapter 9 provided the selection criteria that the Acme management team used to identify the pilot. The FMA project met the conditions of the criteria: it's medium priority, can be completed within 8 weeks, and involves the majority of departments and areas within Acme. Now Acme Media needs to identify a group of employees to look at the idea in more detail and make sure it's feasible to fund the project and identify a full project team.

10.2   *Selecting a feasibility team*

After a project has been endorsed for feasibility analysis, you assign an individual or a team to perform the work. The work can be performed by an individual if the idea is simple, such as a slight enhancement to existing functionality. More complicated ideas should be reviewed from various perspectives, and a team will be required to provide the analysis.

First, you must determine what type of team members are needed to do the feasibility work. Second, you need to review the known requirements with the feasibility team and have the members perform research in their respective areas. The feasibility guide (discussed in section 10.3.1) focuses the team on the areas they should be researching during the phase.

When the team feels they're reaching diminishing returns, or their time limit expires, they will summarize their findings and present them to an approval body. The team will make a recommendation on "go/no go" at the conclusion of the exercise, and the approval body will make the ultimate decision about whether to proceed. Note that an approval body can be as small as a product manager or as large as a steering committee or executive team. In our experience the feasibility team's suggestion is usually followed.

Let's follow Acme Media as it goes through the feasibility phase with its pilot project, beginning with the creation of a feasibility team.

10.2.1 *Selecting feasibility team members at Acme Media*

Acme Media's product manager, Jay Fosberg, and project manager, Wendy Johnson, get together after the FMA idea is named for the pilot project, to determine the types of employees they need to perform the feasibility work. They start—and you will, too—by reviewing the pilot's known requirements or objectives. Jay has a rough concept outlined for the idea. Because the project is medium priority, there has been no reason to go beyond his initial requirements. At first glance, this may seem to be a problem, but in reality it's a blessing. When your company acclimates to the agile mentality, you'll find that you do lighter initial requirements. You'll quickly jump to feasibility and build out your requirements as you learn more along the way. It won't be critical to create a detailed, heavily structured requirements document before determining if the project is feasible. (We'll dive deeper into requirements when we discuss the Planning phase.)

Jay and Wendy spend a few hours reviewing the known requirements and determine that they need three types of team members for the feasibility analysis:

- A *developer*—to provide thoughts about the coding that will be required
- A *designer/UI employee*—to identify any concerns in creating new screens to support the project
- A *customer*—to answer any questions the developer and designer have about scope, requirements, and objectives

They note these needs on the Feasibility Team Checklist shown in table 10.1. We suggest that you create a checklist similar to this one, tweaking it to reflect your organization structure and business model.

In Acme's case, the company has identified the need for a developer, a designer, and a customer to participate in the feasibility process. A project-manager role isn't selected—it isn't even an available option on the Feasibility Team Checklist. Acme did

Table 10.1   Feasibility Team Checklist. A checklist can help prevent an oversight when you're selecting feasibility team members.

Technical		Product/Customer		Other teams	
☒	Developer	☒	Designer	☐	Vendor (i.e. application provider)
☐	Database analyst	☐	Direct customer	☐	Service provider
☐	Architect	☐	End user	☐	Legal
☐	Implementation	☒	Revenue supplying customer (i.e. advertiser)	☐	Finance
☐	Support	☐	Product manager	☐	Quality
		☐	Marketing manager		
		☐	Focus group		
		☐	Usability testers		

this because the company assigns a project manager to a project as soon as it's approved for Feasibility analysis; the project manager stays with the project until it's cancelled or delivered. Wendy will act as the project manager on the pilot project.

We recommend that you follow this process with your methodology. It's excellent to have at least one person on the project team who has been with the idea since

---

Selecting a feasibility team for your pilot project vs. everyday projects

Acme's agile process allows for different teams to be used between the Feasibility phase and the Planning/Development phases. For example, a light team or even one person can do the feasibility analysis. When an idea is through the Feasibility phase, Acme can identify the team for planning and development—the actual project team. Acme chose this design to minimize the impact on the organization until the project has been deemed viable.

In the case of the pilot project, Acme has decided to name the team for planning and development during the Feasibility phase. Only a few team members receive feasibility assignments; the remaining team members sit in on feasibility activities to learn how the process works. This is the beginning of Acme's agile education process. On projects after the pilot, Acme will perform the Feasibility phase as designed, having only needed team members participate.

When you create your lifecycle, you can go either way. If you can free up the entire team for the Feasibility phase, and the entire group is about eight people or fewer, then we recommend having the entire project team involved in feasibility activities. In contrast, you may choose to limit involvement to the minimum amount of employees needed to explore the project for value. Many companies do this because they have a limited number of team members.

inception. This person will understand the vision behind the idea and communicate it to team members as they join the project.

Jay and Wendy select Matt Lee as the developer for feasibility. Matt had coded most of the classifieds functionality, including the merchandise functionality, and he can speak to the complexities the FMA project may encounter.

Ryan Getty is selected as the designer for feasibility. Ryan has been the UI resource for a good portion of the classifieds work. He's good at outlining potential workflows for requirements, which will come in handy during the Feasibility phase.

The customer identified on the Feasibility Team Checklist is the advertiser. The FMA project depends on advertisements from local businesses. Jay (who is the product manager for the classifieds website) has been assigned the customer role for the pilot project. As you may recall from chapter 6, you don't want to expose your new methodology to external customers until the pilot had been completed. But in this instance, it's OK to interview the advertisers. Acme had interviewed advertisers in the past, and they enjoyed participating in discussions about new features.

After you've assembled the feasibility team, it's time to introduce them to the known requirements.

10.3 *Introducing the known requirements to the feasibility team*

If you're working on an agile project, one with volatile requirements or a tight deadline, you won't have deep requirements when you begin the Feasibility phase. A request or idea has been approved for a feasibility investigation, and no one has documented detailed requirements to this point. Your idea is relatively new, and you're working rapidly to either start the project or dismiss it.

The information that is available is presented to the feasibility team. The idea usually has a champion or author who can meet with the team and go over the concept. This person brings in all the information they have at this point, whether it's a diagram on a cocktail napkin, a detailed flowchart, or a mini functional specification. The following items can be analyzed during the Feasibility phase:

- User scenarios
- User stories
- Use cases
- Rough sketches of process flow
- Financial analysis
- Mock-ups
- Storyboards
- Marketing proposals
- Competitive analysis
- A website where a competitor is already using the idea

If your idea comes from within, you may have a white paper created by someone to outline the idea. In Acme Media's case, the idea came from product management, which created a proposal for FMA.

Acme Media starts its feasibility work with a meeting between Jay (the product manager) and the feasibility team. Jay presents the requirements he has gathered so far; see figures 10.3 and 10.4.

Free Merchandise Advertising Proposal

By Jay Fosberg

Project Details

Concept: We have witnessed a 36% decline in merchandise advertising over the last 6 months. Based on surveys of our previous customers and data provided by internet research firms, we have identified 2 competitors who have captured these advertisements.

The first competitor is Craigslist, a centralized network of online urban communities featuring free classified advertisements. We estimate that Craiglist has captured 68% of the lost advertisements. The second competitor is eBay, an online auction and shopping website. eBay has captured the remaining 32%.

The data we have collected shows this trend continuing into the unforeseen future. In the next 6 months we estimate that we will lose another 28% of our merchandise advertisement revenues, for a year to date loss of 64%.

Our objective is to address this issue before our merchandise site is irrelevant to consumers.

The Free Merchandise Advertisement concept explores the idea of allowing sellers to post merchandise for sale for free, identical to the Craiglist model. We believe we can recoup our lost sales and potentially increase our revenue by using contextual advertisements for the site. We will pursue a model similar to the one currently used by Google. Contextual advertisements, labeled as "sponsored links", will be placed in the header and right hand column of the merchandise advertisement pages. (See Google example below).

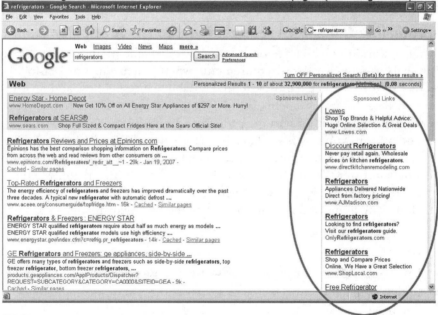

Goals:

- To recover lost revenue on the merchandise classifieds site.
- To increase revenue obtained from the site by shifting to a contextual advertising model.
- To provide another area for retailers to advertise with us.

Figure 10.3   The first section of the FMA proposal outlines the issue and the idea on how to resolve it. It's common to leverage existing functionality to demonstrate requirements. In this instance, Acme Media has used Google's search-results page to demonstrate how sponsored links should work.

Target users:
- Local online buyers and sellers of merchandise such as electronics, appliances, furniture, apparel, tickets, exercise equipment, and sporting goods.
- Local retailers of merchandise such as electronics, appliances, furniture, apparel, tickets, exercise equipment, and sporting goods.

Estimated Timeline:
Detailed concept research and requirements definition – 2 months
Focus groups to review the concept – 1 month
Implementation (design/development/QA) – 2 months
Launch – 1 week

Pricing and revenue model

We will price the contextual advertisements for the number of times we serve them. We will charge $50 for every 1000 ads served. We estimate serving 500,000 ads per month, for a monthly advertisement revenue of $25,000, or $300,000 per year.

Historically we have averaged $180,000 per year on the merchandise site. This revenue was strictly based on the listing fee.

Scope

In scope: general merchandise such as electronics, appliances, furniture, apparel, tickets, exercise equipment, and sporting goods.

Out of scope: job postings, autos, and real estate.

Overview of Features

Since we already have a merchandise site a good portion of the required features already exist. In instances where we have the same features as Craigslist our features appear to be richer. Here are the new features/modifications we know of at this time.

Contextual advertisements support
Modify the existing merchandise classifieds site to support contextual ads in the header and right hand column.

Post without an account
Our current posting method requires the creation of an online account to post an advertisement. This will not be a requirement for the free postings. The poster will only need an email address.

Ad enablement
With free postings there could be issues with fake postings. We will require the poster to enable their posting by sending an enable email to the address they specified.

Post without a payment
We will need to create an ad posting workflow that bypasses the payment processes currently within the workflow.

Limit amount of pictures that can be posted
Today posters can choose 1 to 5 pictures depending on how much they want to pay. We will only allow one photo for the free postings.

Expire ads
The ads that poster paid for could last a variety of days depending on the package they chose. We will have all free postings expire after 7 days.

Flag problem postings
Since free postings will not require a credit card there is more risk of offensive postings. We will need a way to quickly remove offensive postings.

Figure 10.4   The second section of the FMA proposal outlines the target users, revenue model, and key features. This is enough information to initialize a feasibility review.

The team is ready to begin their feasibility investigation.

10.3.1 *What does a feasibility investigation look like?*

When you present your idea to the feasibility team, they will provide initial feedback and subsequent commentary after performing their offline feasibility work. The initial review can provide positive feedback or identify issues immediately. You should inform the feasibility team that candid conversation is not only desired but critical to the process—you don't want to go forward with more extensive feasibility analysis if you don't think the idea is viable.

You should also prepare the idea owner for candid feedback. Encourage the owner to demonstrate their passion for the idea, but at the same time prepare them for frank conversation and a thorough review of the proposal.

The time you spend on feasibility analysis will depend on various factors such as the idea's complexity, the availability of the feasibility team, and dependency on third parties to provide information. An average feasibility analysis begins with a 1- or 2-hour meeting that kicks off the process; at this meeting, one person discusses the known requirements with the feasibility team. The feasibility team reviews the idea with the presenter, and team members ask questions about the customer, the project's value, and potential technology needs. (The next section describes a tool that can help during this process: the Feasibility Discussion Guide.)

This first meeting may provide enough information to make the go/no go decision, but usually a few questions remain that require team members to work offline to get the answers. This offline work may include the following:

- Looking at existing code to see how it can support the request
- Consulting with a vendor about a possible solution for the request
- Doing deeper statistical analysis
- Reviewing competitor functionality to see if they've addressed the same idea

Typically, the team regroups after 2 or 3 days to review their offline work. At this point, they usually have enough information to make the call about whether to continue to the Planning phase.

10.3.2 *Analyzing an idea with the Feasibility Discussion Guide*

A great tool to use during the Feasibility phase is a Feasibility Discussion Guide (see figure 10.5). This guide provides a list of questions that you can use to examine each project, quantify benefits, and identify potential issues.

This feasibility guide is generic enough for practically any company to use; you should modify the questions to better suit your business. For example, if you work in a heavily regulated industry, you may want to add a question or two related to how well the idea helps with compliance.

Feasibility Discussion Guide

Use the following questions to better understand the idea or concept and to determine if it practical to go forward. The answers to these questions will prepare you for the planning phase and kick-start the requirements gathering process.

Customer Requirements and Needs

☐ Who is the customer? Is there more than one type? (ex. Internal, External, Compliance, Consumer, Advertiser, Reader, Business, Employees)
   o Who is the target audience of the project? Describe that target and how they will use the features being developed. Can you identify high level flows, user stories, or use cases?

☐ What customer problems/issues will the product solve? Quantify with examples.

☐ What features are known now? Document those in "ability to" statements, focusing on the customer value of each feature. If possible assign priorities to the known features. Consider the complexity of the features.

Business Value

☐ What are the high-level goals of the project?

☐ What are the success factors associated with the project? How will we know when we are successful? How will we define and measure success?

☐ What are the business reasons/needs for doing the project?

   o What research, traffic stats, company initiative or employee need, webmaster feedback, industry, or competitive knowledge supports the need for this project?
   o What do we know from the industry that dictates or influences what features should be developed?
   o What do we know from the competition that dictates or influences what features should be developed?
   o What is the Return on Investment (ROI) of the features being developed? Consider:
      ▪ Revenue
      ▪ Investment
      ▪ Market Share
      ▪ Advertising Share / Readership
      ▪ Audience Share
      ▪ Customer Retention
      ▪ Customer Satisfaction
      ▪ Cost Savings / Infrastructure

Constraints and Limitations

☐ What constraints exist? Consider resources, funds, technology capabilities, etc.

☐ Should we buy or build this functionality?

☐ What are the outstanding issues, unknowns, and assumptions?

High Level Project Planning

☐ Who are the stakeholders for the project/feature being built? Consider:
   o Decision makers
   o "Non-essential" stakeholders – those people that don't have direct decision-making authority or direct involvement in the project but influence business decisions, resource decisions, or other factors influencing the project.

☐ What project high-level milestones exist at this time?

☐ What type of resources will be needed to continue with the project? (User Interface, Development, Product Management, DBA, Quality, Implementation, etc.)

☐ Maintenance considerations: What will need to be done to maintain and support this functionality?

Feasibility Discussion Guide for APM.doc

Figure 10.5   The Feasibility Discussion Guide provides a list of standard questions to help your team scrutinize a project idea for all benefits and shortcomings.

10.3.3 *Feedback from the Acme Media feasibility team*

As we return to Acme Media, Jay, the product manager, is presenting his idea to the feasibility team. Jay emailed the Feasibility Discussion Guide and the FMA proposal to the three employees in advance of the meeting. We suggest that you follow this approach; you should give the feasibility team members time to review the idea in advance of the first meeting, if possible.

Jay explains the proposal to the team, and the discussion begins. Matt, the developer, is enthusiastic about the FMA idea. He wrote much of the existing merchandise-classifieds functionality and is disappointed that use of the application is declining. He's happy to see product management fighting back.

Ryan, the designer, likes the idea but is skeptical. He understands how free advertising can level the playing field, and he likes the idea of bringing in more revenue through contextual advertisements. But Ryan doesn't understand why a buyer or seller who is currently happy using Craigslist will switch to Acme Media's merchandise-classifieds site. From Ryan's perspective, an equal product isn't a sufficient reason to switch. The contextual advertisements are something different, but they're mainly for commercial businesses to sell their wares—they won't help the typical person looking to buy or sell an item occasionally.

The team knows that the idea is in its early stages, and they aren't surprised that a potential issue was overlooked. Ryan's point is valid: the idea will bring contextual advertising to the site, along with the associated revenue; but advertisers will stop paying for the contextual ads if Acme Media can't guarantee a certain level of traffic to the site. Without buyers and sellers, there won't be any traffic.

At this point, the team stops their feasibility work without proceeding to detailed analysis. Everyone agrees that the idea has a serious issue and the project probably isn't viable. They have two choices at this point: they can go back to the executive team and recommend not going forward to the Planning phase, or they can take some time to see if the issue can be circumvented.

Acme's feasibility team decides to go with the second option. They will spend a few hours trying to resolve the issue before considering cancellation of the project.

10.3.4 *Modifying the idea during feasibility analysis*

Acme's team continues their first feasibility meeting by shifting into a brainstorming mode. How can they modify the FMA idea so that it will not only match the competitor but also provide an incentive for users to leave the competitor?

Wendy reviews the concept white paper one more time and notices that eBay is also taking business away from Acme Media's merchandise-advertising site. She asks Jay why his idea proposal didn't address the lost sales to eBay, too.

Jay explains that eBay is taking only one-third of the business. Craigslist is taking two-thirds of the business, so he decided to focus on Craigslist first.

This conversation piques Ryan's curiosity. He asks Jay about the two competitors' weaknesses. Offhand, Jay can't think of any glaring weaknesses, but Wendy thinks of a few immediately.

The first weakness relates to Craigslist. Wendy has used the site and doesn't like the fact that she can't put her items up for auction: she has to list her items for sale at a fixed selling price. If potential buyers want to offer less, they email her. This happens quite often, and she finds herself flooded with emails asking her if she'll consider a lower offer.

Because of this issue, Wendy often uses eBay. eBay lets Wendy set a minimum price for an item, and often the auction process pushes her final selling price beyond her expectations. But eBay had shortcomings, too: the seller has to pay a percentage to eBay for listing the item, and the buyer never sees the item in person until it's shipped to them. Most sales aren't local, and they involve shipping items after they're paid for. You also have to pay by electronic means, such as a credit or debit card. The Craigslist model lets the buyer and seller choose their method for payment: cash, check, credit, or money order.

The wheels in Jay's head begin to spin. He asks the feasibility team if they will give him the remainder of the day to modify the proposal, and then regroup the following day. The team agrees.

What just happened at Acme is a common occurrence. While reviewing an idea, you may encounter showstoppers and then either find a solution or abort the project. It may be distressing to identify an issue, but at the same time doing so is a good thing. You haven't designed or coded anything yet, so there is no code to throw away. Your investment has been minimal. Also, because the issue has been identified early in the cycle, you have the luxury of aborting or spending a little time to try to overcome the issue.

10.3.5 *Reacting to the feedback*

At Acme the following day, Jay has modified his concept significantly. The feedback from the team helped clarify an opportunity for the company. Figures 10.6 through 10.8 display the modified proposal, with the changes underlined. Jay has renamed the idea: instead of the FMA project, it's now the Online Auction Service (a.k.a. the Auctionator).

Based on the team's feedback, Jay has shifted the project from a free advertising site to a free auction site. A free auction site addresses the weaknesses of both competitors and provides an incentive for buyers and sellers to return to Acme Media's site. Acme's site will allow buyers and sellers to have their cake and eat it, too.

Online Auction Service Proposal (Acme Auctionator)
By Jay Fosberg

Project Details

Concept: We have witnessed a 36% decline in merchandise advertising over the last 6 months. Based on surveys of our previous customers and data provided by internet research firms, we have identified 2 competitors who have captured these lost advertisements.

The first competitor is Craigslist, a centralized network of online urban communities featuring free classified advertisements. We estimate that Craigslist has captured 68% of the lost advertisements. The second competitor is eBay, an online auction and shopping website. eBay has captured the remaining 32%.

The data we have collected shows this trend continuing into the unforeseen future. In the next 6 months we estimate that we will lose another 28% of our merchandise advertisement revenues, for a year to date loss of 64%.

Our objective is to address this issue before our merchandise site is irrelevant to consumers.

The Online Auction Service concept explores the idea of addressing the needs of buyers, sellers, and advertisers, which will lead to an increase in revenue from the merchandise site.

We will address the needs of the advertisers by providing a new option to advertise on our merchandise classifieds site. This site should be lucrative to advertisers because the ads will be contextual to what a potential buyer is searching for.

For example, when someone searches for refrigerators for sale by individuals, we will also return advertisements for refrigerator merchants. These ads will be on the borders of the page, very similar to the Google merchant advertising model. Contextual advertisements, labeled as "sponsored links", will be placed in the header and right hand column of the merchandise advertisement pages. (See Google example below).

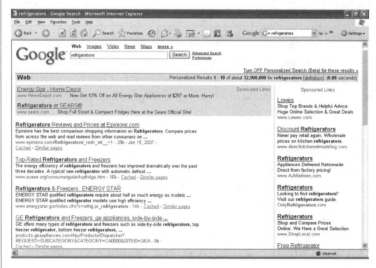

Online Auction Service Concept Proposal Page 1.doc   - 1 -

Figure 10.6   Page 1 of the modified concept for Acme's pilot project, the Auctionator. The underlined area shows how Jay has modified the original concept. Initially, Acme Media was only worried about buyers and sellers; now they will also address the needs of advertisers.

We will address the needs of seller by providing free advertising and a free auction service. Whereas Craigslist provides free advertising, they only support a fixed item price. Whereas eBay provides an auction service, they charge a fee for the service and they only support electronic payment between buyer and seller. We will let the buyer and seller determine their own payment method.

We will address the needs of the buyers by allowing them to inspect an item before paying for it, whereas eBay requires payment before the item is shipped to the buyer. We also believe we will help the buyer by providing a richer source of items to purchase from. We anticipate an increase in seller listings due to the free postings and the contextual advertisements provided by the merchants.

Goals:
- To recover lost revenue from the merchandise classifieds site.
- To increase revenue obtained from the site by shifting to a contextual advertising model.
- *To provide functionality that inspires buyers and sellers to return to our site.*

Target users:
- Local online buyers and sellers of merchandise such as electronics, appliances, furniture, apparel, tickets, exercise equipment, and sporting goods.
- Local retailers of merchandise such as electronics, appliances, furniture, apparel, tickets, exercise equipment, and sporting goods.

Estimated Timeline:
Detailed concept research and requirements definition – 2 months
Focus groups to review the concept – 1 month
Implementation (design/development/QA) – 2 months
Launch – 1 week

Pricing and revenue model

We will price the contextual advertisements for the number of times we serve them. We will charge $50 for every 1000 ads served. We estimate serving 500,000 ads per month, for a monthly advertisement revenue of $25,000, or $300,000 per year.

Historically we have averaged $180,000 per year on the merchandise site. This revenue was strictly based on the listing fee.

Scope

In scope:
- Individual advertisements for general merchandise such as electronics, appliances, furniture, apparel, tickets, exercise equipment, and sporting goods.

- Contextual advertisements for merchants. Their ads should also be for general merchandise such as electronics, appliances, furniture, apparel, tickets, exercise equipment, and sporting goods.

Out of scope:
- Job postings, autos, and real estate.
- Electronic payment methods. Storefronts.

We do not foresee any changes in the business process used to obtain contextual ads from merchants. The ad selling team will just present the new site as an additional option to the merchants.

Overview of Features

We will have two major pieces of functionality work:
1) Modify our seller posting processes to bypass the payment process
2) *Create auction related functionality*

Based on the above, here are the features we have identified so far:

Online Auction Service Concept Proposal Page 2.doc   - 2 -

Figure 10.7   Page 2 of the modified concept for Acme Media's pilot project. Jay now proposes that Acme go beyond free merchandise postings and allow free auctions. This change will let Acme Media fight both of its competitors.

Post without a payment
We will need to create an ad posting workflow that bypasses the payment processes currently within the workflow.
Limit amount of pictures that can be posted
Today posters can choose 1 to 5 pictures depending on how much they want to pay. We will only allow one photo for the free postings.
Expire ads
In the past the ads that poster paid for could last a variety of days depending on the package they chose. We will have all free auction postings limited to 4 days.
Flag problem postings
Since free postings will not require a credit card there is more risk of offensive postings. We will need a way to quickly remove offensive postings.

Alerts for item type

Alert a potential registered bidder when an item they like is posted on Auctionator.

Email a friend

A registered user can email a friend about an item up for bid.

Place an item up for bid

A registered user can place an item up for bid and retract it.

Require registration on the site

Users must register to sell or bid on items. This profile stores preferences, email address, and credit card information.

Contact seller

Contact seller for more information on an item for sale.

Customize my view

A user can pick the fields and colors on their landing screen.

Auction Browser Toolbar

Search Auctionator from your browser without being on the site.

Ability to receive help online
Ability for a user view help on the site

Item bidding
A registered user can bid on an item for sale

Seller feedback
Record feedback to a seller's profile after the transaction.

View seller information

Learn about a sellers past and previous customer satisfaction.

Figure 10.8   Page 3 of the modified concept for Acme Media's pilot project. Jay is starting to get a feel for the major features that need to be supported. This will provide a smooth segue to the Planning phase, when Acme Media will analyze each feature.

10.3.6 *Team review of the modified concept*

The feasibility team reviews the revised proposal and are pleased. To be safe, though, the team goes back to the Feasibility Discussion Guide one last time to see if it can help them identify any remaining weaknesses with the idea.

Matt notes that Acme Media had no experience creating auction functionality and that he'd like to look at some competitor sites to estimate how difficult the work could be.

Matt also notes that he'd feel less at risk if the idea didn't have an e-commerce aspect. Electronic payment can be tricky; and if the idea is to copy Craigslist and not have such payments, then the risk is minimal.

This comment draws a response from Ryan. Ryan likes eBay's electronic payment functionality. He feels protected from fraud when he uses his credit card, knowing he can refuse to pay for bad goods and his credit card company will go after deceitful sellers. Jay records Ryan's concern.

Wendy chimes in next. She notes that Jay specifies a feature to remove offensive postings, because there is a higher probability that offensive postings will occur on a free site. In the past, Acme collected a seller's credit card before an ad was posted, which provided a certain level of security. Wendy is concerned that the new feature alone may not prevent the postings. Jay also notes Wendy's concern.

Jay wraps up the feedback session with a few thoughts of his own. Even though he isn't a project manager, he thinks an online auction service will be a medium-to-large project, and he wonders if it can be completed within the pilot's time constraint.

Wendy agrees but reminds Jay that this kind of issue is what agile is all about: delivering prioritized features within a limited timeframe. They should see what features they can deliver within the 8-week window they've been given.

Jay's last thought relates to marketing the new idea. How can he get the word out to users who have left the site? He has one free outlet for advertising: Acme Media's other websites. He can run ads on those pages, telling buyers and sellers that the Auctionator is a great new marketplace for them. Jay also has free advertising spots on Acme's TV station; he can supplement these ads with other mechanisms such as radio advertising, for which he has a small budget.

Jay asks the group if they're comfortable taking their findings to the executive team and asking for permission to continue into the Planning phase. Ryan and Wendy say yes, but Matt wants a day or two to look at the eBay site and his own code to see how complex the work would be. Ryan also notes that it wouldn't hurt for him to look at eBay's UI while Matt looks at the functionality. Jay is fine with the time Matt and Ryan request.

10.3.7 *Regrouping after technical analysis*

The team regroups 2 days later. Matt and Ryan note that eBay's site is rich with functionality. But the basic functionality needed to support an online auction system won't be overly complex to create. They also note that it would be fun to put some fancy features into the new site, such as store fronts and wireless bidding.

The team asks Jay how rich he wants the new application to be. Jay explains that he wants to deliver minimal functionality until they can prove that the concept will attract buyers and sellers to the site.

Matt also spends part of the 2 days reviewing his existing code for merchandise advertising. He finds that the code is relatively modular and that it shouldn't be difficult to remove the payment process from the workflow. But the auction-related code will have to be created from scratch.

Jay asks Matt if they should consider buying the auction functionality from a third party. Matt replies that if they truly keep the feature set minimal, he should be able to do the work.

10.3.8 Summarizing the feasibility work

The team summarizes their findings into a simple cost/benefit table, shown in table 10.2.

Table 10.2   The cost/benefit analysis summary for the Auctionator. The analysis summarizes the reasons for pursuing a project and the reasons for potentially passing on it.

Benefits	Costs/Risks
Revenue ☒ Recover lost revenue ☒ Generate incremental revenue	**Skill set** ☒ No experience with auction functionality
Customers ☒ Address the needs of buyers and sellers ☒ Provide an advertising opportunity to merchants	**Schedule/Scope** ☒ Desired feature set appears longer than 6 weeks ☒ Some buyers and sellers may desire electronic payment
Expense ☒ We can leverage existing hardware and resources	**Security** ☒ Free auctions may attract fraudulent postings
Ancillary Benefits ☒ Brand awareness and exposure	**Marketing** ☒ A significant marketing effort may be needed to bring buyers and sellers back to the site.

Acme Media uses a simple template to illustrate the pros and cons of pursing the Auctionator. You don't need to be this formal—many teams present their findings with a quick whiteboard discussion.

10.4   The go/no go decision

The Acme feasibility team meets with the executive team to review their findings. The team presents the cost-benefit summary, and the executive team asks several questions.

The first question relates to strategy. Does Acme Media want to be in the auction space? Are there any risks in creating an auction site?

Jay explains that he can't identify any brand issues in pursuing an auction site. As a matter of fact, many readers of the Acme site consider it vanilla and unexciting. An auction site will demonstrate innovation and thinking outside the box. It may help the perception of Acme's brand.

Another executive asks, "Will this tick off eBay? Does eBay do any business with us?" Jay has spoken with the advertising department, and they confirmed that eBay has never advertised on Acme's website or television station. As to whether eBay will be upset, they probably won't worry too much about losing a few auctions to one city. What *will* concern eBay is if other regional websites start creating their own auction sites.

Different ways of approving projects

When you create your own custom methodology, you'll determine the approval level required to pass from the Feasibility phase to the Planning phase. Final approval may come from the project team, or you may decide to have it come from a management group.

It's logical to have different approval levels depending on the scope of a project. For example, a project that can be completed in a few days with existing team members may be blessed by a product manager or project team. Conversely, a project that will take months to complete, with incremental expense, probably needs approval from a management group.

The executives also want to know about expense. Won't auction functionality be expensive to create or purchase? Matt explains that he has reviewed the current classifieds code and spent some time on eBay's site. He's comfortable doing the project if functionality is limited to critical features. Wendy tells the executives that Matt and the other probable team members are already budgeted for, and the only incremental expense will relate to advertising.

What about team size and expense?

Acme Media has a team that is dedicated to their project, but it isn't unusual to have team members working on different projects at the same time. In many environments, executives want to know what types of skill sets are needed and how long you'll need those skill sets. In these instances, the output from your feasibility work should include a high-level estimate of the people you'll need for the project and approximately how long you'll use them. This is especially true if you believe you'll need help from outside the company; outside assistance may require additional funds that aren't budgeted for your team or the platform.

The sponsor asks the team what the estimated advertising expense will be. The team explains that there will be no expense if they limit advertising to the mechanisms available to them at Acme. They can advertise for free on the other sites within Acme's network, and they can also get free spots on the television station. There will be incremental expense if they advertise through other channels, such as radio.

The feasibility team leaves the room to allow the executives to continue their meeting. When the meeting concludes, the agile sponsor tells them that the project has been approved to continue into planning.

Now that the team understands *why* they should do the project, they will use the Planning phase to show them *how* to do it.

10.5   Alternate feasibility paths

Acme Media followed a relatively common process for taking an idea through feasibility. But you can follow several paths to determine feasibility; you can even skip it altogether. Let's look at two additional models.

10.5.1   What people are talking about

Google's employees are allowed to spend one day a week working on a dream project or idea of their own. This leads to the generation of hundreds of ideas each year. It would be impossible for an executive team to review each idea and determine if further analysis was needed.

A few years ago, Google solved this problem with the use of wikis. Google employees submit their ideas to a wiki for all employees to review. Employees discuss the ideas within the wiki, which lets directors and product managers see which ideas are getting the most buzz. The top 100 ideas are then reviewed in more detail and may be sent out for further analysis, feasibility, and usability investigation. This process continues iteratively until an idea is deployed or cancelled. This process has delivered ideas such as the Google browser toolbar.

Your company may not be as big as Google, but an idea wiki is simple to use and usually inexpensive to deploy.

10.5.2   Feasibility for risk management vs. go/no go

We've coached many teams on agile, and we frequently hear teams discuss the lack of a feasibility option. This is usually the case with companies that do one-off projects for their clients.

Greg once worked for a company that agreed to build a proprietary supply-chain management system for GE Supply. The contract was signed with minimal involvement from the development teams. The salesperson walked in and told Greg's team that the work was sold and they had one year to deliver. The go/no go decision had already been made.

This scenario isn't the optimal way to run a business, but sometimes it happens due to the lack of company maturity or the fact that a company is fighting for survival and risks have to be undertaken to survive. Whatever the reasons, it happens, and it's a real constraint.

If you don't have the option to reverse a sale that has been made, you can still use the feasibility process to manage the project's risks. You can identify the areas with the highest risks, ensure that they're started as early as possible, and communicate these risks clearly to the salesperson and other stakeholders. You may be able to use the output from your feasibility investigation to adjust the scope with your client.

Even in instances where your company has a closed-bid contract, your customer is more interested in being successful than watching you fail and taking you to court or asking for their money back. Your customer probably has urgency too, and they should work with you to reach agreement on a feasible project.

10.6 *Key points*

The key points from this chapter are as follows:

- It isn't uncommon for a company to initialize a project without significant justification. This is an issue for all companies, whether they use an agile lifecycle or not.

- In an agile environment, you do not have the luxury of pursuing projects that may never be delivered. Your efficiency in pursuing the highest-priority projects is a component of your competitive edge.

- The Feasibility phase lets you determine if you should continue working on the project, cancel it, or defer it to later. The analysis is performed without a major resource investment in a short period of time. You want to do just enough analysis to see if it's realistic to continue to the Planning phase.

- You need to assign a team to perform the feasibility analysis. This team is composed of experts who work in the areas that will be most impacted by the project. This team usually stays together if the project continues to the Planning phase. If your company is small, it should be relatively easy to determine who to involve in the feasibility analysis. If you work at a larger company, you can use the Feasibility Team Checklist from table 10.1 to assist you with the process.

- The feasibility team reviews the known requirements such as use cases, workflows, financial analysis, and so on to determine whether the idea should be pursued. The Feasibility Discussion Guide from figure 10.5 is a great tool to use for this process. The guide will help you perform a thorough examination of the idea. You should customize the guide to fit your environment.

- The feasibility team can provide extraordinary value. When your employees get comfortable with the process, it will be like having additional product managers. A competent team can identify issues with an idea and can also identify new opportunities that may be overlooked by a product manager working alone.

- If your project is approved, you proceed to the Planning phase and assemble your full project team.

10.7 *Looking forward*

In this chapter, we explained how you review a project idea for feasibility. In chapter 11, we'll show you how to present the approved idea to the project team and go through a process of envisioning the final product. Envisioning provides the team with the information needed to prioritize the work with the customer and begin the initial planning process.

Aligning the pilot
team with the project

How many times have you done one of following?

- Delivered a feature that the customer never used
- Created a detailed specification for a feature and then failed to pursue the feature
- Discovered a problem deep into a project, and had a team member tell you they knew about the issue all along

You can avoid these issues by *aligning* your project team at the start of your projects and *envisioning* the final product.

Alignment does this by uniting the team around a common vision. You involve the entire team in the planning process. If a team member perceives an issue, you learn about it immediately. Developers don't wait until coding starts to voice their issues; they can communicate issues immediately as the team reviews the features at the beginning of the planning cycle.

Collaborative planning is one of the cornerstones of an agile development process. We've seen many companies move to an agile process mainly for the benefits that come from improved project planning. You'll see that value in this chapter as Acme Media performs chartering exercises to better understand the project value and goals.

11.1 Identifying the pilot team

After a project makes it through feasibility analysis, you select the team that will deliver the project. Ideally, you want to begin with your feasibility team and expand that group as needed. Feasibility-team members can share the information from the Feasibility phase with the additional team members; this will kick-start the project team.

Assignments are based on the current estimated size of the project, the type of team members needed, and team member availability. If your company is small, you may have the same people work on every project. You may also have employees who are dedicated to a website or product within your company. If this is true, you have a permanent project team, and you don't need to select one.

A dedicated team?

In support of good planning, you should do everything in your power to dedicate the team to the project during the planning and development cycles. Dedicated team members are part of the agile process and a tenet of good project management. In some environments, not all team members can be dedicated 100 percent to projects. In these instances, you should make it clear what percentage of time each team member will be working on the project; doing so removes ambiguity for team members and their managers.

We've seen companies where the functional leads or managers determine the team members who are assigned to projects or features. In these environments, the leads are given an overview of the project and its known requirements, and then they assign people from their team based on the criteria mentioned earlier. In these cases, the functional leads act as their own resource and capacity managers.

Acme Media uses a resource pool for its projects. This provides flexibility and also increases the tribal knowledge throughout the team. There are specialists for each area, but team members may be assigned to any product or project depending on company need and the employee's desire to learn about a new area or technology.

Table 11.1 lists the project team members that were selected for Acme Media's Auctionator project.

As you may recall from chapter 6, the core team is composed of employees from various areas and with various titles. When the pilot project is chosen, chances are that some core-team members will be on it due to their functional jobs. But the majority of pilot-team members probably won't be from the core team. You need to review your pilot-team roster and determine whether the team has enough core-team members to support mentoring and hand-holding during the pilot.

If the pilot team does not have enough mentoring, you should assign a few core-team members to assist them. These core-team members must be present for all major meetings and check in daily with the team.

Table 11.1   The pilot project team for the Auctionator/Online Auction System. (OAS). Asterisks indicate core-team members. Your pilot project team will have various levels of agile knowledge.

Pilot project role	Name	Background	Pilot project role
Project manager	*Wendy Johnson	Wendy is part of the core team. She looks forward to seeing how the project-manager role works in an agile environment.	Project manager
Developer	*Roy Williams	Roy is part of the core team.	Developer
Developer	Matt Lee	Matt usually supports development of applications for the Classifieds group.	Developer
UI	Ryan Getty	Ryan has a lot experience doing prototype work, which should bode well for the agile process.	UI
QA	Gina Wallace	Gina is curious to see how much she'll be involved in planning the pilot project. Her peer, Vijay Kumar, is on the core team, and she'll ask Vijay for mentoring during the pilot.	QA
Operations	Tom Klein	Tom works for Matt Shiler, who is on the core team. Tom has no agile experience.	Operations
Requirements	Rich Jenkins	Rich has spent a lot of time learning about agile from his peer on the core team, Wes Hunter.	Requirements
Architecture	*Keith Gastaneau	Keith is part of the core team.	Architecture
Customer	Jay Fosberg	Jay is a product manager for the Classifieds group and proposed the concept of Free Merchandise Advertising. Jay will play the role of the customer for the pilot.	Customer

Acme Media has three core-team members working on the pilot project. A good rule of thumb is to ensure that the pilot team includes two or more core-team members.

Acme also has a bonus in that one of the core-team members on the pilot is the project manager. She will be involved in almost every aspect of the project and available to provide mentoring to the pilot team.

Jay Fosberg will be the proxy for the customer during the project, which isn't a stretch for him. Jay has always been a strong supporter of the customer and an advocate for application usability.

After you identify the pilot project team, you need to train them and orient them on the process you're going to assess.

11.2   Preparing the pilot team

In addition to providing mentoring to the pilot team during the project, you also need to prepare the team in other ways. You need to train the pilot team on agile practices and principles, and provide a method for feedback during the pilot.

11.2.1 *Ensure everyone is trained on agile*

The untrained pilot-team members go through a process similar to that followed by the core team. They need an overview of why the company is pursuing agile, training on the agile principles, and an understanding of the process they're to use on the pilot.

If possible, have your agile coach provide the pilot team's training, with core-team members contributing to the discussions. This process training takes one or two days and is slightly different for the pilot team. In addition to the fundamental principles and practices of agile, they also need training on how the core team has represented those principles in the custom methodology. For example, they need to see how the core team's new process supports the agile principle of *customers and developers working together daily*. If core-team members are attending the fundamentals training with the pilot team, they can show the pilot team how the principles are reflected in the custom methodology.

You should expect the untrained team members to have some cynicism and negativity related to using the new process. Their concerns usually relate to the following:

- *A misunderstanding of agile principles*—Common misconceptions are discussed in chapter 1.
- *A belief that the current process works fine*—Project team members may be unaware of the issues that the new methodology addresses.
- *Lack of detail in the agile process*—In the past, you may have prescribed every step in the development process. Now, the team is asked to participate in selecting the processes that add the most value, and that can be a shock.

If your environment has been controlling in the past, the last item will take time to resolve. Agile doesn't assign employee A to do step B; it tells the employee to deliver value to the customer as quickly as possible and provides tools and processes to reach that goal. The team works together to determine logical steps and assignments during the project.

No matter what the feedback is, listen to the pilot team with an open mind. Where applicable, show them how the new design takes their concerns into account.

You may receive enough feedback from pilot-team members to tempt you to make another update to the methodology. But unless the feedback identifies a showstopper, we suggest holding off on any changes—the pilot will provide plenty of feedback, and you can incorporate the pilot-team feedback when the pilot project is complete.

11.2.2 *Providing a mechanism for feedback*

When the pilot project kicks off, you need to provide a way to gather feedback from the pilot team. The best way to do this is to invite them to the weekly core-team meetings and give them the floor. The core team can listen, see how the methodology is working, and provide guidance to the pilot team.

You should expect some apprehension from the pilot team during the first few meetings. The pilot team knows they're providing feedback to the group that customized the methodology. Do your best to create an environment where egos are checked at the door and the pilot team feels comfortable sharing their feelings.

11.3 Envisioning the product

When you have your project team together, you'll perform a series of exercises to orient the team on the product idea and bring them up to speed on the feasibility work that has already been performed. In some circles, this work is referred to as *chartering*.

Chartering synchronizes the customer and the project team on the project's value and goals. The group also works together to define the scope of the project and the project stakeholders.

Let's start by creating an elevator statement for the Auctionator.

11.3.1 Creating an elevator statement

If team members appreciate the value of a project, it will increase the likelihood of their buy-in and support. If they don't believe in the value, they may not apply themselves, and they may undermine the project. You can provide clarity around the value by having the team work together to create an elevator statement.

An *elevator statement* allows you to condense the project concept into a short, compelling paragraph. The idea is that if you're asked about your project in an elevator on the bottom floor of a building, you should be able to describe the project in a concise, intriguing way before you reach the top. This is a great tool for communicating the value of the project to those outside the team, and it centralizes everyone on the benefits that should be delivered.

You begin the exercise by having the team review the known requirements and the desired deliverables. Then the team works together to answer the following questions:

- Who is the customer?
- What do they need?
- What is the category of the product or service?
- What are the most compelling benefits to the customer?
- Can you quantify the benefits?
- What differentiates your product from existing alternatives?

We also find it helpful to show the team a few examples of elevator statements to get them started. We frequently use an elevator statement that we created for the iPod. We have no idea if Apple uses elevator statements, but we took a guess at one the company may have created before they pursued the iPod project:

Apple iPod Elevator Statement
For: music lovers
Who: desire a simple way to listen to and manage their songs

The: iPod

Is a: portable digital music player

That: provides intuitive, easy to use controls.

Unlike: other MP3 players

Our: product provides seamless integration with a world-class music store (iTunes).

This example quantifies what is different and better about Apple's product. It will lure consumers away from MP3 players that have confusing interfaces, or those players that don't integrate with an online music store.

Now it's time for Acme to quantify what is better about its product. The project team reviews the outputs from the Feasibility phase to help them create their elevator statement. The two artifacts they have are the concept proposal and the cost/benefit summary. (You can review these items in chapter 10.)

After a few hours of collaborating and discussing the project, the Acme Media project team creates the following elevator statement for the Auctionator:

Auctionator Elevator Statement

For: internet buyers and sellers

Who: would like to sell their items locally within an auction framework

The: Acme Auctionator

Is a: local online auction system

That: allows the purchase of goods.

Unlike: eBay

Our: product allows the winning bidder to pay in person using cash or check.

And unlike: Craigslist

Our: product allows the seller to put an item up for bid, as opposed to selling at a fixed price.

Acme's elevator statement is somewhat unique in that it has two *unlike* bullets. There is nothing wrong with this; it reflects how Acme will deliver a product that is better than the offerings from both of its competitors.

Now that Acme has an elevator statement, the team is ready to identify the project's key features.

11.3.2 *Introduce the team to the features*

As you may recall from chapter 10, Jay, the product manager, presented product highlights to the feasibility team. These highlights are stated from a perspective of what the user will have the ability to do, or *ability to's*. For example, one of the ability to's for the Auctionator is "The ability for a seller to put an item up for bid." These ability to's will be the basis for defining the features.

When Acme concluded the Feasibility phase, the team recorded the product highlights/ability to's into the project worksheet (see table 11.2).

Highlights (ability to...)
Place an item up for bid
Bid on an item
View seller feedback
Contact the seller to ask questions
Flag problem postings
Expire auctions
Post an auction without payment

Table 11.2   Original product highlights identified for the Auctionator

These highlights are good for starting the transition to feature identification. They're missing some attributes, such as "Who is the user of the feature?" and "What is the business priority of this feature?" but they provide enough information to get started.

Acme Media has a one-day break between completion of the Feasibility phase and the start of the Planning phase. During that time, Jay, the product manager, reviews the features and adds more detail to them.

You may recall that the Auctionator is a medium-priority project for Acme Media. Because it is *not* high priority, Jay has only outlined light requirements. This works well for the pilot because most agile projects are initiated with light requirements.

Customer diligence

You should encourage the customers on your projects to do as much research as they can before the kickoff meeting. Your team will welcome all the details they can get about the requirements. The team will spend many hours trying to understand and define the features over the life of the project, and the customer can reduce this time by performing as much diligence as possible before meeting with the team.

After spending a few hours reviewing the project concept and cost/benefits summary, Jay identifies additional features for the Auctionator and adds more detail to each feature. He summarizes his findings in a document he labels Feature Description Document (see figures 11.1 and 11.2).

As you review the Feature Description Document, notice that Jay has increased the number of features from 7 to 14. He's also added user types, such as buyer and seller. And he's identified a key piece of functionality that he overlooked earlier: the ability to search for items that are up for bid. The rest of the features will be useless without this capability.

Online Auction Service
Feature Description Document

Major Required Features

The primary required features for the *Online Auction Service* are summarized below. The priorities have been assigned by our marketing department after surveying our existing customer base (buyers and sellers). The priorities represent value to the customer/end user.

Product Features and Priorities

Customer Priority	Feature (Ability to)
High	# 1 Flag problem postings
Medium	# 2 Create alerts for item type
Low	# 3 Email a friend
Critical	# 4 Place an item up for bid
Critical	# 5 Register on the site
High	# 6 Contact the seller
Low	# 7 Customize my view
Low	# 8 Use an Auction Browser Tool Bar
Medium	# 9 Receive help online
Critical	# 10 Bid on an item
Medium	# 11 Record seller feedback
Medium	# 12 View seller information
Critical	# 13 Search by category
Medium	# 14 Perform advanced search

Figure 11.1 **A summary of the features for the Auctionator project. Planning starts now as the team scrutinizes the priority of the features.**

In our experience, there is usually time to refine feature information after an idea makes it through the feasibility gateway. On occasion, you may have a project that must go directly from feasibility to planning; this may be due to project urgency, or a project may be so small that refinement can occur during the Planning phase.

Feature 1: Flag problem postings

Since free postings will not require a credit card there is more risk of offensive postings. We will need a way to quickly remove offensive postings. The buyers and sellers on our site will be able to to identify inappropriate postings for speedy removal by using the flagging feature located on each auction. If a post receives enough negative flags it will automatically be removed.

Feature 2: Alerts for item type

Alert a potential registered bidder when an item they like is posted on Auctionator. Acme Media uses a third-party for all email alerts. The company, *eLertz*, provides an API for Acme to pass the email address and alert information to them. Today eLertz sends alerts related to breaking news and when an automobile goes for sale that matches a potential buyer's criteria.

Feature 3: Email a friend

A registered user can email a friend about an item up for bid.

Feature 4: Place an item up for bid

A registered user can place an item up for bid and retract it. The seller can enter a title, description, price, location, and two images.

Feature 5: Require registration on the site

Users must register to sell or bid on items. This profile stores preferences, email address, and credit card information. We should be able to do this with some light enhancements to our existing registration functionality.

Feature 6: Contact seller

Contact seller for more information on an item for sale. There will be a free form text field for the question. The contactor can request that their email address be hidden.

Feature 7: Customize my view

A user can pick the fields and colors on their landing screen, show their favorite sellers and searches, and list their recent purchases.

Feature 8: Auction Browser Toolbar

Search Auctionator from your browser without being on the site. The toolbar will embed in the browser itself and also provide buying/selling status and alerts.

Feature 9: Ability to receive help online

Ability for a user view help on the site, more than likely an FAQ that can be accessed from any page.

Feature 10: Item bidding

A registered user can bid on an item for sale. The system will automatically bid up to the maximum amount specified by the bidder.

Feature 11: Record seller feedback

Record feedback to a seller's profile after the transaction. The system will asking the winning bidder to complete the feedback.

Feature 12: View seller information

Learn about a seller's past and customer satisfaction with previous purchases.

Feature 13: Search by category

A general search box that also allows filtering by category.

Feature 14: Advanced Search

Search by category, price, location, and option to only show items with pictures.

Figure 11.2   The features outlined for the Auctionator project. The team will start with this raw list and shape it into a prioritized release plan during the Planning phase.

11.3.3 *Common understanding of the features*

Jay presents the Feature Description Document to the project team at the kickoff meeting and discusses each feature. The team asks questions to better understand the scope of the project.

Table 11.3 lists some of the questions the team asks Jay, and his responses.

Table 11.3   A great way to start the project is to have the customer or product owner discuss the features and take questions from the project team. The question-and-answer session synchronizes the team on the scope of the project and also validates the value of the project.

Question	Answer
Feature 8 describes an auction browser toolbar. Will this toolbar need to support all major browsers?	The toolbar will need to support current versions of Internet Explorer, Firefox, Safari, and Chrome.
Feature 7 describes the ability to customize your view. Do you envision this being done with a cookie, or will the user have to be a logged-in, registered user?	We want the user to register with us and be logged in before they have the option to customize their view.
Feature 1 describes the automatic removal of a posting if it receives enough complaints. Couldn't this feature create problems, if fake complaints are created to get an auction removed?	Yes, this could be an issue; but the user must be registered to file a complaint, which I hope will minimize the issue. Do you (the team) have any ideas how to solve this issue?
Feature 4 describes the ability to place an item up for bid and retract it. Will the user have the ability to edit the posting too?	Yes. I overlooked that. I'll create a new feature card (#15) for this feature.
Won't we need a way to remove and edit postings ourselves? Some kind of admin tool?	Good point. I'll create another feature card (#16). Maybe we can use our existing code for removing merchandise postings. Our goal is to start with light functionality for the Auctionator, so maybe we can get by with a tool that only allows us to remove postings.

The juices get flowing at the start of this meeting—this is good. You want the team engaged and energetic, so they own this project and bring it to completion. You've started down the path to ownership by immediately asking them for their feedback.

At this point, the team is starting to understand the features but doesn't have enough information to support the planning objective. You need sufficient information to assign the features to development iterations. The Acme team will help you reach this objective by creating feature cards in chapter 12; the feature-card exercise will examine each feature in more detail, identifying risks, quantifying value, and more clearly defining feature scope.

11.4   *The tradeoff matrix*

Many projects begin without the team identifying the most important priority. Everyone involved in the project needs to know whether the highest priority is ensuring delivery of scope, delivering the project by a specific date, or delivering the project with a set amount of resources/team members.

Your project sponsor will usually say that all three are equally important; but when the project comes under duress, they will be forced to prioritize. The goal of creating a *tradeoff matrix* like that shown in table 11.4 is to be honest from the start and let the

	Fixed (1)	Flexible (1)	Highly flexible (1–n)
Resources		X	
Schedule	X		
Scope			X
Costs			X

Table 11.4   The tradeoff matrix is a simple tool that communicates a project's priorities. In this example, Acme Media states that it must deliver the project by the target date, with other areas being compromised if needed.

project team know what the priorities are in advance of any issues coming to light. Completing this exercise increases the probability of project success.

When you create a tradeoff matrix, only one item can be the number-one priority. For the Auctionator, Acme Media has set a completion date 8 weeks out to ensure that the pilot doesn't run on indefinitely. Therefore, Acme marks Schedule as Fixed, or inflexible.

Acme's second priority is minimizing the need to use employees beyond the named project team. Because the project is a pilot, Acme doesn't want to complicate it by involving third parties. Acme marks Resources (project team members or contract help) as Flexible, meaning that if things get tight, the company will let a few additional people be added to the project.

If the project-team size and schedule are the first two priorities, then all other components must be highly flexible. This means Acme must be flexible about feature scope and project expenses. The feature set can't be rich if Acme Media wants to meet its number-one goal, delivering by a specific date. In addition, Acme must be flexible with the project budget, potentially spending beyond the estimates to ensure on-time delivery.

NOTE   The third column of the tradeoff matrix shows 1–n. You can add as many components as you like to this column, but they all must be viewed as highly flexible/lower priority.

The tradeoff matrix is the last item you need before you aggregate all the information you've collected into a charter document called the *project worksheet.*

11.5   *Project worksheet*

After your project idea has been scrutinized by the project team, you can aggregate the information collected into a project charter document. We call our charter the *project worksheet.* Similar to a charter, the worksheet is a useful tool for collecting project highlights and presenting them to a product manager, sponsor, or other interested party. The charter can also be posted on a prominent wall to remind the team what they signed up for.

A different spin on the tradeoff matrix

A few years ago, Greg worked on a project that would allow employees to view their benefit and pay information online. The goal was for employees to be able to verify their benefit selections and review their most recent pay stub online. The functionality would be available to 20,000 employees.

Being a typical project manager, Greg quickly identified a due date for the project and started working the critical path to ensure on-time delivery. The project team identified the critical features and major tasks to be accomplished and then kicked off the project.

As the project drew closer to the deadline for code completion, Greg began hearing a consistent concern: several project-team members were worried about the fact that they were exposing personal and intimate data via the application. They were concerned that the application could be hacked, or that one employee could see another employee's information.

Greg called a quick team meeting to discuss the concern with the project sponsor. The sponsor made it clear that a security breach of any type was not acceptable. The personal data had to be guaranteed secure, or the application wouldn't go live.

After the meeting, the team outlined all possible ways the data could be accidentally exposed or hacked. They also created a dummy database and asked an internal security expert to try to breach the application.

All these efforts extended the project beyond the original schedule; but as the team learned from the sponsor, *schedule was not the number-one priority.*

If the team had created a tradeoff matrix at the start of the project, they would have avoided some stress and planned differently. They would have been in tune with the project's main priority: data security. Instead, they assumed it was a typical project that was focused around delivering on time.

A tradeoff matrix for the project would have looked like this:

	Fixed (1)	Flexible (1)	Highly flexible (1-n)
Resources			X
Data Security	X		
Scope		X	
Costs			X

Greg learned two lessons: always be clear about your priorities before you begin the project, and don't assume that schedule is always the number-one priority.

Acme's new methodology suggests populating the worksheet with the information that comes out of the Feasibility phase and then enriching that information after reviewing the project with the project team. The information on the sheet can be reviewed quickly by people interested in your project, whether they're executives or the project team itself.

Sticking with the mentality of "just enough," the project worksheet contains only enough information to make the call about whether to proceed to the Planning phase. The document is simple, it's light, and it adds value to the process.

Figure 11.3 shows project worksheet for the Auctionator after the Feasibility phase. Let's take a moment to review the sections of the project worksheet that we haven't covered so far.

PROJECT NAME: Online Auction Service (The Auctionator)   Last Modified: 05/04/2010

Project Worksheet

Project manager:
Wendy Johnson

Team members (for Feasibility):
Product Management: Jay Fosberg

Development: Matt Lee

User Experience: Ryan Getty

Project objective statement:

The objective is to convert our existing merchandise advertising site into a free auction site. The conversion needs to be operational by 10/5/2010 using identified team members and contract help as needed.

Trade-off matrix:

	Fixed (1)	Flexible (1)	Highly Flexible (1-n)
Resources		X	
Schedule	X		
Scope			X
Costs			X

Issues and risks:

Scope could get out of control.

Migration of existing, non-auction advertisements.
Free auctions may invite fraud.

May need a significant marketing effort.

The pain of re-creating an auction if someone does not pay.

Technical considerations:
No experience with Auction functionality

Need to consider ways to prevent fake postings.
Success - If the idea takes off will our platform be able to scale to the volume?

Stakeholders:
Sponsor: Steve Winters (CIO)

Stakeholder: Jay Fosberg (Product Manager - Classifieds)
Stakeholder: Roy Williams (Program Manager - Registration)

User/customer benefits:
Free postings for sellers.

Auction functionality to ensure best possible price for sellers.
Eliminate the need for "offer" emails for buyers and sellers.
Item inspection before purchase.

A consolidated marketplace for buyers.

A new advertising channel for merchants.

Highlights: (Ability to...)
Place an item up for bid

Bid on an item

View seller feedback

Contact seller to ask questions

Flag problem posting

Expire auctions

Post auction without payment

Major milestones:
Go Live 10/5/2007

Project elevator statement:

For Internet buyers and sellers who would like to sell their items locally within an auction framework, the Acme Auctionator is a local online auction system that allows the purchase of goods. Unlike eBay, our product allows the winning bidder to pay in person using cash or check. And unlike Craigslist, our product allows the seller to put an item up for bid, as opposed to selling at a fixed price.

Project Worksheet - Feasibility Phase

Figure 11.3   The project worksheet after the Feasibility phase. One of the best things about the project worksheet is the contents usually fit onto one page. Interested parties will enjoy seeing all of the information in a quick snapshot.

11.5.1 *Team members*

The first two sections are simple. They list the assigned project manager and the team that has been working on the project prior to kickoff.

11.5.2 *Objective statement*

The objective statement is the most rudimentary summary of what the project needs to do. It also speaks to the constraints the team has assumed so far. In this instance, they believe the project must be complete by the middle of June, using internal employees and contract resources as needed.

11.5.3 *Issues and risks*

Acme summarizes the project risks it's identified so far. It's common for this list to grow as the project progresses. The Planning phase may also identify features needed to mitigate the risks. It's important to note that although we're mainly focusing on feasibility at this point, the Acme team has already started thinking about deployment processes such as migrating existing advertisements.

11.5.4 *Technical considerations*

The technical considerations section identifies specific risks to the application itself. These issues can relate to scalability, security, storage, new technologies, performance, usability, firewalls, browser compatibility, and recovery.

11.5.5 *Stakeholders*

Stakeholders are people who have an interest in the project, but they aren't the direct customers. For Acme's project, the sponsor definitely has an interest in the outcome. Jay Fosberg also cares, because he is the product owner for the classifieds website. Roy Williams has been listed as a stakeholder because the feasibility team believes the Auctionator may use the existing user-registration functionality, which Roy manages for Acme.

11.5.6 *User/customer benefits*

The user/customer benefits are tied to end users and other revenue-providing customers such as advertisers. These are the main benefits identified so far.

11.5.7 *Highlights*

The highlights section lists the high-level features identified so far. Jay, the product manager, has given the features simple descriptions in his Feature Description Document You want the team to begin looking at the features from more of a user perspective now, so they're relabeled in terms of "Ability to." For example, instead of saying "The system will support placing an item up for bid," the label reads "The ability to place an item up for bid." The change is subtle, but it starts the transition to user-centric analysis. In effect, it transitions the feature to a high-level user story. Make sure you describe the value, not the task.

11.5.8 *Major milestones*

At this point, the team hasn't identified many milestones. The only one currently known is the target completion date. The team will flesh out more milestones during the planning phase.

In conclusion, the project worksheet should provide enough information to determine whether the idea is feasible. Ideally, you want all the information to fit onto one page, but on occasion you may find an additional page is needed.

11.5.9 Elevator statement

We will keep the elevator statement on the project worksheet so we are always reminded of our main business goals during the project.

11.6   Key points

Key points from this chapter are as follows:

- Once your idea has been approved, you should run it by the project team as soon as you can. The team will provide valuable feedback on the idea and also normalize around the scope and goals of the project.
- Many projects get sidetracked by passive-aggressive behavior. You can eliminate this issue by creating an environment where team members can challenge the value of the project without repercussions.
- You may want to hold off on selecting project team members until an idea has passed through initial feasibility analysis. In the spirit of lean, you don't want to risk wasting valuable employees on an idea that may not go forward.
- You'll receive invaluable feedback from the pilot team as they test the processes defined by the core team.
- The pilot project will also serve as excellent training for the pilot team and start the evangelism of the new process throughout your organization.
- Be prepared to provide mentoring to your pilot team via your coach and your core-team members. You should mix a few core-team members into the pilot team to provide support.
- Perhaps no one exercise is more valuable than the product-envisioning exercise. The team and the customer will reach consensus about the value of the project.
- A tradeoff matrix will help your team when you encounter constraints during a project. Does schedule win? Does budget win? Your matrix should make it clear what wins before the constraint is encountered.
- A project worksheet provides a great summary for stakeholders and others who need an overview of the project and its value proposition.
- When you complete your team alignment work you'll create feature cards, which are covered in chapter 12.

11.7   Looking forward

In this chapter, we introduced the project team to the project idea and the customer. The customer and team began to envision what the delivered project will look like, and together they're ready to begin detailing specific features. In chapter 12, we'll identify the features and create supporting feature cards to quantify the risk and value of each feature.

Part 4

Populating the product backlog

Once we know the overall goals of a project, we can examine the project in more detail and identify features. These features will go into our backlog, be prioritized, and be added to an iteration if they are of high value.

A product backlog holds features that tie to the product. These features could include bug fixes, product suggestions, refactoring work, nonfunctional requirements, migration work, or content setup.

For a one-time project the backlog is initially populated after team alignment. If you are doing steady-state releases, your backlog already exists and you are in a state of constantly reviewing it before proceeding with your next iteration or release.

Once you have a running backlog, anyone can populate it. The largest contributor is frequently your customer or product owner, but the queue can be populated by the project team, executives, or support groups within your company.

When folks populate your backlog, they may put in requests that equate to an entire project or work that could take several months to complete. You and your team will need to break down the requests into features that can be completed in 10 days or less, or else your project will lose transparency and you will have deliveries that have to cross many iterations to be completed.

Let's get started by seeing how Acme Media populates its backlog by creating its initial feature cards for the Auctionator project.

Feature cards:
a tool for
"just enough" planning

When we plan an agile project, we try to do so in a lean fashion. We want to gather the minimal information needed to prioritize, sequence, and estimate a feature, so we can deliver high-value features as soon as possible. We can do this without creating detailed functional specifications and without guessing at all the tasks that we may need to complete, by creating *feature cards*

Feature cards start the discussion between the customer and the project team and support reaching common agreement on what a feature entails. In this chapter we will show you how much information to place in a feature card and how to involve your team in the creation of the cards; we will also discuss the limitations in using cards.

To help you better understand feature cards and the feature-card exercise, let's look at the structure of a card.

12.1   *The structure of a feature card*

Feature cards are similar to the *user stories* used in Extreme Programming (XP) development. We also often use the term *feature shell* to describe a feature card. The card provides enough information to plan a feature and discuss it quickly. The size of the card also makes it easy to track a feature and re-plan when necessary.

Let's look at a completed feature card (see figure 12.1).

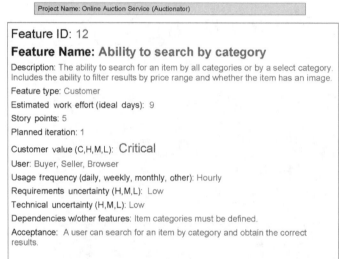

Figure 12.1   **A completed feature card for the Auctionator. A feature card provides just enough information to prioritize a feature. Additional dialogue or documentation is usually needed to support coding.**

The following are the feature card's fields:

- *Feature ID*—A unique number assigned to the feature. Numbering becomes more important in large projects, when features can have similar names.
- *Feature name*—A high-level description of the feature. It should describe the value of the feature to the customer. As we mentioned in chapter 11, the words *ability to* are frequently included in the name to indicate what the user has the ability to do.
- *Description*—A deeper description of the functionality.
- *Feature type*—Whether the feature is for the customer or for the system itself (a technical feature type). An example of a customer feature is the ability to bid on an item. An example of a technical feature is "create an email web service."

- *Estimated work effort (ideal days)*—Total labor estimated to be needed for the feature. It's a summary of the task estimates on the back side of the card. This field is used only for the first iteration of a project.
- *Story points*—A measure of the relative size of the feature, not an estimate. Story points will be your main metric for determining capacity as the project proceeds.
- *Planned iteration*—The iteration in which you plan to build the feature.
- *Customer value (C,H,M,L)*—Critical, high, medium, or low. The customer's or user's perspective of the value this feature provides. Critical means the customer doesn't see the value of the project if this feature can't be completed. Customer priorities frequently change after the team discusses all possible options for supporting the requirement outlined in the feature.
- *User*—Similar to an actor in a use case. For a pilot project, the most common users are buyers and sellers.
- *Usage frequency (daily, weekly, monthly, other)*—Another way to help you determine the value of the feature. Frequent use often implies high value to the customer.
- *Requirements uncertainty (H,M,L)*—High, medium, low. How comfortable the project team is with the customer's awareness of their need. After the customer described the feature, were you confident they truly understood their need, or was the customer still trying to clearly state the need? If a feature has high uncertainty, it's difficult to outline a design and the potential code needed. Conversely, if the uncertainty is low, the team should be able to outline a design and build the feature.
- *Technical uncertainty (H,M,L)*—High, medium, low. Tied to the technical risk associated with the feature. Does the project team have a vision for the technology that is needed to support this feature? Do you have experience with this technology? High technical risk means you don't have experience with the technology, or the technology itself isn't stable.
- *Dependencies w/other features*—Do you need any other features in place, or designed, before you can build this feature? For example, your project has a feature that lets you view a seller's feedback from their previous transactions. Before you create this feature, you need to create a feature that lets you record buyer feedback onto the seller's record.
- *Acceptance*—An outline of a high-level user acceptance test. What tests will this feature have to pass before it's deemed complete?

We frequently hear project teams ask how they can go from a feature card to working code. Many teams are used to receiving a detailed functional specification. A feature card doesn't have the detailed information they have received historically.

The answer is that *feature cards aren't supposed to replace functional specifications.* The feature-card exercise helps your team assess the level of documentation or information that is needed to build the feature. This documentation may include use cases, wireframes, mockups, usability studies, or other requirement artifacts.

> ### How much documentation for requirements?
> We've seen teams build simple features from the information on the feature cards. As features become more complex, teams bring in additional tools such as use cases, workflow diagrams, wireframes, screen mockups, prototypes, and information-flow diagrams. This is where agility and team knowledge come into play. The methodology doesn't dictate the documentation needed for each feature: the team does.

12.1.1   *The right amount and type of information*

Teams also want to know when a feature card is too big and when it should it be split into separate features. The best way to determine this is to walk through the steps needed to support the feature.

Project-team members grab a feature card during the feature-card exercise and walk through it on a whiteboard. They review potential workflows to support the feature and the steps needed. This workflow discussion usually identifies hidden features, and the team can create additional feature cards. You'll see an example of this process when Acme Media performs its feature-card exercise.

You can also use these guidelines to determine whether your feature cards contain the correct amount and type of information:

- The functionality described is understandable to users.
- The card describes functionality, not an implementation task.
- There is enough information to estimate the implementation effort.
- The card generally represents 1–10 days' worth of effort, or it fits in your story point scale (which we'll discuss later in chapter 14).
- Each card is as independent of the others as possible.
- The card is testable.

With experience, you and your team will develop a good feel for when the information is sufficient.

12.1.2   *Additional feature-card benefits*

In addition to providing the correct amount of information to initiate planning, feature cards also provide these benefits:

- *Customer focus*—Many requirement-gathering processes can quickly turn into task meetings. When this happens, the focus becomes how to build a feature, not what the customer needs. Feature-card titles focus on the customer. You provide the "ability to" for the customer. Your titles are user centric, and so are your acceptance tests.
- *Identifying risks early*—Feature cards have two fields that ask the team how uncertain they are about requirements and about the technology that will be needed.

In many environments, these risks wouldn't be identified until functional specifications were complete and the team started working on detailed design. In an agile world, the developers and other team members are involved early in the process to identify risk. This gives you more time to work through the risks, or an opportunity to cancel risky, noncritical features.

- *Common understanding*—We've worked on many projects that had highly documented requirements, but whose team was still confused about the feature. This frequently happens when one person writes the detailed specifications and then tries to explain a 30-page requirement document to the team. The feature card starts the requirements process by letting the entire team see the direction the feature is taking. This common understanding leads to quicker delivery and quicker decisions, because the team doesn't have to constantly reference and interpret requirements documentation.

Now that you have a feel for the structure and benefits of feature cards, let's look at the process you use to create them.

12.2 A team approach to creating feature cards

One of our favorite agile practices is the team creation of feature cards. The exercise lets the team discover features together. The project team uses an *organized brainstorm* to refine product highlights and convert them into feature cards. At the conclusion of this exercise, the feature cards contain enough information to be prioritized, sequenced, grouped, and estimated. You'll use this information to create your release plan.

You can expect the following things to happen during the exercise:

- Feature scope will become clearer.
- Additional feature dependencies will be identified.
- Many feature cards will be split into more granular features.

Team members grab blank index cards and enter the information from the Feature Description Document (explained in chapter 11) and additional information gathered from the customer. Acme Media gathered this information in chapter 11 when Jay, the product manager, introduced the project team to the project's features.

At this point, your feature cards are *born*, but they aren't complete. Figure 12.2 displays a feature card for the Auctionator after the initial conversation with the customer.

Acme needs to complete the following fields on the card:

- Usage frequency
- Requirements uncertainty
- Technical uncertainty
- Dependencies

Let's join the Acme Media team as they complete their feature cards.

Project Name: Online Auction Service

Feature ID: 10

Feature name: Ability to bid on an item

Description: A registered user can bid on an item for sale. The system will automatically bid up to the maximum amount specified by the bidder.

Feature type: Customer

Estimated work effort (days):

Story points:

Planned iteration:

Customer value (C,H,M,L): Critical

User: Bidder

Usage frequency (daily, weekly, monthly, Other): **?**

Requirements uncertainty (H,M,L): **?**

Technical uncertainty (H,M,L): **?**

Dependencies w/other features: Registration. Any others **?**

Acceptance: A registered user can place a bid on a live auction. The system performs automatic bid increments up to the bidders specified maximum bid.

Back of card:

Tasks	Ideal days	Group	Assigned

Figure 12.2   A feature card after Acme's first discussion with the customer. You need to complete the question areas before you can prioritize this feature.

12.2.1   Creating a feature card at Acme Media

You complete the feature-card fields by discussing the cards as a team. As each team member creates a feature card, they act as an investigator and speak to other team members and the customer. To see this in practice, let's watch a team member at Acme Media complete the additional fields.

Gina Wallace is the tester assigned to the pilot project. Gina grabs the feature card for *ability to bid on an item* (shown in figure 12.2) and considers the four empty fields. Based on the information Jay, the customer, provided during the feature introduction, Gina knows this feature is at the core of the application and will be used frequently. Gina writes *high* in the category for *Usage frequency*.

Gina also remembers that Jay said a user must be registered to place a bid on an item. Gina records feature 4, *require user registration*, as a dependency for this feature.

Continuing to think about dependencies, Gina also realizes that a user can't bid on an item unless the item is posted. Gina records feature 10, *place an item up for bid*, as another dependency.

Next, Gina considers the requirements uncertainty for the feature. How well did Jay describe the feature when the team asked him questions about it? Did Jay have a good feel for the feature's scope? After spending a few minutes thinking about the card by herself, Gina realizes she still has some open questions, so she asks Jay for more information:

- Will we have a way to refresh the bidding screen so the bidder can keep track of how much time is left to bid, or will the bidder have to refresh their browser on their own?
- Will a bidder have an option to *buy it now*, meaning can they place a bid so large that the auction automatically ends and they win the item?
- Will a bidder be able to view the bid history for an item up for bid?

Jay considers Gina's questions within the overall vision for the project. The main vision is to get live quickly with a minimal feature set so Acme Media can stop the competition from eroding the company's customer base. With that vision in mind, Jay tells Gina that the bidding screen won't refresh automatically. Jay also feels the *buy it now* functionality will make a great future feature, but they won't pursue it in the current release. Jay adds the *buy it now* feature to the product backlog.

Jay also thinks about the ability to view bidding history. He considers his own experiences when buying items on eBay: he cares about seeing the highest bid but not about seeing the entire bidding history. Jay decides that the ability to view the bidding history will also go into the product backlog, but it won't be considered for this release.

Gina records the additional information on the feature card and then revisits the question of requirements uncertainty. To her, it seems that the customer has a good feel for this feature and that the basic requirements are well defined. Gina writes *low* for *Requirements uncertainty* on the card.

Next, Gina considers the last field: *Technical uncertainty*. The customer can't help her a lot here, but she knows Matt, the developer, was involved in the feasibility investigation and can assist. Gina walks across the room and speaks with Matt.

Matt shares the information he's collected from his feasibility work. He tells Gina that a level of concern exists because the team has never created auction functionality before, but he's researched competing sites and found free auction source code on the internet. Matt has also looked at the existing merchandise applica- tion code and feels the auction functionality can be added to it without much technical concern.

Speaking to the *ability to place an item up for bid* specifically, Matt feels this feature isn't technically complex. Matt tells Gina that he'll mark the feature as having *low* technical uncertainty. Gina records the information on the card.

Gina needs to complete only one more field. How will she describe an acceptance test for this feature? She goes back to Jay to ask what he will consider a successful deployment of this feature. Jay and Gina identify two acceptance tests for the feature: a bidder's auction will be successfully recorded into the system, and the bidder will receive a bid-confirmation notice. Gina records the tests onto the card.

She has now completed all the fields she can; see figure 12.3.

As Gina has been completing her card, other team members have been doing the same thing. The room has been abuzz with conversations. When all the feature cards are complete, each team member will describe the feature they documented to the group for feedback and thoughts.

Project Name: Online Auction Service

Feature ID: 10

Feature name: Ability to bid on an item

Description: A registered user can bid on an item for sale. The system will automatically bid up to the maximum amount specified by the bidder.

Feature type: Customer

Estimated work effort (days):

Story points:

Planned iteration:

Customer value (C,H,M,L): Critical

User: Bidder

Usage frequency (daily, weekly, monthly, other): Daily

Requirements uncertainty (H,M,L): Low

Technical uncertainty (H,M,L): Low

Dependencies w/other features: Registration, The ability to place an item up for bid

Acceptance: A registered user can place a bid on a live auction. The system records the bid and provides a confirmation performs automatic bid increments up to the bidder's specified maximum bid.

Assumptions: - *Buy now* and, *view bidding history* are out of scope for this feature.

            - The system will not refresh the screen for the bidder.

Back of card:

Tasks	Ideal days	Group	Assigned

Figure 12.3   A feature card after completion of the feature-card exercise. For now we won't address the fields for estimated effort and planned iteration. This will come after you perform prioritization and estimation work.

Why not design the feature right now?

As you create feature cards, you'll begin to imagine potential design options and constraints. It may be tempting to turn the feature-card meeting into a full-blown design session. Don't do it.

What if you discover that a feature has a low priority, or the customer decides the feature isn't needed after all? If this happens, you'll have wasted precious time designing a feature that will never be delivered.

You must also consider the time needed to design each feature. The feature-card exercise is time-boxed and is usually completed in one day. You're gathering just enough information to prioritize the work, not complete it. Designing every feature in detail could take several days. You have urgency to evaluate and prioritize the work before engaging in detailed design. You'll go deeper into the features before and during the development iterations.

12.2.2   *Reviewing the feature cards as a team*

To complete the feature-card creation process, each team member presents their card to the team at large for feedback. When the whole team reviews the cards, additional issues are discovered, additional assumptions are added, and you give everyone on the team a voice. It's also common for team members to challenge the customer on the value of some features.

When Gina reviews the ability to bid on an item, various members of the team ask questions:

- Keith from architecture wants to know the feature's service-level requirements. How much time will the system have to record a bid and then allow all bidders to see the increase? Gina defers the question to Jay, the customer, who says the system needs to reflect a new bid after five seconds. Gina records this assumption on the card.

- Ryan, the designer, wants to know about the user interface. He asks Jay if they can use the existing site-navigation theme, or if the team will need to create a new look and feel for the Auctionator. Jay responds that he wants to keep the project as simple as possible and use the existing navigation if possible.

- Tom from operations asks how long a bid must be stored after an auction is closed. Also, will they need to store all bids or just the winning bid? Jay replies that he wants all bids for an auction to be stored for one month. Jay also tells the team that he's working on legal disclaimers for the site, to protect Acme Media from any issues associated with disgruntled bidders.

Acme Media continues the feature-card exercise by reviewing and discussing all the other features. As the end of the day, they have enough information to prioritize and sequence the work.

12.3 Feature cards compared to...

Feature cards are at the heart of the agile case study we're using. You may wonder how they compare and contrast to other requirement and planning tools frequently used for software development. Let's take a moment to compare feature cards to three popular tools.

12.3.1 User stories

Some of the people we've worked with refer to feature cards as user stories on steroids. We believe this is an accurate description.

Feature cards share the same goals as user stories. You aren't looking for requirements; you want information to help you plan. You aren't looking for formal requirements to review; you want to interact with the customer *verbally* to better understand their needs. You also want to gather just enough information to understand the scope of the system. User stories and feature cards collect conversations with customers. Feature cards also aim to represent a piece of work that can be completed within an iteration. And feature cards and user stories both collect the tests needed to verify a feature is complete.

The main thing that makes feature cards different is the additional fields for uncertainty, dependencies, and frequency of use. By adding these fields, you make it easier for the team to prioritize and sequence features after the initial customer conversations.

12.3.2 *Use cases*

Use cases have been an essential requirements-gathering tool for many years. We've used them on many projects, and they can provide a good process for documenting a system's detailed requirements. But if use cases are used too early, they can create issues for a project:

- A use case can imply technical-design details and bias the team toward implementation. You can easily lose sight of what the customer needs and begin rushing down the path to building the application.
- A use case can define a large scope of functionality. You want to see all your features defined as pieces of work that can be completed within an iteration. Many times, a use case exceeds this timeframe.

Let's look at the first issue and how design can creep into the discussion with use cases. A few years ago, Greg worked on a project that let employees update their personal benefits information online. Greg and a developer worked with the customer and quickly documented the main use case (see figure 12.4).

In this example, the use case didn't have an extreme bias toward design details, but hints were starting to surface. Greg's team was already thinking about using PeopleSoft and a SQL database. This team also assumed there would be separate screens for each benefits area and that the customer would receive a change confirmation via email. Such assumptions may end up being correct, but they steer the customer away from a conversation about their needs and into a discussion of implementation details.

It's important to note that there are two types of use cases: *essential* and *real.* An *essential* use case is closer to a feature card; the interaction listed is at a high level and isn't implementation specific. A *real* use case describes the detailed interaction with the system, naming screens, databases, triggers, and other system artifacts.

Returning to the second issue with use cases, let's see how scope could become large for an Auctionator feature (see figure 12.5).

Use Case:
Update Personal/Benefits Information

Use Case Name: Employee <u>updates</u> personal and benefits information via intranet

Actors:

Factory and Service Employees

Pre-conditions:

- Employee record exists in database (PeopleSoft and local SQL DB)
- Employee has an assigned employee number
- Employee has successfully logged into the global network
- During the authentication process, the employee responded "yes, they knew they were about to view personal information"

Steps:

1. Employee selects screen to update (contact info, insurance info, 401K info)
2. Area is displayed
3. Employee inputs new data
4. Employee may select another area to update
5. Employee inputs new data
6. Repeat as many times as necessary
7. When all revisions have been made, employee will select "submit changes".
8. Data will be sent via e-mail to appropriate contact within HR
9. Employee will receive message informing them that their changes will be reflected within the next 24-48 hours.
10. Employee logs out of application

Post-conditions:

- PeopleSoft database has an updated employee record.
- Employee has been notified via email of the change.

Exceptions:

- Employee is not set up in PeopleSoft
- Employee not downloaded to SQL database
- Employee has an incomplete record in the database

Figure 12.4   A use case can create issues for a project when it's used too early. The format can bias the team toward implementation planning versus trying to understand the true user or business need.

The Acme Media team could probably complete the main use case for *place a bid* within 10 days, but other use cases that could come from the exceptions probably wouldn't be completed within the same 10 days. Frequently, it takes more time to create an exception feature than it does to support the main, *perfect world* flow.

In conclusion, we think use cases are a great requirements-gathering tool, but they should be used in conjunction with feature cards or after feature cards are complete.

12.3.3 *Functional specifications*

In our experience, a functional specification is a deep, detailed document that speaks to how a requirement will be delivered. Functional specifications frequently include use cases, wireframes, interaction diagrams, formal business requirements, and entity-relationship diagrams.

Functional specifications are common in a waterfall environment. We usually see the following flow around a functional specification:

Use Case:
Place a bid for an auction

Use case name: A bidder can bid on an active auction.

Actors:

A registered bidder can bid on an active auction

Pre-conditions:

- The auction is in the database and active
- The bid amount is higher than the current highest bid
- The bidder is registered and signed in

Steps:

1. Bidder selects auction
2. Bidder enters bid amount into textbox
3. Bidder submits bid
4. The system confirms the bid

Post-conditions:
- The bid is confirmed to the user
- The highest bid is incremented in the database

Exceptions and alternate flows:

- Auction expires before bid is entered
- Bid placed is not above the current highest bid
- Bidder is not logged in
- The buyer is prompted for seller feedback

Figure 12.5 Alternate flows and exceptions can make a use case large and hard to consume within one iteration.

1. A business-requirements or marketing-requirement document is created.
2. A functional specification is created from the business-requirement document.
3. A technical design document is created from the functional specification.
4. A test plan is created from the functional specification.

The process can be formal, and each document is created in series. In some cases, the customer may not be consulted as the documents are being created; this process is common with fixed-bid work.

The team is trying to deliver to a requirement document and to use statements such as "The system shall...." If the customer did not detail their requirements correctly, you don't care—you get paid as long as you deliver to their specifications. This approach is different from the agile mentality of learning as you go and engaging in frequent customer interaction.

If you contrast a feature card to a functional specification (FSP), you'll notice the following differences:

- A feature card starts a requirements conversation. An FSP tries to cover all requirements immediately.

- A feature card is used to record conversations. An FSP doesn't include conversations but focuses on documenting how a documented business requirement will be met.

- A feature card focuses on verbal communication, common understanding, and synchronizing the team on the customer goals. An FSP focuses on documenting the functional details and having team members read the FSP to understand what they should do.

- A feature card focuses on gathering just enough information to prioritize, sequence, and estimate the work.

Note that we don't see an issue with creating functional specifications, but we *do* see issues with the process that usually surrounds them. In our experience, we've witnessed four weaknesses with the processes typically used with a formal FSP:

- A functional specification focuses on delivering what was requested at the beginning. In our experience, what the customer wants changes as they see the product demonstrated. Feature cards begin the process of identifying what is needed at the end, not the beginning.

- A functional specification can position the customer as an enemy, with definitive statements such as *the system shall*. The customer is also somewhat inhuman when their needs are presented on paper versus via a face-to-face conversation.

- The process around functional specifications can delay the ability to get early estimates for the project. An FSP may take weeks or months to complete, and then it's passed to developers for technical design and ultimately development estimates. It may take months to get an estimate for project duration.

- When estimates do come in, you may realize that you've completed functional specifications for features that you won't have time to complete. This FSP work will be wasted effort.

There is value in FSPs when you work with offshore resources, or to help you support traceability requirements. It's also great to have a document that holds all the information about a feature in one place, especially if you don't have a dedicated team room or a place to hold your whiteboard diagrams and flow. We've seen some teams take pictures from their whiteboard-modeling discussions and store them in the FSP. This is a great idea because team members usually understand diagrams better than requirements statements. The main point is that you don't want to start your initial planning process by creating detailed functional specifications.

12.4   Limitations in using feature cards

Switching to a feature-card-based planning process can be a big cultural change. You may have constraints that make it difficult for you to make the conversion. Let's look at some of the most common constraints.

12.4.1 *Project complexity*

We once worked on a huge project to deliver an online real estate site. The project was estimated to have four major phases and take a year to complete. In addition, we were outsourcing most of the functionality to a real-estate site service provider. The provider wanted us to provide complete functional specifications for all our requirements before they would provide a cost estimate. Our team had agile experience, but we didn't see how we could use feature cards for a vendor who didn't want to work in an agile fashion.

Since this time, we've learned that the best way to deal with large projects is to focus on identifying the critical features first and then use the feature-card process for the critical work. When we need to estimate all the work, we discuss themes for future phases and provide high-level estimates to stakeholders, but we don't try to estimate a huge project in detail. This approach has worked well for us because we often find that once phase 1 critical features are delivered, the customer may change their mind about what is needed next and may cancel subsequent phases. You'll also find that the world isn't static during your project, and a change in the business climate can make a customer redirect you to a new need.

12.4.2 *The customer isn't available*

An integral part of creating feature cards is dialogue with the customer or product owner. On occasion, we've worked with teams that were able to complete the feature-card exercise with minimal customer interaction during the exercise. Here's an example.

Once we worked on an intranet platform that had multiple customers per release. Some customers were available for the feature-card exercise, and others had only an hour or two to give. Some customers were totally unavailable due to vacation or illness. If a customer had only an hour or two, we interviewed them intensely for the time they were available and then used a proxy to continue the process. The proxy was frequently a business analyst who spent time with the customer before the feature card meeting. As the feature-card discussions continued without the customer, the analyst provided feature requirements and decisions; later, they reviewed the discussion with the real customer.

In cases where the customer wasn't available at all, we debriefed them before the session and had someone on our team named as a proxy in advance of the meeting.

Ultimately, you want high customer involvement in your development process. Assuming your customer was highly involved in the creation of business-requirement documents in the past, your customer should have time for the feature-card exercise now that you won't require detailed business requirements to initiate the project.

12.4.3 *Compliance and traceability*

In many environments, you must provide requirements traceability and support compliance programs such as Sarbanes-Oxley (SOX). Let's discuss traceability first.

If you use feature cards, you may find it difficult to go through them for an auditor to prove you supported a requirement. In these instances, you may want to have an electronic version of the card (see section 12.5) with a unique ID that can be referenced to show support for the original requirement. In our experience, we've gone a step further and created an electronics requirement package that auditors can reference. These packages contain customer discussions, wireframes, interactions diagrams, workflow diagrams, and sometimes use cases. We've also stored a record of test results and customer approval. The good news is that our feature cards, and everything we do in an agile environment, are focused around acceptance testing. Other than documenting results in a place they can be referenced, you shouldn't need to make any process changes.

Agile is also good for compliance environments because projects (releases or iterations) are small and make results easier to view and comprehend. An agile process also lends itself to transparency, which most regulatory bodies desire.

Perhaps the biggest thing to address with agile and compliance is how you document your process. We've found that companies often harm themselves by documenting a process they don't follow. In these examples, teams rush to create artifacts that support compliance but provide no value to the project.

We've also worked in ISO environments; one of the famous quotes from ISO auditors is "document what you do, and do what you document." Many large companies have teams dedicated to corporate methodology, and these teams document what they think you do or should do. You need to work with these teams so they document the true agile process that you use, so you're always in compliance.

12.5   *Hard-copy cards vs. electronic cards*

The spirit of feature cards is to increase verbal communication with the customer and enhace the team's understanding of features. Using physical cards encourages face-to-face communication and also helps the team better remember what a feature is about, because a team member writes the conversation notes on the card in their unique handwriting (see figure 12.6).

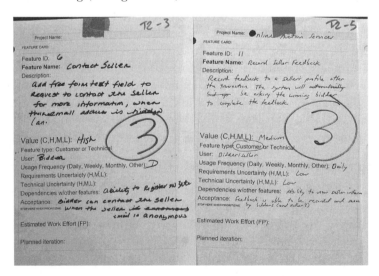

Figure 12.6   Features are easier to remember when they're created by hand and always on the wall for team members to reference and edit.

You should make it easy to discuss, reference, and modify feature cards if needed. A physical card simplifies this process. Physical cards also work well when you begin prioritizing and sequencing the features for a release: you can move the cards around and view them as the team discusses sequencing.

But sometimes you may also want an electronic representation of your card. For example, if you're working with distributed employees, you may want to show them the features via a wiki or collaboration website, as in figure 12.7. You may also have a queue for customer requests, where your customers complete an electronic form that populates your backlog. You can print these cards for the feature-card exercise and update them online after the exercise if necessary.

Some teams don't have a dedicated team room, and an electronic tool lets the team view feature information at their desks or other remote locations.

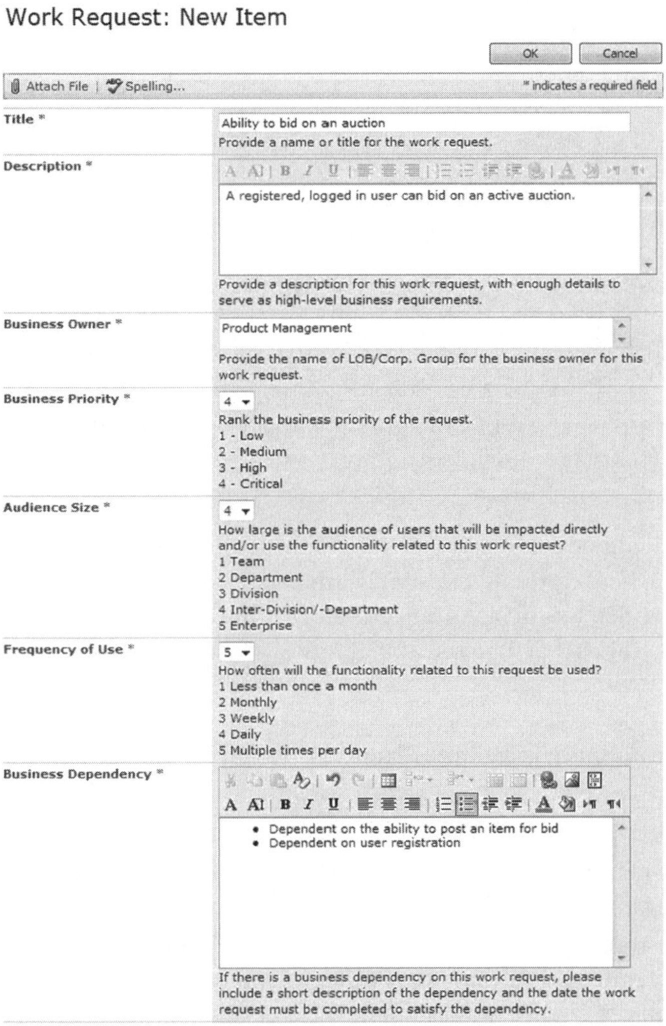

Figure 12.7 Tools such as SharePoint let you create feature cards electronically. Electronic cards can be used to supplement the use of physical cards and make it easier to distribute feature information to offshore teams or across a large enterprise.

A case study from a real project manager using both physical and electronic cards

When I was initially trained on agile processes, I was told to always use index cards or paper for the feature cards. The team could quickly create, edit, view, and move index cards. The physical paper was also conducive to collaboration and conversation. I totally support this approach, and I can attest that paper works great for the feature-card exercise.

On occasion, though, I've had issues with paper after the feature-card exercise. I've worked in several environments where we couldn't get a dedicated team room, so we couldn't leave our artifacts on the wall. In those instances, we brought a computer and a digital camera with us to the team room. We created the feature cards in Microsoft Word and used a digital camera to take a picture of any sequencing work. We then posted the information on a team website that all team members could go to whenever they wanted—they didn't have to find the physical feature cards. When necessary, we printed out the feature cards and went back to work passing them around physically and writing on them.

Going electronic has also helped me with capacity planning. I've used tools such as SharePoint, VersionOne, and Rally to enter features into an electronic list. This list lets me aggregate team capacity and story-point estimates for a quick comparison. This helps me assign features to iterations during release planning.

I've also created a feature-card template in Microsoft Word. I print a stack of these blank cards before the feature-card exercise and hand them out to the team when we start breaking down the features. The template contains all the fields in which to record feature information. This also helps people remember what data they should collect.

I suggest that you experiment with paper and electronic methods and then outline a custom process that works for your team.

Do all you can to use physical cards that are viewable at all times, preferably in a dedicated team room. Physical cards are extremely important for the feature-card exercise and later for release and iteration planning. Use electronic cards to supplement physical cards if you have constraints that limit the availability of physical cards to team members.

12.6   Key points

The key points from this chapter are as follows:

- Feature cards let you plan a project without creating detailed functional and technical specifications.
- Feature cards help you prioritize your work and avoid wasting time on features that may never be needed.
- Feature cards aren't meant to be the only source of requirements information. After initial planning, you may want to supplement the cards with additional artifacts to support feature development.

- Features need to be broken down into a size that allows delivery of working code within 10 days. If you pursue large features that take weeks or months to complete, you may fall back into a waterfall process and lose your ability to evaluate project status.

- Feature cards are all about the customer. The cards should describe the value that will be delivered to the customer.

- A completed feature card holds initial estimates, but you don't perform estimation until you determined priorities and sequence. You'll do this in chapter 16.

- Involve your entire project team in the feature-card exercise, unless the team is too large. If your team has more than 12 people, you may need to have representatives by area.

- Involving the entire team ensures consistent understanding and buy-in. If anyone has doubts about feature value, they can share their concerns directly with the customer.

- A feature card is similar to a user story. The main difference is that a feature card has fields to remind team members about information to collect related to risk and value.

- Use cases can assist you during the feature-card creation process, but you need to make sure the use case speaks to the business need and not a specific implementation of the need.

- If at all possible, use physical feature cards for the feature-card exercise. Physical cards encourage you to interact with the customer and place a focus on verbal communications, which helps you understand the customer's need. Try to limit the use of electronic cards to supporting the physical cards or passing the information to distributed groups.

12.7 Looking forward

In this chapter, we fleshed out the features for the pilot project. You should be starting to understand the value and the risks of each feature. In chapter 13, you'll learn how to use this information to prioritize your work. After your work is prioritized, you can estimate the features; then you'll be ready to lay out your overall release schedule.

Prioritizing the backlog 13

Have you ever run out of time on a project and started skimping on testing, training, or usability? Have you ever delivered a project and then been amazed that the customer only used about 20 percent of the functionality? These common issues illustrate the need for prioritizing features within a project.

When you prioritize features, you ensure that you deliver the most valuable functionality to your customer first. You do this by iteratively building feature sets and deploying these features after each iteration if needed. For example, you may find that you need three iterations of work to complete your project. In this instance, you put the critical, minimum functionality needed in iteration 1, followed by high-priority features in iteration 2, followed by medium-priority features in phase 3. Each iteration concludes with usable features that could be deployed to your production environment if needed. The power in this approach is you can still deliver critical parts of your project if issues are encountered along the way. You won't need to compromise on the quality of the features you deliver, and the customer can still receive a usable system.

In this chapter, we'll discuss the guidelines for prioritizing features, and you'll see these guidelines in action as Acme Media prioritizes its project/product backlog for the Auctionator project. At the conclusion of this exercise, Acme Media will have a prioritized backlog that is ready for initial estimation.

13.1   The art of prioritizing, sequencing, and grouping features

After you complete the feature-card exercise, you need to determine the logical build sequence. There are dozens of ways to do this; we'll walk you through a process that has worked well for many project teams in various industries.

However your project team chooses to do this process, follow the way you do it consistently so your team can focus on building the application. You want the team to get familiar with a sequencing process so that it becomes intuitive.

Here are the guidelines we suggest for prioritizing, sequencing, and grouping features:

- Determine what features are most important to the user/customer.
- Determine which features go together to provide value to the customer. If possible, avoid splitting features across groupings when both features are needed to provide value to the user.
- Think about features that are high value and high risk. It's usually good to get them up front in the sequence so you can make the call on removing them from the project or have the luxury of being able to work on them in every iteration.
- Interfaces always present risk. As a rule of thumb, feature cards that involve an interface should have technical uncertainty marked as *high.*
- Third parties (vendors/partners) also represent high risk, especially if you've never worked with them before. You want features related to third parties early in the sequence also.

After you have the guidelines for prioritizing, you need to determine who will take part in the prioritization exercise. In most agile environments, the customer or product owner prioritizes the backlog. We agree with this practice for initial prioritization, which is based on anticipated business value. But after the customer has prioritized the features, you should engage the entire project team in an exercise of reviewing the priorities based on additional attributes of the feature cards, such as frequency of use, technical/requirements uncertainty, and dependencies.

Our suggestion is to tape all the feature cards to a wall, in the order of business value, and then have the team move the cards around. The highest-priority items are on the left, and the lesser-priority items are on the right. The team looks at the

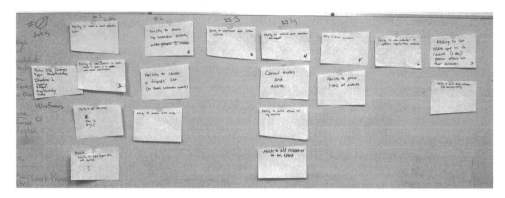

Figure 13.1   You'll prioritize your feature cards based on business value, risk, dependencies, and uncertainty.

features as a group, and team members are allowed to move cards based on their perception of value, risk, and usage. Figure 13.1 shows a whiteboard with features taped to it; a team has just concluded the prioritization exercise for their project.

NOTE   The X axis displays value, from left to right. If two features are at the same place on the X axis, they're of equal value, and you stack them one on top of another. The Y axis position is irrelevant and has no relationship to value.

To see these concepts in practice, let's spend a few moments with Acme Media as the team prioritizes their product backlog.

13.2   *Prioritizing the backlog at Acme Media*

Acme Media has just completed its feature-card exercise with the customer. The product manager, Jay, is the customer. Acme Media hasn't started the prioritization process yet, but it has the information it needs to begin; see table 13.1.

Table 13.1   Acme Media has a product backlog after completing the feature-card exercise. The work hasn't been prioritized yet, but the team has the information they need. Note that you should assign unique IDs to features to prevent confusion when you have features with similar names.

Customer value	ID	Feature name (ability to)	Requirements uncertainty	Technical uncertainty	Usage	Dependency	Comments
High	1	Flag problem postings	Low	Low	Low	4	
Medium	2	Create alerts for item type	Low	High	Low	4	Feature requires an interface
Low	3	Email a friend	Low	Low	Low	4	

Table 13.1   **Acme Media has a product backlog after completing the feature-card exercise. The work hasn't been prioritized yet, but the team has the information they need. Note that you should assign unique IDs to features to prevent confusion when you have features with similar names.** *(continued)*

Customer value	ID	Feature name (ability to)	Requirements uncertainty	Technical uncertainty	Usage	Dependency	Comments
Critical	4	Place an item up for bid	Low	Low	High	5	
Critical	5	Register on the site	Low	Low	High		Ties into existing registration functionality
High	6	Contact the seller	Low	Low	Medium	4, 5	
Low	7	Customize my view	Low	Low	Low	5	
Low	8	Use an auction browser toolbar	Low	High	Low	5	No experience with browser toolbars
Medium	9	Receive help online	Low	Low	Medium		
Critical	10	Bid on an item	Low	Low	High	4, 5	
Medium	11	Record seller feedback	Low	Low	Medium	5	
Medium	12	View seller information	Low	Low	Medium	11	
Critical	13	Search by category	Low	Low	High		
Medium	14	Perform advanced search	Low	Low	Low	4	
Low	15	Retract a bid	Low	Low	Low	5	
Medium	16	Purchase an item immediately	Low	Low	High	5	
Critical	17	Auction engine	Medium	Low	High	4, 10	Processes to support the auctions

Note that we've aggregated the feature information into a table to make it easier for you to follow the process. At Acme Media, the team uses their hard-copy cards and the wall for the prioritization exercise.

13.2.1 *Prioritizing by value*

Acme Media's first step is to make sure the business priorities are unchanged after the feature-card exercise. The customer may want to reassign the priorities now that you have more information about the features.

The Acme Media project team asks their customer, Jay, if he still agrees with his initial value assessments. Jay notes that the *purchase an item immediately* feature is predicted to have high usage. Looking at it now, he'd label it as high or critical business value. Jay decides to mark the feature *high*.

After making the change that Jay requests, the team sorts the cards by customer/business value. You can see the results from the initial sorting in table 13.2.

Table 13.2   **Feature cards sorted by customer value. You sort by customer value first because delivering valuable software "early and often" is your main objective.**

Customer priority	ID	Feature name (ability to)	Requirements uncertainty	Technical uncertainty	Usage	Dependency	Comments
Critical	4	Place an item up for bid	Low	Low	High	5	
Critical	10	Bid on an item	Low	Low	High	4, 5	
Critical	5	Register on the site	Low	Low	High		Ties into existing registration functionality
Critical	13	Search by category	Low	Low	High		
Critical	17	Auction engine	Medium	Medium	High	4, 10	Processes to support the auctions
High	16	Purchase an item immediately	Low	Low	High	5	
High	1	Flag problem postings	Low	Low	Low	4	
High	6	Contact the seller	Low	Low	Medium	4, 5	
Medium	2	Create alerts for item type	Low	High	Low	4	Feature requires an interface
Medium	9	Receive help online	Low	Low	Medium		
Medium	11	Record seller feedback	Low	Low	Medium	5	

Table 13.2 Feature cards sorted by customer value. You sort by customer value first because delivering valuable software "early and often" is your main objective. *(continued)*

Customer priority	ID	Feature name (ability to)	Requirements uncertainty	Technical uncertainty	Usage	Dependency	Comments
Medium	12	View seller information	Low	Low	Medium	11	
Medium	14	Perform advanced search	Low	Low	Low	4	
Low	3	Email a friend	Low	Low	Low	4	
Low	7	Customize my view	Low	Low	Low	5	
Low	8	Use an auc-tion browser toolbar	Low	High	Low	5	No experience with browser toolbars
Low	15	Retract a bid	Low	Low	Low	5	

This first sort of the feature cards lets the team understand which features are critical, high, medium, and low. Note that another way of viewing the critical features is to say they're the minimum features needed to deliver a functional application. Although you aren't creating a release plan yet, the *critical* label gives you early insight into what the first iteration will probably contain.

The next sort relates to dependencies. Which features have a high dependency placed on them? What features tie to each other?

The Acme Media team looks at the Dependency column and sees that eight features are dependent on feature 5, *the ability to register on the site*. As a matter of fact, the only critical feature that doesn't require user registration is *search by category*. Based on this, the team moves *the ability to register on the site* to the far left, indicating it's the first feature in the sequence.

13.2.2 Evaluating risk

The Acme Team follows the dependency evaluation by reviewing feature risk. The team looks for high-risk features, knowing that they must be removed from the project or moved to the top of the sort.

You have three options for dealing with high-risk features. Here are our suggestions:

1 *High risk and critical/high business value*—Move the features to the top of your sort, and pursue them early in the project. By doing this, you'll be able to use the entire length of the project to work out issues related to the risk.

2 *High risk and medium business value*—You have to make the call on a case-by-case basis. You can work on the feature early, in the middle of the project, or at the end of the project. We suggest that you review the value again with the customer

and see which way the feature is leaning. If the customer leans toward high value, pursue option 1. If the customer leans toward low business value, pursue option 3.

3 *High risk and low business value*—Move the feature to the bottom of your sort, or consider removing it from the project.

For us, risk is tied to uncertainty. Which features do you have doubts about? Are the requirements still vague for any features? Are you questioning what technology to use for any features?

If you do a quick review of Acme Media's list, you can see a few features that meet this uncertainty criterion. Feature 17, the *auction engine*, has medium requirements uncertainty and medium technical uncertainty. This feature is also considered critical.

Ideally, Acme would like to move this feature closer to the top, but it's dependent on other features. The *ability to place an item up for bid* (4) and the *ability to bid on an item* (10) need to be understood at some level before Acme can build the auction engine. Based on this, they move this feature above search but below features 4, 5, and 10.

Another feature with a risk implication is *ability to use an auction browser toolbar* (8). This feature has high technical risk because the development team has never tried to embed functionality into a browser. This feature is also marked as a low priority to the customer. High-priority / high-risk features go to the top of the sequence list. Low-priority / high-risk features go to the end of the sequence. Acme makes the auction browser toolbar the last item in the sequence list.

The last item with a level of risk is *the ability to create alerts for item type* (2). This feature is labeled as high risk because it requires an interface to a third party. Acme has used this vendor in the past and is familiar with the vendor's API. The risk is probably lower than indicated, so the team leaves this feature where it is in the sequence.

Let's review Acme's sequence after these changes; see table 13.3.

Table 13.3   **Feature cards sorted by customer value and risk. You sort high-value/high-risk items to the top to ensure time for resolving the risk. You sort high-risk/low-value items to the bottom.**

Customer priority	ID	Feature name (ability to)	Requirements uncertainty	Technical uncertainty	Usage	Dependency	Comments
Critical	5	Register on the site	Low	Low	High		Ties into existing registration functionality
Critical	4	Place an item up for bid	Low	Low	High	5	
Critical	10	Bid on an item	Low	Low	High	4, 5	

Table 13.3 Feature cards sorted by customer value and risk. You sort high-value/high-risk items to the top to ensure time for resolving the risk. You sort high-risk/low-value items to the bottom. *(continued)*

Customer priority	ID	Feature name (ability to)	Requirements uncertainty	Technical uncertainty	Usage	Dependency	Comments
Critical	17	Auction engine	Medium	Medium	High	4, 10	Processes to support the auctions
Critical	13	Search by category	Low	Low	High		
High	16	Purchase an item immediately	Low	Low	High	5	
High	1	Flag problem postings	Low	Low	Low	4	
High	6	Contact the seller	Low	Low	Medium	4, 5	
Medium	2	Create alerts for item type	Low	High	Low	4	Feature requires an interface
Medium	9	Receive help online	Low	Low	Medium		
Medium	11	Record seller feedback	Low	Low	Medium	5	
Medium	12	View seller information	Low	Low	Medium	11	
Medium	14	Perform advanced search	Low	Low	Low	4	
Low	3	Email a friend	Low	Low	Low	4	
Low	7	Customize my view	Low	Low	Low	5	
Low	15	Retract a bid	Low	Low	Low	5	
Low	8	Use an auction browser toolbar	Low	High	Low	5	No experience with browser toolbars

Now Acme's team has a good sort of their features. Critical features are first in the list, where they belong. Risky features have been sorted accordingly and either moved up front to buy the team time to work out the risk or moved to the end because they have low customer value.

13.2.3 *Grouping related features*

The last step in Acme Media's sorting exercise is grouping features. Acme needs to group features that must be used together to provide value to the user/customer.

For example, the customer won't care if Acme delivers the *ability to bid on an item* (10) if no one has the *ability to put an item up for bid* (4), because there won't be any items to bid on. These two features need each other to provide value to the customer. Acme places them together and calls them Group A.

If you review the features, another logical grouping stands out. Users can't *view seller information* (12) if they don't have the *ability to record seller feedback* (11). These two features needed to be delivered together to provide value to the customer (Group B).

Let's take a final look at the feature list after Acme establishes the groupings; see table 13.4.

Table 13.4 **Feature cards sorted by customer value and risk, with logical groupings. Groupings show you features that must be delivered together to provide value to the customer.**

Customer priority	ID	Feature name (ability to)	Requirements uncertainty	Technical uncertainty	Usage	Dependency	Comments
Critical	5	Register on the site	Low	Low	High		Tie into existing registration functionality
Critical	4	Place an item up for bid	Low	Low	High	5	Group A
Critical	10	Bid on an item	Low	Low	High	4, 5	Group A
Critical	17	Auction engine	Medium	Medium	High	4, 10	Processes to support the auctions
Critical	13	Search by category	Low	Low	High		
High	16	Purchase an item immediately	Low	Low	High	5	
High	1	Flag problem postings	Low	Low	Low	4	
High	6	Contact the seller	Low	Low	Medium	4, 5	
Medium	2	Create alerts for item type	Low	High	Low	4	Feature requires an interface
Medium	9	Receive help online	Low	Low	Medium		
Medium	11	Record seller feedback	Low	Low	Medium	5	Group B

Table 13.4 Feature cards sorted by customer value and risk, with logical groupings. Groupings show you features that must be delivered together to provide value to the customer. *(continued)*

Customer priority	ID	Feature name (ability to)	Requirements uncertainty	Technical uncertainty	Usage	Dependency	Comments
Medium	12	View seller information	Low	Low	Medium	11	Group B
Medium	14	Perform advanced search	Low	Low	Low	4	
Low	3	Email a friend	Low	Low	Low	4	
Low	7	Customize my view	Low	Low	Low	5	
Low	15	Retract a bid	Low	Low	Low	5	
Low	8	Use an auction browser toolbar	Low	High	Low	5	No experience with browser toolbars

Now that the team has determined their priorities, sequence, and groupings, it's time to estimate the features. This process is covered in chapter 14.

We suggest that you hold off on estimating features until you've completed the sequencing exercise. The reason is you may identify several low-value items that you may want to remove from the project. If you remove them, you don't need to waste time estimating them.

You can use estimates to assist in prioritizing the backlog

As noted in this chapter, we suggest performing initial estimates after you've determined the priority of each feature. Our suggestion is based on the time needed to estimate each feature. You don't want to waste time estimating a feature that you may never pursue.

In the last few years, however, we have crossed paths with teams who do a quick initial estimate and use it as another factor in the sequencing/prioritization process we've outlined in this chapter. We don't have an issue with this approach, as long as you time-box the estimating window. It's easy for a team to want to do a first pass at designing features before providing estimates. This can be a time-consuming process and may delay the start of developing features that are known to be critical to the project.

Working with the customer, you can review the sequenced features and see if any low-priority features should be removed. You especially want to consider features that are low value and high risk. In the case study, one feature stands out: the *auction browser toolbar* (8). It's low value and high risk. The Acme Media team discusses its value and risk with Jay ,the customer, and he agrees to remove the feature from the project. Jay understands how the feature could be technically complex and distract the team from the most important features.

13.3 *Other ways to prioritize features*

As we mentioned at the start of this chapter, there are many ways to prioritize features. Section 13.2 demonstrates a common way to perform prioritization; let's contrast it to another approach.

We have a friend, Tim, who once worked for a small startup company that was fighting for survival. The company provided commercial software to other companies; similar to Acme Media, the company delivered to a product market, not a specific customer.

Tim's team performed the feature-card exercise but used a slightly different approach for determining feature value (see figure 13.2). Tim's company looked at three factors when determining feature priority:

- How close is this feature to the target market? This is the most important ranking attribute; multiply the score of this value by 4.
- How much effort will this feature take to complete? Multiply this score by 3.
- How much organizational impact will this feature have? In this instance, *organizational impact* means the feature will make the company more attractive to potential investors.

Notice that Tim's team didn't score the items 1 to 10. Every item had to be scored as 9, 3, or 1. This scoring method was used to push the team to start thinking about priorities immediately and to avoid having all items reach a similar score.

When Tim's team concluded this exercise, they didn't consider the sorting process complete. They used the output of the Excel spreadsheet as a starting point for dialogue on how they would prioritize the items. The scores influenced their decisions, but ultimately the team made the call about priorities.

Customer Facing Features	Ratings			
External	Market (x4)	Effort (x3)	Org Impact (x1)	Total
User-purchased gift certificates	9	9	9	72
Buy-X get Y free promotion	9	9	9	72
Save-your-shoppingcart	9	3	9	54
Promotion Mgmt.	9	3	9	54
Menu of 3-4 different page flows (express, etc)	9	1	9	48
OrderHistory - Change ship-to address prior to export	3	9	9	48
Single-purchase coupons	3	9	9	48
Enhanced Billing UI	3	9	9	48
Affinity points	9	3	1	46
Dynamic personalized upsells/xsells	9	1	3	42
VIPC Lite	1	9	9	40
OrderHistory - Self-service returns	3	3	9	30
Buy-now, ship-later	3	3	3	24
Gift Cards & personalized messages	3	3	3	24
Gift Wrap	3	3	3	24
Wish Lists	3	3	3	24
WAP/WML support	3	1	9	24
HTML Emails	1	3	9	22
Auctions	3	1	3	18
OrderHistory - show "real" shipments	1	3	3	16
Configurable Multiple Ship To	1	3	2	15

Figure 13.2 An Excel spreadsheet is used to weight and sort features for a release.

13.3.1 *What about technical features?*

You may have noticed that most of the features/user stories in the Auctionator are customer facing. We've done this to make it easier to follow the case study, but we understand that every project/release you perform includes some level of technical work, and this work must be prioritized with the customer-facing features.

Returning to Tim's small company, figure 13.3 shows how his team prioritized their technical/refactoring features.

Refactoring Features	Ratings			
Internal	Benefit (x4)	Effort (x3)	Org Impact (x1)	Total
Email service	9	9	1	64
Table shipping algorithm service	9	3	9	54
HTML/UI friendliness cleanup and enhancements	9	3	9	54
Modularize promotion arbitration process	3	9	9	48
Close existing bugs before adding new features	3	9	9	48
Refactor abstract servlet hiearchy	6	6	3	45
Order-placement and payment-processing service	3	3	9	30
Distributed webcart	3	3	9	30
Multi-site support	3	3	9	30
Allow cart operation even if tax and fraud aren't ava	3	3	9	30
Clean up the Validation Infrastructure	3	3	9	30
Simplify/refactor rendering components	3	3	9	30
Rewrite logging functionality	3	3	9	30
Shipping service table algorigthm > 150 lbs	3	3	9	30
Completion of FedEx table support	3	3	9	30
International shipping	3	3	9	30
Change taxing to accept multiple items in one netw	3	3	3	24
Site/Merchant/Supplier/Shipping configuration gui	3	1	9	24
Shipping calculation service	3	3	1	22

Figure 13.3 Every project will have features that are related to architecture and refactoring. This work is prioritized with the customer features, and your release will be a mixture of both types of features.

In this example of architectural features, the team used similar attributes to rank the backlog. The main difference was removing the *Market* column and replacing it with a column that measures how valuable the feature is to the platform.

Your technical features will be stored in the same backlog as the customer-facing backlog; but similar to Tim's team, you may use different attributes to rank the features.

Technical features frequently correlate to refactoring work and consolidating redundant programs. In this example, Tim's company had four product groups, and each had created its own email engine. The team realized how much work was being wasted in maintaining four sets of similar code, so they decided to work together to create one email service that they could all use.

13.4 *Key points*

The key points from this chapter are as follows:

- Prioritizing features helps you deliver value to your customer sooner.
- Prioritizing features lets you stop a project before it's complete and still deliver the critical features.

- Customer value is the main attribute for determining prioritization, but you use other factors such as risk, frequency of use, and dependencies to create your final prioritized backlog.

- The customer or product owner can provide the business priorities, and then the team and the customer should work together to complete the sorting process. This step aligns the team on the priorities and contributes to team buy-in.

- Some features need to be delivered together to provide value to the customer. When these features are identified, you group them together, and they have equal priority.

- You can customize the prioritization at your company to meet your unique needs. You should start with customer value and then consider other areas that are of value in your environment. These areas can include market share, usability, feature expense in time and or money, investor value, and innovation.

- You backlog will consist of features that are customer facing and features that may be considered refactoring. You'll review both types of features when prioritizing your product backlog.

13.5 *Looking forward*

In this chapter, we explained how to prioritize features based on business value and technical risk. In chapter 14, we'll show you how to estimate the prioritized work so that you can assign features to iterations.

Estimating at the right
level with the right people

Estimating software is a mystery for most teams. Teams can spend huge amounts of time breaking down features to create their estimates, but the actual time needed is usually a vastly different number. The issue lies in two areas: techniques and expectations.

Most teams use traditional estimation and capacity-planning techniques. Traditional techniques are dependent on constants and repetitive work. A traditional planning process wants to know how much time it takes to build a widget, how many machines are available to build the widgets, and how many hours a day the machines can be used for building the widgets.

As you probably know, each piece of software is unique, and it's difficult to estimate something that is being built for the first time. We never build the same widget twice. It's also hard to treat a developer like a machine and predict their output on a daily basis. Communicating this to sponsors and stakeholders is also challenging; many experienced software professionals still believe incorrect estimates are more closely tied to incompetence than to the realities of software development.

Agile estimation techniques won't remove uncertainty from your early estimates, but they will improve your accuracy as the project proceeds. This is true because agile estimation methods take actual work into account as the project progresses. Your work mix may be diverse, but if you measure at an aggregate level you can still identify an average that you can use for estimating your capacity. We'll demonstrate this process as we follow the Auctionator through its development iterations.

The estimation process covered in this chapter is based on the teachings of Mike Cohn in *Agile Estimating and Planning*. Mike is a founding member of the Agile Alliance and one of the most knowledgeable estimation experts in the agile community. We highly recommend reading *Agile Estimating and Planning* to gain a deeper understanding of estimation techniques.

Let's start by seeing how a project team usually gathers the information needed to create estimates.

14.1 Contrasting traditional and agile estimation techniques

An average software project begins when a team or person outlines a project and receives approval to go forward. The project may be started by a product manager with an idea for an existing product, or by a customer request, or by the signing of a contract.

In the early stages of a project, someone guesses how long it will take to deliver. This person may be a salesperson, project manager, or development manager. They may make a guess based on their experience, or they may have some quick chats with seasoned employees and solicit their opinions.

When the timeline guess is in place, the project begins. If the project is related to a product, there may be marketing requirements to reference. If the project is for a customer, there may be a statement of work to reference. In either case, it's common for an analyst team to convert the information into functional specifications.

After the functional specifications are completed, a conversation begins with the development team, designs begin to evolve, and some teams may document a technical design and architectural plan. When this work is complete, the development team provides estimates based on the anticipated approach. The team also estimates their capacity by resource type. Then the estimates, capacity, and known dependencies are entered into a project plan. At this point, the team has a schedule that they feel confident in, and they share it with the stakeholders.

This exercise may take several weeks or months to complete. If a project is time-boxed, the team may find that there isn't enough time to deliver all the features for which they created functional specifications, designs, and estimates. The team then has to scope back the features for the project to meet the timeline, realizing they've wasted valuable time in estimating features that won't be pursued.

Agile estimation techniques address the shortcomings of this method. You don't design and estimate all your features until there has been a level of prioritization and you're sure the features are needed. You used a phased approach to estimation, recognizing that you can be more certain as the project progresses and you learn more about the features.

At a high level, the phased process looks like this:

1 Estimate the features in a short, time-boxed exercise during which you estimate feature size, not duration.

2 Use feature size to assign features to iterations and create a release plan.

3 Break down the features you assigned to the first iteration. *Breaking down* means identifying the specific tasks needed to build the features and estimating the hours required.

4 Re-estimate on a daily basis during an iteration, estimating the time remaining on open tasks.

Agile estimating is also different in that you involve the entire team in the estimation process. Let's take a moment to look at the value of whole-team estimation.

Are traditional estimation techniques really that bad?

For some software projects, requirements rarely change and timely delivery isn't critical. Other times, a project sponsor may be more interested in schedule accuracy than delivering while a need still exists. In still other cases, a long-term, fixed-bid contract must be supported, and you can't risk identifying additional expenses after the contract is signed. In these and many other instances, traditional techniques are worthy and valuable.

But if you're reading this book, there is a good chance you have volatile requirements, your customer needs to receive valuable software soon, and you must deliver your project in a lean method with limited waste. If this is true, you need an agile estimation process.

14.2 The importance of whole-team estimation

Every year, Best Buy Corporation tries to predict how many gift cards will be sold at Christmas. The typical process is to solicit the opinion of upper management and internal estimation experts to forecast a number.

In 2005, the CEO of Best Buy decided to try an experiment. The CEO followed the normal process for obtaining the estimates but also sent an email to approximately 100 random employees throughout the company, asking them how many gift cards they believed would be sold. The only information provided to both groups was the sales number for the previous year.

After the Christmas season was completed, the predictions of both groups were reviewed. The expert panel was accurate within 95 percent of the actual number of cards sold. The random group of employees was accurate within 99.9 percent of the number of cards sold (see figure 14.1). How did a random group beat the internal estimation experts?

In his book *The Wisdom of Crowds*, author James Surowiecki makes a case that a diverse set of independently thinking individuals can provide better predictions than a group of experts. Surowiecki qualifies this assertion by stating that the diversity needs to be in the way a group views problems and the heuristics each individual uses to analyze a problem or question. For example, a person's age can greatly influence their perspective on an issue.

Figure 14.1   Best Buy Corporation realized improved estimation accuracy by querying a large, diverse group of employees. The diverse set of employees consistently delivered better estimates than the in-house estimation experts.

Surowiecki's work draws many parallels to the issues with estimating software development. We often get together a group of specialists or experts to estimate the work that needs to be completed. These experts may be managers or leads who facilitate the work of their various teams. The fact that all the experts may be a part of management limits their diversity in opinion. And the fact that these experts may work together frequently may lead to standardized thinking, also known as *groupthink*.

In an agile environment, you increase the accuracy of your feature estimates by estimating the features together as a team. Estimates aren't limited to managers or leads but also include developers, testers, analysts, DBAs, and architects. The features are viewed from various perspectives, and you merge these perspectives to create a common, agreed-on estimate.

Entire-team estimation has additional benefits beyond diverse opinion. First, you get estimates from people who are closer to the work. Team members' opinions may be diverse, but they provide better estimates because they know your existing code, architecture, and domains and what it takes to deliver in your environment.

A second benefit is team ownership of the estimate. If a manager provides the estimate, they hope the team supports the estimate and buys into it. If the team provides the estimate, they're immediately closer to owning the estimate, and they feel more responsible for making the dates they provided.

Moving to team-based estimation isn't easy. Managers may not welcome additional input, and team members may be reluctant to challenge the experts and instead echo whatever the experts say.

It will take time to overcome these hurdles, but you can do one thing to expedite the change: when you perform team-based estimation, have the meeting facilitated by an indirect manager such as a project manager or ScrumMaster. This person can treat all people as equals regardless of title and proactively query team members who are reluctant to contribute. You can also use the planning poker process discussed in the next section to prevent one person's estimate from influencing another's.

My team is huge; how can I involve everyone?

We've worked with development teams that included 20 people or more. It's difficult to involve a group this size in one estimation session. The teams we've worked with have addressed this issue in three ways.

Some teams send a lead to the estimation meeting. Instead of providing estimates, the lead records the information about the features and then returns to their team to review the features. The lead may represent development, QA, business analysis, implementation, or other functional areas. The functional areas then do their own story-point estimation for the feature, and the lead takes that estimate back to the smaller leads-estimation meeting.

A second way we've seen this addressed is via conference phone. A small group of leads or other representatives discuss the features with the customer, and other team members listen in over the conference line and put in their perspective on how large the feature is.

Finally, some companies assign features to subteams within a team at large and allow the subteams to estimate the features they're assigned. A project manager or other resource then aggregates the information from several teams into one release plan.

14.3   A step toward agility: estimating size, not effort

As we mentioned in section 14.1, one of the main issues with traditional estimation techniques is the fact that team members really don't believe their project timeline until they've completed detailed analysis of the features. They don't feel comfortable until they've completed functional specifications and correlating technical designs. Then, when they complete this work, they're often surprised and have to notify stakeholders that they can't make the timeline without a decrease in scope or other project adjustment.

It's easy to see why stakeholders want you to estimate a delivery date immediately. The project may have a constraint or deadline that must be met, or the project may require funding that needs to be tied to a duration. You may also need to identify when shared employees are needed so you can reserve them. How can you improve the accuracy of your initial estimate without doing weeks or months of detailed feature analysis? The answer is *story points*.

14.3.1   Using story points for quick estimation

Story points are a different way to look at estimating features. They aren't a measure of the time needed to complete a feature but a measurement of a feature's *size* relative to other features. This approach is powerful because you may not have enough information to estimate the time to create a feature, but you can immediately begin to compare the sizes of features to each other to determine a relative size (see figure 14.2).

Figure 14.2   Similar to features in a project, the buildings in a city have various sizes and attributes. Can you look at the buildings and determine how long it took to build each one? Probably not. But you can compare the sizes of the buildings to each other. This is the main premise of story points.

To demonstrate, let's pretend you're making passenger cars instead of software. The cars are listed in table 14.1. Because you've never built cars, you don't know how long it takes to create one, but you can estimate how large a car is compared to other cars. For example, you know a Mini Cooper is probably the smallest car of all. You know that a Camry is a medium-size car, and you know that a Town Car is probably the largest of them all.

You can convert these size assumptions to numbers by using an estimation scale. A popular scale for estimating feature size is the Fibonacci scale, which sums the previous two numbers to derive the next number in the sequence. The sequence looks like this: 1, 2, 3, 5, 8, ... The main benefit of the Fibonacci scale is that enough separation exists between the numbers to prevent the team from squabbling over slight differences. For example, if the scale was 1, 2, 3, 4, 5, 6, 7, 8, 9, 10, team members might debate whether a feature was a 7 or an 8. It's easier for team members to reach agreement if the scale jumps from 5 to 8.

When you have a list of cars or software features to compare, Mike Cohn suggests that you first identify an item that is a 2 and then an item that is a 5. By selecting a 2, you still have room to list an item as smaller; if you identify a 5, you have room to estimate another feature as larger, and you also have the ability to compare a list item to two other list items (the 2 and the 5).

In the example in table 14.1, we quickly identified the Civic as a 2 and the Impala as a 5. You can use these two reference points to relatively compare the other cars and estimate their size.

Now that you have size estimates, you may wonder how you can convert them into work estimates. Initially, *you can't convert them*. In relation

Table 14.1   Comparing the relative size of various automobiles

Car	Story points
Mini Cooper	1
Camry	3
Town Car	8
Civic	2
Prius	2
Accord	3
Beetle	2
Impala	5
Crown Victoria	5

to the first iteration you perform, the story-point estimates won't help at all. But after you complete the first iteration, you'll know how many story points you completed, and you can use this number to estimate your story-point capacity for forthcoming iterations. You'll measure story-point throughput after every iteration going forward and use those historic numbers to determine the average story-point capacity for forthcoming iterations.

To follow through with our example, let's say you've identified 10 days as the standard iteration length. In those 10 days, you completed the Camry (3), the Prius (2), the Beetle (2), and the Impala (5). You were able to process 12 story points' worth of features in an iteration. For now, you'll assume that you can complete 12 story points in iteration 2, and you'll assign 12 story points' worth of cars to iteration 2. In effect, you're saying that your iteration capacity is 12 story points' worth of features.

When iteration 2 is complete, you'll see how many story points you put through that iteration. Average that number with 12 from iteration 1, and use the result as your new capacity estimate for iteration 3. You'll continue this process forever. Over time, your story-point capacity estimates will become more accurate because they're based on several real production iterations.

NOTE Your initial estimation using story points is to help you quickly provide an estimate to stakeholders and to let you lay out a high-level release plan. We'll cover release planning in chapter 15. You also plan in more detail right before an iteration begins. This detailed planning includes identifying tasks and estimating the time needed to complete the tasks. Iteration planning will be covered in chapter 16.

With classic estimation, you examine the major work tasks to derive an estimate. With story points, the team doesn't examine tasks, but they do compare the size and complexity of features. To improve the accuracy of your story-point estimates, the team uses *planning poker* to ensure individual opinions.

14.3.2 Planning poker

In planning poker, each team member has index cards with 1, 2, 3, 5, and 8 printed on them. One team member (preferably the customer or product owner) kicks off a discussion of a feature, and the whole team asks questions and normalizes on the scope and breadth of the feature. When the conversation is complete, a vote is taken: all team members hold up an index card with their estimate on it. It's important for everyone to do it at the same time so they aren't influenced by their peers. If everyone holds up cards with the same number, the estimate is official, and you record it. If you don't have consensus, you investigate why. Let's see this in action with an example from Acme Media.

14.4 Estimating story points at Acme Media

The first thing the Acme Media team needs to do is establish two reference points for all features. They do this by identifying a feature that is 2 story points in size and a feature that is 5 story points in size. After a review of the features, the Acme team concludes that *Search by category* is 2 story points and *Receive help online* is 5 story points; see table 14.2. Acme Media's team then reviews all the features against *Search by category* and *Receive help online* to determine if the other features are the same size, smaller, or larger. As additional features are estimated, they're also used as reference points to compare the nonestimated features.

More help with story points and estimating

As we mentioned at the start of this chapter, Mike Cohn is a superb authority on agile estimation and planning and has written a book with that same title. Mike also has a free website you can visit to learn more about planning poker: http://www.planning-poker.com/.

After the Acme Media team completes the planning-poker exercise, they have a prioritized, estimated product backlog. Now the question becomes, how many features can they complete within the project timeline? We'll rejoin Acme Media in chapter 15 to see how they answer this question.

ID	Feature name (ability to)	Story points
5	Register on the site	3
4	Place an item up for bid	3
10	Bid on an item	3
17	Auction engine	8
13	**Search by category**	**2**
16	Purchase an item immediately	2
1	Flag problem postings	2
6	Contact the seller	3
2	Create alerts for item type	3
9	**Receive help online**	**5**
11	Record seller feedback	5
12	View seller information	2
14	Perform advanced search	8
3	Email a friend	2
7	Customize my view	8
15	Retract a bid	2

Table 14.2 Story points let you evaluate capacity and throughput without performing detailed task analysis in advance.

14.5 Key points

Key points from this chapter are as follows:

- Software estimates are prone to high error rates when they're created early in a project. Based on this premise, you should time-box early estimation exercises, realizing that there are diminishing returns after a day or two of estimating.
- Software development is unique, but you can still identify trends that let you estimate your project timeline.
- Many teams limit software estimation to managers, leads, or other experts on the team. The accuracy of your estimates will improve if you involve the whole team in the process. In addition, you'll increase team buy-in and support of the estimates.
- You can reduce the time needed to obtain initial estimates by using the story-point estimation technique. You may obtain better estimates by spending weeks analyzing features, but story points allow you to quickly transition to a working iteration and pursue delivery of critical features immediately.
- The story-point technique lets you outline your overall release schedule sooner and update stakeholders on the ability to meet pre-established deadlines.
- Planning poker can add fun to your estimation process while ensuring independent estimating by team members.

14.6 Looking forward

In this chapter, we explained how you can estimate features in terms of relative size. The work performed here will let you lay out an overall release schedule in chapter 15. In chapter 16, we'll do more detailed estimation, identifying the specific tasks for the first iteration.

Part 5

Enough information for scheduling

When chapter 14 concluded, Acme Media had a prioritized and estimated product backlog. In this section we will take the backlog and assign the features to iterations, which will allow us to provide our first pass at a release schedule.

In the following two chapters we will discuss how to create an overall release plan and how that plan is enriched before each iteration begins. We will also discuss obtaining team commitment for the iteration by involving the members in the detailed iteration planning process.

You may recall one of the main agile principles, *responding to change over following a plan*. This is especially true when it comes to creating release and iteration plans. We do create plans, but we do not fall in love with them. We know they are temporary and will be adjusted. We are so confident of change that we will create windows of time for adapting between the iterations.

Release planning: envisioning the overall schedule

If you work with a smaller team doing smaller projects, it may be relatively easy to create a release plan: you define the iteration length and see how many iterations will fit into the window of time allotted for the project. But as projects grow in size, complexity increases, and so does the need for coordination. Our case study is emulating a medium-size project team working on a medium-size project. We'll stay within the medium-size context as we discuss the pieces of a release that most teams need to consider when creating their release plan.

If we reflect for a moment, Acme Media has spent one week taking its medium-size project through feasibility, chartering, and creation of feature cards. In this chapter, you'll watch as Acme Media gathers additional information and outlines its release schedule.

Sometimes, confusion exists about the terms *release* and *project*. In the instance of your pilot project, *release* and *project* are synonymous. Although every iteration of the Auctionator will deliver releasable software, the initial goal of the project is to wait until all iterations are complete before releasing.

Acme Media still needs to gather some additional information before outlining a release plan. Let's start the chapter by finding this information.

15.1 Defining the pieces of a release plan

Once you have a prioritized, estimated backlog, you still need a few more pieces of information to create your release plan. You need to determine the length of iteration 0 (zero), the length of your development iterations, how much time will be needed between iterations, and the project deadline. Let's look at how you obtain each item.

15.1.1 Iteration 0 length

Iteration 0 represents the time needed to prepare the project for development iterations. This work can include completing contracts with third parties, preparing development environments, preparing development machines, setting up a project wiki, obtaining funding, and organizing support tools such as bug trackers. Iteration 0 is discussed in detail in chapter 17.

You determine the time needed for iteration 0 based on how long it takes to get these items completed for your project. In Acme Media's case, the Auctionator doesn't require extensive time for preliminary setup work. The development environments are already in the correct state for development, and incremental funding isn't needed for the project. Acme Media decides to complete four items before the development iterations:

- Create a new project within Acme's bug-tracking tool
- Begin testing the API provided by the messaging vendor to make sure connections and firewalls work correctly
- Continue to envision and model the architecture
- Hold a project kickoff meeting

The project manager, Wendy Johnson, discusses the items with the team, and together they estimate that the preliminary work can be completed in one week. Acme records one week for iteration 0 in its release plan.

15.1.2 Development iteration length

If you're working on your first agile project, like Acme Media, you don't know what a *good* iteration duration is for your project. You know that you want to build the critical pieces of the system as soon as you can, but how long will it take?

Fortunately, thousands of agile projects have been completed across many industries, and you can learn from them. Extreme Programming (XP) environments frequently have iterations of 1 to 2 weeks in length. Scrum teams like to do a sprint/iteration every 30 days. More than likely, a number between 1 and 4 weeks will work for your environment.

We suggest that you start with 2-week iterations and see how that timeframe works for you. It may be good to use this 2-week iteration length for several projects before making the call on whether it's successful. If you find that your features are too large to complete in 2 weeks, you can examine your features to see if you've broken them down to their true, essential requirements; alternatively, you can try a longer iteration length. Acme Media has followed this advice and created its release plan assuming 2-week iterations.

15.1.3 *How long do you need between iterations?*

Scrum has a structured process for completing a sprint/iteration and getting back to work quickly. When an iteration is completed, the product is demonstrated and (you hope) accepted. The team then goes through the following steps to initialize the next iteration:

1 Perform a sprint retrospective.
2 Return to the backlog, which may have changed while the team was in the sprint. If it has changed, the product owner is asked to prioritize the work.
3 Plan the next iteration based on estimates and the estimated iteration capacity.
4 Begin working on the next iteration.

Many Scrum teams complete this work in 1 or 2 days, which is somewhat amazing. If you're just becoming agile, it will be difficult to wrap up a sprint and start a new one in 2 days. A 1- to 2-day turnaround demonstrates a mature team with a well-oiled process. It will take time for your team to develop this rhythm.

As a starting point, we suggest that you space iterations approximately 1 week apart until your team matures around your agile process. You won't be well oiled right out of the gate, and a week between iterations will let you breathe a little as you're adapting to your new methodology.

We also find that many projects need the additional time to wrap up an iteration. Here are the tasks we frequently see between iterations:

- Completion of acceptance testing
- Load testing of a completed iteration
- Demonstrations to the customer and stakeholders
- Usability testing
- Iteration retrospective
- Review of the backlog, and planning for the next iteration

As you can see, a lot of work may take place between iterations, and completing it in 2 days can be difficult.

Some agile coaches would say that the work you list as "between iteration" work is part of the iteration. The argument is that acceptance testing, performance testing, and re-planning are iteration activities. We don't have an issue with this perspective, but we've chosen to model our case-study iterations without these tasks. If you wanted to, you could include these tasks and say that Acme Media has 3-week iteration windows. Now that Acme Media has determined its iteration length, the company can proceed to outline an overall timeline for the project.

Who is watching the store while you're in the iteration?

In our early experience, most discussions of agile suggested that the project team was dedicated to the project, and some other group took care of any issues encountered in the production environment. In recent years, we've seen a shift in that mentality; many people now factor in production support when determining team capacity for an iteration. Many companies have only one team for projects and production work.

In 2004, Greg worked with the internet team at the Seattle Times Company. The Seattle Times team factored production support into their capacity estimates, but they also decided to add a support buffer to their break between iterations. Although the team needed only 2 to 3 days to review one iteration and continue to the next, they added an additional 2 days to address production issues that could wait. The 5-day window allowed the team to plan for the next iteration while cleaning up any noncritical issues.

15.1.4 *Determining the overall timeline*

Most projects are constrained by time, and the overall schedule is built to support this constraint. Here are some typical causes for a time constraint:

- Your sales team sells a project to a customer.
- You need to put something in place to meet a regulatory timeline.
- You have an ongoing release schedule, and you must complete the work within the predefined window.
- You have only a limited amount of time to use employees on a project (employees may come from a shared pool).
- You have a fixed budget, and once that money is spent, so is your time.
- You need to beat your competitor to market.

To determine your timeline, you must review the total time available for your project. In most instances, your timeline starts with today and ends on the date requested by the customer or stakeholder. For our purposes, *today* is equal to the day you complete the story-point estimates for your features.

You can see the constraint model applied if we return to the Auctionator project. For the Auctionator, *today* is equal to April 20. Acme Media's stakeholders have asked that the project be completed in 8 weeks, which means the Acme Media team has from April 20 to June 15 to deliver the project.

Once Wendy has the overall timeline, she takes the other information she's collected (time for iteration 0, iteration length, and time needed between iterations) and begins outlining an iteration-by-iteration schedule in Microsoft Excel (see figure 15.1).

Wendy uses Microsoft Excel because she's comfortable with the tool and can post the schedule on the project wiki. But Wendy understands the importance of keeping

Iteration 0	Iteration 1	Adapt week	Iteration 2	Adapt week and deployment preparation	Go live
4/23 - 4/27	4/30 - 5/11	5/14 - 5/18	5/21 - 6/1	6/4 - 6/14	6/15
Architecture planning	Design	Iteration retrospective	Design	Iteration retrospective	
Testing with vendor	Technical investigation	Technical reviews	Technical investigation	Technical reviews	
Project kickoff	Coding	Usability testing	Coding	Final testing	
	Feature refinement	Acceptance testing	Feature refinement	Prepare for deployment	

Figure 15.1 A release plan will begin to take shape after you've determined your overall project window, iteration length, and time spent to prepare between iterations. Most teams need extra time at the end of a project to prepare for deployment.

the schedule in front of the team, and she uses an office plotter to print the schedule and post it prominently in the team area.

Now that Acme Media has an outline for the project timeline, the team can complete their project plan by plugging the features into the schedule.

Just two iterations?

Acme Media has only two iterations in its pilot project, which is a minor change from the company's previous development process. In theory, you want more iterations so you can demonstrate and react to new information sooner. But in the case of a pilot project, two iterations are fine. The team is just learning agile techniques, and they can increase the number of iterations on subsequent projects.

15.2 Completing the release plan by assigning features to iterations

After you've identified your release schedule, you can assign features to the iterations. This process isn't difficult because you've already prioritized and estimated your features (see chapters 13 and 14).

You assign features to iterations based on the velocity you've demonstrated in the past. For example, if you've historically averaged delivering 25 story points per iteration, you'll use 25 story points for your capacity when scheduling new releases.

If you're doing a pilot or first-time agile project, you don't have any history on which to base your capacity. In this instance, you proceed to detailed planning of your first iteration. In detailed planning, you'll have the team break down each feature into tasks and perform estimates at the task/hours-needed level. You'll see this in practice in chapter 16. After you complete detailed planning of the first iteration, you can see how many story points are assigned to the first iteration and use that number as your capacity for subsequent iterations.

Completing a release plan is a little more complex than assigning features based on capacity. You also want to consider the following guidelines during the assignment process:

- *Deliver usefulness to the customer in every iteration.*   In a perfect world, each iteration would be released and provide some level of value to the customer. Acme Media will do this for iteration 1 of the Auctionator. The company will deliver the minimal set of features needed for a working system.

- *Consider dependencies between features.*   Features may be dependent on each other to provide value, so you shouldn't split them across iterations. For example, *the ability to record seller feedback* is of no value unless *the ability to view seller information* is also completed.

- *Put high-priority, high-risk features in early iterations.*   You want high-priority, high-risk features to go into early iterations so you have more time to work out the issues that correlate to the risk. Acme Media understands that features dependent on third parties are always high risk, and the team begins testing their vendor's interface during iteration 0 to get a jump on potential risks.

Let's rejoin Acme Media to see the guidelines in action.

15.2.1 Assigning features to iterations at Acme Media

When Acme Media completes detailed planning for iteration 1, the team finds that they've assigned 19 story points into the iteration. For now, 20 points will be used as the capacity number, so they plan iteration 2 to hold 20 story points.

Acme Media's features were prioritized, grouped, and estimated in chapters 13 and 14; the main work remaining is to load up each iteration with 20 story points.

> **Projects without time constraints**
>
> The Auctionator is time-constrained to represent the most common projects we encounter when working with agile teams. But on occasion, we see a project that is driven by feature richness, meaning the project goes on for as long as it takes to deliver all the features requested. In such an instance, you lay out a project plan with as many iterations as needed to complete the work.

Wendy, the project manager, loads up the iterations based on the work the team provided (see figure 15.2).

Now that Acme Media has a release plan, the team is ready to hold a kickoff meeting and share the information with stakeholders, executives, and support groups they will depend on.

Auctionator Release Plan

Iteration number:	Iteration 0	Iteration 1	Adapt week	Iteration 2	Adapt week and deployment preparation	Go live
Iteration dates:	4/23–4/27	4/30–5/11	5/14–5/18	5/21–6/1	6/4–6/14	6/15
Iteration theme:	Initial architecture modeling Prepare development environment Test with vendors	Core, critical functionality coded	Iteration retrospective Technical reviews Usability testing Acceptance testing	Create and integrate secondary features	Iteration retrospective Technical reviews Usability testing Acceptance testing	Go live; deploy to production

Features

API setup with eLertz	X					
Register on the site		X(3)				
Place an item up for bid		X(3)				
Bid on an item		X(3)				
Auction engine		X(8)				
Search by category		X(2)				
Purchase an item immediately				X(2)		
Flag problem postings				X(2)		
Contact the seller				X(3)		
Create alerts for item type				X(3)		
Receive help online				X(5)		
Record seller feedback				X(3)		
View seller information				X(2)		

Sideline (features that can come in if others go out, currently at the top of the backlog)

Perform Advanced search						
Email a friend						
Customize my view						

Figure 15.2   The completed release plan for the Auctionator project. The numbers in parentheses represent story-point estimates. Acme Media has estimated its story-point capacity at 20 points per iteration. After loading, iteration 1 holds 19 points, and iteration 2 contains 20 points.

15.3 *Communicating the release plan with a kickoff meeting*

Acme Media has involved the entire project team in creation of the release plan, so the team is up to speed on why the project is being pursued, the overall timeline, and the features assigned to each iteration. Acme still needs to bring other groups on board to make sure the project is supported and to create awareness about support that may be needed.

The first objective of the kickoff meeting is to bring stakeholders and sponsors up to speed. The project team shares the information gathered during the feasibility and chartering exercises, including scope, benefits, key dependencies, constraints, risks, and the release schedule.

In a traditional environment, the presentation may be performed by a project manager or development manager. In an agile environment, you should try to get as many team members to present as feel comfortable doing so. At Acme Media's kickoff, four team members present: Wendy, the project manager, Jay, the customer, Gina, the tester, and Roy, the developer.

A second objective of the kickoff meeting, and perhaps the most important, is to bring support groups up to speed so they can see when their help may be needed. Some of the support areas typically discussed during a kickoff meeting are as follows:

- *Operations*—These teams will support your application once it's deployed, and they need to know what type of maintenance will be required to keep the application working correctly.
- *Security*—In larger companies, your application may need to be reviewed to make sure it complies with corporate standards.
- *Load testing*—In larger companies, you may need to reserve load-testing equipment.
- *Load balancing*—You may have specialized groups that manage load-balancing environments, and you'll need their support for your project.
- *Hardware and storage*—If you're doing a project that requires new equipment, you may need help from hardware teams.
- *Documentation*—If your project will require supporting documentation, you may want to invite documentation teams to your kickoff.
- *Marketing*—If you need to do public announcements or advertising, you must bring this team up to speed with your release plan.
- *Training*—If your project will require training for employees or customers, you should invite this team to the kickoff.

NOTE   If you work with a small team, all of this work may be covered by the same team that does development. But if you work for a larger company, you probably already have experience dealing with support groups and can relate to the support categories we've outlined.

You can expect questions during the kickoff meeting, and there may even be discoveries that force you to adjust your release plan. Many teams create their release plan and rarely modify it during the project; but you should plan to modify your release plan frequently. Discoveries and adaptation will occur throughout your project. This is part of the value of having your release plan physically represented on a status wall. You can move pieces around quickly when things change, without needing to go into a tool such as Microsoft Project.

You know that dates will change as you make discoveries during your project. Use the project kickoff meeting to stress this point with stakeholders. Acme Media reminds stakeholders that June 15 is the current estimate, *not* a guaranteed hard date.

> **Tools for creating a release plan**
>
> You can document your release plan in a multitude of ways. You can sketch it on a whiteboard, use butcher paper and index cards and create it on a wall, or go electronic and use tools such as Microsoft Excel and Microsoft Project. You can also pursue tools that were made just for agile development, such as those available from VersionOne and Rally Development.
>
> In our experience, you should choose the tool that is easiest for you to maintain while still making it possible to keep your team and stakeholders up to speed on timing and status. This may include using additional tools such as burn down charts.
>
> A good rule of thumb is the larger the project, the more need there is to create the plan electronically so that it can be distributed and viewed throughout the enterprise. If the project or your company is relatively small, you can have stakeholders visit the team room to review the release plan.

Mike Cohn makes a good suggestion, that you should not even propose a delivery date, but instead provide a delivery range so that expectations aren't set for a specific date. For example, the Acme Media team will go into the kickoff meeting and say that they expect to deliver the project sometime between June 8 and June 22.

15.4   Key points

The key points for this chapter are as follows:

- The main driver for your release schedule is the length of your development iterations. You must experiment to see what length works best for your work mix and team. A good length is usually somewhere between 2 and 4 weeks.
- You need time between iterations to demonstrate, adapt, and re-plan. Some teams can do this work within 2 days. Teams new to agile should allow more time, taking as much as 5 days between iterations.
- Most projects are constrained by a target-completion date. You can create your release plan by working backward from this target date.
- Features are assigned to iterations based on priorities and estimated size. One person can do the assignments and review them with the team, or the team can assign the features together.
- In larger organizations, you need to communicate the release plan to stakeholders and support groups.

15.5   Looking forward

In this chapter, we laid out the overall release schedule and kicked off the project. In chapter 16, we'll examine the features assigned to iteration 1 in more detail and identify the tasks needed to complete the work.

Iteration planning: the nitty-gritty details

When you plan for a release, you estimate features at a high level using story points and measuring relative size. This lets you envision the entire release and communicate the timeline to parties who have an investment in the project.

When an iteration begins, you should understand the work being pursued in detail so the team can understand the tasks and feel confident that they can deliver the features assigned to the iteration. The team will increase their confidence by estimating the identified tasks in hours needed to complete the work, and they will compare the estimates to how much capacity they have in hours available for the iteration.

A key part of iteration planning is a clear definition of what complete or done means. Let's start our discussion of iteration planning by defining *done*.

16.1 Clearly defining the goals: what is "feature complete"?

When you create your feature cards, you record acceptance tests. These acceptance tests help you focus on delivering to the minimum requirement and also verifying that a feature is complete.

We suggest reviewing the acceptance tests at the start of iteration planning. The team needs to have a good understanding of what success means before breaking down the work and identifying the tasks needed to complete it.

A good way to kick off iteration planning is to have the customer explain the acceptance tests that have been recorded on the feature card. The team can ask more questions about the tests, and a tester can document the tests in more detail during the discussion. This may mean creating the tests in a testing tool such as TestDirector.

NOTE The tests you create should be in boolean terms, meaning that the test results can be viewed from a true or false perspective.

For many teams, the customer can't be available for every build and can't test every feature as it's delivered, so a tester performs the daily tests. If a feature passes, it's queued for eventual approval by the customer. In the case of Acme Media, the customer performs user acceptance testing at the end of each iteration.

16.2 *Using feature modeling to identify and estimate tasks*

To this point, Acme Media's team has struggled to not jump into a detailed design session for each feature. Even though they've been performing just enough planning to create a release plan, it's natural for a team to begin envisioning technical solutions as soon as they see a feature description. When your release plan is complete and you need to start working on the first iteration, you turn the team loose and let them break down the features into detailed tasks and estimates.

We cannot prescribe one perfect method for breaking down your features. You may be able to understand the required tasks through team discussion, or you may find that you need to create wireframes or mockups to understand the work that will be required. Some teams can effectively identify tasks by creating use cases for the feature cards and envisioning the system needed to support the use cases.

One process that we've found effective is *feature-card modeling*. This technique is focused around user interaction and screen design, and many teams find that the exercise lets them learn enough about a feature to identify the required tasks. Here are the steps you follow to perform a modeling session with your project team:

1 Select a feature card.
2 Outline a workflow for the feature.
3 Create new feature cards for features that are discovered in the workflow.
4 Outline the screens needed to support the feature.
5 Add detail to the screens, considering user and system interaction.
6 Identify the major tasks needed to build the feature.
7 Estimate the identified tasks.

If modeling is new to your team, you should involve the entire team the first time you use it. After this training, they can break into subgroups in future sessions and model several features concurrently.

The customer should be highly involved in the modeling sessions. The project team will have many questions for the customer as they probe for deeper understanding of the requirements.

Let's watch Acme Media as it models one of the features for the Auctionator.

16.2.1 *Outlining the workflow for a feature*

Acme Media will model feature 10, *the ability to bid on an item.* The first thing the team does is outline how a buyer arrives at the bid screen.

The team envisions that the buyer will perform a search from the auction home page. The search will bring back a list of results the buyer can choose from. The buyer will then choose a listing and view the details of a specific auction. The team outlines this workflow on the whiteboard (figure 16.1).

Figure 16.1   A first pass at a workflow to support a feature

The team then discusses what the buyer can do once they arrive at an auction detail page. They note the following:

- The buyer must be logged in to place a bid from the auction detail page.
- After the buyer places a bid, they will want to watch the auction and monitor the status of their bid.
- The team thinks about the ability to retract a bid. Is that functionality required? Jay, the customer, listens in and determines there is a need to support bid retraction.
- The team also discusses the ability to "buy now." In essence, that's what Acme's classifieds site does. With input from the customer, the team determines that they will have "buy now" functionality.
- The team notes that several processes must be triggered when an auction closes.

You can see their whiteboard notes in figure 16.2.

One of the common occurrences during this exercise is the identification of previously hidden features.

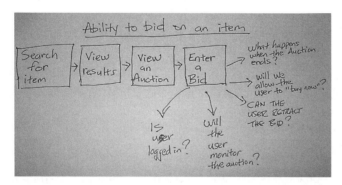

Figure 16.2   The workflow surrounding the ability to bid. As the team discusses the feature, additional questions surface about system interaction.

16.2.2 *Discovering new features*

The team now lists the additional feature cards that have been discovered during their workflow exercise (figure 16.3). These features aren't on the current list provided by the customer; they need to be encompassed in existing cards, or new cards must be created for them.

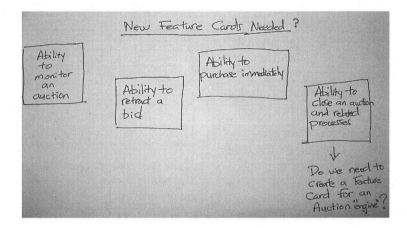

Figure 16.3
Identifying new feature cards after reviewing the workflow

The team decides that *the ability to monitor an auction* is an intrinsic part of the bidding process. Monitoring and viewing auction details will be included in the scope of *the ability to bid* feature. The team creates new feature cards for the other discoveries:

- *Feature 15*—The ability to retract a bid.
- *Feature 16*—The ability to purchase an item immediately.
- *Feature 17*—An auction engine. The team has identified several processes that the system needs to manage, such as tracking the highest bidder, emailing the winning bidder and seller, notifying the seller if no one bids, and tracking the time left in the auction.

The team now has a clear understanding of the scope of *the ability to bid* feature. They will take ownership for viewing auction details, entering a bid, and monitoring an auction/bid (see figure 16.4).

With the additional features defined, the team is ready to examine the user screens in detail.

Figure 16.4   Outlining the scope of a feature

16.2.3 *Outlining the screens for a feature*

With the scope defined, the team outlines the screens that will be needed to support bidding. They envision four screens to support the process:

- *A screen to view auction details*—The buyer will arrive here after selecting an auction from the listings provided by the search feature.
- *A screen to enter a bid*—The screen will tell the buyer the amount needed to be the high bidder. The bids will be in graduated amounts.
- *A screen to review and confirm a bid.*
- *A bid confirmation from the system to the buyer.* The team isn't sure whether to provide a confirmation via the screen or to append it to the auction-detail screen to confirm the bid.

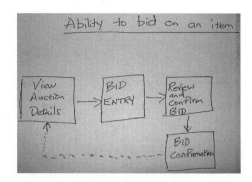

The screens are shown in figure 16.5.

After you define your screens at a high level, you can begin to define detailed system interactions.

Figure 16.5   Identifying the screens needed to support a feature

16.2.4 *Adding details to a screen by considering user interaction*

Now that you know the scope of your feature and the probable screens, you're closer to your goal of identifying the tasks that will be required to build the feature. The final step is breaking down each screen to understand user and system interaction in more detail. Let's start with the View Auction Details screen shown in figure 16.6.

The team outlines the fields for the auction detail screen. The picture (photo), text description, and location will come from another feature, *the ability to place an item up for bid*. The seller provides this information when they put their item up for bid.

The team envisions receiving the current bid and time remaining from the auction engine.

The other items on the screen are links to functionality that will be delivered from other features, such as the *ability to send an auction to a friend*, the *ability to contact the seller*, and the *ability to view seller feedback*. The team also envisions a search box to let the buyer search for other auctions.

The only remaining item is the link to *place bid*. This will take the buyer to the screen for placing a bid.

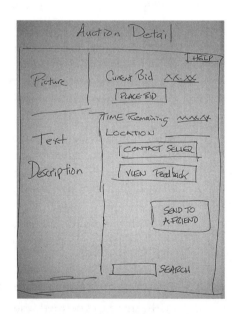

Figure 16.6   Adding details and fields to a potential screen. A detailed screen increases the understanding of a feature, which leads to more accurate work estimates.

The team goes through this exercise for each screen related to *the ability to bid on an item*. Then they go through the exercise for each feature. At that point, the team can identify all the tasks needed to complete the feature.

It is important to reiterate that the modeling work is happening just before an iteration begins, and the work is performed for only the current iteration. We do not want to waste time modeling features that may never be pursued because of the customer changing their mind or the scope of the project changing.

16.2.5 Is modeling worth it?

Some people will review the modeling exercise we've just outlined and question the effort. You tie up the entire project team for one day to model all the features. At the end of their work, the team has created no code, written no HTML, and performed no database work. The team spends the whole day *talking* about features. What is the value?

Here it is:

- The team has a deep, common understanding of the customer's needs.
- The team has a feel for the scope of each feature and what they need to do to support the feature.
- The team has contributed to the discussion and identified issues before development starts.
- The team has a feel for how the features tie together.

The improvement in team performance due to the modeling exercise easily outweighs the time lost doing "actual work." This exercise *is* necessary work—it's every bit as important as coding, and maybe even more so. Code is worthless if it does not support the customer's needs.

We've noticed a funny thing: we see teams skip modeling and then get confused about features mid-iteration. The team calls a quick, impromptu meeting and begins modeling a feature without realizing it. We suggest that you accept feature modeling as a reality of software development and do the work up front. It will reduce your overall cycle time for delivering features.

16.3 Identifying and estimating tasks

In the modeling exercise, you identify the screens needed to support the features. We also discussed how those screens interact with the application at large. You use this information to create your estimates. Your team reviews the workflow and screen layouts to identify the tasks they need to complete to build the feature. After they identify the tasks, they estimate them. To see this in action, let's review the feature card that Acme modeled: *the ability to bid on an item*.

Acme has identified four screens for this feature:

- View auction details
- Bid entry
- Bid review
- Bid confirmation

The team has also laid out the fields for each one of these screens and discussed system interaction related to the screens. Based on this information, the team enters their tasks and estimates for each feature. You can record the information on the back of the feature card or in a project tool; Acme Media's team recorded the estimates for *the ability to bid on an item*, as shown in table 16.1.

Table 16.1   Recording tasks and estimates for a feature during modeling

Tasks	Group	Assigned	Estimate
HTML for four screens	UI	Ryan	16 hrs
Design data model	Dev	Roy	16 hrs
Code to handle insert, update, delete	Dev	Roy	8 hrs
Create tests	QA	Rich	2 hrs
Interface with user registration	Dev	Roy	4 hrs
Error handling	Dev	Matt	8 hrs

The team does this task-identification exercise for each feature, starting with the features ranked as the highest priority by the customer. The team repeats this exercise, estimating and adding features to the iteration, until they believe the iteration is full and they can't take on any more work. The team is *committing* to doing the work versus having a schedule forced upon them.

The team still uses a process to help them determine how much work they can take on, but they make the ultimate decision about what to take on regardless of what the estimate and capacity tools imply.

Task assignments aren't permanent

Some people suggest not making any task assignments before an iteration begins. They prefer to have team members pull tasks as they're available, working their way through the backlog of tasks without formal assignments.

In our experience, we've seen this approach work; but two items affect the value of ad hoc assignments. First, you'll probably have team members with specialties when you begin using an agile process. You won't have the capability for *anyone* to take on *any* task—you'll have to assign certain tasks to certain team members. Related to this issue, if you work in an enterprise environment, it may take several years to develop the knowledge needed to be effective in delivering software in your environment.

Second, when teams model features, they may break up into groups and model several features in parallel. When this occurs, the team members participating have a more detailed understanding of the features, and they're better candidates to work on those features.

We suggest developing your team to a point that anyone can do any task, but this will take time and is rarely possible when you're first moving to agile.

Let's look at how you determine iteration capacity.

16.4 Determining the hours available in an iteration

The first step in determining iteration capacity is looking at how many hours are available in an iteration. Advanced teams will measure hours available for the whole team. Teams new to agile will measure hours available by specialization. When you first move to agile, you probably won't have interchangeable team members; instead, you'll have people with development skills, analyst skills, HTML skills, database skills, and other specializations. Over time, the team should cross-train and lose dependency on specific people for specific tasks; but on day one, specialization will probably be a reality, and you must plan capacity around that reality.

Acme Media knows that the team has 10 working days within their iteration. They use this information to determine how much capacity each team member has available (see figure 16.7).

Iteration 1 - Team Capacity	People	Days	Unfactored manhours	Factored manhours	New dev manhours	Maint manhours	Notes
Development							
Dev - Roy	1	10	80	72	68.4	3.6	
Dev - Matt	1	10	80	72	68.4	3.6	
Dev - TOTAL	2	20	160	144	136.8	7.2	
Implementation							
Implementation - Robert	1	5	40	32	16	16	Robert at TechEd 3 days
Implementation - Jim	1	5	40	20	10	10	
Requirements							
Reqs - Rich	1	13	104	83.2	74.88	8.32	
Reqs - TOTAL	1	13	104	83.2	74.88	8.32	
Ux							
Ux Design							
Ux Design - Ryan	1	9	72	57.6	46.08	11.52	Ryan will be at TechEd -1 day
Ux Design - offshore	0	0	0	0	0	0	
QA							
QA - Functional							
QA Functional - Gina	1	10	80	64	38.4	25.6	
QA Functional - offshore	0	0	0	0	0	0	
TOTALS							
Implementation Total	2		80	52	26	26	
Dev Total	3		240	216	205.2	10.8	
QA Functional Total	1		80	64	38.4	25.6	
Requirements Total	1		104	83.2	74.88	8.32	
Ux Design Total	1		72	57.6	46.08	11.52	
Total	8		576	472.8	390.56	82.24	

Figure 16.7 Acme Media determines its capacity for iteration 1. The spreadsheet takes implementation support into account and includes notes about other events that may affect the capacity of specific individuals.

Once the team understands their capacity, they begin loading up the iteration with features and tasks (see table 16.2).

Table 16.2 As features are added to an iteration, the team can see the impact by functional area.

	Est. Req.	Est. Ux	Est. Dev.	Est. Impl.	Est. QA	Est. Arch.	Sum
Ability to bid on an item	24	40	40	16	24	4	**148**
Ability to place an item up for bid	16	24	40	8	24	4	**116**
Ability to search by category	40	24	16	8	32	16	**136**

As Acme Media adds features, Wendy, the project manager, use a spreadsheet that calculates the difference between iteration assignments and team capacity. The team can see the workload by area and adjust the iteration features to keep everyone at approximately 100 percent usage (see figure 16.8).

	Estimate of Effort by Team ▾	Total	New Dev Capacity	Utilization Delta	Utilization %
3					
4	Estimate of Effort by Team ▾	Total	New Dev Capacity	Utilization Delta	Utilization %
5	Architecture	100	0	(100)	0%
6	Development	438	448	10	98%
7	Engineering	0	0	0	0%
8	Front-End Development	308	115	(193)	267%
9	Implementation	296	444	148	67%
10	Quality Assurance	500	646	146	77%
11	Requirements Analysis	330	484	154	68%
12	Search Analytics	112	72	(40)	156%
13	User Experience	328	158	(170)	207%
14	Sum of Est. Total	2412	2209	1881	15%
15					
16					
17	**Engineering Total**		0	16	
18	**Implementation Total**		297.6	580	
19	**IPG Dev Total**		266.76	86	
20	**QA Functional Total**		754.78		
21	**QA Load Total**		41.6		
22	**Requirements Total**		209.088	344	
23	**Ux Total**		231.84	248	

Figure 16.8 The team can compare capacity to estimates as they add features into the iteration. In this example, the features assigned to the iteration are almost perfect for the developers, pushing them to 98% of their capacity. But the user experience group is booked way beyond their capacity at 207%. The team can back out features to get everyone closer to 100%, or they can disregard the calculation and choose to go forward if they feel comfortable doing so.

After the team reaches agreement on the features, they can commit to the iteration plan. Let's look at some of the ways the iteration plan can be recorded.

16.5 Bringing estimates and capacity together to complete the plan

When your team reaches agreement on the features for the iteration, you can use a multitude of tools to share the iteration information. In the simplest form, you can place all the tasks on a wall with index cards and let the team move cards over from the task backlog to the completed backlog.

Some teams use a combination of cards and online tools. The Acme Media team loads the iteration plan into a tool called a *burn down chart* that lets them view the iteration plan and present it to stakeholders and other parties who may not be on-site or have easy access to the team work area (see figure 16.9).

You may also find that your iteration becomes complex due to dependencies and that it's hard to keep track of all the work using an iteration wall or a burn down chart alone. In those instances, you can use tools such as Microsoft Project.

Some people believe that if you're using a tool like Microsoft Project, you aren't agile. Many people believe that tools like Project imply formality and overhead, and they're good only for traditional projects. We can tell you that this definitely isn't true. It isn't the tool that takes away agility but the way the tool is used. Let's look at an example.

As we've mentioned, Greg is a project manager, and his team releases new software every 8 weeks. Greg typically uses tools such as an iteration wall and burn down charts. But his team noted that on some iterations, it was hard to keep track of

	B	C	G	H	I	J	K
1			▼ 10 Days Remaining	9 Days Remaining	8 Days Remaining	7 Days Remaining	6 Days Rem
2	Description	Area	Stand Up #1	Stand Up #2	Stand Up #3	Stand Up #4	Stand Up
3	**Feature - Ability to bid on an item**						
4	HTML for screens	UI	16				
5	Design data model	Dev	16				
6	Code insert, update, delete	Dev	8				
7	Interface with user registration	Dev	4				
8	Create tests	QA	2				
9	Error Handling	Dev	8				
10	**Feature - Ability to place an item up for bid**						
11	HTML for screens	UI	8				
12	Auction engine interface	Dev	8				
13	Bid refresh function	Dev	4				
14	Validate registration	Dev	4				
15	Confirm auction via email	Dev	6				
16	Create tests	QA	4				
17	**Feature - Ability to search by category**						
18	Define search scopes	Dev	4				
19	Develop crawl logic	Dev	8				
20	Faceted search filters	Dev	4				
21	Category edit tool	Dev	8				
22	2 search screens	UI	4				
23	Create tests	QA	8				
24	**Feature - Auction Engine**						
25	Expire auction logic	Dev	16				
26	Alert winner	Dev	4				

Features / Burn Down Chart \ **Iteration Tasks** / Iteration Days /

Ready

Figure 16.9   Acme Media enters its iteration plan into a burndown chart that lets them track the work remaining as the iteration progresses. An electronic tool makes it easier to share status with the rest of the company or the customer.

dependencies. Greg's team asked if he could record the dependencies into a plan so the team could track them during the iteration. Greg moved the iteration plan into Microsoft Project, and the team found the tool valuable, especially because they still had a level of specialization. Microsoft Project not only helped the team deal with complexity but also showed the team estimated hours needed by each member during the iteration.

Returning to Acme Media, project manager Wendy debates whether to enter the iteration information into a tool such as Project. Wendy decides that little labor is required to enter the information into the tool; plus, her team is familiar with it. You can see Acme Media's iteration plan in Project in figure 16.10.

Now that the Acme team has their iteration plan, they're ready to get started with their feature work.

16.6   *Making status visible*

Historically, there are two issues with measuring status on software projects:

- How do you make sure the code is complete?
- How do you make it easy for the team to see and understand project status?

Project teams have struggled with these issues for years. They frequently prepare to deploy code and at the last second realize something is missing.

Let's delve into these two issues and see how Acme Media simplifies status measurement and makes status transparent to the team.

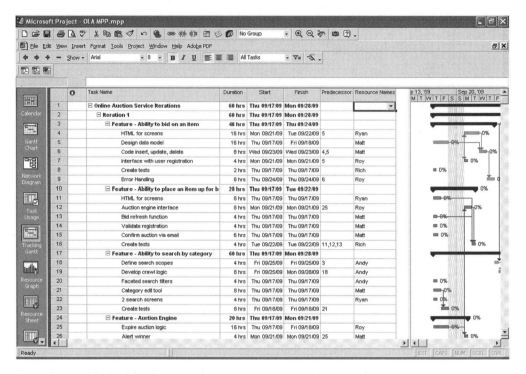

Figure 16.10   Microsoft Project isn't usually viewed as a tool used by agile teams, but it can help with agility when an iteration becomes complex or team members need to anticipate how much work they must deliver. The key to using a tool is to make sure everyone knows that assignments are tentative and to ensure that the plan is highly visible and updated daily.

16.6.1 Visibility within an iteration

As we mentioned, Acme Media has entered its iteration tasks into a burn down chart, which projects how much work should be completed as the iteration progresses. On a day-by-day basis, the team can see if they're on track, running behind, or running ahead of schedule (see figure 16.11).

Acme Media estimates 152 hours of tasks to complete for the iteration. The burn down chart shows that this number needs to be down to 138 hours of work after day 1, 120 hours of work after day 2, and so on. On the last day, the team should have no hours of work remaining.

Software development doesn't care if it's being tracked in a nice linear chart. In reality, the work comes in surges, with the team sometimes stuck on an issue or problem and not making any progress. Figure 16.12 shows Acme Media's burn down chart after 7 days of work.

Many teams collect the estimates for remaining hours of work at their daily stand-up meetings. This is where the *days remaining* line comes from in the chart. Day 1 represents the task estimates before work has begun, and day 2 represents the estimates after the first stand-up meeting. The Acme Media team has started work, and now they believe the

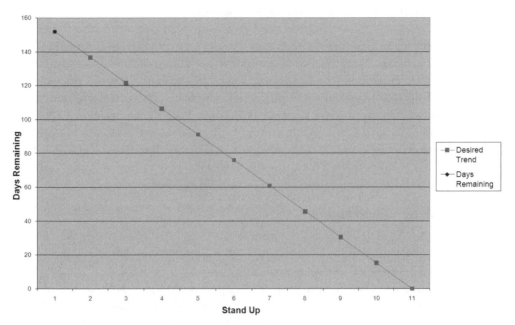

Figure 16.11   A burndown chart tells you how many hours of work you should have remaining as the iteration progresses.

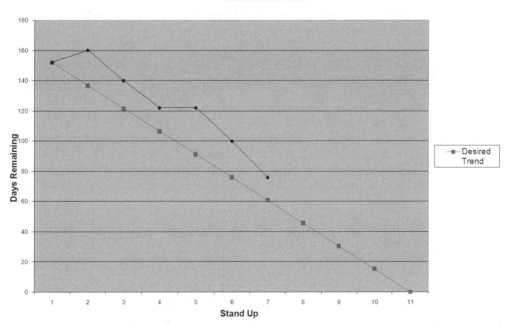

Figure 16.12   As the iteration progresses Acme Media sees status on a daily basis. In this example they're running behind after seven days of work, but they're trending to get back on schedule.

work is larger than originally estimated. What was originally estimated at 152 hours of work is now estimated to be 160 hours of work.

This is a common occurrence: after your team gets deep into the code, they may encounter surprises and need to increase their estimates for hours of work remaining for some tasks. They will also discover new tasks that you'll need to record into your burn down chart. The positive here is that some tasks will also be easier than expected, which will help your team stay on track toward completing the work within the iteration. Your team will also appreciate knowing the status of the iteration on a daily basis.

Acme's situation also illustrates another common occurrence: as the team progresses from day 4 to 5, the amount of work remaining doesn't change. This happens when a team gets stuck on an issue. The team may be investigating options or doing technical research, so no code is created during this time.

16.6.2 Tracking release status

As your team tracks status for the iteration, a person such as a project manager or ScrumMaster may be keeping track of the overall release. Let's look at how Acme Media keeps track of release status.

Historically, Wendy the project manager used Microsoft Project to track release status, but team members frequently didn't reference the tool because they found the plan hard to decipher or didn't have Project installed on their PCs.

Wendy decides to go with a lighter tool for her team: a tool that will be easy to decipher and one that everyone can access. She creates the tool using Microsoft Excel, which makes it easy to post on the project wiki site and also easy to print. She calls the new tool the Progress Matrix (see figure 16.13).

FEATURES	Functional Requirements	Code Written	Unit Tested	System Integration	Functional Testing	Customer Approval	Load Test	DR Code Release	Production Code Release
Iteration 1									
Ability to register on the site	✓	✓	✓	✓	✓	✓	N/A		
Ability to place an item up for bid	✓	✓	✓	✓					
Ability to bid on an item	✓	✓	✓	✓	✓				
Auction Engine Logic	✓	✓	✓	✓	✓				

Figure 16.13   The Progress Matrix makes status easy for the whole team to comprehend quickly. Feature status is viewed from a binary status versus percentage complete.

The Progress Matrix allows Acme's team to quickly digest status. The columns in the matrix convey completeness at each stage. The fields Wendy has decided to track are as follows:

- *Functional requirements*—If the team feels they understand the initial scope of the feature, they mark this field as complete. The customer can still request changes later in the cycle.
- *Code written*—The code is complete from the developer's perspective.
- *Unit tested*—The developer has executed the code locally, and it has passed the unit tests.
- *System integration*—The code has been integrated into the system test environment and didn't break other features in the existing code base.
- *Functional testing*—If a feature passed integration testing, Acme has built the feature into the User Acceptance environment, and a tester has performed functional testing.
- *Customer approval*—Acme's customers review and test features during the adapt week. This box is selected when the customer approves the feature.
- *Load test*—Acme's development team load-tests features to make sure there is no unforeseen effect on performance.
- *DR code release*—Acme Media has created a Disaster Recovery (DR) environment in case the Production environment ever goes down. The first step in a production code deployment is to put the new code into the DR environment.
- *Production code release*—This indicates that a feature has been deployed to the Production environment. In theory, the project is over at this time; but Acme sometimes deploys code to the Production environment in advance of exposing it to users. This lets the team verify that the code works correctly in the Production environment.

We personally enjoy using tools like the Progress Matrix. They give management and the team quick insight into release status. When we introduce the matrix to teams and project managers, they frequently ask us if this is the only tool we use for release status. Our answer is, "it depends."

16.6.3 *Finding tools that work for you*

Similar to the agile team, the agile project manager looks at the project and determines the best tools for tracking a project. If you're tracking a project, the Progress Matrix is the lightest tool you can use. The project needs to be straightforward and mainly focused on development.

If the project becomes more complex, you can pursue a supplemental tool to help track all tasks, not just those tied to development. We have a friend who was the project manager on a medium-complexity project a few years ago. She wasn't comfortable relying on the Progress Matrix or the iteration plan alone; she wanted another tool to make her more comfortable with tracking the project. Our friend disliked Microsoft Project and decided to track the project with an Excel spreadsheet (see figure 16.14).

	A	B	C	D	E	F	G	H
1	**VACATION 3.0 TASKS**	**BEGIN DATE**		**DUE DATE**		**PERSON**		**DONE**
2	**Focus groups**							
3	Draft mockups for focus groups reviewed with Janet			9-Sep		Julie		X
4	Second mock review with Janet			24-Sep		Amy/Julie		X
5	Final mockups for focus groups to Janet			28-Sep		Amy/Julie		X
6	Props for focus groups - screens, handouts			28-Sep		Julie		X
7	Conduct focus groups	10/12, 10/14				Janet		X
8	Debrief	15-Oct				Mike/Janet		X
9	First draft report			1-Nov		Julie		X
10	Final Report			10-Nov		Julie		X
11	Retrospective			8-Nov		Team		X
12	**Advertiser tool**							
13	Document fields and functionality			4-Nov		Julie		X
14	Design mocks of advertiser tool	5-Nov		19-Nov		Sam/Amy		X
15	ePay business rules and decisions	15-Nov		10-Dec		Julie/Greg		X
16	User agreement finalized	15-Nov		15-Jan		Mike		
17	Review mocks	22-Nov		24-Nov		Cheryl/Mike/Team		X
18	Build advertiser tool templates	29-Nov		10-Dec		Sam/Amy		X
19	QA Templates - make fixes	9-Dec		9-Dec		Cindy/Sam		X
20	Engineer advertiser tool	13-Dec		12-Jan		Jessie		
21	Ad tour	1-Dec		5-Jan		Julie/Cheryl/Amy/Sam		
22	QA tool/make fixes	13-Jan		18-Jan		Cindy/Sam/Team		
23	**Yellow pages feed**							
24	Choose YP provider			1-Nov		Scott/Julie/Team		X
25	Finalize pricing and contract			1-Jan		Scott		X
26	Prepare DB to take YP feed and additional fields from advertiser tool	8-Nov		24-Nov		Jessie		X
27	Put YP feed into DB			7-Jan		Jessie		
28	Map SIC codes to categories	22-Nov		17-Dec		Julie		X*
29	**Front-end**							
30	Draft front-end functionality	27-Oct		10-Nov		Julie		X
31	Design front-end mocks	11-Nov		3-Dec		Amy		X
	Finalize front-end fields and							

Figure 16.14   You can use tools such as Microsoft Excel to track project status. Tracking tools need to be easy to use and simple for your team to digest.

So many tools, so little time

Numerous off-the-shelf tools are available for tracking the status of agile projects. We've used many of the tools provided by Rally Software, VersionOne, and Thoughtworks. As you've seen in our case study, there are other tools, such as SharePoint, that weren't made specifically for agile work but that can be configured to support tracking features, iterations, and releases. Many tools also require no hardware on your side: you can use the tools on the vendors' servers.

You can use various tools to track project status. The key is to pick a tool that makes it easy to display status to the team and to those who need to manage the project. We like the simple spreadsheet our friend created. It made it easy for her to track status on multiple tasks and still use the Progress Matrix to verify code completeness.

But what if a project runs for many months and has a multitude of dependencies and complexities? What tools should you use to measure such a large, complex project? It happens that Greg recently participated in such a project.

The project Greg worked on was slated to run 18 months. His company upgraded its intranet platform and migrated content for more than 40,000 system users. The team had been together many years and had adopted many agile techniques and processes. These agile processes were used to deliver a new release to the platform every 7.5 weeks. For the most part, Greg's team leveraged the existing infrastructure and provided new features and enhancements with each release.

The team started the 18-month project using the same techniques they had used for the enhancement releases. They broke the 18-month project into releases and set out to do the work. During those 18 months, Greg's team encountered many issues with applying release techniques to a large project, including these:

- Many features took longer than a release to complete, such as procuring and installing hardware.
- Features sometimes had as many as 10 dependencies that needed to be completed before work could begin.
- The large project include 20 to 30 mini-projects. A given release could have as many as 1,000 tasks to be completed.
- A good portion of the project was dependent on a third-party software provider. The team could submit bugs to the vendor, but they couldn't control when the bugs were fixed. Many times, the fix spanned several releases.

The complexity of this project pushed Greg's team to keep track of tasks and features. They soon found that they needed three tools to keep track of issues, feature status, and the project at large. The team continued to use a Progress Matrix to track feature completeness, but they supplemented it with a list of outstanding vendor issues and a Microsoft Project plan. This plan provided a roadmap for the project and made it easier to see the dependencies associated with a feature or piece of work (see figure 16.15).

In essence, Greg's team created the correct level of agility for their project. They still delivered iteratively, received frequent customer feedback, and quickly adapted to change.

ⓘ	% complete	Task Name	Duration	Start	Finish	Predeces
✓	100%	⊞ Release 2.0	36 days	Mon 03/12/07	Mon 04/30/07	
✓	100%	⊞ Release 2.1	43 days	Tue 04/03/07	Fri 06/01/07	
✓	100%	⊞ Release 2.2	43 days	Tue 05/01/07	Fri 06/29/07	
✓	100%	⊞ Release 2.3	43 days	Wed 05/30/07	Mon 07/30/07	
	77%	⊞ Release 2.4 Last Custom Code Build for UAT and Failover testing	31 days	Wed 06/27/07	Thu 08/09/07	
	23%	⊞ Release 3.0 - Migration Ready on 10/19/07	80 days	Thu 06/28/07	Thu 10/18/07	
	0%	⊟ Release 3.1 -Go Live on 12/06/07	74 days	Fri 08/24/07	Thu 12/06/07	
	0%	⊞ Scoping	34 days	Fri 08/24/07	Thu 10/11/07	
	0%	⊞ Requirements (inc UEG)	16 days	Thu 10/11/07	Thu 11/01/07	
	0%	⊞ Development (inc Front End Dev)	19 days	Tue 10/23/07	Fri 11/16/07	
	0%	⊞ Configuration Mgmt	9 days	Thu 11/08/07	Tue 11/20/07	
	0%	⊞ QA	13 days	Fri 11/09/07	Wed 11/28/07	
	0%	⊟ Customer UAT	8 days	Mon 11/19/07	Thu 11/29/07	
	0%	Customer UAT Window	8 days	Mon 11/19/07	Thu 11/29/07	290
	0%	⊟ **Deploy v3 (early)**	2 days	Fri 11/23/07	Mon 11/26/07	
	0%	Deploy 3.1 to DR	1 day	Fri 11/23/07	Fri 11/23/07	296
	0%	Deploy 3.1 to Prod	1 day	Mon 11/26/07	Mon 11/26/07	303

Figure 16.15   Complex projects frequently require the use of tools such as Microsoft Project to track timelines and dependencies. Using such a tool isn't anti-agile. Agile is all about using the correct level of documentation and process. In a complex project, a tool such as Microsoft Project provides the correct level of support.

16.7   Key points

The key points from this chapter are as follows:

- Acceptance tests are defined at the start of iteration planning to make it clear to the team what *complete* means.
- Feature modeling is an effective practice for identifying the tasks needed to support a feature.
- After tasks are indentified, iteration planning becomes similar to traditional planning. Capacity is estimated and compared to detailed task estimates.
- The project team can use tools to determine their capacity, but ultimately the team makes the call about the amount of work they can deliver during an iteration.
- Many teams are initially constrained by skill sets and capacity planning and have to take available skills into account.
- Many agile teams list their iteration tasks on a wall so they're easy to view and move during an iteration. Teams can use additional tools such as burn down charts, Microsoft Project, and project wikis if iterations become complex or if the information needs to be shared with distributed locations.

16.8   Looking forward

In this chapter, you broke down the features for iteration 1. Now you're ready to begin construction. In some projects, especially in a steady-state release environment, work will begin immediately; for other projects, some precursor work needs to be performed. We call this pre-work iteration 0, and we'll discuss it in chapter 17.

Part 6

Building the product

This section begins with a discussion of iteration 0—the time needed to set up development environments, finalize vendor contracts, and prepare the team for the project. We then move to the development phase and discuss the agile principles and how Acme Media has embraced them. You will see the principles in action in chapter 18 as we follow Acme through its development iterations. We will conclude this section with testing and the importance of identifying issues early.

As you read this section you will notice a mind shift compared to traditional development. We will not take our requirements and go about building and testing code without customer involvement. We will surface our work to the customer frequently to validate that we are building what they asked for. The customer will also have a chance to verify that the working code addresses the business needs they have.

We will conclude this section by discussing testing in an agile environment. We will go beyond customer validation and discuss unit, integration, and exploratory testing.

Start your engines:
iteration 0

At this point, the Acme team has performed feasibility and planning work for the pilot project. Many people in the agile community label this pre-development work *iteration 0*. Iteration 0 work is foundational work that is performed prior to development starting.

For our purposes, *iteration 0* is the foundational work performed after initial planning but before development begins. Iteration 0 work usually runs for about a week, but it can take less or more time depending on project complexity. Let's look at some of the typical tasks performed during this timeframe.

17.1   *Initial vision for the architecture*

The Acme Media team performed a high-level analysis of the architectural needs for the Auctionator when they performed their feasibility work. They will take one more look at the architectural needs before they begin development. This makes sense, because they just came through the feature-card exercise. They have more information about each feature, and they can use that knowledge to outline an initial architectural model.

Assessing and modeling your architectural needs offers numerous benefits. Here are a few:

- *Confirmation of costs*—You get a better feel for hardware and licensing needs, and you thus minimize surprise expenses during development.
- *Better understanding of third-party needs*—You can identify dependencies with other departments and begin planning with them early.
- *Better communication*—Documenting your initial model gives you a tool for interacting with other departments, vendors, and software providers.
- *Reduced technical risk*—Outlining your initial architecture identifies areas where you may lack technical skills or technology needed to support the project.

You might think that this exercise would slow you down and prevent you from jumping into the code. In reality, you outline an architectural vision to ensure quick delivery. Your architectural work helps identify areas of risk that could prevent deployment at the end of development. You also focus on making the architecture flexible, so you can be agile in supporting future needs and requirements.

Here are the technical artifacts that may be created during architectural assessment:

- Infrastructure diagrams
- Application flow diagrams
- Logical component diagrams
- Security model/requirements
- Performance requirements
- Availability requirements
- User interface flow

What is your source for this technical information? Usually, an architect gets all the developers in a room to discuss the architectural approach for a project. A customer advocate is usually involved, too, to provide clarity on business needs.

We've seen some companies perform architectural modeling without a customer advocate in the room. This is possible, but it's critical to have the requirements drive the architecture, not the other way around.

17.2   *Completing contracts with third parties*

We can't remember the last time we worked on project that didn't require services or software from a third party. Iteration 0 is a great time to take care of contracts related to obtaining these services. Here are some examples:

- *Additional licenses*—We see this a lot when working with Microsoft products. You may need to obtain additional application or SQL server licenses to support additional users or processes.

- *Data feeds*—Ahmed once worked on a *Do Not Contact* marketing application, and his team had to obtain the *Do Not Contact* names from several vendors. We've also worked on directory-type applications where we had to obtain business listings from Yellow Pages providers and load them into a database.

- *Email services*—Some companies will manage user alerts for you. Acme Media uses eLertz for its various alert needs; eLertz will notify users when an item they desire comes up for bid. Many companies will also manage online subscriptions and pass articles or other information to your users based on their profile.

- *Search services*—So many good search options are on the market that it frequently makes sense to buy this functionality instead of creating it. We've worked at companies that purchased the Google Search Appliance or another off-the-shelf search application and installed it in their environment.

- *Contract help*—You may work on projects where you need to beef up your team to address a skill set that you don't typically require. We recently helped a team with a project where they needed to create a web-based training module for users. This wasn't a normal need for their projects, so the team hired a contractor who specialized in creating training modules.

- *Specialized applications*—Similar to search, it doesn't make sense for you to create some other kinds of applications, because good, affordable products are already on the market. These include stock tickers, weather widgets, blog applications, mapping software, content-management systems, and online forms.

When you're squared away with third parties, you can make sure your development environments are ready to go.

17.3 *Preparing environments and support tools*

As you come out of initial planning, you're thinking about the customer, their feature requests, and how you're going to design and create the features. It's easy to get so caught up in this moment that you forget to prepare the environment from a technical and project-management perspective. Iteration 0 is the perfect time to make sure you're ready to develop, build, test, manage, and track code.

Let's start with the development aspect. What do you need to do to make sure you're ready to build code? You should set up some of the following areas:

- *Version control*—Set up a new branch or project in your version-control system such as Subversion or Perforce.

- *Automated builds*—Get CruiseControl or your tool of choice to support daily builds and continuous integration. Make sure all developers can monitor the builds.

- *Workstations*—In addition to build tools, make sure the developer workstations are good to go. Be sure framework and development products are installed and configured correctly for the project you're pursuing.
- *Defect tracking*—If you use a bug-tracking tool, create a new project in the tool before you begin recording issues.

When the development environment is prepared, you must consider all the ancillary tools and processes required to support the project. Here are the ones we frequently see teams use:

- *Automation testing*—Prepare your build-verification tools for the forthcoming builds. This usually involves reviewing your latest release and seeing what additional scripts must be created to regression-test the application.
- *Load testing*—If your initial planning indicates that some features may have high volume or place a heavy load on the system, you need to plan for load testing during development. This involves using load-testing tools such as LoadRunner to simulate many users hitting the system concurrently. You must create scripts that will test your features and verify that the system will perform at the required level.
- *Content testing*—What kind of content or data do you need to test the features? You'll probably need to create the content before testing, so try to create it during iteration 0. Even more important, make sure you have a process for refreshing the data during testing and keeping data consistent across all test environments.

After ancillary tools, you need to make sure all the project-support tools are set up or established. You may be using these types of tools:

- *Time tracking*—Time tracking is needed to measure how much of a project budget has been used or to bill a client for time and materials. Time tracking seems like an anti-agile activity, but it frequently has to be done on a project and it's one of the constraints many teams have to accept.
- *Status tracking*—How will you track risks, code completeness, build notes, and iteration status? These tools also need to be set up during iteration 0. Tools such as burn down charts and iteration plans can be posted on your project wall, configured in your wiki tool, or both.

If you have your tools and environments set up, what else do you need? Money!

17.4 *Obtaining funding*

One of the things we enjoy when working for small companies is having little overhead. We usually have only one product, one project, one project team, and one budget. It's easy to focus on the goal of delivering value to the customer.

When we work for larger companies, we see more overhead, bureaucracy, and rules for initializing a project. One of those hurdles is obtaining funding.

Acme Media doesn't have many hurdles in funding the Auctionator project. The company has a dedicated project budget for the team, and the Auctionator doesn't require additional funds beyond the team's annual budget.

Funding becomes more difficult when a significant capital investment is required to support a project. If you need to buy more servers or expensive licenses, your company may require the completion of financial forms and spreadsheets. Greg currently works in such an environment.

In Greg's workplace, several groups compete for capital dollars needed to support their projects. The teams all present their business cases to an executive review group, and the executives make the call about which projects to fund. As you can imagine, this process can take some time: completing forms, going to review meetings, waiting for the executive decisions, and finally waiting for an account to be opened so orders can be placed.

Greg's company has realized that this formal process can jeopardize projects that need to be delivered quickly to ensure benefits. To remove this issue and become more agile, Greg's company has created a process that lets a team receive early funding before a project is formally approved. The team doesn't receive enough funding to pay for the entire project, but they get enough money to keep working on the project while the final decision is being made and the value is validated.

17.5   *Finalizing and dedicating the project team*

Let's take a moment to review the current state of Acme's project team and how the team got where it is:

- Acme started with a project idea from the product manager (who acts as the customer advocate).
- The product manager and project manager worked together to determine what type of employees were needed to perform feasibility. They added a developer and a UI resource at that time.
- After feasibility, the team had a better feel for the types of employees that would be needed to bring the project home, and they brought several more people into the project: an additional developer, a QA resource, an operations resource, a business analyst, and an architect.

Now that development is about to start, how does the team change? First, Acme lets the representative from the Operations team, Tom Klein, return to his job. Tom won't be involved in development, but the team will invite him to demonstrations so he can provide feedback and share any concerns he sees from an operations perspective.

The team also lets the architect reduce his involvement with the project. We typically see architect involvement reduced by half after a project goes through initial planning. The architect will come back for several design sessions and to help Acme's team resolve issues related to performance or scalability. This also frees the architect to work with other project teams that may just be getting started.

The remaining team members need to be dedicated to the project. In a perfect world, you'll have a product-development team and a production-support team. The development team shouldn't have any issues focusing on the project work at hand.

In the not-so-perfect world—and in the situation we see the most—the development team is also in charge of supporting the production environment. This means they're dedicated to the project unless a high-priority production issue interrupts them. We say *high priority* because we encourage agile teams to wait until the adapt period between iterations to look at noncritical issues that may have occurred in the production environment.

The main thing to remember is that collaboration and communication are critical during an iteration. Make this the number-one priority for all team members. Try to put off competing projects or issues until after the iteration is complete.

17.6 *Cheating: starting the work early*

We're avid supporters of *project cheating*. We're always looking to take advantage of opportunities to start an activity early, test early, demonstrate early, adapt early, and deliver early. Iteration 0 is a great time to cheat. In theory, you aren't officially working on an iteration, but you can still use this time to remove risk and increase understanding.

Development environments may not be ready yet, but you can still pursue activities that reduce risk and increase feature understanding. Some of the tasks you can start during iteration 0 are as follows:

- *Continue scoping*—It's doubtful that you got all the information needed to develop features during the feature-card exercise. Continue interacting and modeling with the customer to refine feature requirements and understanding.

- *Start modeling and prototyping*—In our experience, the development environment isn't required to create prototypes. You can outline prototypes with pure HTML, Photoshop, whiteboards, and even sketches on a piece of paper.

- *Test interfaces and APIs with vendors*—If your project involves any type of interface, you should begin testing it as soon as possible. Interfaces usually represent the highest risk to project timelines.

- *Initialize test cases*—Related to scoping, you probably didn't come out of the feature-card exercise with a crisp definition of how you'll test each feature. You can get a jump on this work in iteration 0.

- *Work issues and risks*—What items could potentially derail or delay the project? Will you need sign-off from a compliance group before deploying? Will you need support and maintenance processes in place before you go live? Do you need to reserve shared resources for the project, such as a load-test environment? Use iteration 0 to get started on these items.

- *Training*—Will you need to deliver training materials at the end of the project? Iteration 0 can be used to jumpstart these.

- *Communication planning*—Who will be affected by your project? Iteration 0 is a great time to identify your audiences and the messages you need to send to them during development, deployment, and (potentially) migration from the old system to the new one being delivered.
- *Marketing plan*—Your product or project may require a marketing plan to roll it out. For example, Acme Media needs a marketing plan to support the Auction-ator. Acme has faith in the product, but the company needs a way to advertise to the customers they've lost to eBay and Craigslist.

When the development environments come online, you can stop cheating and begin your development iterations in earnest.

17.7 Key points

The key points from this chapter are as follows:

- One-time projects may require set-up and foundation work before development can begin.
- Initial architecture modeling can bring the team together on a design vision and speed up development.
- Many projects require the services of third parties. You may need to complete contracts or obtain vendor licenses before beginning development.
- You may need to set up your environments before work begins. This pre-work could include setting up machines, organizing load-test environments, and preparing test content.
- Larger projects may need tools set up to support the project. These can include time-tracking systems and status tools.
- Many projects require funding to get started. You may have to present your feasibility findings to a funding body and obtain approval before proceeding with development.
- Although your development environments may not be ready to go, you can still do other value-add work for the project. This can include feature modeling, estimating, training preparation, and working on your communication plan.
- Work for a project does not have to start at a prescribed date or time. If team members have capacity, they can begin design and investigation work before an iteration formally begins.

17.8 Looking forward

In this chapter, we covered iteration 0 and the precursor work that is required to get development started. In chapter 18, we'll join Acme Media as the team starts development work and learn what development really means in an agile environment.

18
Delivering working software

If the Acme Media team decided to track their pilot project in a project tool, they would say that the project is around 50 percent complete. Fifty-percent complete sounds good. You're halfway there. You can tell your stakeholders that you're on schedule and they don't need to worry about anything. But this is where things change in an agile environment.

In an agile environment, you measure status by working code. Knowing if a project is feasible is a good thing. Doing initial planning is a good thing. But to this point, you haven't delivered any value to the customer. From a customer perspective, you have a project status of 0 percent.

In agile, you get to working code quickly by using iterative development and building to the minimum specification. You deliver the most valuable software in prioritized batches. You do your best to make each batch contain enough functionality for it to be a deployable subset of features.

Iterative development works because it supports the realities of software development. You can't forecast all the variables, but you can make sure you deliver critical functionality as quickly as possible.

This chapter begins with a discussion of the agile development principles and how Acme Media has embraced them. You'll see the principles in action as we follow Acme through its development iterations. We'll contrast these principles to Acme Media's legacy processes.

The game of rugby provides a nice visual example of how the process works. In rugby, one of the team formations is called a *scrum*. The scrum formation involves many players meeting at the same point on the field and literally interlocking their heads. The same thing is true during agile development. All team members, regardless of title or area of expertise, work together to deliver working software. Their minds are interlocked with a singular purpose: to deliver high-value functionality to the customer as quickly as possible.

In the past, Acme Media delivered all software, both high- and low-priority features, in one delivery at the end of the project. The entire team didn't help during development; it was solely up to the programmers to bring the features home. In this chapter, Acme will use its new iterative approach and deliver the highest-value features first. The team will deliver working software in batches until they run out of time or the customer need is satisfied.

18.1 Supporting the agile principles during development and testing

Acme Media moved to an agile process because the company wasn't delivering projects quickly. The development team had a history of constantly moving out milestones and missing deadlines. With the newfound popularity of web advertising, the team was overwhelmed, and customers were taking their advertisements to other websites that could turn them around quickly.

Acme Media made the correct choice in deciding to move to agile. The following ten agile principles discussed in this chapter focus the team and the company on delivering early during the construction phase:

1　Satisfy the customer through early and continuous delivery of valuable software.
2　Have business people and developers work together daily throughout the project.
3　Whenever possible, communicate face to face.
4　Pay attention to technical excellence and good design.
5　Focus on simplicity and the art of maximizing the amount of work not done.
6　Welcome changing requirements, even late in development.

    7 Test early, and test often.

    8 Continuously integrate code changes.

    9 Obtain customer feedback as early as possible.

    10 Minimize team distractions during development iterations.

Let's look at each principle separately.

18.1.1 Satisfy the customer through early and continuous delivery of valuable software

Acme Media never delivered early in the past, but the company's new iterative approach will let it get key features out to the customer early. The planning process the team followed in chapter 8 also ties to this principle. The team will deliver more quickly because they didn't have to create functional specifications before they created their iteration plan. They saved time because they didn't document requirements for features that won't be pursued.

18.1.2 Have business people and developers work together daily throughout the project

In Acme Media's previous process, the business analysts worked with the customer to document requirements. Frequently, an internal product manager communicated the needs. After the requirements were documented, the analyst passed them to the developer and determined whether there were any questions.

In Acme Media's new process, the developers have already had direct interaction with the customer. The entire team participated in the feature-card exercise, and the developers gained clarity on some customer needs by asking questions directly. The customer (in this case, the product manager) will also be available during the development iterations and can clarify their needs and be consulted if issues are encountered.

Notice how the principles stress *business people*, not just customers. In our experience, several individuals beyond the customer and the development team care about a project, including people in marketing, legal, security, implementation, support, documentation, and training. In an agile environment, the development team interacts with these teams throughout a project.

18.1.3 Whenever possible, communicate face to face

This principle is difficult for Acme Media to embrace. The team enjoys using email and Instant Messenger. They rarely do face-to-face discussions during development. The repercussion from this style is that team members frequently get into email hell, where a message goes around and around with as many as 20 responses.

We live in an age of Blackberries, texting, instant messaging, and blogs. Some people like to wear headphones when they work. There are more and more ways to communicate indirectly. Basically, we're allowed to communicate on our own schedule, at our leisure. The convenience of communicating whenever you want to can be helpful, especially when a team member has to travel or be away from the work area for a while. But during development, these methods should be the *exception*, not the norm.

This is where an agile coach or manager can help. A good coach will always be observing the process and looking for ways to ensure collaboration, quick decision making, and common understanding within the team.

Acme Media's agile sponsor, Steve, saw this issue at Acme after he received his training on agile. Steve worked with the management team to create a physical environment at Acme Media that supports face-to-face communication:

- A few team members weren't in the main development area, and these team members were relocated to be with the main group.
- Acme had standard cubicles with walls 5 feet high. When team members wanted to chat, they had to get up and walk around to see each other. Steve had the cubicle walls lowered to 3½ feet so the team can communicate face to face without taking a walk.
- Steve cleared out a large area next to the development area and called it the *bullpen*. It's dedicated to the development team, and team members can meet there at any time and post anything they want on the walls. Wendy, the project manager, uses the wall to post status information for the features that are in progress.
- Steve purchased several rolling whiteboards so the team can have quick discussions within the cube areas.

These changes don't force the team to work face to face more often, but you'll find that it happens naturally. Team members may find it a bit silly to IM or email a person who is visible to them.

18.1.4 Pay attention to technical excellence and good design

Acme Media has the classic issue that most teams do: they need to deliver early, but they also need to make sure their design and architecture are scalable. How do you solve this problem? You don't.

This struggle continues in an agile environment. If you rush a product and deliver it without any reflection on future needs, you may have to start from scratch to support a simple enhancement. Your lack of foresight may prevent you from delivering value quickly.

Conversely, it's easy to spend a lot of time pursuing the perfect design: one that is scalable for any situation; that can't be critiqued for any flaws; and that takes so long to create that you ship your product late, after the opportunity is gone.

Technical excellence involves balancing these two areas and delivering valuable software frequently while minimizing the cost of future change. This isn't simple to do, but it's a reality of software development. Developing software is complex, and for many of us this is the challenge and joy in doing our work.

Acme Media had this issue before they pursued agile. The main difference for them now is that designers and architects know that a perfect design can cost the team a delivery. After several missed deliveries, the company and their careers could be in jeopardy. Consistent delivery ensures customer satisfaction and income.

18.1.5 Focus on simplicity and the art of maximizing the amount of work not done

Some days, Ahmed gets under the skin of his clients. They know that sooner or later they will hear his trademark questions: "Why are we doing this feature, and what happens if we don't?" Ahmed works with his teams during the feature-card exercise, and he usually remembers what the customer requested during the session. When Ahmed sees the team pursuing feature richness beyond that vision, he questions it.

It's easy to have scope drift within your team. It's natural to want to create great software and go beyond a customer's minimal requirements. Greg once worked for a company whose mission statement said it would "meet and exceed customer requirements in an effort to delight them." This is a dangerous approach to take in software development. Getting code to a state where it can be deployed is challenging enough without adding bonus functionality.

Focusing on simplicity also lets you demonstrate to the customer sooner. The sooner you demonstrate, the sooner you know if you're in synch with their needs. This prevents waste and minimizes rework.

Acme Media never thought about this principle in the past. The developers received a functional specification, and they determined feature richness. The developers could even use a feature request to test new technology or add functionality they thought the customer might request in the future. In the new agile world, the development effort is time-boxed, and the team is encouraged to surface their work as soon as possible for customer review.

18.1.6 Welcome changing requirements, even late in development

We can't lie. We don't welcome changing requirements. We embrace agile, and we know the roots of this principle, but we haven't been able to convert to a mode of *welcoming* changing requirements. What we *do* welcome is a process that expects change and doesn't add to the issue by pretending change doesn't exist in a software project.

We've worked in environments where we had to create a change request for every variation during a project. The change request was associated with guilt and poor project management. In reality, all projects have changes in requirements. These changes typically come from the customer seeing a working product and identifying an oversight, or from a technical discovery after programming begins.

Acme Media has lived in the guilt world. It thought other companies didn't have these issues. It thought it had wishy-washy customers and a poor project manager. In the new environment, the company may not embrace changing requirements, but it understands that they're inevitable and can't be planned out of a project.

18.1.7 *Test early, and test often*

Acme Media used to perform its testing at the end of development. The company thought this was a good approach. If the team ran short on time, they could cut back on testing and still finish development.

The issue with this approach is that when you do find bugs, it takes longer to trace them. The magnitude of a bug can be greater too, potentially requiring a rewrite of code in several areas.

To mitigate this risk, an agile team tests as soon as possible. In some sense, testing begins during the feature-card exercise. A QA employee should be in the room during the exercise to identify inconsistency in requirements, potential integration issues, validation of performance needs, and other technical constraints.

Advanced agile teams take this concept even further by using a process called Test Driven Development (TDD). A TDD process has the developer create a unit test before writing any new code. The test is executed to validate that it failed, and then the developer begins writing code until the test passes. This approach usually shortens the overall delivery cycle.

Acme Media won't pursue TDD out of the gate, but the team will begin testing early and pursue a goal of daily builds and a build-verification test.

18.1.8 *Continuously integrate code changes*

Related to testing early and often is the principle of *continuous integration*. Developers need to continually integrate their code changes to verify that their latest change hasn't broken the code. Continuous integration also ensures that the entire team is working from the same version of base code.

Historically, integration has been an infrequent event during development, and integration issues have been discovered late in the cycle, making them harder to find and jeopardizing ship dates. Acme Media didn't integrate often in the past, and this added to the company's issue of missing delivery dates. Integration of every change requires discipline, and Acme Media's developers didn't want to be that disciplined. Acme will move to daily integration during the pilot, with a long-term goal of integrating every code change.

18.1.9 *Obtain customer feedback as early as possible*

In the past, Acme Media sought feedback from the customer after development was complete. Using this approach, Acme Media's team frequently found the customer had functionality issues with the code that was developed. The issues went beyond bugs: they frequently tied to the customer saying the code didn't meet their needs. Acme tried to address as many issues as possible before going live, and if major issues couldn't be fixed quickly, they delayed shipping the product.

Acme Media's new approach is to demonstrate to the customer as soon as the team has functioning code. The customer won't have to wait for the final product to provide feedback. Issues will be discovered early, before layers of code are applied.

Does scope creep exist in an agile environment?

Acme Media's development team has never enjoyed change requests. Whenever the customer asks for a change, team members go back to their desks and mumble about "scope creep." After their agile training, team members have a new perspective. Let's look at an example.

If a customer asks for an alarm clock, and during a demonstration they notice that they forgot to ask for a snooze button, then they have experienced a natural occurrence in software development. Sometimes you miss a feature detail during a requirements discussion, and a demonstration exposes what was overlooked. This type of change should be embraced.

On the other hand, if a customer asks for an alarm clock, and after a demonstration they request that the alarm clock also be usable as a coffeemaker, then you have a radical change in requirements and potentially a new project. Some might call this scope creep, but we think the issue ties to the need to ask "why?" during the feature-card exercise. If the root business need is known, it's doubtful that a major functionality shift like this will take place during development.

As we've mentioned, we do embrace change, and if the customer truly needs an alarm clock/coffeemaker we'll deliver it. But we want to make sure we understand the fundamental need.

Acme Media's new development model has a formal adapt phase between iterations, during which the team demonstrates to the customer. These demonstrations will occur every 2 weeks. The team has also adopted an approach of surfacing work in advance of the adapt window if pieces are ready early or if the feedback will help them make design decisions.

18.1.10 *Minimize team distractions during development iterations*

During development iterations, the team needs to be 100 percent focused on the work at hand. Everyone must be available to clarify requirements and to collaborate on and solve solutions. In our experience, issues discovered during development can be solved in a multitude of ways, and involving the team at large makes this possible. Customers can modify or reprioritize requirements, developers can code around an issue, a product can be configured differently, or hardware can be modified.

Because you're on a tight schedule for an iteration (usually around 2 weeks), you can't spend time trying to trace down team members and orchestrate a meeting in the next day or two. You don't send emails and wait for people to respond. You need to work issues promptly and stay on schedule for delivery at the end of the iteration.

In a perfect world, the team would have no distractions and could focus solely on the project at hand. Some companies have development groups that work only on projects. But most teams we work with have to deal with distractions. Many teams are also in charge of maintaining the current production environment, and if a production issue occurs they must work on it. This is true for Acme Media.

Acme Media's development team works on projects and maintains the three existing websites. In addition, they have daily maintenance activities, and they frequently work on mini-enhancements that don't require a project team. These supporting activities have contributed to Acme Media's failure to deliver in the past.

The development team must continue to perform their support activities, but in their new development model they will try to defer maintenance and support activities until the adapt week. During development, they will be interrupted only for critical production issues.

Acme also realized that the company had become *people dependent* in several areas. Experts existed for every area, and developers didn't cross-train with each other. When a production problem occurred, frequently only one person had the skills to work the issue. Acme identified this problem when the company outlined its new agile process and created a plan to cross-train the developers. The cross-training will spread skills throughout the team and let the developer with the most free time address the issue, which will minimize project interruptions.

Now that you have a feel for the agile principles, let's see them in action.

18.2 Where to begin?

When we left Acme Media, the team had just completed their iteration plan. They outlined one item for iteration 0, modifying the contract with eLertz to support an additional alert needed for the Auctionator. With this work out of the way, it's time to focus on the features that are assigned to iteration 1.

The work backlog, shown in figure 18.1, contains both features and tasks. The team first identified tasks during their feature-modeling exercise, when they identified the high-level work required to support each feature. The team identified additional tasks during iteration 0; now that they're in a development iteration, they will finalize and complete the tasks.

Even in an agile environment, you can't anticipate all of the tasks until you begin working on the features. We've often heard people say, "Development doesn't really start until we open the code." In our experience, we've found this to be true. Let's look at an example with Acme Media.

	B	C
2	Description	Area
3	**Feature - Ability to bid on an item**	
4	HTML for screens	UI
5	Design data model	Dev
6	Code insert, update, delete	Dev
7	Interface with user registration	Dev
8	Create tests	QA
9	Error handling	Dev
10	**Feature - Ability to place an item up for bid**	
11	HTML for screens	UI
12	Auction engine interface	Dev
13	Bid refresh function	Dev
14	Validate registration	Dev
15	Confirm auction via email	Dev
16	Create tests	QA
17	**Feature - Ability to search by category**	
18	Define search scopes	Dev
19	Develop crawl logic	Dev
20	Faceted search filters	Dev
21	Category edit tool	Dev
22	2 search screens	UI
23	Create tests	QA
24	**Feature - Auction engine**	
25	Expire auction logic	Dev
26	Alert winner	Dev

⊞ ◂ ▸ ▸⊦ \ Features ╱ Burn Down Chart ╲ Iteration Tasks ╱ Iteration Days ╱
Ready

Figure 18.1   Acme Media's backlog of work for iteration 1. In a perfect world, team members grab a task and begin working. In Acme Media's world, the team is constrained by specializations, and some tasks can be completed only by certain team members or groups. Acme Media will cross-train, but it will take time for the team to mature to a point of no specializations.

When Acme did the initial planning for *Search by category*, the team identified four major tasks:

- Create a screen to enter search criteria.
- Create a screen to display search results.
- Create a screen to display an item up for bid.
- Define the process for crawling and indexing items up for bid.

When Ryan, the user experience designer, starts working on the search screen, he notices that the search categories haven't been discussed with the customer. The customer, Jay, the product manager, gives Ryan the categories, and they have a quick discussion about searching in general. It occurs to Jay that Acme Media serves a wide geographic area and that buyers will want to filter by location when performing a search. Ryan can add that functionality to the search screen without a significant change in his effort, so they agree he should do so. They share this decision with the entire team to see if it has any effect on designs for the other features.

18.2.1 *Sequence within an iteration*

We frequently hear team members ask, "In what order should we pursue the features during an iteration?" The answer is twofold. First, you'll often need to deliver all the features assigned to an iteration to take the application to a state where it provides value. From an end-user perspective, all features are equal—the customer needs them all for a minimal functioning system.

Second, from a coding perspective, it comes down to technical dependencies. Do some parts of a feature have to be in place before a related feature is pursued? For example, the Acme team members who create the search functionality will probably need some level of the auction functionality in place first. They must know what attributes are associated with an auction and then build out the correct search logic and indexing process.

In our experience, the sequence we build in is rarely serial. Team members evolve features together as everyone normalizes on what the system is. We frequently hear a team member say, "I've completed my first pass" at a task or feature, acknowledging that work on other features may require them to revisit their work. This approach is normal. Just be sure you don't label a feature *complete* until everyone agrees it is.

18.2.2 *Making assignments*

In the past, Acme Media made assignments at the start of a project. The team hammered out the tasks they thought they could do, and department leads assigned people to the tasks.

Acme Media has made a subtle change with the new process. The department leads assigned people to participate in the planning phase based on the information that came out of the feasibility work. The planning team identified tasks during the modeling exercise, and Wendy, the project manager, recorded the tasks on her iteration plan (figure 18.1). Team members follow their areas of expertise and experience and put their names on the tasks that they identified.

The planning-team members also got a feel for the features and which tasks each one of them will probably perform. Wendy recorded this information with the tasks and went over it with the department leads at the end of the initial planning phase.

In our experience, a team that works together for a while develops a feel for who should do what on a given feature. Team knowledge and experience with each other allows team members to make quick decisions and interact with each other in an agile way. Acme Media's development team has had some interaction, but that interaction hasn't matured to a point where they're self-directed. The managers at Acme Media will be tasked with taking the team to a more self-directed level in the coming months and year.

It's also important to note that assignments aren't permanent—they can be changed on a daily basis if needed.

18.3   *Completing a feature*

Development begins by reviewing the features in the iteration plan. Team members come together to determine the most logical place to start. If your team has a large enough staff, you may be able to begin work on all features concurrently.

In Acme Media's instance, the team isn't large enough to begin all features at the same time, so they focus on features that are at the core of the functionality. They start with *Ability to place an item up for bid*, *Ability to bid on an item*, and the *Auction engine*. The tasks associated with these features are started one by one as the team begins doing the work.

Where are your functional specifications?

As you may recall from chapter 1, an agile team and their coach choose the processes needed to support each project. They use their team experience and coaching to determine which tools and practices to use. Acme Media decided to create a functional specification for one feature in iteration 1, the Auction engine.

Acme Media's team viewed the auction engine as complex, and they wanted to have a deep understanding of each use case, the actors involved, and the business rules. They didn't think a feature card and accompanying story could store all the information they would want to reference and share during development.

When the team created the functional specification, they decided to embed the feature-card information into the specification. This information was still valuable, and it would be great to reference it while reviewing the deeper functional requirements. The team also took digital pictures during their whiteboarding sessions and embedded the photos into the specifications for reference.

Acme Media's approach is in line with a major agile concept. Greater levels of documentation are expected if the project or feature requires greater ceremony. This means you should create documentation if it helps the team get the job done or if you have a customer for the documentation. Agile teams must be careful to make sure they don't skip creating documents because they consider paperwork anti-agile.

We've noticed one other thing during development, and you probably have, too: many features are so dependent on each other that they must be built in parallel. For example, it may be hard for the Acme team to create logic for *search* if they don't know the attributes of an auction. Conversely, they may want to change the data structure of an auction if it impedes search engine performance. It's common to iteratively build out features in parallel as team members discover feature dependencies.

18.3.1   *What the work looks like*

Agile development begins when a developer pulls a task from the iteration plan and then works with other team members to complete a feature. This work can take many forms:

- *Reviewing design and technology options*—Every requirement can be addressed in several ways from a technical perspective. Developers can choose a framework they have experience with or experiment with a technology that may support the need. The development team will review their options and reach agreement before proceeding.

- *Working a problem*—We're confident more time is spent working on issues than on any other task during development. When the code is open, you'll frequently discover constraints. Developers spend a lot of time reading blogs and posts about issues they encounter. They also spend time discussing issues with other developers and soliciting second opinions.

- *Continuing to scope and refine the work*—Even though the developer discusses the requirements with an analyst or the customer, scope discussions continue. Similar to Acme's issue with search categories, the developer sees details that the analyst couldn't anticipate or places where two requirements contradict each other.

- *Working on alternatives with the customer*—Frequently, the customer will have a requirement that can't be met without a major expense. For example, Greg once worked with a customer who wanted a guarantee that the system would be available 99.95 percent of the time. Greg's team estimated that the additional architecture and hardware needed would cost around $500,000. The customer decided to go with an up-time requirement of 99.50 percent instead, for no additional expense.

- *Creating content to test the application*—This part of development is frequently underestimated. Good content needs to be established to provide an accurate test of the application, and the content must be consistent across environments. You get a jump-start on this work in iteration 0 and then finalize the content needed during the development iterations.

- *Creating unit tests*—Developers will create unit tests to verify their individual functions are working correctly. In a test-driven environment, the unit tests are created before construction begins.

To continue this discussion, let's look at the model of feature development in figure 18.2.

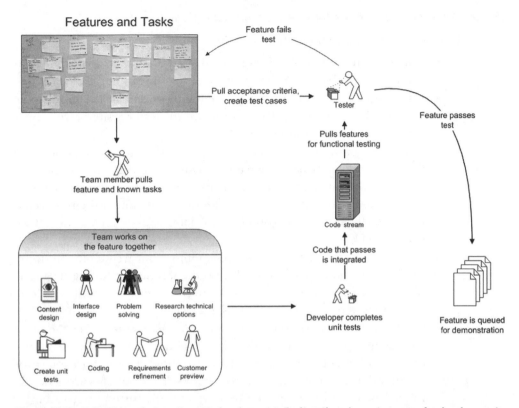

Figure 18.2   Following a feature through development. An iteration plan sets you up for development, and you pull tasks and complete them as a team. The team needs to work together to ensure consistent understanding and to be aware of how tasks interact with each other.

After the team completes their work, the developer performs a unit test to make sure the feature is working as requested and then integrates their code into the mainline code stream.

As the team is completing their work, a tester is preparing test cases for feature testing. This work starts during initial planning. Acme Media's tester, Gina Wallace, was in the room during the feature-card exercise and began envisioning the tests needed at that time. Gina also asked the customer questions about nonfunctional necessities such as performance requirements.

As features are completed, Gina pulls a feature and tests it. If a feature passes, it's labeled *test complete* and put into a queue for demonstrations at the end of the iteration. (We'll cover demonstrations in chapter 20, when we discuss adapting and user acceptance.) If a feature fails the test, it's put back into the list of features and tasks.

18.3.2   *Other considerations for development iterations*

Here are a few items to note when reviewing this workflow:

- The developer will probably create unit tests incrementally for the code they're creating. Unit tests are usually created at the function or class level.
- It's common for the customer or analyst to work with the tester to create the functional tests. In an agile environment, the tester is sitting with the team and can ask clarifying questions quickly.
- There are several ways to manage features that fail. You can put bugs on the iteration backlog or hold a separate bug-triage meeting before putting the bug into the work queue. We personally like the triage meeting. Much of the time, we find that a bug isn't a bug but a misinterpretation of the requirement or an issue with the testing environment. Working bugs as a team can get to the root cause quickly.
- Unit and functional tests are more common, but frequently we do other tests for features and applications. We also do acceptance testing during the adapt phase, and we may do usability and performance testing if we see the need. (We'll look at testing in detail in chapter 19.)
- You'll formally reserve time to demonstrate the features after the iteration, but you can also preview your work as you're building it. An agile team plays this by ear. If you spend too much time demonstrating, you can hurt your productivity. We find that the best balance is to demonstrate or discuss areas that have high requirements uncertainty, or when a feature is turning out to be technically expensive. In these instances, you can demonstrate and discuss alternatives with the customer.

This chapter covered the flow for a normal development cycle. Unfortunately development is rarely normal. We realize this, and we will discuss all of the complications that can happen during development in chapter 20, "Adapting: reacting positively to change."

18.4   *Key points*

The key points from this chapter are as follows:

- Projects can be measured in terms of percentage of tasks complete, but the ultimate metric is the demonstration of working code.
- Books like this one can help you understand what agile is about through a case study, but the main goal is to make sure the processes and exercises you use support the agile principles.
- A mature organization can pull tasks from the project backlog as team members are available. Teams with specialists will have to do more planning for task assignments.

- Features are often dependent on each other, and you may need to iteratively construct features in parallel.
- *Work* is a subjective term in an agile environment. Many times, you'll spend more time resolving issues and researching technology than you'll spend on coding.

18.5 *Looking forward*

In this chapter, we discussed what development looks like in an agile environment. We looked at testing from a high level and explained how testing fits into the overall flow. In chapter 19, we'll discuss testing in detail, looking at all the types of testing that can occur during a software release.

Testing:
did you do it right?

Cease dependence on inspection to achieve quality.
Eliminate the need for inspection on a mass basis by
building quality into the product in the first place.
                                          —W. Edwards Deming

Greg's career began in manufacturing. The company he started with focused on using lean manufacturing techniques. *Lean manufacturing* focuses on eliminating waste and improving process flow when building a product. One of the people who influenced the creation of lean manufacturing was W. Edwards Deming, a noted statistician and manufacturing consultant. In his book *Out of the Crisis*, Deming outlines 14 points for management. One of those points appears at the beginning of this chapter and has resonated with Greg his entire career.

Building quality into the product sounds clichéd and has been overused by many marketing departments. But in an agile environment, the concept is real and tangible. Consider the following.

In an agile environment, you get the tester in the room before programming begins. The tester and the whole team try to break the product's design before you start building. You do your best to understand the customer's core needs before

244

beginning production. When you do start production, you demonstrate frequently and try to prevent defects versus focusing on managing them.

Related to this point, you try to mistake-proof the development process. Consider, for example, two digital cameras that Ahmed owns. Both cameras have rechargeable batteries. One camera lets Ahmed put the battery in two different ways; the only way Ahmed can find out if he put it in correctly is to try to turn on the camera. The other camera has a battery that is shaped so it will go in only one way—it's impossible to put it in incorrectly. The manufacturer has made the process mistake-proof. In agile, you try to mistake-proof the process by integrating code continuously and automating testing devices. Advanced agile teams use Test Driven Development (TDD) to mistake-proof the process, writing code until the test passes.

To see how you can add agility to your testing process, let's look at how Acme has modified its approach to quality.

19.1 *Unit testing*

When Acme Media reviewed its existing processes, the company noted that the developers already did unit testing. They began doing unit testing after a history of passing nonworking code to the testers. As the development team learned more about agile testing, they realized their unit testing process could be improved.

Acme's existing unit testing process meant the developers reviewed the requirements and manually executed the code to see if it passed. *Passed* meant the developer didn't detect any code issues and that from their perspective the code functioned correctly.

This was a good improvement for Acme, because it reduced issues for the testers and increased their confidence in the code they received. This change also reduced issues with code integration and breaking the builds.

> **More resources**
>
> Numerous excellent resources can help you with unit testing. One of our favorites is *The Art of Unit Testing* by Roy Osherove. Roy focuses on three major principles: that a test should be maintainable, trustworthy, and readable.

But Acme still had some issues. When a tester encountered a bug, it still took time for the developer to find the issue. The developer would try to remember how they manually tested the code and then dig into the components to find the problem area.

In the last few weeks, Acme's development team has learned more about unit testing and how some teams create code to test the functions, procedures, and classes. To agile teams, unit tests mean testing scripts that exercise the code and log errors. If Acme follows this approach, it will gain additional benefits:

- Developers can get quicker feedback on code issues, making it much easier to identify and repair the code.
- The unit tests can be used during refactoring, to make sure improvements or changes to the code didn't break the existing work.

- The unit tests can be automated because they're actual code.
- The unit tests can be exercised by anyone on the team.
- The unit tests can be passed with the functional code during system integration and make the integration test more robust.
- This work will be foundational to using TDD, if the team chooses to do so in the future.

During agile training, Acme learned that some teams create their own unit testing system but that most teams use open source testing frameworks such as JUnit and NUnit. Acme decides to use the pilot project as an opportunity to create true unit test scripts. The Auctionator is an enhancement to the existing classifieds functionality, which uses .Net technology; so one of the developers, Matt Lee, downloaded the product during iteration 0 and started to get a feel for the tool (see listing 19.1).

Matt will find out if creating unit tests provides the same benefits to Acme that he learned about during training. He will write the tests after he creates the code, as opposed to writing them in advance. As Matt becomes more familiar with unit tests, he'll increase his ability to use TDD in the future.

19.2   *Integration testing*

Acme Media is relatively happy with its existing integration process. All of the integration tests are automated, and the team revisits the tests after every project/release. Tests are added to exercise new functionality and removed for features that are no longer used. The team also puts a lot of thought into identifying tested module interaction across the system.

After agile training, Acme identified a few weaknesses that it wanted to improve. In the past, the team performed an integration build based on the capacity of the QA team. At the start of a project, QA estimated how many features they could test at a given time and requested project builds based on that capacity. The issue with this process was that the team might go as long as a week before integrating their code and a subsequent integration test. Several issues were usually uncovered during the build, and it took a while to trace the root issues.

Acme learned about continuous integration during agile training and understands the value. Because the team is used to going 5 days before integrating, integrating daily will be a big cultural shift. They also learned that another issue was concealed by the fact that they built every 5 days: there was almost no automation of the build process. A build took from 4 to 6 hours and pulled a developer away from their work.

Acme decided on a twofold attack on the integration issue. First, they will go to more frequent builds, building every Tuesday and Thursday. Second, they will work on increasing the automation of the build process. The team knows some places where automation can be added, and they pursued those changes during iteration 0.

The last change relates to unit testing. Matt Lee plans to pass his unit tests along with his code during the builds. The QA team needs to make sure they have a process in place to exercise the test code that Matt sends across.

19.3 *Functional testing*

Related to integration testing, historically Acme Media tested features in groups every 5 days. The QA team met with the development team and saw what features would be delivered in the forthcoming build. They then pulled the functional specifications and began documenting test cases and scripts. This approach had two issues.

First, features weren't delivered by priority—they were delivered by how quickly they were completed. The first build for the project might be limited to low-priority features. This issue was resolved by Acme's new iterative planning process: the first iteration now contains the most critical features, and subsequent iterations contain the next-highest-priority work.

The second issue was acclimation. In the past, the QA team was almost viewed as a group outside of development. The first time they saw the features was after the functional requirements were complete. In Acme's new agile model, the tester is in the room during the feature-card exercise and during feature modeling. The tester can bring up risks before the coding begins. In a way, this is early testing; you might even call it *design* testing. The tester can influence how the feature is created and so reduce the chance of bugs or issues with nonfunctional requirements, such as performance or up time.

Acme's QA team began creating test cases during iteration 0 and will continue to do so until the last iteration is complete. Test cases are created in the order they will be delivered in the iterations, with the highest-priority features' test cases created first. See figures 19.1 and 19.2.

Acme performs functional testing as soon as a build is integrated. The team refers to the integration build as a *build verification test* (BVT). If the code passes the rudimentary tests, then it's in good enough shape to begin functional testing.

In a perfect world, functional testing for each iteration would be complete at the end of the iteration. In reality, a few features usually still need to be tested, and testing for those can be wrapped up during the adapt week between iterations.

Step	Description	Expected Result
Step 1	Login to the portal as the valid user.	User should be able to login to the portal.
Step 2	Verify the presence of custom global navigation header UI ribbons.	Global navigation header should consist of following UI ribbons: 1. Admin 2. Navigation 3. Search
Step 3	Login to the portal as the valid user.	User should be able to login to the portal.
Step 4	Verify the presence of global navigation header links. [Note: Navigation ribbon should be left aligned relative to the display settings.]	Navigation ribbon should consist of the following links: i) Search ii) Help iii) My Auctions

Figure 19.1 The complexity and criticality of your application determine how detailed and formal your testing needs to be. In this instance, the team has gone formal, documenting the expected results in detail.

View Topic

1. You are now viewing your selected topic. From here, you will be able to see and do:

    a. The logout navigation will be in the upper-right corner of this page.
    b. In the upper-left corner is a link back to the forum you came from along with the current topic title.
    c. You can post a new topic by clicking the 'New topic' buttons.
    d. The posts window shows the author and the message for each post. The author consists of the user's real name, the total number of posts they have made, and their location (city and state). The message contains an optional title, post date and the message itself.
    e. You can reply to the topic by clicking the 'Post reply' buttons.
    f. You can reply to a specific post in the topic by clicking the 'Reply' button next to the desired message post.
    g. At the bottom of the posts table is an option menu for date-limiting the posts displayed.
    h. At the bottom of the page is a link to watch this topic for replies. By clicking this link, an e-mail will be sent to you when someone replies to this post. If this is turned on, the link will change so that you can click it again to turn it off.
    i. If this topic had a poll that you had not voted on, you would be given then option to vote. If you had voted, it would show you the poll results.
    j. **Administrators can also delete, move, lock (and unlock), or split the topic from this page. They can also edit or delete a specific post.**
2. Click the 'Reply' button next to a post.

Figure 19.2   In this instance, the team didn't need a formal test case, and they listed the test case in terms of a user scenario.

Note that user-acceptance testing and nonfunctional testing are covered in chapter 21.

19.4   *Exploratory testing*

As we've mentioned throughout the book, Acme Media has a unique practice: a company-wide bug stomp. In many circles, this is known as *exploratory* testing. Exploratory testing is different than functional testing. Functional testing tries to make sure the software does what it's supposed to. Exploratory testing tries to make sure the software doesn't accidentally do things it isn't supposed to do.

For example, a few years ago Ahmed worked on a team that created an application, tested it internally, and then invited users from outside the company to test it. The application was supposed to be functional without any online help or training for the user. In this instance, the user was creating a new event listing: for example, information about a concert, such as the artist, the location, and the date and time. For the test, users were told the application was for entering event information and to create a fake event record. No other instructions were given.

All the users began entering records, and nine out of ten had a consistent issue: they couldn't enter the event date in a format the application would accept. Every user had to try to enter the date several times before the system accepted the record.

Ahmed's team researched the issue and uncovered the root cause. The company standard for entering dates was mm/dd/yyyy. All the developers knew this, and so did all the testers. Internally, no one had to *think* when entering a date—they knew the correct format to use. But externally, real users didn't know the standard, and they all had different experiences for entering system dates. Because the user group had no preconceived notions, they were able to expose this usability issue (see figure 19.3).

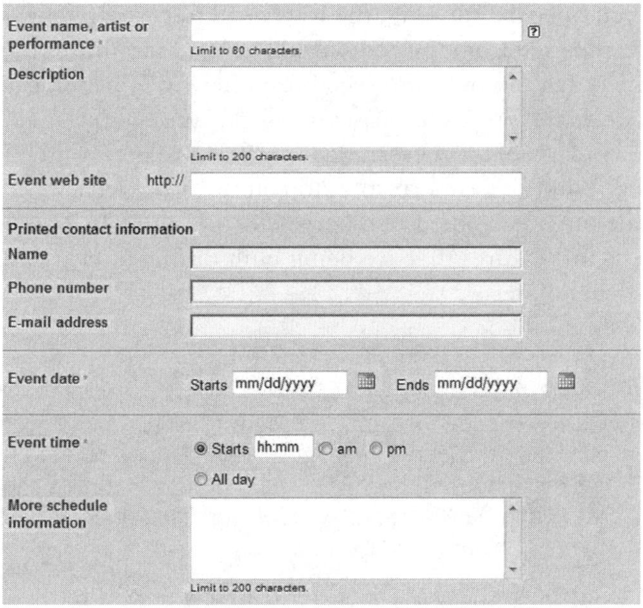

Event name, artist or performance
Limit to 80 characters.
Description
Limit to 200 characters.
Event web site
http://
Printed contact information
Name
Phone number
E-mail address
Event date
Starts mm/dd/yyyy
Ends mm/dd/yyyy
Event time
Starts hh:mm
am
pm
All day
More schedule information
Limit to 200 characters.

Figure 19.3 A usability issue is resolved by providing a format for the user in the date field.

Usability testing is great for finding issues that may be blind spots for your team. If you've been living with a feature since idea conception—which is true in an agile environment—you may not be able to objectively scrutinize the application.

We can see an example of this at Acme Media. Acme Media decided to send the Auctionator out for usability testing. Figure 19.4 indicates how organized the Auctionator site was, as viewed by actual end users. The Acme Media team had grown used to the site and knew how to navigate to all the features. End users still saw areas to improve, with 30 percent of the sample saying the site was at least somewhat disorganized.

How organized is the site?
50%
25%
0%
21%
49%
23%
6%
1%
Very organized
Organized
Somewhat organized, somewhat disorganized
Disorganized
Not organized at all

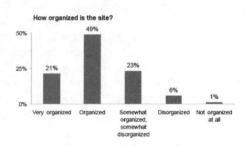

Figure 19.4 Your team may be blind to how the system is viewed by users. Usability testing reveals what the end-user experience is like.

We highly suggest that you use some method of exploratory testing before releasing your product to the public.

19.5 Test automation

As we discussed in the introduction of this chapter, you want to prevent defects if possible; and if you can't prevent defects, you want to find them as early as possible to ensure that your code is always in a deliverable state. To support this objective, let's look at test automation.

Test automation is a widely discussed subject. The main question is always, "Does the time I take to automate the tests provide return?" Many people find that automation is tedious to set up and that once it's running, the tests need to be frequently changed, especially if the tests are separate from the code. You'll need to scrutinize your specific situation, and your agile coach can help you recognize where automation can help.

In our experience, we've followed a few basic tenets on automation.

First, automation is a great tool for regressing code. If you're performing build verification tests with every build, it's superb to automate tests for legacy code that is already in place, to make sure new code doesn't break the old code. In a perfect world you could automate tests for features that are being built during a release, once they have successfully passed all unit tests.

Automation to save money

Greg recently worked with a company that used offshore testing. The company outsourced testing to a vendor that provided two onshore test leads and up to eight offshore workers to support the actual testing. The onshore leads were in the room during feature-card creation and had direct interaction with the customer. The onshore leads also performed the build-verification tests.

The company encountered tough financial times, like many companies today, and decided to reduce its testing expense by eliminating one of the onshore leads. The development team knew how critical it was for the tester to be involved in feature creation, but they realized QA interaction would be compromised now that there was only one lead.

The team investigated automating the build-verification test to a point that it could be run by the offshore testers, thereby leaving the onshore lead free to work with the team during feature-card creation. After weeks of piloting and trying various tools, the onshore QA lead was able to automate 95 percent of the build tests, and the offshore team took over running them every night. QA still wasn't able to attend every feature discussion, but the loss of one test lead was minimized by automating the build test and passing it to the offshore team.

Our main belief is that you should get return on automation, and it may not make sense to automate every test. Acme Media has developed a practice of enhancing its automated build-verification scripts at the conclusion of every release. A sampling of representative scripts is added to the build test to make sure features in the new release didn't break existing features that were certified in the previous release. The scripts that are automated meet the following criteria:

- The thread selected is a good test of the overall feature.
- The test can be automated. The sequence is consistent, so that it can be automated.
- Automation doesn't change the behavior of the software. Many times, automation tools can't emulate true user interaction.

Acme Media is happy with its process for updating the build test at the end of each release, but during the team's next pilot they will test the ability to continuously enhance the automated build test *during* the release. This will be another step toward agility and will also provide more time for the QA team to do exploratory testing. (See an example automation tool in figure 19.5.)

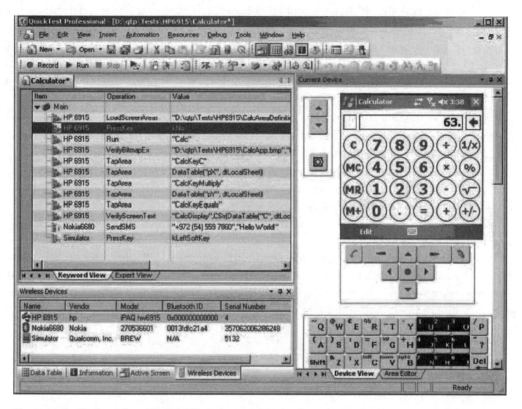

Figure 19.5   Tools such as HP QuickTest can make test automation easier.

Our last point related to automation is that you need to have a consistent environment, consistent configuration, and consistent test data to support automated scripts. You should create a process that lets you reset your test environment to a known configuration before testing begins.

19.6   Key points

The key points from this chapter are as follows:

- Do your best to create a process that minimizes the ability to create defects.
- Testing should begin as early as possible to minimize the impact a defect can have downstream.
- A defect is harder to find if it's been in the code for several builds.

- In a perfect world, you'd create unit tests before development starts. This is a great goal, but it's a reach for teams just becoming agile.

- If you can't create unit tests first, at least consider automating them after they're complete. Automation will help with refactoring and regressing the code with each build.

- You should have a goal to build every day, but move toward this goal in small steps. Give your team time to acclimate to a more frequent build process.

- Just as you select which processes to use during a project, you must decide how much testing is needed. Some applications, such as medical software, require more stringent testing, whereas less-critical applications, such as checking out a book from a library, may not require as much testing.

- Testing usually doesn't conclude at the end of an iteration. Usually a few items are still open that must be resolved. You need to close these items or clearly document them before pursuing user acceptance of code.

- Functional testing tells you whether the code supports the requirements. Exploratory testing tells you if the code accidentally supports a bad scenario or has other issues if not used as designed.

19.7   *Looking forward*

When you complete development and testing, you'll be ready to demonstrate the completed work to your customer. During the demonstrations, you'll make discoveries, and you'll need to adapt accordingly. In chapter 20, we'll discuss adapting during and at the conclusion of an iteration.

Embracing change

General Dwight D. Eisenhower said, "The plan is useless; it's the planning that is important." Eisenhower knew that you could plan all that you wanted to, but something could and would still go wrong. It was more important to be able to react and re-plan than it was to lay out the initial plan.

This is not to say we do not create an initial plan in an agile environment, but to say we understand that all possible scenarios cannot be anticipated and we must have a process that allows us to triage issues and recover. We cannot lament how the original plan did not work, but instead we must be able to re-plan and continue to pursue success.

In the following three chapters we will discuss adapting to change, learning as we go, and ensuring successful delivery of our project along the way.

Adapting: reacting positively to change

So far, every chapter in this book has emphasized being agile and adapting to change. Acme Media adapted to a revised product vision during feasibility and reacted to feature discoveries during planning. In this chapter, we'll discuss how to react and adjust to information you discover during development iterations.

No matter what methodology you use, you'll always have to deal with issues and challenges during development. Your advantage is that you're expecting change and you have tools and processes in place that support and embrace adaptation.

Managing changes and decisions during development is still a difficult feat. You're trying to stay on schedule, meet the customer's needs, and support nonfunctional requirements such as performance needs. Discoveries require diligent, collaborative decision making. You'll refine requirements, reprioritize the work, and re-plan based on what you encounter.

Teams that are new to agile often have questions about the timing of adapting. Here are three common questions:

- *Can we adapt at any time?*   Yes, you can and do adapt at any time. We'll discuss this in detail in section 20.2.

- *If we adapt all the time, how do we get any work done?*   This is a superb question. Many anti-agile folks want to know how we get any work done if we spend all our time talking about it instead of doing it. That is a fair question. The answer is that there is a fine line between work labeled *adapting* and work labeled *development*. Are you adapting when you're stuck on a technical constraint and you're Googling for a workaround? Are you performing development when you refine requirements with a customer or analyst? At the end of the day, it's all work that supports delivering the correct solution to the customer. This will be demonstrated in sections 20.2 and 20.3.

- *How do we adapt at the end of an iteration?*   We'll cover this question in section 20.3. Acme Media will demonstrate a solid process for gathering feedback at the end of an iteration and recalibrating the project based on the customer response.

Let's start by discussing common reasons for adapting.

20.1   Common reasons for adapting

When you need to adapt, you go back to one of the agile core principles: *How can you deliver the most important features early?* You still want to hit iteration delivery dates, and you still want to hit your deployment dates, but your main goal is to deliver value as soon as you can within the reality of your constraints. The common reasons for adapting are illustrated in figure 20.1.

Figure 20.1   Adapting occurs throughout an iteration and following an iteration review by the customer.

Here are some common issues that come up during development and some of the ways we've seen teams adapt to them.

20.1.1   Feature is larger than expected

Frequently a feature will surprise you when you start developing it. The code takes longer than expected, or you underestimated complexity. We also see this when teams are working with an off-the-shelf application. Sometimes the software provider promises functionality that isn't quite there, and you have to figure out how to close the gap. Here are some of the ways we've seen teams adapt to feature overrun:

- *Work with the customer to prioritize the functionality in the feature and potentially reduce the scope.*   Try to deliver the highest-priority functionality within the iteration schedule.

- *Accept the discovery and continue the work into the next iteration.* Try to demonstrate the state of the feature at the end of the iteration if possible, with a test harness or limited user interface.
- *Cancel the feature, and re-evaluate the feasibility of the project.* If a feature is too large, the cost may exceed the benefit, and the feature shouldn't be pursued. But if a critical feature is cancelled, the value of the project may be lost. The team needs to reassess the project's viability.

Another reason a feature could grow is that a customer begins to understand their needs more and they need to refine their requirements. Let's look at this issue in more detail.

20.1.2 *Customer refinement of requirements*

This may be the most frequent reason to adapt. Similar to our bathroom-remodel example in chapter 9, you frequently don't know what you want until you see it. On occasion, we've worked with teams that fought the customer during refinement discussions. Because a refinement request could make the project run longer, these teams worked hard to talk the customer out of the request.

An agile team takes a different approach. You want to be good listeners and make sure you understand the request. If the request will have an impact on your capacity, you can adapt:

- *Revisit the entire scope of the feature.* Can other parts of the feature be sacrificed for the refinement request?
- *Delay other work.* Explain the impact to the customer, and show them how other work may be delayed or pushed into subsequent iterations.

When you kicked off your project, the customer provided their priorities in the tradeoff matrix (schedule versus resources versus costs, and so on). You can use this matrix to help the customer decide how to react to the change in requirements and how to best triage the discovery.

20.1.3 *The business need changes*

The world doesn't care about your project and goals. Frequently, the playing field will reset during your project. Imagine what would happen if Craigslist decided to start offering free auctions while Acme Media was building the Auctionator. How would Acme Media adapt to this mid-project? Would the company cancel the project or identify a feature that would still separate it from the competitor?

Another example that comes to mind is desktop search functionality. Many people started using Google's desktop search utility a few years ago. The utility was superb and free. It was a great marketing tool for the Google brand. We're confident the folks at Microsoft cringed at seeing Google invade their world and be successful. We believe desktop search was a medium-priority feature at Microsoft, with no urgency to get it to market. Google changed all that with its success; 2 months later, Microsoft released its own desktop search utility. We believe Microsoft adapted to the change in the competitive climate and reprioritized the feature midstream, moving it up to an earlier iteration/release.

Here are some ways we see teams adapt to a change in the business climate:

- Reprioritize features, just like Microsoft did.
- Add a new feature.
- Cancel a feature. Sometimes a feature loses its value during a project.

In drastic situations, you may find that the need changes enough to cancel the entire project.

20.1.4 *A technical constraint is discovered*

This issue is related to a feature being larger than expected. How many times have you encountered a technical issue during a project? Perhaps a better question is, how many times have you *not* encountered a technical issue?

We've seen issues with performance, browser compatibility, security, and product compatibility. The list of issues you can encounter is infinite.

Here are some ways you can resolve technical constraints:

- Speak to software vendors for guidance.
- Look at blogs and internet postings where others have solved the issue.
- Research other technology options.
- Have a discussion with the experts within your company who may be able to help.

If the issue can't be resolved within the iteration, you can

- Ask the customer if you can remove the feature from the project.
- If the feature is of a critical or high priority, discuss extending the work into the next iteration.
- Delay the feature for another iteration.
- Remove the functionality from the requirement that leads to the technical constraint.

As we mentioned in chapter 18, dealing with technical constraints is a common part of the development process.

20.1.5 *A team member is unavailable*

What do you do if a team member becomes unavailable during an iteration? What if they're sick, or they have to address a production issue? If you lose a team member, is the iteration in jeopardy?

If a team member misses a day or two, the team can frequently keep the iteration intact. Other team members may be able to take on some of the work, or the work may get reprioritized to work around the missing team member.

In a worst-case situation, an iteration may have to be stopped and restarted when resources can re-engage. We've seen this happen for serious production issues, where the majority of the team was tied up for days when a server or database went down.

20.1.6 *A third party doesn't deliver*

As you may recall from chapter 16, third parties are the highest-risk area for any project. If you have an issue internally, you can triage however you like; but if you have an issue with a third party, you have limited control.

Note that *third party* means any group outside your project team. You may have little influence on groups that support your project. This is common in large companies where individual groups control areas such as data centers, load balancers, system monitoring, or shared infrastructure such as virtual machine environments.

Your focus should be to work with third parties as early as possible to give you the most time to resolve issues. But what do you do if they still don't deliver?

One option is to do the work yourself. Does the third party provide a service that you can't perform or choose not to because it isn't a core competency? A few years ago, Greg worked with a team that created an online advertisement site for travel businesses. If you were a hotel, you could create your own website and advertise in a major online travel directory. The team Greg worked with decided to outsource the application because they didn't want to make a heavy technology investment. The travel directory was a beta test for future directory models, and they didn't want to create code that had potential for being disposed. But after the project started, the vendor came up short on critical requirements such as integration with the existing user-registration application. Greg's team was halfway through iteration 1 when they made a decision to release the vendor and develop the travel directory in house.

20.1.7 *Team throughput is lower than expected*

We've discussed story points and how you can use them to determine your capacity for an iteration. Even though your capacity estimate is based on real work, sometimes you'll underestimate the time needed to complete an iteration. This isn't an exception. Your velocity will fluctuate with each iteration. Over time, you'll have more consistency, and your estimates will become more accurate; but there will always be iterations that exceed or beat your estimate.

For example, say you average 30 story points per iteration but only complete 20 in a particular iteration. A few features are in a partial status or not started. What are your options?

You're fighting two agile goals when you can't complete all the work in an iteration. First, you're trying to deliver the minimal level of functionality needed to support a release. If you don't complete all features, you probably don't have a releasable product.

Second, you want to demonstrate status to customers and stakeholders at the end of an iteration. That is difficult to do when features are incomplete.

Here are three common strategies we see teams use when the work isn't complete by the target date:

- *Continue the incomplete features into the next iteration.* When you do this, you should still demonstrate status of the incomplete work. You need to have a feel for the work remaining so you can estimate it for the next iteration. You should also get feedback from the customer. Anything you can demonstrate will help you with this goal. Teams frequently create temporary user interfaces or test harnesses to demonstrate status on incomplete features.

- *Stretch the iteration.* As a rule of thumb, this isn't a good practice. The team will give less respect to the deadline if it can always be stretched. But if this is your last iteration, you must stretch the iteration or reach agreement on leaving out features or pieces of their functionality.

- *Remove the feature(s), or deliver them in a partial state.* This is frequently a customer and team decision. The team outlines the repercussions for removing or partial delivery, and the customer makes the call about what they want to do. Partial delivery is usually an iffy proposition. If a feature is incomplete, it will probably need some level of cleanup to be usable.

You may also wonder about determining capacity for the forthcoming iteration. If you underestimate this iteration, what stops you from underestimating the next?

Because your capacity estimate is based on real work, this release should be an anomaly. The team will discuss this during the adapt week and see if a resource change or other area has affected the accuracy of the running capacity estimate. At a minimum, this low throughput iteration will be averaged into the existing capacity algorithm, and your estimate for the next iteration will be lower.

20.2   *Adapting during an iteration*

We've seen two schools of thought about adapting during an iteration. One viewpoint is that you can adapt for technical issues, but you don't want a lot of customer interaction during the iteration because the customer will get confused by seeing a partial product and won't provide valuable input. Teams that take this approach also like to provide a level of isolation for the development team. The developers are given a 2-week timeline to deliver a working product. The team feels that if the developers have frequent customer interaction, they will lose momentum and miss the deadline.

The second school of thought is that you embrace customer interaction in parallel with dealing with technical issues. You demonstrate your work during the iteration, ask the customer clarifying questions, and try to deliver the iteration on schedule.

Which method is the best? If your customer is new to agile, you may be better off going with the first method and gathering customer feedback during the adapt week. You may also find that your development team is more productive if they can be isolated and allowed to focus on delivering code.

But if you stop and look at this approach, you may wonder if we're discussing an agile process or a waterfall approach broken into iterations. If developers are isolated from the customer, how can you build the solution together? Your goal is to build the desired solution on time. Meeting the deadline provides no value if the result is not what the customer needs.

We have empathy for teams when the customer is too involved and hurts the process more than helps it. We've seen this on occasion, and we believe it's more about training the customer than the fact that the customer is involved.

Should you hide the developers?

On occasion, we've supported having a developer work from home when they needed uninterrupted focus. But over the last few years, we've seen developers adapt to a collaborative environment and learn how to get their privacy while sitting with the project team. Some developers put on headphones to isolate themselves, and others set their IM status to Busy.

We do a lot of interaction with developers by walking up and asking them if they have a moment to discuss a feature. In the old days, everyone was polite and said "Sure." These days they frequently ask if we can come back later because they're in the middle of solving something. We like this new attitude. Although no one likes to hear "No, I don't have time to speak with you," we like the fact that developers are performing self-management and looking out for the project.

It reminds Greg of a manager he worked with 10 years ago. On occasion, the manager got under a tight deadline and hung a sign on his cubicle entrance that read, "Unless my cubicle is on fire, don't disturb me!!" If you peeked inside his cube, you saw him with headphones on, hammering away on the keyboard.

As much as agile is about collaborating, there are times where you need to give the developers the privacy they need to bring home a solution.

We personally embrace customer involvement during an iteration. Just like the team, the customer needs to be trained on how to be collaborative and productive. You can achieve this over time.

20.3 *Three ways Acme Media adapted during its first iteration*

To illustrate adapting during an iteration, let's return to Acme Media. We'll start by looking at a request to modify the search feature.

20.3.1 *A change in feature scope*

As you may recall from chapter 16, Ryan, the designer, noticed that the customer, Jay, hadn't requested *the ability to filter searches by location.* After a quick discussion, Jay agrees that the filter is needed. Ryan feels the additional work can be completed with minimal effort and the feature doesn't need to be re-estimated. Ryan discusses the change with the project team, and everyone agrees that the additional work is minimal and can be easily added to their existing tasks.

20.3.2 An issue with performance

As you may recall from chapter 4, Acme Media had been burned by not performing load testing on features in the past. During iteration 1, Matt, the developer, identifies a potential load issue with the auction engine.

Matt and Jay, the customer, estimate that as many as 100 people can be bidding on an item concurrently. Matt uses the load-simulation tool to simulate concurrent bidding and notes that the server is maxing out at around 75 concurrent bidders.

Matt creates a queuing process for the bids to minimize the impact to the end user, but bids can take as long as 10 seconds to process when 100 people are bidding at the same time.

Matt researches various technical options and notes that he's doing little caching and that every request is going to disk. Matt finds that he can cache most of the bidding page, which reduces the peak response time to 5 seconds. Jay agrees to this performance level and doesn't think it will be a usability issue. Jay will be happy if they get as many as 100 people bidding at one time.

20.3.3 Underestimating the registration need

Acme Media wants to let potential buyers bid on items without creating an account. They can bid by providing their email address, and by design the Auctionator will encrypt their email address and store the bid. The encrypted email address will represent the bidder ID during the auction.

The issue is that the bidder has no idea what their encrypted ID is. If they view the bid list for an item, they can't tell if they're the highest bidder. They only see an encrypted string.

Matt discusses this issue with Jay. They think of two options:

- Email the bidder, and tell them their encrypted ID so they can recognize it.
- Require registration to perform bidding.

The first option will work, but even then it may be hard for the buyer to discern their encrypted bidding ID when viewing bid history.

The second option is more palatable. Requiring registration for users will make it easier to design the overall system and provide benefits to the user. The user won't have to submit their credentials for every bid if they're registered and logged in. Jay, the customer, agrees to this option, and the team pursues creating a system that requires registration for bidding.

20.4 Adapting at the end of an iteration

When an iteration ends, you focus on four areas:

- Demonstrating and gathering feedback
- Re-evaluating priorities
- Reviewing team performance and velocity
- Re-planning

Let's look at each of these in detail.

20.4.1 Demonstrating and gathering feedback

Demonstrations can take many forms. The most common forms are as follows:

- *Impromptu*—This type of demonstration usually happens during development. A developer or designer can show the customer working code, a proposed UI, or anything where feedback will help guide the team. We also see informal presentations between team members during a project. For example, developers can review early functionality with the team to discuss usability and performance.

- *Structured*—Greg was taught to use a more prearranged demonstration technique at the end of an iteration. This format works well when you have a short amount of time for review and you want to quickly gather feedback from many customers and stakeholders.

- *User Acceptance Testing (UAT)*—This technique is great for getting focused feedback from the customer. It also works well in a regulatory environment where formal approval is required.

Which technique is best at the end of an iteration? Similar to the menu you use at the start of a project, the team should make the call about the best way to demonstrate. Smaller teams and smaller projects can probably go informal throughout the project. As projects get larger and have more customers and stakeholders, it may be best to do formal demonstrations in conjunction with User Acceptance Testing.

Let's consider Acme Media's Auctionator project. The project has several stakeholders and one person playing the customer role. The project team is composed of nine people. We consider this a medium-size project.

When the Acme team reviews the project, they decide to present structured demonstrations and customer UAT at the end of the iterations, due to project size and the number of people affected. The entire team and stakeholders will participate in the formal 1-day review at the end of each iteration, and the analyst will lead a UAT session with the customer in subsequent days. You'll see this combination in action when Acme goes through the demonstration cycle in section 20.5.2.

20.4.2 Re-evaluating priorities: what are your options?

In a perfect world, you'd go through the demonstration cycle, and the customer would be 100 percent satisfied. In the real world, you'll see some of the following:

- The identification of issues, both functional and technical
- Requests to modify features in progress
- Requests for new features
- Requests to decrease the scope of features

Managing and prioritizing all this information is a cerebral process. How do you determine what is truly critical and what adds minimum value? What foundational information can you use to help triage? You need to go back to the tradeoff matrix that you created in chapter 11.

In Acme's case, the tradeoff matrix indicates that the schedule is fixed. The team must meet their project date. They have light flexibility with their resources and high flexibility with scope. They should focus on delivering the minimal amount of functionality needed to support the Auctionator. The date is critical, and they may enhance the functionality with a future project or release.

Reviewing priorities is critical to this triage process. The team needs a guiding light, or they may get lost in a sea of potential options for each issue. With date being the driving force, and knowing that adjusting resource levels won't help much at the end of an iteration, they need to focus on scope. What does the team have to deliver to go live with the project? What is the minimal set of functionality they must deliver?

Figure 20.2 illustrates this point.

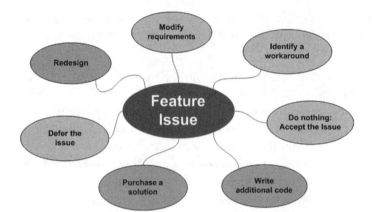

Figure 20.2   When you discover an issue, you have many options. The team uses their collaborative knowledge to choose the best solution.

You have many options as you review issues within your team. Some common options are as follows:

- *Modify the requirements.*   This may sound unusual, but if you encounter a constraint that can't be realistically overcome, the customer may change their requirements. This happens frequently when you're constrained by a commercial software package and you don't have the ability to modify it.

- *Identify a workaround.*   In many applications, you can accomplish an objective more than one way. For example, if you create a search engine and can't get the category functionality to work, the user may be able to perform a workaround by entering a category title with their search string.

- *Do nothing.*   You'll often do nothing when an issue is low priority, such as a barely noticeable cosmetic issue. There isn't enough value in pushing out the project to make a fix for a minor issue.

- *Write additional code.*   Sometimes you have to edit or create more code to meet basic need. This can be caused by identifying a missing critical requirement during demonstrations.

- *Purchase a solution.* In some cases, a missing requirement can't be easily supported in house. You may have to buy some functionality to support the requirement.
- *Defer the issue.* Deferring is different than doing nothing. Sometimes you'll defer an issue until you see how forthcoming features relate to it. A feature that is being delivered in subsequent iterations may remove the issue.
- *Redesign.* A requirement may change so completely that you can't use any of the work you completed during the iteration. You'll need to revisit the design and start coding from scratch. These types of changes are usually driven by a change in the business environment rather than the customer.

NOTE As you review these ways to adapt to change during development, you may be thinking, "I already do these." That makes sense; these are common ways to adapt regardless of whether you follow agile principles. What is unique is that you identify the issues much earlier than with classic techniques, and you highly involve the customer in the triage process.

Now, let's look at another aspect of adapting: analyzing team performance during the iteration.

20.4.3 Reviewing team performance and velocity

When you complete an iteration, you measure how many story points you've completed. As mentioned in chapter 14, you continually measure the number of story points you complete and add them into your running average. Your running average is the number you use to determine capacity for the next iteration you pursue. For this process to work, you must keep your iteration length consistent and the people on your team the same. If you lose or gain a team member, you should begin recalculating your run rate based on the team change.

Acme Media didn't have a running average for its first-ever iteration, but the team estimated their story points so they could initiate the averaging process.

20.4.4 Re-planning and reacting

After you finish gathering feedback and reviewing team performance, you review the existing plan for the next iteration and make appropriate changes. Your changes are based on discoveries during development, feedback and testing at the end of the iteration, team performance, and changes in the business climate. You may remove features previously assigned to the iteration or add new features based on your discoveries.

20.5 How Acme Media adapts during adapt week

In chapter 15, Acme Media decided on 2-week development iterations with 1 week for adapting between iterations. Acme decided on the 1-week interval to allow time for maintenance of the current production environment and to provide a window of time for feedback and User Acceptance Testing.

In this section, Acme will do the following:

- Review the work that was completed during the iteration
- Demonstrate the work and gather feedback on it
- Perform user acceptance testing on the work
- Review the identified issues
- Reprioritize the work based on their findings
- Re-estimate new features identified
- Review velocity and determine capacity
- Modify the iteration plan for iteration 2

Acme has outlined the following schedule for the adapt week:

- *Monday*—Team cleanup on features; complete testing
- *Tuesday*—Structured demonstration to customers, stakeholders, and the team at large
- *Wednesday/Thursday*—UAT with Jay
- *Thursday*—Review discoveries from UAT; review team velocity
- *Friday*—Review and re-plan; update plan for iteration 2

Let's rejoin Acme Media to see common of ways of adapting at the conclusion of an iteration.

20.5.1   *Reviewing the work completed*

Acme Media assigned features to iteration 1, as shown in figure 20.3.

Most of the features have been completely unit tested and are going through final testing in QA. The auction engine is running late, and the team needs to find out if it's in a state where it can be demonstrated to customers and stakeholders.

Matt the developer has just completed the final unit tests on the auction engine, and he's confident it will demonstrate all the functionality. The feature was delivered late because he had to make architectural changes to support caching. (Caching is required to support up to 100 concurrent bidders.)

A retrospective now?

In chapter 22, we'll discuss retrospectives/lessons-learned sessions that you can hold at the end of the project or between iterations. It's a good idea to perform a quick retrospective between iterations. These meetings are typically informal, and the team can quickly identify areas to improve before the next iteration kicks off. To take this even further, you may find that you need to stop during an iteration and review what is going on, especially when feature delivery is running late or when major process issues are being encountered.

FEATURES	Requirements	Functional	Code Written	Unit Tested	System Integration	Functional Testing	QA Testing	Customer Approval	Load Test	DR Code Release	Production Code Release	Notes/Comments
Iteration 1												
Ability to register on the site	✓	✓	✓	✓	✓	✓	✓	N/A				- Jay has approved the feature - Scope was expanded to include bidder registration - QA has executed all tests
Ability to place an item up for bid	✓	✓	✓	✓	✓				✓			- QA estimates one more day of testing
Ability to bid on an item	✓	✓	✓	✓	✓				✓			- QA estimates one more day of testing
Auction engine logic	✓	✓	✓	✓	✓							- Unit testing was completed today - QA still needs to test several scenarios, estimate needing 2 more days - Need a final load test
Search by category	✓	✓	✓	✓	✓	✓			✓			- QA estimates one more day of testing

Figure 20.3   The status of the work for iteration 1. Most of the features are going through their final tests, but the auction engine is running late. It isn't uncommon for a feature to run late during an iteration, even with daily management. The main question is whether you can demonstrate all the features.

The first day of the adapt week involves reviewing all the features to make sure they're in a demonstrable state. Acme Media has been integrating and stabilizing the code during the iteration, but it's hard to envision the entire system until all the features are complete.

20.5.2 *Demonstrating the work*

Acme Media dedicates half a day to presenting the iteration work to the customer, stakeholders, and anyone in the company who wants to see the how the project is going. Stakeholders include anyone with a vested interest in the project. (Typical stakeholders include executives, support organizations, investors, and technical partners such as analytics.)

Acme outlines a demonstration schedule during day 1 of their adapt week (see figure 20.4).

Acme creates a tentative schedule for the demonstrations so that stakeholders can choose when to come by if they aren't available for the entire day.

You should note two items when reviewing Acme's demonstration plan. First, the plan is somewhat formal and structured. Acme decided to go with a more structured demonstration because the project affected several areas. Second, this is a high-level

Start Time	Presenters	Topic	What to demo, what's exciting, what's the scope	Demo tools	Attendees: Customers/Stakeholders
9:00	Jay, Wendy	Iteration theme, our objectives for the iteration, overall status	Show competitor websites, discuss how we are going to get our customers back, discuss minimum functionality to get live quickly	Competitor sites, PowerPoint slides	Project team, CIO, Company President, Stakeholders, Support teams
10:00	Matt, Ryan	Ability to place an item up for bid	Item description options, image upload, activation, expiration	Code in SIT environment	Project team, CIO, Jay
10:30	Roy	Search for an auction	Simple search , using categories, maintaining categories, "sounds like" functionality	Code in SIT environment	Project team, CIO, Jay
11:00	Matt, Ryan	View and bid on an auction	Ties to search screen, entering a bid, winning bid screen, notification	Code in SIT environment	Project team, CIO, Jay
11:30	Roy	Registration integration	When registration is required, new screen for existing registration, session limits, relationship to cookies	Code in SIT environment, Graphic that compares new registration process to the existing one.	Project team, CIO, Jay
12:00	Matt	Auction engine logic	Auction tracking, performance, discuss potentially purchasing this functionality in the future	Code in SIT environment	Project team, CIO, Jay
12:30	Gina, Matt	Stability of the features	Outstanding issues, test coverage, performance results	Bug tracker reports, demo bugs	Project team, CIO, Jay

Figure 20.4   Acme Media demonstrates the iteration features during the team's demo day. The demonstration synchronizes the company on the current state of the project and provides an opportunity for feedback. The entire team participates in the demonstration, with developers, designers, project managers, and testers describing status from their perspective.

demonstration for stakeholders and customers. The team will perform a more detailed demonstration when they perform UAT with the customer, Jay.

One agile principle states, *as complexity increases, the project will require higher levels of ceremony.* If the Auctionator project was smaller, the demonstration process could be informal and include the UAT at the same time.

Demonstration day is a special time for a project team. The team knows their work is valuable because people want to see it and ask questions about it. The demonstration also adds transparency to feature status. True status is evident to everyone.

20.5.3 *Personality types and demonstrations*

In the early days of software development, the only people who spoke in front of customers were managers and leads. Everyone else was a worker bee and did their job silently back at their desk. Because these team members didn't do presentations, management usually worked with leads if they had feature questions.

In the last few years, we've seen a change in this area. More and more worker bees enjoy talking about their work and presenting to the team at large. This bodes well for a collaborative environment. High interaction is required and desired in a high-performance agile team.

But sometimes a reclusive worker really doesn't want to present. We've seen these folks forced to present, and they stutter, sweat, and stumble through their presentations. Such individuals may become physically ill when asked to present. What do you do if you're trying to become agile and a team member isn't cut out for high social interaction?

You can work around a team member who doesn't want to present. Another person who worked on the feature can present the feature, or two people can co-present. Another team member can lead the discussion, and they can both respond to questions. Co-presenting frequently works well for people who dread public speaking—it takes the pressure off them to lead the discussion, but they can still contribute value.

20.5.4 Demonstrating incomplete features

There are two types of incomplete features: planned and unplanned. In a planned scenario, you start the iteration knowing that you aren't going to complete a feature but that you'll take the feature to a certain state. For example, Greg once worked with a team that was creating a dynamic organizational-chart feature for their intranet. The team released new software every 7 weeks, and they didn't think it was possible to deliver a solid product within that window of time. The team broke the feature into three subfeatures that they delivered across three releases. In the first release, they created mockups and performed usability testing. In the second release, they delivered the product to the production environment. In the third release, they did refactoring based on what they learned in the production environment. This refactoring work included creating a web service to distribute the load across more servers and improve the performance of the feature.

In the unplanned scenario, you don't complete your work by the end of the iteration date and the feature isn't in a demonstrable state. What can you do? Here are some options we've seen teams use:

- *If the feature infrastructure is complete but the interface is missing, create a test harness to exercise the feature's inputs and outputs.*   A test harness can demonstrate the status of the feature and verify that the coded logic is working correctly. There is a good chance you can use existing unit tests to demonstrate the feature to the customer.

- *If the UI is complete, present it to the customer and simulate the fields being populated.*   This demonstration can help identify usability issues.

- *Demonstrate in the development or system integration environment.*   You may not consider a feature complete until it's tested in a user acceptance environment, but you can still use other environments to demonstrate and obtain feedback.

Acme Media uses the last option with the auction engine feature. The feature isn't built into the user acceptance environment when the demonstrations begin. Acme demonstrates the feature from the system integration test (SIT) environment while they build to the user acceptance environment.

The most important thing to remember is that you need to demonstrate, period. It's easy to fall into a behavior where you never demonstrate features unless they're complete. You may worry that the customer can't comprehend an incomplete feature and will only ask questions about the missing components: if you take this approach, you may erode sponsor and customer support. Everyone needs to see that you're making progress toward delivery.

20.6   *User Acceptance Testing*

Acme Media chooses to do more detailed demonstrations with the customer after the public demonstration. The additional testing allows the customer to ask more detailed questions and try the features hands on. The testing is another validation of feature completeness.

When smaller project teams perform UAT, the whole team participates. Everyone can hear the customer's feedback and questions. This is the ultimate way to perform the testing so you keep everyone on the project synchronized on the state of the system and issues the customer may be encountering or the discovery of new requirements.

As projects increase in size, it becomes more difficult to have everyone participate in the testing. Team members may be pulled away for production issues; and it can be hard to coordinate the testing with a large group in the room, even in a large team room.

What Acme does—and what we've seen many larger teams do successfully—is have an analyst lead the UAT. The analyst leads the customer through testing all the features and includes the team members who worked on each feature. For example, the Auctionator has one analyst assigned to it: Rich Jenkins. Rich spends 2 days going over the features with Jay as Jay tests them. As they test each feature, Rich invites the team members who worked on the feature to join them; this usually includes the designer and the developer.

Although not everyone is required to attend UAT, the meeting is an open invitation to everyone on the team. The acceptance testing is performed in an open area adjacent to the team, and everyone is welcome to stop by and listen in on the testing discussion.

20.6.1   *Acme Media's UAT approach*

Some teams treat UAT as a free-for-all. These teams turn the customer loose and let them do whatever they like with the system in whatever sequence they desire. Other teams are more formal with UAT and go through the features one by one to verify functionality.

Acme Media chooses a hybrid model. Rich leads Jay through testing and analysis of each feature, but then he turns Jay loose on the system to look at any area he desires.

On some features, such as the *auction engine*, Rich also uses a light functional specification to help with the testing.

20.6.2   *Output from Acme Media's UAT*

Acme schedules 2 days for UAT, but the team wraps up their work with Jay after a day and a half. The issues shown in figure 20.5 are recorded at the end of the session.

Acme Media identifies several potential issues but nothing that prevents the iteration from being releasable. Issue 2 could be a distracting user experience, but the system is functional and Acme can put text on the posting screen that tells sellers it takes 10 minutes for items to display.

	Discovery	Discussion	Resolution
1	Lost the ability to "buy now"	The existing merchandise site supported immediate purchases, the new auction site does not.	Create an enhancement request in the product backlog. Pursue in a future project/release.
2	Search engine is refreshing too slowly	It takes as long as 10 minutes for a posted item to show up in search results.	Roy thinks he can make a change to the search crawl configuration setting to resolve this issue. The work will be a potential feature for iteration # 2.
3	There is no limit on photo size	Large photos can take a long time to load and take up storage space.	We will do nothing for this release. We will see how many people load images that are greater than one meg after we go live. We may put in a size limit in the future.
4	The search results page displays merchant advertisements when there are no search results	Advertisements are rendering down the right side of the results page, and the rest of the page is empty.	Jay will review this issue with some of our prominent advertisers to see if they consider it an issue. We will not make a change at this time.
5	User Registration does not work with cookies disabled	Our registration design requires cookies to be enabled. Approximately 10% of our existing customers have them disabled.	Our research shows that our competitors are using the same cookie technique and it has not hurt their volume. We will leave registration as is.

Figure 20.5 Acme Media identifies five issues during UAT. The team doesn't identify any showstoppers for the iteration, but they do identify areas that require additional research and potential features for iteration 2.

Acme will also consider resolving the search-engine issue in iteration 2. The issue is a potential feature for iteration 2 because they haven't yet compared it to the other priorities for the iteration.

Team agility comes into play in the way the team manages issues during an iteration. The team uses their experience to determine whether an issue can be fixed quickly and immediately or if the scope of the work is large enough to qualify as a new feature that should be pursued in a subsequent iteration. In the instance of issue 2, Roy thinks the work and research may take a day or so, and he asks that the work be treated as a new feature.

20.7 *Changes in the business climate*

One of the things we tout in an agile environment is delivering the project needed at the end, not necessarily what was requested at the beginning. If the business climate changes during your project, you react and adapt.

Acme encounters a small change in business climate during iteration 1. One of their competitors, Craigslist, decides to allow merchants to post their own auctions. The merchants can label their auctions as being from a dealer, and they could also list business information in the auction.

Acme Media has to decide whether this change lowers the attractiveness of the advertisement space they're going to offer merchants. Will a merchant still pay for a contextual advertisement if they can post auctions for free on Craigslist?

Jay, the product manager, does a few hours of research on the change and notes the following:

- Craigslist merchant auctions will be more attractive to mom-and-pop businesses. These types of businesses don't have a budget to buy contextual advertising, so there should be no effect on Acme's business plan.

- Merchants can still post auctions on Acme's auction system. The only difference is that the auction won't have an attribute that labels it as being from a dealer. A user can't limit a search to dealer auctions.

- Merchants can still list their business information in the description field on Acme's auctions.

Jay concludes that the impact is minimal and the team should stick with the same business plan and feature set.

20.8 Reviewing the findings and revising the plan for the next iteration

Acme is ready to plan for iteration 2 when UAT is complete. Re-planning requires Acme to review the following information:

- *Team velocity*—How many story points did they complete? How many can they expect to complete in iteration 2?

- *Demonstration feedback*—Did the demonstration identify any new work?

- *UAT*—Did Jay identify anything that needs to be addressed in iteration 2?

- *Features originally slated for iteration 2 at the start of the project*—Are these features still valuable based on what the team learned during iteration 1?

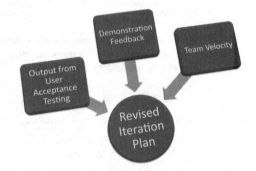

Figure 20.6   After you complete your first iteration, you use discoveries and evaluation of team velocity to adjust your plan for iteration 2.

These variables are shown in figure 20.6.

Let's take a moment to look at each variable.

20.8.1 Evaluating team velocity

Acme estimated that the features for iteration 1 were worth 19 story points. Table 20.1 shows the estimates for each feature.

Feature	Story points
Register on the site	3
Place an item up for bid	3
Bid on an item	3
Auction engine	8
Search by category	2
Total	**19**

Table 20.1   Acme Media measures actual velocity for the first time by seeing how many features were completed in iteration 1.

The team completed all the features in iteration 1, so they can say they average 19 story points per 2-week iteration with the current project team. Based on this real-world throughput number, Acme says their capacity for iteration 2 is 19 story points.

Acme's capacity estimate for iteration 2 is based on a low sample rate—only one iteration—which marginalizes the reliability of the estimate. The capacity estimate will become more reliable over time as Acme delivers more iterations and the capacity estimate reflects an average.

What would have happened if the team hadn't completed all the features in iteration 1? For example, what if the search feature needed additional work? Would the team include only a portion of the story points toward the completion total? There isn't a blanket rule for how to approach this issue, but we suggest the following:

- If a feature runs longer than expected due to additional scope, and the original scope is complete, record the story points in the completion number.
- If the feature stayed closer to the original scope/vision, and it isn't complete, then don't record the story points in the completion sum.

Agile is all about adapting, and there is fine line in saying *original scope*, but you do have to consider the scope you envisioned when you created your original estimates.

20.8.2 *New work identified during the iteration*

Acme identifies one new feature that it wants to pursue in iteration 2: an issue with search crawling. Because this feature is new, the team doesn't have an estimate for it, so they review it as a group against the criteria they used to estimate the other features. As you may recall from chapter 8, Acme used a story-point model to estimate features. A feature represents 1, 2, 3, 5, or 8 story points.

Roy, the developer, looks at the potential feature during customer UAT and thinks the work will be easy but will take a day or so to perform. When Roy reviews other features for the iteration, he thinks the search-crawl work is a little easier than the search-by-category work. Searching by category is rated at 2 story points, so Roy suggests that the crawl work be rated at 1 story point. The team agrees with Roy, and the feature will be reviewed with other open features to see if it will make it into iteration 2.

20.8.3 *Features originally slated for iteration 2*

Acme outlined an overall release plan before they began working on the features. The original plan called for two iterations, with the minimal feature set needed to go live in iteration 1 and secondary priority features in iteration 2. You can see features originally slated for iteration 2 in table 20.2.

Feature name (ability to)	Story points
Purchase an item immediately	2
Flag problem postings	2

Table 20.2   The initial plan for iteration 2, before the discoveries from iteration 1

Feature name (ability to)	Story points
Contact the seller	3
Create alerts for item type	3
Receive help online	5
Record seller feedback	5
View seller information	2
Total	**22**

Table 20.2   The initial plan for iteration 2, before the discoveries from iteration 1 *(continued)*

You'll notice that we say *originally slated*. These features were considered valuable to the system before Acme started. Now the team needs to re-evaluate the features against three criteria:

- Are these features still valuable based on what the team learned during iteration 1?
- Are these features the same priority as new work discovered during the demonstrations?
- Will these features fit into the story-point capacity for the iteration?

Acme's project team reviews the features after the demonstrations. Jay, the customer, feels that all the features are still valuable. The goals of the project haven't changed significantly during iteration 1, and Jay doesn't see a reason to pull any of the features from the original iteration 2 plan.

Acme also identified one new feature during the iteration: they need to do some work to improve the speed of search crawls. How will this work compare in priority to the original iteration 2 features?

Jay and the team review the features and discuss how much impact the slow crawl speed will have on users. They compare the impact to the value the other features provide, and they determine that the *ability to flag problem postings* is of lower priority. If they need to reduce the feature set for the iteration, they will pull the flag feature before the search-crawl improvement feature.

Do they need to remove anything? Their capacity for an iteration is 19 story points. If they include all the features originally targeted for iteration 2 plus the search enhancement, they will be at 23 story points (see table 20.3).

Feature name (ability to)	Story points
Purchase an item immediately	2
Flag problem postings	2
Contact the seller	3
Create alerts for item type	3

Table 20.3   A potential new plan for iteration 2

Feature name (ability to)	Story points
Receive help online	5
Record seller feedback	5
View seller information	2
Search-crawl enhancement	1
Total	**23**

Table 20.3   A potential new plan for iteration 2 *(continued)*

Acme could accept the additional points and try to squeeze them in, but that would be going against an agile principle. Agile is all about transparency and honesty. If you start fudging your numbers and saying you can exceed your capacity estimates, you'll soon be exceeding team capacity on a daily basis, and overtime will become a norm rather than an exception.

Another option is to extend the iteration. If you make the iteration 12 days instead of 10, will you have enough capacity? How will that affect the numbers you use to determine your capacity? How will you average the story points that come out of an iteration if the number of days isn't constant?

Another issue with modifying your iteration length is the effect on the team. A project has many variables around it, and you're flexing and adapting to all the discoveries. If you can keep iteration length consistent, the team can develop rhythm and not have to adapt to variable iteration length.

Our suggestion for this dilemma is to assign only the number of features you estimate you can process in the iteration, and then make the other features *sideline* features. If the team has more capacity than they expected, because a feature is cancelled or is completed more quickly than expected, they can pursue a sideline feature during the iteration.

Acme Media takes the sideline approach and chooses the most important features that will take up the 19 story points available (see table 20.4).

Table 20.4   Acme Media revises the plan for iteration 2 based on the discoveries during iteration 1.

In or sideline?	Feature name (ability to)	Story points
In	Purchase an item immediately	2
Sideline 1	Flag problem postings	2
In	Contact the seller	3
Sideline 2	Create alerts for item type	3
In	Receive help online	5
In	Record seller feedback	5

Table 20.4   Acme Media revises the plan for iteration 2 based on the discoveries during iteration 1. *(continued)*

In or sideline?	Feature name (ability to)	Story points
In	View seller information	2
In	Search-crawl enhancement	1
	Total In	**18**

Acme has completed its adapt week by creating a revised plan for iteration 2. The team is ready to perform the last iteration and then switch to delivery mode.

20.9   Key points

The key points from this chapter are as follows:

- Regardless of methodology, most projects have to deal with features running late, technical limitations, missing requirements, or a change in the business environment.
- Agile teams adapt to discoveries by performing diligent and collaborative analysis of issues.
- Adapting happens throughout a project, not only after demonstrations and feedback sessions.
- How you adapt is usually tied to the priorities identified in your tradeoff matrix.
- You'll re-plan between iterations. The re-planning is based on customer feedback, discoveries, and evaluation of team performance.
- Interacting with the customer can be stressful for team members who don't typically lead discussions. You'll need to slowly develop presentation and interaction skills with team members who don't have interaction experience.
- You'll encounter a variety of potential issues during your projects: customer discoveries, technical constraints, changes in the business world, issues with third parties, and occasional problems with the team.
- Adapting at the end of an iteration concludes by revising the plan for the forthcoming iteration. You review the issues, determine which features are still valuable to the project, estimate your capacity, and create an iteration plan that supports your capacity estimate.

20.10   Looking forward

In this chapter, we discussed adapting during and after an iteration. When all your iterations are complete, you'll perform final preparations and deploy your code to a production environment. Deployment and delivery are covered in chapter 21.

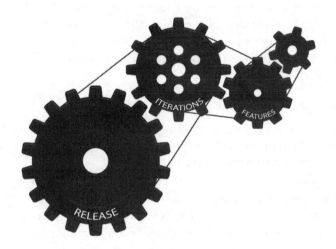

21

Delivery:
bringing it all together

At this point you may be thinking, "Why are you talking about delivery?" Isn't delivery easy in an agile environment? After all, you make sure each iteration is production ready. If each iteration is deployable, deploying should be a piece of cake.

The fact that your code is in a deployable state is a plus; but in reality, releasing code can be a major effort. In some environments, releasing code can be more complicated than building code.

For the purposes of this chapter, we'll discuss delivery from the perspective of a complete project or release. We'll look at deploying a set of features with a synchronized delivery to the production environment. This type of deployment is common for teams that release on a synchronized schedule, or when you deliver a project with several interdependent features. This is the case with the Auctionator for Acme Media: several auction features work together to bring value to the end user, so they must be deployed at the same time.

When you build code, you're working with a small group, and it's easier to manage the project. When you release the code, you'll affect end users, customers, marketing, support, stockholders, stakeholders, training teams, and help desks. In some companies, a compliance group must be engaged to release the code.

In this chapter, we'll go through all the steps that Acme Media (and potentially you) may go through when deploying a project. You'll complete your testing, prepare support groups, train end users, turn on your marketing plan, and deploy the code into the production environment.

21.1   *When to release*

A production release can be triggered by a deadline, by a predetermined release schedule, or when there is enough value. You may also release to production to perform a beta test of a product or application.

Let's take a moment to look at the various constraints that may drive the release of your product.

21.1.1 *To support a constraint*

Four common project constraints are customer deadlines, regulatory requirements, resource limitations, and competitor-driven deadlines. Let's look at each.

SUPPORTING A CUSTOMER CONTRACT

Although contracts and agile development aren't the best of partners, you may still find yourself working with a customer who requires a contract. In these instances, you'll still use your tradeoff matrix to help the customer understand the compromises required to support the fixed date. You and your team will focus on delivering to the date.

One of the agile principles is *Customer collaboration over contract negotiations*. If you follow this principle, your customer will pay you iteratively as you deliver value and as they develop a better understanding of their needs.

When we coach agile teams, we emphasize this point. Our clients agree with the principle but often tell us that they work in a contractual environment and that there is no easy way to leave that environment. They can collaborate with the customer during the project, but there is still a looming contract deadline.

We've seen this in our own work experience. In our early years of work, a sales or marketing group would make an outlandish commitment to a customer to secure a sale; then they would come visit our development team and tell us about the miracle we had to pull off.

In recent years, we've worked on contractual projects, but the sales teams have become more collaborative and involve the development team in the estimation process.

This helps the team buy into the project and also minimizes over-commitment and the potential for creating a death-march project (a project destined to fail).

SUPPORTING A REGULATORY DEADLINE

Projects are often driven by the need to meet a compliance deadline. In recent years, many companies have scrambled to deliver projects that support the Sarbanes-Oxley Act. In 1999, we all scrambled to deliver systems that supported Y2K.

In the past five years, we've worked on compliance projects for Basel II (control over financial reporting and supporting processes), the Health Insurance Portability and Accountability Act (HIPAA; integrity and confidentiality of health records), and Hazard Analysis and Critical Control Point (HACCP). Regulatory compliance is a project reality for many teams.

SUPPORTING A FINANCIAL OR RESOURCE DEADLINE

Larger projects require a commitment of capital funds, and the fund commitment is usually tied to a budget. In these instances, a project must be completed before the funding expires.

You may also find that you have a budgeted amount of time for the project team. This is usually true of consulting resources or shared resources within your company.

MEETING A DEADLINE FROM YOUR COMPETITION

One of the main strengths of agile is helping you quickly deploy functionality to catch and overcome a competitor. You've seen this in action with the Acme Media case study. Acme Media needed to catch its competitors before the company's merchandise site became obsolete.

Deadlines related to a competitor aren't usually date specific but are focused on delivering enough functionality and excitement to make customers reconsider your product. Acme Media has followed this approach, and the first release of the Auctionator will stop the bleeding; subsequent releases will allow Acme to separate itself from the competition.

21.1.2 *To meet a predetermined schedule*

Many companies release new products on a regularly scheduled basis. Greg's current team releases a new product every 7½ weeks. The great thing about a regular release schedule is it gives you one solid reference point in a world of moving parts. The team acclimates to the deployment cycle, and the customer knows there is always another bus coming if a feature request doesn't make it into the current release.

A fixed-release schedule also works well with a product backlog. You can see an example in figure 21.1.

If you release products consistently, you'll review the backlog consistently and develop a rhythm for evaluating features and scoping the forthcoming release with the customer.

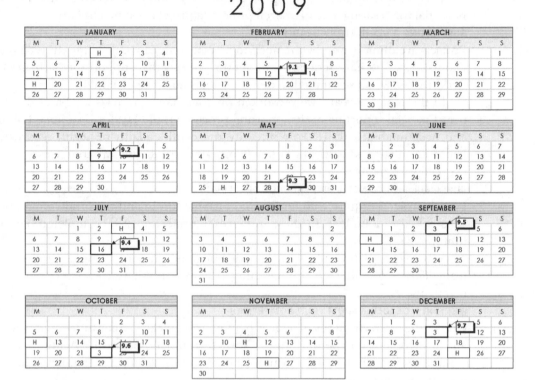

Figure 21.1   Many teams follow a predetermined release schedule to provide rhythm for the team and the customer. A predetermined schedule lets you schedule iterations in advance and also removes customer anxiety when a feature isn't completed in a given release. The customer knows the "bus schedule" and can get their feature on the next bus.

21.1.3   When there is enough value

The preferred method for releasing any project is when your customer says there is enough value to deploy. Because customers are highly involved in agile projects, they can say whether enough value exists at the end of each iteration.

> **Why not release every iteration?**
>
> The potential complexity of releasing explains why teams seldom deploy each development iteration. Releasing each iteration can be expensive, and the cost of doing so needs to be justified. The expenses can include additional labor and blocking customers from accessing the system during deployment.
>
> The Acme Media team didn't deploy their code at the end of iteration 1. Iteration 1 provided enough core features to support a minimal system, but Jay, the customer advocate, wanted the team to spend two more weeks completing the secondary features so that a robust system could be deployed. From Jay's perspective, they have

> ### Why not release every iteration? *(continued)*
>
> only one shot to get their customers back from the competitors, and Jay wants the system to provide a solid user experience. The features provided in iteration 2 will support that goal.
>
> Acme Media also understands the expense of deploying. Although many of Acme's publishing systems support real-time deployment, the architecture of the Auctionator is more complicated and requires a unique deployment plan and additional mechanisms for operations and support.

Some agile teams use charts to indicate how much value has been delivered. These charts are a great visual for the team and help support common understanding of status, but determining whether there is enough value to deploy is a subjective exercise. We frequently find that the customer makes the decision to deploy based on their perspective of status as much as what our tools indicate.

21.1.4 *To test the product*

In theory, you don't deploy until the product is stable, but in some cases you have to deploy to validate stability. Sometimes you deploy to the production environment because you can't simulate the final experience within your test environments.

For example, how many companies can afford to have a load balancer in their test environment? How well can a load simulator emulate a real user? How many PC configurations can you simulate in your test environment?

All the tests you do before you go live try to emulate what will happen when you deploy. But at the end of the day, there is no way to be 100 percent sure what will happen until you put the code out there.

In recent years, we've worked with many teams that understood this reality and designed *soft launch* plans to test the code in production. Note that these teams didn't expose the functionality to all users but to a small subset who piloted the functionality and provided feedback.

> ### Making sure a constraint is real
>
> Understanding constraints in detail often reveals that the constraint isn't as demanding as you imagined. We'll illustrate with a story from Greg.
>
> Greg recently worked on an intranet application with his team. They were given a deadline for turning a new application over to their customer, and they began delivering iterations to prepare for deployment. As the deadline drew near, they identified a shortcoming in the design for load balancing. The issue would make it impossible to send email alerts to users. They revisited the design, came up with a workable solution, implemented the design, and began testing. Unfortunately, this last-second change cut into the team's burn-in period. They wanted to run various performance tests with the system before deployment, and they estimated a month for this work. After the design change, they had only 2 weeks left.

> **Making sure a constraint is real** *(continued)*
>
> The team spoke with the customer and found they had only one true deadline. Part of the functionality the team was delivering was to support a feature that was being lost when a vendor's data center was shut down. If they could deliver that functionality as scheduled, they could continue to burn in and test the system and then deploy all features 2 weeks later than scheduled. That is exactly what they did.

Companies like Microsoft do this for every major product release. They offer the product to a beta group with limited support and noted risks, and then they review the feedback that comes in. Subsequent releases involve major customers and larger groups; then the product is released to the public at large.

21.2   *Final testing*

Although every iteration is a releasable subset of the product, you still have to complete final testing before deployment. Potential areas for final testing are as follows:

- *Functional testing of the last development iteration*—You test code as it's iteratively delivered during a development iteration, but you may still need time to complete functional testing of the final features.
- *Final User Acceptance Testing (UAT)*—Some teams must go through a customer acceptance process before deployment. You may have to do this for regulatory reasons or because of the way the software development lifecycle is managed in your company.
- *Final performance analysis*—Many teams also do final performance testing before releasing. The last iteration allows us to test performance across all features and identify areas that may affect usability.

Before we look at each of these tests in detail, let's discuss the relationship between quality level and the release decision.

21.2.1   *What about quality level?*

We've sat through many bug-review meetings where we discuss bug criticality level, potential workarounds, and how much the bug affects usability. We also estimate how much work is required to fix the bug. If a bug will take more than a few minutes of work, we label it a feature and then prioritize it with the other features in the current backlog.

In the early days of software projects, we had hard rules like "We won't deploy with any level-3-severity bugs." This was a nice rule, and we tried to follow it; but at every release, push came to shove, and we had to make the call about whether to miss our date or let some level-3 bugs go out with the deployment.

We'd love to tell you how agile makes this decision easy, but even agile has limited influence on the release decision. No matter what methodology you use, there will always be questions about whether quality is good enough to allow deployment. The good thing about agile is we have baked in quality with each iteration so there should be fewer issues with the quality level.

Related to this question, we're amazed that we can still find articles on the internet today that look at this quality-level question from a binary perspective. We recently read an article by a person with a significant development background, who said they would rather ship late than risk putting a buggy system into production. We appreciate this perspective and consider the thought noble, but we have trouble supporting it from a real-world perspective. We've worked at several startups, where the difference between shipping on time and delaying for improved quality can mean closing the company doors. Customers may go somewhere else, and investors may pull funds.

Conversely, we've worked on projects where the company wasn't at risk, but we felt pressure to release early and put out a product so buggy that it hurt our reputation and affected future sales.

Agile does help with this dilemma by directly involving the customer in the release decision. You don't have to guess what the customer would say; they tell you directly, and that has an impact on your decision. In cases where the customer is represented by a proxy, such as a product manager, the decision becomes more difficult. In these instances, the project team and stakeholders focus on understanding each other's point of view and then reaching a consensus. On rare occasions, we've seen teams truly split on what to do; in those cases, a person such as the platform owner makes the call about whether to deploy.

21.2.2 *Completing functional/usability testing*

Although you test iterations as you go, you may do slightly different testing before releasing. You may do tests outside of the team, such as usability testing and experimental testing. When you're part of the team, you know the requirements, and you're always looking to test against that vision. People outside the team haven't been pre-programmed on what to expect and will find things you never thought of.

Usability testing involves bringing in members of your target audience and watching them use the application, frequently without instruction. The testers may be given light instruction of the ultimate goal, but you try to turn them loose to see if they use the system the way you intend them to. You do usability testing during iterations too, but that testing may be limited to prototypes and workflow simulation.

One of the interesting things about usability testing is you don't always act on the discoveries. For example, if a user will use a feature multiple times per day, you may want to see how they adapt to a feature after using it several times.

Acme Media also has a good way to do experimental testing with minimal expense. As mentioned in chapter 20, they invite the entire company to join in a bug stomp. The team prints out test scenarios and asks everyone to test a use case. If an employee finds an issue, they email Jay, the product manager, who determines whether the system is acting as designed or whether the employee has discovered a true defect. This exercise is also a great way to spread product knowledge throughout the organization.

21.2.3 *Completing the user acceptance process*

Although you've demonstrated the product to the customer during each iteration, it isn't uncommon to have a final approval process prior to releasing. Common reasons for final acceptance testing are as follows:

- This is the first time the customer has been able to view the entire system.
- The project is tied to a contract that necessitates validation of requirements.
- The demonstrations to date have been with a customer advocate, and there is a desire to expose the system to a broader audience of end users.

Acceptance testing can follow many formats; see section 20.6 for more details.

After the customer verifies functional requirements, you need to make sure non-functional requirements are also supported.

21.2.4 *Validation of nonfunctional requirements*

Before you release, you need to make sure the underlying system performs as required. System requirements are frequently overlooked by the customer, and the project team can coach the customer in determining nonfunctional requirements.

System requirements don't match up to a user story or specific functionality; instead, they represent the overarching ability to support service requirements. For example, Dairy Queen may have to support a user story where a customer orders and receives an ice cream cone. The user story steps may include *customer orders the cone, employee creates the cone with the ice cream machine,* and *the employee delivers the cone.* The user story meets the needs of one user, but it doesn't say how many ice cream cones the system can support during a day. How many cones you must deliver in a day is an example of a nonfunctional requirement.

Nonfunctional requirements are as critical as the ability to support a specific user story. If the system fails, you won't be able to support any user stories.

Experienced customers understand the importance of nonfunctional requirements, usually because they have paid the price for not specifying them in the past. These customers provide service-level requirements that are used to create a service-level agreement (SLA). The SLA helps the customer and the team reach agreement about realistic expectations of the system.

Here are some common areas to validate before going live:

- *System availability*—How much downtime is acceptable for system maintenance and system issues? If the system goes down, how long is acceptable? This number is usually specified as a percentage, and this percentage maps to the number of hours a system can be down in a given time period. Acme Media has a platform availability target of 99.5 percent. This means the company's sites can be down for approximately 400 hours in a year.

  Note that increasing uptime percentage usually increases platform expense. For example, Acme Media feels it can support 99.5 percent uptime with its existing platform. If Acme wanted to pursue an uptime of 99.9 percent, the company would have to double the number of servers used and implement a complicated redundancy system. In effect, this would double the cost of the infrastructure.

- *Data-recovery requirements*—If the system goes down, how much data can you afford to lose? The metric for data recovery is Recovery Point Objective (RPO), which is specified as the number of minutes of data that can be lost during a failure. Acme Media determined that it can accept 10 minutes of data loss for the Auctionator.

- *Downtime for a given failure*—System availability relates to how much time you can be down for a given timeframe. Your Recovery Time Objective (RTO) specifies how long you can be down for an individual failure. Many companies have a second environment they can switch to in case of a failure. The RTO usually ties to how quickly you can switch to the Disaster Recovery (DR) environment. RTOs can range from a few minutes to a few hours, depending on the criticality of the system and how much money your company can invest in a recovery system and process.

- *System response time*—When a user requests a page, how long should it take for the system to respond? How long is beyond your usability threshold?

- *Maximum concurrent users supported*—What is the maximum number of users that can access the system at one time before performance begins to degrade? A recent example is from the 2007 holiday shopping season. Macy's website couldn't support the surge in traffic it received during the holiday season, and potential customers were welcomed with a web page saying "We'll be right with you" (see figure 21.2).

- *Archive and purging requirements*—Over time, your system may become loaded with historical transactions and other data. How long does this data have to be available to the system? When you remove it from the system, do you have to store it for a period of time because of regulatory or other requirements? Acme Media doesn't have a regulatory need to store the Auctionator transactions, but the company thinks it will be prudent to keep the log files for 1 year in case there are any questions.

We'll be right with you.

It's a little crowded in here right now, and to make sure everyone enjoys shopping with us, we're asking new visitors to wait here a few moments while other shoppers finish up. We'll refresh your browser and welcome you in momentarily. Thanks for your patience!

- 1-800-BUY-MACY (1-800-289-6229) 9am-6pm Monday-Saturday and 11am-7pm Sunday to order by phone.
- Visit macysweddingchannel.com to shop or create a wedding registry.
- Use the Store Locator to find a store near you.
- Visit CheckFree.com to pay your bill online

Figure 21.2 Nonfunctional requirements, such as the maximum number of users that can be supported, are just as important as the features themselves. Macy's probably has a great user experience behind this screen; too bad the system can't take any more customers at this time.

In many cases, nonfunctional requirements are determined by the company providing the service (you) versus an individual customer. For example, Acme Media's product manager identifies the nonfunctional requirements for Acme Media's platform based on what he feels will be acceptable to customers.

21.3   *Preparing support groups and processes*

Whether you use agile or not, all projects need to have support processes in place before you go live. The main difference with agile projects is you think about maintenance and support starting on day 1 of the project. Agile teams often use a template to record maintenance concerns along the way. Let's look at an example.

21.3.1   *The running maintenance and support worksheet*

Acme Media labels its maintenance scratchpad the Maintenance and Support Worksheet. The Acme team noted their first maintenance concerns when the product was being examined for feasibility, and they recorded their final maintenance concerns during the last development iteration.

Some typical items recorded on a maintenance worksheet are as follows:

- *Location of supporting documentation*—Acme stores its support documentation on a network drive.

- *Marketing information*—This information may include a marketing plan or other information related to publicizing the application you're about to release. Note that marketing a project goes beyond external customers. If you're delivering an internally consumed application, you should still look for a way to advertise it to your users. This may include discussions at user group meetings or a notice/advertisement on your intranet.

- *Known issues or limitations*—What bugs or defects will be outstanding when you go live? Document these for support people and to make sure they're included in your help documentation.

- *Support for analytics*—Many companies use an analytics tool such as Sage Analyst or WebTrends.

- *Supporting jobs and processes*—What jobs need to run nightly, weekly, or at other intervals to maintain the system? For example, the Auctionator requires a job to send out nightly email alerts to users who want to be notified only one time per day.

- *Archiving*—Production systems can become bloated with old data if they aren't purged frequently. Acme Media establishes a nightly job to archive transactions that are 1 year or older.

- *Search support*—Many applications have a search engine tied to them. You may want to update the search engine for the application or feature you're about to release.

Acme's completed worksheet appears in table 21.1.

Table 21.1 Maintenance concerns are recorded through all phases of a project via the maintenance worksheet.

Maintenance and Support Worksheet	
Location for supporting documentation	N:\acmemedia\open\Marketing\OLA
Marketing URLs	http://www.acme-media.net/OLA
Known issues and limitations	Defect #1211: Auction doesn't refresh with Firefox v1.12
Redirects	http://www.acme-media.net/merchandise to http://www.acme-media.net/OLA
Analytics tracking	This project should be tracked as a new channel called "online auction service"
Support jobs	Nightly archive of auctions older than 1 year Email alert job for daily and weekly alerts
Support and help articles	See help functionality delivered in iteration 2
Archiving	Auctions older than 2 years to be stored in /acmemedia_working/archive/auctions/
Search indexing	Add keywords for quick hits on *auction, classifieds, merchandise*

Just like the other templates we've discussed in this book, you can use your worksheet as a starting point and then modify it to match the maintenance areas you need to track during a project.

21.3.2 *Finalizing help materials and support processes*

Acme Media treats its end-user help materials as a feature and delivers them in iteration 2. This is common with online web applications, where minimal user help is provided. In other environments, you may have a person or team dedicated to technical writing and the creation of support materials.

Acme's help desk also has an escalation path so they can pass an issue to the development team if the issue can't be addressed with their help documentation. If the issue isn't severe, the help desk sends an email to the team. If the issue is severe, the help desk has a call tree and can work their way through it until they can find a person to work the issue.

21.3.3 *Enabling system monitoring, and creating an escalation process*

Most companies monitor their networks to make sure the infrastructure is up and running. This includes monitoring database activity and server performance. In addition, many companies have tools in place to measure the user experience, including page-response time and application availability.

Acme Media uses a tool for measuring and monitoring the user experience. This tool, HP SiteScope, emulates a web browser and identifies potential issues before users are affected. Acme modifies the configuration of SiteScope so it will monitor various aspects of the Auctionator and trigger alerts to the team if potential issues are identified.

After you've established monitoring, you need to outline a process for managing alerts. Acme Media has a standard triage process for alerts so the correct people are notified if an alert is triggered by the Auctionator. Non-severe alerts go to the development team inbox. Critical alerts go to the development team and support team inboxes, and the support team calls development if they don't receive a response within a specified period of time.

21.3.4 *Enabling maintenance and background processes*

Acme Media notes two jobs that need to run to support the Auctionator: the first job archives auction transactions that are more than a year old, and the second sends out alerts to potential buyers on a daily and weekly basis.

The software projects you pursue may have many background process needs. In addition to the ones Acme Media identified, you may need support jobs for expiring content, data-warehouse population, reporting, refreshing content or data-search crawling/indexing, or pre-building cache on your servers.

21.4 *Communication and training*

Agile development understands the importance of communication, and that is why you put team members in close proximity to each other. It's also important to communicate with individuals who aren't a direct part of the project team. Let's look at a few typical messages communicated during a project.

Table 21.2 lists potential audiences and messages for a given project. To give you context, we've listed the audiences and messages that Acme Media addresses during the Auctionator project.

Acme Media has a diverse group to communicate with, but you may have additional groups unique to your project. For example, if you work in a regulated industry, you may have to communicate to governing bodies such as the FDA and OSHA. You may also need to create communications that validate Sarbanes-Oxley (SOX) compliance for your project.

Table 21.2 Acme Media outlines its training and communication plan before going live.

Audience	Message or training needed
End users: ■ Current users of the merchandise site ■ Users lost to competitors	■ Notify users that the current site is being decommissioned and that they can begin using the auction site, for free, on September 21. ■ We need to advertise the new auction service on our other websites (news and travel). Marketing will also run a TV advertisement.
Paying customers: ■ Merchants	■ We need to notify merchants that they have a new, targeted advertising option.

Table 21.2 Acme Media outlines its training and communication plan before going live. *(continued)*

Audience	Message or training needed
Internal employees and stakeholders: ■ Internal sales team ■ All employees ■ Help desk ■ Environment support	■ We need to train the sales team so they can sell auction site advertising to merchants. ■ Send a notice to all employees outlining why we're doing the project and when it goes live. ■ Orient the help desk on the new functionality, alert them to when we go live, and make sure they have a clear understanding of where and how to route issues. ■ Alert the network team so they can change DNS and add in the new URLs for the auction system.
Support groups: ■ Advertising support team ■ Analytics	■ Have the advertising team program the new advertisements to begin showing up on the Auctionator site when we go live. ■ Make sure the web analytics team has our new URLs and the categories associated with them so we can analyze traffic on the new auction site.
Stakeholders' sponsor: ■ CIO	■ Meet weekly with the sponsor to discuss status.

The Auctionator is a medium-size project for Acme Media, so the communication required is also at a medium level. Acme chooses the level of documentation needed for each project based on variables such as audience size, project duration, and the level of ceremony required. You should do the same on your projects.

21.5 Ready to release

Now that you have all the support areas and processes ready to go, you need to make the final decision about going live and then plan the deployment steps in detail.

21.5.1 Deciding to go live

Although every iteration you deliver is deployable, teams often need to obtain approval from customers, stakeholders, support groups, network teams, testers, and change-management groups before deploying code to a production environment.

We've covered common go-live criteria in this chapter. You'll consider code stability, outstanding defects, readiness of support groups, system performance, and user readiness. You can analyze these areas from a statistical perspective, but the ultimate decision may be based more on how you feel about the project than on empirical statistics.

Acme Media analyzes the state of its project. The team, the customer, and the sponsor all agree to go live, noting only one concern: the auction functionality doesn't work correctly with an older version of Firefox. The team reviews server-log information and determines that few users have the old Firefox version. They also note that the version isn't included in their list of officially supported browsers. You can see Acme Media's implementation checklist in table 21.3.

This discussion may seem simple for a go-live discussion, but it's important to remember that Acme Media is working in an agile environment now. The company has been building and stabilizing the product with frequent builds and iterative creation of features. Acme works to make each iteration solid, so a go-live conversation is closer to a formality than a requirement. There shouldn't be many surprises or unknowns at this time.

Now that you know you're going forward, let's plan the deployment steps.

Table 21.3 An implementation checklist helps everyone grasp the state of the project and contribute to the go-live decision.

Questions	Yes	No
Have all the requirements in scope been met?	☒	☐
If not, has agreement been reached for those elements not satisfied?	☐	☐
Does the product support segregation of duties—the division of roles and responsibilities to reasonably prevent a single individual from subverting a critical process?	☒	☐
Are there any business or regulatory changes that would prevent implementation of the product(s) of this project?	☐	☒
Do you agree to accept all documented risks associated with deploying this product? This may include potential risks to existing systems or business operations.	☒	☐
Do you understand the outstanding defects and their possible consequences as described in the Technical Test Results (as applicable) and in the User Acceptance Testing results?	☒	☐
Are all employees who will use or support or be otherwise affected by the product(s) prepared for implementation?	☒	☐
Do you agree to move the product(s) into implementation?	☒	☐
Has all User Acceptance Testing been completed?	☒	☐
Have all business functions specific to this application been tested?	☒	☐
Have all SOX control tests relevant to this application been tested?	☒	☐
Have all nonfunctional tests been completed?	☒	☐
Has performance testing been completed, including load, stress, and capacity testing?	☒	☐
Has security testing been completed?	☒	☐
Has recoverability testing been completed?	☐	☒
Has usability testing been completed?	☒	☐
Have workarounds for known defects been documented and communicated to all affected parties?	☒	☐
Have all the required Business Continuity (BC) / Disaster Recovery (DR) deliverables been successfully completed?	☒	☐

21.5.2 *Planning the deployment steps*

You may remember that during the development iterations we discussed code completeness. You make sure the code can be demonstrated, that it is tested, and that it supports nonfunctional requirements. Many features also require you to design a process for their deployment. This process may require that you write scripts and configure the system to support the new feature. In our experience, deployment scripts and processes are a part of the deliverables during a development iteration.

When you deploy your iterations to the production environment, you need to create an overall process and sequence for deploying the features.

> #### Yes, you can deploy instantly
>
> You may be reading this chapter and thinking, "This is ridiculous. We release code every few days!" We're sure this is true for many people.
>
> This chapter is focused on a medium-size project, and we're implying a certain level of ceremony to give you a feel for the options available during a deployment. We've worked in environments where we deployed new features daily (an online newspaper), and we've worked on projects where it took a year to deploy (software for medical devices).
>
> Deploying quickly is a good thing. The sooner you get your code in place, the less chance there is that you'll miss the need or opportunity. But if you work on larger projects, you may find interdependencies between features, and deploying may not make sense until the bulk of these features are in place. We're demonstrating this model with Acme Media in hopes of helping you when deployment becomes more complex due to a larger audience or dependencies on outside groups.

Many times your architecture will influence the process you use. This is true with Acme Media. Acme developed its deployment process around two realities of the production environment. Let's look at the realities Acme Media had to take into consideration.

21.5.3 *Deployment considerations*

Acme Media developed its deployment plan around the realities of the company's environment. Let's look at unique areas for Acme Media.

ARCHITECTURE

Acme's architecture has two elements that influence the deployment plan:

- *Disaster recovery*—Acme maintains a DR environment to fail over to in case of an emergency. This backup system is maintained in a data center across town. Acme always deploys to the backup center first as an additional test of the code and as a test of the deployment plan.
- *Load balancer*—Acme uses a load balancer to equalize the load across the company's servers and to ensure the site stays up if one server goes down. Acme uses the server pool during deployment to allow the site to stay up while new code is installed onto each server.

SAFE WINDOW TO DEPLOY

Acme must also consider other variables when choosing the day and time for deployment. The team goes over the following checklist to determine the best window:

- *Holidays*—Acme avoids deploying on holidays because support groups aren't available.
- *Other deployments*—The team chats with other departments to make sure they aren't doing deployments or infrastructure work that could block a deployment.
- *Resource availability*—Acme has to make sure the types of employees needed for deployment aren't on vacation or in training during the deployment window.
- *Blackout windows*—Acme has windows of time where deployments aren't allowed. These windows usually correspond to month-end or year-end financial processing.
- *User activity*—Acme times releases so there is minimal affect on users. This means avoiding peak usage windows in case an issue is encountered.

Although it doesn't affect Acme Media, we've worked with teams that deploy only when the customer is available to test the product in the production environment.

MIGRATION AND CONVERSION

The Acme Media team doesn't have to worry about migrating or converting data when they deploy, but they do have to create a plan for phasing out and decommissioning the old merchandise site.

21.5.4   *Creating a deployment and backout plan*

Acme Media creates deployment scripts and processes as a part of code delivery during the development iterations. The team reviews these scripts during deployment planning and also lays out a logical sequence for running the scripts.

Acme uses a collaborative process to create a deployment plan for each release. Wendy, the project manager, organizes a meeting to discuss the timing for deploying the code.

In the spirit of being agile and productive, Acme doesn't follow the same exact process for each deployment. For example, the load-balancer architecture allows Acme to deploy to the production environment without blocking user access to the system. Individual servers can be removed from the load-balancer pool and then reinserted after they've received the new code. When the team has a slight change to make to the production environment, they do it during normal hours and without splashing the site (see table 21.4).

When the Acme team outlines the deployment plan for the Auctionator, they consider the complexity of the deployment scripts, the time needed to put the code into production, and the risk associated with the deployment. They also consider the complexity of backing out the code if an issue is encountered. They decide to do a deployment in the evening when website traffic is down, so that if an issue is encountered there will be minimal impact to site visitors.

Table 21.4 Acme Media's deployment plan for the Auctionator

Time	Activity	Expected result	Action	Go/no-go decision	Owner
5:00PM-7:45PM	Back up SQL Server databases.	Databases backed up successfully.	DBA verifies that database backup is complete.	Stop deployment.	Aaron
1:00PM-4:00PM	Begin server pre-validation (restart) of all servers.	All servers restart successfully.	Ensure servers are ping-able / apps online.	QA confirms the functionality works via BVT.	Jim/Gina
7:45PM	Run SQL script, and remove SQL hardening.	Script runs successfully.	DBA verifies that script completes without errors.	Rerun script.	Aaron
8:00PM	Remove Set A production servers from application pool.	Set A servers aren't accessible via FQDN .	Ensure all Set A servers aren't in the load-balancer pool.	Confirm all Set A servers aren't accessible.	Jim/Gina
8:05PM	Clean up and deploy Auctionator code to Set A production servers.	New Auctionator code functioning.	Ensure correct Auctionator version was installed to each server.	QA confirms new functionality works as expected.	Jim/Gina
8:50PM	Add Set A production servers back into application pool.	New Auctionator code functioning.	Ensure all Set A servers are back in the load-balancer pool.	QA confirms new Auctionator functionality works as expected.	Jim/Gina
9:30PM	Remove Set B production servers from application pool.	Set B servers aren't accessible via FQDN.	Ensure all Set B servers aren't in the load-balancer pool.	Confirm all Set B servers aren't accessible.	Jim
9:30PM	Clean up and deploy Auctionator code to Set B production servers.	New Auctionator code functioning.	Ensure correct Auctionator version was installed to each server.	QA confirms new Auctionator functionality works as expected.	Jim/Gina
9:35PM	Apply redirects to old merchandise site URLs.			Verify redirects to auction site.	Ryan
10:35PM	Verify merchant ads are serving correctly.				Gina
12:10AM	Reapply SQL hardening.				Gina/Aaron
12:30AM	All sets added back in; announce deployment.				Wendy

Acme Media will also have a chance to test the deployment plan when the team deploys the Auctionator to the DR environment.

21.5.5 Reducing risk with a pilot

Acme Media minimizes deployment risk by deploying to the DR environment first. Many teams don't have a DR environment and need another way to test with minimal risk. For these teams, a pilot deployment or soft launch can start an iterative deployment process.

You can perform a pilot by deploying to your production environment but limiting access to a small audience. The small audience provides feedback and is aware of the risks that come from piloting, such as limited support and the possibility that their data could be lost. A pilot is also frequently used on projects where quality is the number-one priority.

21.6 Enough planning; let's deploy

As we mentioned in an earlier sidebar, deployment can happen relatively quickly on smaller projects or where the architecture lends itself to a quick process. The Auctionator will take several hours to deploy, so the team will do it in a collaborative fashion.

Acme Media's team members sit relatively close together at their desks, but for deployments they all go into a conference room and sit at a table face to face. This setup allows the team to tell each other when they're finished with a step during the deployment. It also accelerates troubleshooting if an issue is encountered. The whole team can hear the issue at once, and each team member can investigate the issue from a different angle.

If you saw the movie *Apollo 13*, you may remember the scene in which the crew experienced an issue and alerted ground control. In real life, flight director Gene Kranz asked each group to analyze the problem from their perspective. One person investigated a potential sensor malfunction, another person looked to see if the issue was consistent across all systems, and another person tried to figure out what was going on by studying the biosensors on the astronauts.

When we participate in deployments, we see similar troubleshooting methods when we encounter an issue. For example, if a web page isn't displaying correctly, the user experience designer verifies that the stylesheet installed correctly, a network engineer verifies that the web servers are running, and an implementation engineer verifies that the database scripts run correctly.

When Acme Media completes its deployment, Wendy sends out a notice to the company so everyone can prepare to support the new application.

21.6.1 Celebrate!

Acme Media doesn't have a history of celebrating deployments. Many of the company's projects never reached completion, or teams weren't proud of the work they did release.

The Auctionator is one of Acme's best accomplishments. For once, Acme isn't deploying features that provide minimal value, and they've also hit their timeline for deploying the critical features. Acme is also happy because the whole team agrees that the project was valuable and worth pursuing.

When you deliver a project like the Auctionator, you need to celebrate. Although a lot of people say "it's just work," we all put a lot of personal effort into delivering a project, and we take pride in what we've overcome and what we've delivered. It's important to celebrate the achievements of the team, the issues that were resolved, and the fact that you delivered the functionality that was needed at the end. It's also a moment for management to tell employees that their work is valued and important.

Every company has a different way of celebrating, whether it's a party or an offsite gathering. The critical piece of the celebration is timing: you should celebrate while the project is still on everyone's mind, before you shift to the next project. We've worked on several projects where we couldn't find time to celebrate at the end or delayed the celebration for one reason or another. In those instances, the celebration seemed a little hollow and staged, and we'd forgotten some of the hard work we performed and why we were entitled to a celebration.

You've probably been to celebrations where a group of people congregated in a corner and started whispering, "Why are we celebrating? Were we really successful?" Many projects take off without clearly defining what success means. You may recall that you avoid this issue by defining success when you go through the feasibility discussion guide, discussed in chapter 10. The celebration is a great time to revisit this list.

Acme Media defined success as stopping the steady decline of customers to eBay and Craigslist and increasing site revenue by adding merchant target advertising. Acme celebrates a few days after deployment and doesn't have significant data to determine if customers are returning. But the company does have a list of merchants who've signed contracts for targeted advertising. These merchants were pursued as the project was being completed, and the initial number that signed up for the advertising program is in synch with the numbers Jay envisioned for the first month of the new site.

21.7 Key points

The key points from this chapter are as follows:

- You create software in deployable units during each development iteration, but you don't deploy after every iteration because of the ceremony required to release. Your environment may make it easy to deploy code, but many software projects require training, communications, and final acceptance testing before features can be released.
- Code can be released to support a deadline, according to a predetermined release schedule, or when the team and customer agree there is enough value to deploy.

- For many companies, additional testing and validation must take place before releasing. This can include final functional testing and testing of nonfunctional requirements such as system response time.

- Many companies overlook validation of nonfunctional requirements. Such companies frequently fail dramatically during a product release.

- Many projects require the creation of new processes and documentation for support. You create the support processes and train your support team on them before deployment.

- Many teams need to document their go-live plan, especially when deploying new technology. This plan integrates the deployment and configuration steps created during each iteration.

- You may find it valuable to iteratively roll out your project to the audience it's intended for. A pilot or beta group can assist with this iterative process and reduce deployment risk.

- If your team doesn't use a team room on a daily basis, establish one for the day of deployment. Having everyone co-located during deployment helps resolve issues quickly by collaboratively working the issues.

- Always celebrate your projects quickly after deployment. It's easy to get distracted once you go live, either due to go-live issues or pursuit of the next project. If you don't celebrate, you'll dilute your accomplishments and possibly reduce team morale.

21.8   *Looking forward*

In this chapter, we discussed delivering and celebrating. You also need to stop and reflect on what went well and what could be improved. You'll do this with a project retrospective, which we'll cover in chapter 22.

The retrospective: working together to improve

All agile methods, whether Scrum, Extreme Programming (XP), or custom, support stopping to reflect on the process on a regular basis. A project retrospective normalizes the team on the issues encountered and provides an opportunity for improvement, which everyone desires.

The inherent flaw with retrospectives and postmortems is they often turn into complaint sessions, and participants leave without a clear plan of attack. This chapter provides a process to eliminate these problems.

First, you'll give participants time to reflect on the project before the retrospective meeting. Second, you'll collect opinions from the team before the meeting, aggregate the information, and publish the results back to the team to review before the meeting. Finally, you'll prioritize the issues identified during the retrospective and post them prominently in the team work area.

In this chapter, we'll follow the Acme Media pilot team as they perform a project retrospective for the first time. This retrospective will be the last step the pilot team performs in testing the new process. When the retrospective is complete, the core team will review all steps of the new process and then decide how to scale the methodology across the rest of the organization.

You've probably participated in a project postmortem or retrospective. We've participated in dozens of these meetings, and we've rarely seen them obtain optimum results. We believe these meetings don't go as well as possible for four reasons:

- The retrospective happens too late, and participants forget the issues encountered.
- The participants don't separate personal/performance issues from process issues.
- Participants aren't provided enough time to gather their thoughts and observations.
- The output of the meeting isn't documented or followed up on.

Over the years, several people have given us advice about how to address these issues; we'll share them in this chapter.

22.1 *Setting expectations for the retrospective*

You can prepare your team for the retrospective by providing guidelines in advance. We use the guidelines outlined in figure 22.1; they set expectations before you perform the retrospective and get the team thinking about the process and not personal issues.

Your retrospective will have two main objectives, and the guide encourages your participants to start thinking about them:

- Identify what went poorly so you can address it.
- Identify what went well so you can repeat it.

Acme Media's development team will stay together for subsequent projects. When they get a good feel for the behavior expected, they won't need to review the guidelines before every retrospective.

Conversely, you'll probably have folks from other departments or teams attend your retrospectives on an ad hoc basis, depending on their level of involvement in the project. Make sure you send the retrospective guidelines to newcomers every time.

NOTE   You may wonder what is unique about retrospective behavior in an agile environment versus a traditional environment. In our opinion, there is no difference. No matter how you develop software, you should always strive to be professional in the workplace, avoid blaming individuals, and instead focus on enhancing the development process as a team.

Another critical item during the retrospective is to make it clear that you're meeting to review the process, not to measure whether the project was successful. You want to know if you have an effective process when you review the project. You aren't evaluating whether the project is making money, whether your marketing assumptions were correct, or whether you captured your target market. There is a time for such a review, but the retrospective is focused on the methodology.

Project Retrospective Meeting Guidelines

Purpose
- Define what went well on the project so we can repeat on future projects.
- Define what didn't work or could have gone better so we can learn from our mistakes and improve on future projects.
- Document the surprises we encountered so that we watch for these risks on future projects.
- Improve our development process.

Meeting Preparation
A questionnaire should be filled out by each participant prior to the meeting and sent to the facilitator. It lists specific areas of discussion and asks people to describe what went well and what did not go well on the project. The facilitator should summarize the results and present them to the group to focus the discussion on key areas of success or concern.

Optimal Outcome
Generate a prioritized list of process-specific lessons learned and root causes. Convert highest priority items into action items and delegate for action.

Ground Rules for Meeting
- When identifying what worked and didn't work, give some thought to the root causes and potential solutions for what didn't work.
- If you are representing others in this meeting, please get input from them.
- Respect other people's perspectives – everyone's opinion is valid, even if you may not agree with it.
- Avoid blaming people for past events. The goal is to learn from mistakes, not to lay blame or find fault. It's easier to look back and identify issues with a project than it is while a team is engaged in the project. Everyone is trying to do their best job under the circumstances.
- Focus on understanding, learning and looking ahead.
- Feel free to ask for clarification on what is communicated.

General Topics of Discussion
- Discuss the questions on the pre-meeting survey, focusing on highest and lowest scores.
- What was the single most frustrating part of our project? How would you do things differently next time to avoid this frustration?
- What was the most gratifying or professionally satisfying part of the project?
- Which of our methods or processes worked particularly well?
- Which of our methods or processes were difficult or frustrating to use?
- If you could wave a magic wand and change one aspect about the project, what would it be? What would you like to remain the same?
- How clearly defined were the objectives for your work?
- Did you feel adequately involved in the project planning and decisions?
- Was the project significantly delayed/hampered by outside dependencies?

Figure 22.1   Retrospective guidelines. A retrospective may involve members outside of the normal group, and the guidelines provide expectations and orientation for the meeting.

22.2   *Time to digest: a survey in advance*

When team members understand what is expected in the retrospective, a project manager or other team member should survey the team before the retrospective meeting. Surveying the team in advance gives them time to reflect on the project and consider what went well and what can be improved. The survey can also be completed at the convenience of the team member. As a rule of thumb, we like to send the survey out 3 days before the retrospective meeting and give participants 2 days to respond.

Here are some items that make the survey a good tool for project analysis:

- *Scoring*—Team members must say whether they agree or disagree. Many surveys allow a neutral answer, and many people choose the neutral answer to be safe. This weakens your ability to determine whether you're doing well or poorly in a given area. Do allow N/A if a team member didn't personally participate in a given area.
- *Tailored questions*—The questions are tailored to your environment. Acme Media cares about project management, development, and delivery. Other companies may want to focus on cost, speed, or efficiency.
- *Allow supporting comments*—The survey lets participants enter supporting comments on each question. These comments will help start the dialogue during the retrospective meeting.
- *Anonymity*—Acme Media uses an online questionnaire tool that lets team members respond anonymously. As time goes on, the team will become more comfortable about revealing their thoughts to each other, and anonymity will become less of a need.

Figure 22.2 shows Acme Media's survey.

After the survey results are in, the facilitator can aggregate all the information into a results page and email the results to the team before the retrospective meeting. Team members enjoy reviewing the survey results before going in; the information puts them in the right frame of mind for the meeting.

This is a good time to point out why you do all of this prep work before the retrospective meeting. You've probably attended such meetings and witnessed scenes like the following. The facilitator gets everyone together and reorients the team on the project. The facilitator asks people to list things that went well and things that went poorly. One or two people speak up, and the facilitator writes their thoughts on a whiteboard and asks other team members for their thoughts. Eventually, other team members start to chip in as they recall events that happened during the project. With 10 minutes left in the meeting, you start to get good commentary, and the facilitator rushes to get the thoughts on the whiteboard and discuss root causes and potential solutions for the issues. The most important part of the meeting is hurried, and the result is a marginal list of items that went well or poorly. The team will rush to document corrective actions when they should be thoughtful about identifying and resolving the root issues.

The preparatory work we outline in this chapter should get your team engaged in relevant conversation the minute the meeting starts so you don't have to hurry documenting the main issues and what you'll do to improve them on the subsequent project.

Project Retrospective Questionnaire

Please fill out prior to retrospective meeting and send to facilitator.

1	strongly agree
2	agree
3	disagree
4	strongly disagree
n/a	not applicable

PROJECT MANAGEMENT

Question	1	2	3	4	n/a
Project objectives and goals were clear?					
Project risks and trade-offs were well understood?					
Roles and responsibilities were clearly defined?					
Stakeholders assisted in meeting objectives?					
Stakeholders were updated on status in an adequate fashion?					
Customers were clearly defined?					
Customers' needs were clearly defined?					
Customers were adequately involved throughout the project?					

DEVELOPMENT

Question	1	2	3	4	n/a
Project tasks were well defined?					
Project tasks were appropriately assigned?					
Appropriate specs and/or mockups were provided to assist in planning?					
Project goals were attainable within the timeframe?					
Post implementation plan was defined and effective?					
QA testing was thorough and completed on time?					
Changes were reasonable and prudent throughout development?					
Team collaboration was high throughout the project?					

DELIVERY

Question	1	2	3	4	n/a
Project was deployed in a reasonable timeframe according to scope?					
Training & support was adequate and timely?					
Support was informed and properly trained?					
Stakeholders and affected teams were properly informed prior to launch?					
Delivery fallout was handled in a timely manner within teams?					

Additional comments:

Figure 22.2   The project retrospective survey covers the main areas of the project. Acme Media chose areas that meant the most to its environment. Your retrospective survey should cover the areas that are important to your team, company, and customer.

22.3 *Conducting the retrospective meeting*

When the team has reviewed the survey, you can get them together for the retrospective meeting. If you have a team room or shared area, you can conduct the survey there, but sometimes it helps to find a conference room or other venue to pre- vent distractions.

Most teams have limited time for the retrospective meeting and usually complete it in 60 to 90 minutes. Because time is limited, you should discuss the most important areas first. The most important items to focus on are *things you're doing well* and *things you're doing poorly.* You can highlight these items in the survey so the team knows you'll begin with them (see figures 22.3 and 22.4).

Retrospective Questionnaire: Auctionator Project

PROJECT MANAGEMENT

Question	Strongly Agree	Agree	Disagree	Strongly Disagree	n/a
1) Objectives and goals were clear?	3	7			
2) Risks and trade-offs were well understood?	2	8			
3) Stakeholders assisted in meeting objectives?	1	6	1		2
4) Stakeholders were updated of status in an adequate fashion?	2	5			3
5) Customers were clearly defined?	4	4	1		1
6) Customers were adequately involved through out the project?	2	5	1		2
7) *Customers' needs were clearly defined?*		6	3		1

PLANNING AND DEVELOPMENT

Question	Strongly Agree	Agree	Disagree	Strongly Disagree	n/a
8) *Features were well defined?*	1	5	4		
9) Priorities were clear to the team?	1	9			
10) The team adapted well to discoveries during development?	1	8	1		
11) *Project goals were attainable within the timeframe?*		5	4	1	
12) Post implementation plan was defined and effective?	2	7			1
13) *Testing was thorough and completed on time?*		8	2		
14) Changes were reasonable and prudent throughout development	1	8			1
15) *Team collaboration was high throughout the project.*	5	5			

DELIVERY

Question	Strongly Agree	Agree	Disagree	Strongly Disagree	n/a
16) *Project was deployed in a reasonable timeframe according to scope?*	3	6	1		
17) Training & support was adequate and timely?	1	1			8
18) Support was informed and properly trained?	2	1			7
19) Stakeholders and affected teams were properly informed prior to launch?	2	4			4
20) Delivery fallout was handled in a timely manner within teams?	2	4			4

Figure 22.3 The retrospective survey results. A facilitator highlights the areas the team should spend the most time on during the meeting, focusing on areas where the team agrees they're doing well, where they have issues, and areas where they're split. The Auctionator retrospective has 10 attendees, so each row totals 10. Each vote equals one attendee.

- 've addressed risks early and it was clear what the release entailed.
- The feasibility work helped quantify the value of the project.

Q2: Project risks and trade-offs were well understood?
- Early risk assessment meetings were helpful.
- I scored it "agree" but it can be improved. A list of application specific features and their risks would be an improvement.

Q4: Stakeholders were updated of status in an adequate fashion?
- Wendy and Jay did a great job of keeping stakeholders informed and accountable.

Q5: Customers were clearly defined?
- It was clear that Jay represented the end users of the system.
- We did a good job of identifying the other customers of the project, such as the paying customer (the advertisers) and ourselves.

Q6: Customers were adequately involved throughout the project?
- Jay was involved and the team is struggling to get used to this. We are used to guessing what the customer wants and deciding on our own.
- I felt I was involved too much. I sat through discussion on server load estimation and maintenance jobs. I think we need to figure out when to involve the customer so we do no waste their time. (This is Jay).

Q7: Customers' needs were clearly defined?
- We made several discoveries during development, such as the need to register bidders. I'm not sure if we did enough due diligence before coding began on the bidding feature.
- We did a good job of prioritizing discoveries during the release, but the process was chaotic and required a lot of meetings.
- I liked the fact that we kept asking what was critical for delivery every day. We did not assume initial priorities were the same after we made discoveries.

Q8: Features were well defined?
- We had lots of discoveries with the bidding functionality.
- We had overlap on some features and we had to work out who did what work. This was true with registration and the bidding process.
- I thought we defined the features the best we could before we dived into them.

Q11: Project goals were attainable within the timeframe?
- We could not do all of the original work we intended to do after we made discoveries, but Jay helped us reassign priorities and still deliver the critical work.
- We booked more than we could do. Maybe this will get better now that we have measured velocity.

Q13: Testing was thorough and completed on time?
- We had open issues but we continued into iteration 2.
- Rich was able to get defect information to us early since we did frequent builds.
- We went live with known defects, but for the most part we agreed that they were not critical issues.
- This was a complicated application and some tradeoffs were made to give emphasis to core functionality.
- We struggled to find the correct level of requirements documentation to support testing. The feature card was too little, but a complete functional specification would be overkill on some features.

Q15: Team collaboration was high throughout the project?
- QA, Dev and Analysts met regularly to discuss the direction of the project. This was vital given that everything was pretty fluid to the end.

Q16: Project was deployed in a reasonable timeframe according to scope?

- The scope changed but we delivered what Jay needed.

Figure 22.4   Team members can add comments to their survey responses to support their evaluation of a given area. The facilitator can use the comments to jumpstart the retrospective meeting if team members don't contribute initially.

How frequently should you do a retrospective?

Acme Media chose to do a retrospective at the end of each project, but you may alter the frequency to best support your needs. For example, the Scrum process suggests a retrospective at the end of each sprint, which typically runs 30 days. The end of a sprint may correlate to the end of a project, or it may only tie to one iteration of development work that will eventually support a completed project. Some teams choose to do both: they have a small, quick retrospective after each iteration and then a more detailed review at the end of the project.

You should also consider the size of your project when determining how often to do the retrospective. If your project runs for 4 days and involves two people, a formal retrospective may not be needed. Conversely, if you're working on a project estimated to run 6 to 12 months, you should identify logical times to stop and review the process.

It's also good to analyze areas where the team is split. If half the team thinks you did well understanding the customer's needs and the other half doesn't, you need to find out where the difference in perception is coming from.

22.4   *What to expect during the meeting*

Retrospective meetings tend to take on a mind of their own. Similar to a weathervane in a storm, when several team members are participating, the conversation can go anywhere.

What about the facilitator?

Picking the correct person as facilitator helps the retrospective immensely. Good characteristics for a facilitator are as follows:

- Has good communication skills.
- Has background in analysis or process control.
- Knows something about the project and its history.
- Doesn't intimidate the team. For example, executives frequently have the skills required, but they influence how the team responds.
- Has the team's respect.

Facilitators are frequently ScrumMasters, project managers, agile coaches, or development managers. If the facilitator also worked on the project, they should wait until the team has contributed to the discussion before sharing their own thoughts. This helps the facilitator focus on facilitating and also ensures that the whole team contributes during the meeting.

Many teams try to find someone outside of the project to be the facilitator. This helps maintain a neutral perspective on the issues as they're discussed, but you may also waste a lot of time orienting the facilitator.

A project retrospective provides insight into the team's maturity level. A mature team jumps into dialogue immediately and begins to constructively analyze the issues that occurred. The majority of the team participates in the discussions, and analysis of issues doesn't turn into attacks on individual performance.

Conversely, an immature team is quiet and requires prodding from the facilitator. Long periods of silence may occur until one person speaks up. Others may be uncomfortable sharing their thoughts with the team at large. If your culture isn't open, and team members aren't solicited for their opinion, it will take time for them to gain confidence that their thoughts won't be shot down.

Most teams fall somewhere in the middle. These teams have one or two members who usually do all the talking, a handful of people who speak their mind on occasion, and a few people who almost never speak. Acme Media falls into this category. To provide contrast for your own team, you can see how the pilot team folks behave in Acme's retrospective in table 22.1.

Although you have feedback from the team in advance of the meeting, you can expect additional issues to come up when the group discusses the project together.

Table 22.1 **A retrospective includes a variety of perspectives and personality types. A good facilitator obtains constructive feedback from all participants and helps the team gel around improvements that should be implemented.**

Project role	Name	Retrospective behavior
Project manager	Wendy Johnson	Used to leading process improvements with the team. Wants to contribute to every discussion during the retrospective. Wendy thinks about process issues every day and looks forward to the chance to review them in detail at the retrospective. Wendy is careful to limit her contribution during Acme Media's first retrospective so that other team members can learn to contribute.
Developer	Roy Williams	Roy was a lead developer at Acme Media for a while and is part of the core team. Roy has always been outspoken and doesn't like his ideas to be challenged. He contributes freely during the meeting, but the facilitator asks other team members for their thoughts after Roy speaks. Some team members do speak up, and a few have different perspectives than Roy. Over time, Roy will have to learn how to collaborate with the team versus having them acquiesce to his ideas.
Developer	Matt Lee	Matt has a history of being the junior programmer. He's been quiet in the past but shares his thoughts when the facilitator queries him directly during the retrospective.
User experience	Ryan Getty	Ryan is used to speaking in front of the team and has great skills for being an agile team member. Ryan frequently leads discussions with the team and uses a whiteboard to illustrate designs with the team. He leaves his ego at the door and does a great job of collaborating with the team and aggregating ideas. Ryan speaks up during the meeting but provides space for others to contribute. He also focuses on issues and avoids personal attacks on others.

Table 22.1   **A retrospective includes a variety of perspectives and personality types. A good facilitator obtains constructive feedback from all participants and helps the team gel around improvements that should be implemented.** *(continued)*

Project role	Name	Retrospective behavior
Quality assurance	Gina Wallace	Testers have been second-class citizens at Acme Media for a while, and Gina had given up on suggesting ideas that were always disregarded. The new agile process gives her hope, though, especially because testing isn't delayed until the end of the project. Gina contributes in depth during the retrospective and finds that her previous suggestions are in line with the new agile process they're pursuing.
Operations	Tom Klein	Tom works in a department that doesn't have plans for using an agile process. As a pilot-team member, he was trained on the new process, but he doesn't quite *get* agile yet. Tom is comfortable making suggestions, though, and points out some areas for improvement in the deployment process.
Requirements	Rich Jenkins	Rich is a by-the-book analyst and feels that everything should be documented. During a discussion of missing requirements, Rich blames the new agile process, saying that everything should be documented to prevent misunderstandings in the future. Rich believes the Sunday paper shouldn't go out until Monday if the quality isn't perfect.
Architecture	Keith Gastaneau	Keith is a seasoned architect and has learned that agile methods are the best way to deliver software. He takes a Socratic approach to the retrospective and asks the team insightful questions.
Customer	Jay Fosberg	Jay acted as the customer advocate during the project and enjoyed the respect that the customer title received with the new process. But Jay discusses the fact that he may be too involved in the process, in that he was invited to all team meetings and lost time for some of the other work he needed to accomplish on his own.

What about personal performance issues?

We've participated in retrospectives where the project was affected by an individual's poor performance. In these instances, the team could use the meeting to humiliate the employee and discuss how their performance hurt the team, but the retrospective isn't the place to criticize personal performance.

Employee performance should be addressed by management away from the team. The whole team may realize where a person failed, and they can give the person feedback during the project, but the retrospective isn't meant to address personal performance issues.

A manager can dig deeper into the performance issue and may also know that the issue relates to a personal issue the employee is experiencing. The manager can create performance plans if needed and also provide a level of tolerance if the individual is experiencing personal problems related to their health, family issues, or substance issues.

22.5 *Converting the feedback into action*

After all the issues are documented, the facilitator works with the team to prioritize the issues. It may sound corny and a little like 1980s business philosophy, but the facilitator works with the team to find the root cause of each issue. Similar to identifying a customer's root need, you must look at each issue and ask "Why?" several times.

During the retrospective, Rich discusses the fact that he had a hard time testing the bidding functionality. The facilitator and the team ask Rich if he didn't look at the feature card or if he didn't listen when the customer discussed the feature. Rich said he did listen, but the bidding functionality was complex and he couldn't keep track of all the permutations.

After digging deeper into the issue, the team identifies two root issues. First, the team isn't creating feature cards at the correct level of detail. There are several flavors of bidding, such as "buy now" and "expiring bids." The team should have gone more granular on the feature and created separate cards for the unique functionality of each type of bid.

Second, everyone assumed that feature cards were all you create in an agile environment. Because face-to-face is the most effective means of communication, the team ran with feature cards and customer discussions. This model didn't work well for the bidding functionality when Jay, the customer, forgot some of the many business rules involved. It also made it hard for Rich to envision an encompassing test plan.

The team forgot one of their own rules: deciding the level of documentation needed throughout the project. In retrospect, they should have created additional documentation to support the bidding feature and its complexity so that it could be tested thoroughly and to keep everyone in synch with the feature's details.

Acme Media identifies several additional issues from the project and then sets about documenting action items for improving the process on the next project. Figure 22.5 summarizes the findings and action items. Acme Media will review this list at the end of the next project to see if the team has successfully addressed the key issues.

This list will be reviewed at a subsequent retrospective to validate if the changes were effective.

Recommended Changes from Auctionator Retrospective

Priority	Suggested Changes	Who	When
A	Determine the correct amount of documentation to support testing and development. We went with an enhanced feature card in the previous release and it did not provide enough detail. We need to examine each feature and estimate the depth of documentation we will need.	Team	Immediately
B	Be more selective when inviting the customer to meetings. Invite the customer to meetings where the information will help them or their input is needed.	Team	Immediately
B	Demo during the iteration if we have something the customer can provide feedback on. In our first project we waited until the end of the iterations.	Developers	Immediately
B	We need to make sure we understand the customer's core need when creating the feature cards. We rushed on some in our previous project and had discoveries that would have been exposed with a more diligent discussion.	Team	Immediately
B	Continue to refine the estimation process. We underestimated the work for the last project. Our actual throughput measurement should help with this issue.	Wendy and the team	Immediately
C	We need to look for overlap on the features and work to better define the scope of each. We got confused with overlapping work during the last project.	Team	Immediately

Figure 22.5   A retrospective ends with a prioritized summary of the key issues and action items to address them. Prioritization helps the team identify the changes that need to happen immediately versus changes that will make a marginal difference in performance.

22.6   *Key points*

The key points from this chapter are as follows:

- You should review your development process on a frequent basis to look for areas to improve and as an act of preventive maintenance.
- You can perform retrospectives after every iteration or at the conclusion of each project, with a goal of reviewing the process at least every 2 months.
- You need to do pre-work before the retrospective meeting to ensure success. This pre-work includes setting expectations for participants and surveying participants before the retrospective meeting. The pre-work provides the foundation needed to ensure a successful meeting and the early exposure of any issues you may have encountered.
- Use the pre-work to focus the meeting on the top areas to discuss. You'll focus on areas where the team is in consensus that there is an issue, where they agree you're doing well, and where the team is divided about how you're doing.

- The retrospective meeting requires a strong facilitator who works well with the various personality types of the team. The facilitator makes sure that no one person dominates and that introverts also express their opinions.
- The retrospective concludes with a list of prioritized improvements. The improvements are put on display in a visible place: a team-room wall, a project wiki site, or both. You'll review the output at the subsequent retrospective to see how well you addressed the issues identified.

22.7 Looking forward

At this point, we've taken our case study completely through a project, from concept to delivery to retrospective. In chapter 23, we'll discuss the next steps after a pilot project and logical ways to scale agile across larger companies.

Part 7

Moving forward

Chapter 22 concluded our case study. We followed Acme Media as it researched agile development, created a new process that introduced agility, and tested the new practices with a pilot project. Acme concluded its pilot with a project retrospective, which is the last step in its new process.

Similar to a project retrospective, Acme Media's core team needs to perform a retrospective on the new process, determining where it worked, where it needs to be changed, and how to scale agility across the company. In this section we will follow the core team as they review the pilot, and we will discuss how Acme Media can move from project-level adoption to enterprise-level agility.

23

Extending the new process across your company

Creating a successful Scrum team is only the first step on the road to an Agile company. In most enterprises today, you must create a successful product portfolio delivered by distributed/outsourced teams. Even then, to win in a market segment, an Agile approach to the enterprise product strategy is needed to dramatically improve opportunity for success.

—Jeff Sutherland, co-creator of the Scrum development process

Chapter 22 concluded our case study as we wrapped up the project with a retrospective. With the pilot under your belt, it's time to look at what you've learned and what you need to do to scale the new process across your company.

As we've mentioned throughout the book, the pilot project may be all that is needed for a smaller company to get started with agile, but larger companies will need to do additional work to achieve enterprise-wide adoption. In this chapter, we'll help you continue with scaling by discussing common findings and how to increase your agility level through the use of the Sidky Agile Measurement Index

(SAMI). The SAMI will help you measure your current level of agility and determine logical places to continue improving your process. The SAMI is similar to Capability Maturity Model Integration (CMMI) in that it uses levels, but the purpose of the levels is to help you measure where you are, not to act as a scoring mechanism.

> **What is CMMI?**
>
> Per the Software Engineering Institute at Carnegie Melon: "The Capability Maturity Model Index is a process improvement approach that provides organizations with the essential elements of effective processes. It can be used to guide process improvement across a project, a division, or an entire organization. CMMI helps integrate traditionally separate organizational functions, set process improvement goals and priorities, provide guidance for quality processes, and provide a point of reference for appraising current processes."

Let's get started by looking at common findings at the conclusion of a pilot project.

23.1   Common findings after a pilot

Every company has a unique experience when moving to agile. But we've witnessed some trends that tend to span almost all migrations. Let's review some of the common outputs from a pilot test.

23.1.1 Slower than the old process

We once worked with a project manager who had to create a weekly status report for executive management. When the project manager began in her position, she had to learn how the report was generated. First she had to make sure every department entered their status information, then she had to run a query from the time-tracking system, and then she had to aggregate the data into a Word document and export it to Acrobat. When the project manager was trained, she wrote down every step to make sure the report came out correctly. On average, the report took 4 hours to generate. As the weeks passed, the project manager looked less at her notes and began to perform the steps from memory. Her time went from 4 hours down to 1.

Most teams doing an agile pilot will seem more like the 4-hour project report than the 1-hour project report. During the pilot, team members flip through notes from agile training, read books (like this one), and try to be agile more by process than by feel. This is to be expected. You need to make sure everyone who is supporting your move to agile understands that progress will be slower at first.

23.1.2 Confusion about the process

As mentioned in the previous section, many team members will be reading their notes from training as you're going through the pilot process. Team members usually hear the training in different ways, and during the pilot these different perceptions come out.

For example, one team member at Acme Media thought he heard the agile coach say you should estimate features before prioritizing them, and another team member heard that you should estimate after prioritizing. You'll encounter similar examples during your pilot.

This confusion is a good thing, in that it brings questions to the surface and gives your team a chance to normalize on what agile will mean in your company. In the process we've outlined, these questions are discussed weekly with the core team and your agile coach during the pilot, and the group can reach consensus on the practices and approaches you'll use.

The negative about this confusion is that it makes things somewhat chaotic and provides ammo for anyone in your company who is looking for a reason to say agile won't work. In addition, your pilot project will be slowed down while the team stops to figure out process issues and reach agreement about how things should be done. All these things are normal: you should set expectations with your pilot team and your sponsors that confusion is to be expected on the first few projects and that the process will solidify and improve over time.

23.1.3 *Team polarization*

As your pilot concludes, your team may split into two camps: one that believes the pilot was successful and agile should be used throughout the company, and another that believes the pilot demonstrated that agile doesn't work and provides no value.

At the start of this book, we discussed agile detractors and how to involve them in the process. This includes using their feedback to improve the process and giving detractors a role in the migration. If your pilot concludes, and the detractors aren't embracing agile, you'll need to investigate and find out why. You'll have a difficult time scaling agile if employees are split on whether to use it.

Note that there is a difference between finding areas to improve and making a blanket statement that agile doesn't work. Your detractors will probably find areas that need to be fixed during your pilot, which is a good thing; but if the detractors are simply saying, "Agile doesn't work," you must address this via management or coaching.

We're assuming your company has needs that drive the use of agile, such as tight deadlines, volatile requirements, and the need to deliver what the customer really requires. If this is true, then agile should work for you, especially if you've created a process that recognizes and addresses the constraints of your environment.

Some team members may never embrace agile, but they will accept it as a reality and over time may be converted. Other team members may never buy in—agile may be too radical a change for them. In these rare instances, we've seen employees leave companies or management ask employees to leave.

23.1.4 *Starting to feel agile*

Your pilot will also turn guesses about what agile is like into reality. Every time something new comes out, we all want to know more about it. Quite a few years ago, the new thing was XML—we all went to XML training and created a few applications that used XML, and then we said "Ah, that's what XML is." The same thing is true of agile.

Until you do a project with agile, it's just a buzzword, hype, and conjecture. You can read books like this one, take training, and enlist the help of a coach. But until you do an agile project, you don't know what agile means.

As your pilot project wraps up, you and your team will discover what it means to collaborate on decisions. You'll understand what it takes to deliver in an incremental manner. You'll know what's required to let the customer into your back office and involve them in the development process.

Perhaps the greatest benefit that will come from your pilot is that your team will begin to reach agreement on what agile means. It isn't important for you to agree with the agile community or the authors of this book—it's only important for you and your team to reach agreement about what practices provide value in your environment.

Finally, we'll contradict ourselves for a moment. We've said you can't tell someone what agile is: they need to experience it. We—Ahmed and Greg—have different backgrounds and agile experiences, but we both recognized one thing at the end of our first agile project: we both thought, "This is how it's supposed to be done." We've all worked on projects where we felt bad at the end and knew the process partially contributed to the issues. But when we concluded our first agile projects, we felt that we were using a process that supports the realities of software development. It felt good!

23.2   *What the Acme Media team learned from their pilot*

To better illustrate the findings from a pilot, let's review what Acme Media learned at the conclusion of the company's pilot. We'll analyze how Acme did in comparison to the five agile enablers discussed in chapter 1. We'll also compare how Acme did in relation to the company's goals for moving to a more agile process.

The team that performed the pilot project performed a retrospective at the end. The core team reviews the results from the pilot retrospective but also looks at the pilot from a global perspective. The core team evaluates the pilot against the agile enablers they were trained on and considers the best way to continue moving the company to a better development process.

To help you follow along, we'll score Acme Media against the agile enablers. Scoring is definitely subjective, but it helps teams understand where they are and where they can improve. We'll score on a scale of 1 percent to 100 percent, where 100 percent represents perfect support of an agile principle.

23.2.1 *Embracing change to deliver customer value*

Acme Media delivers code iteratively now, which lets it adapt during projects. The team holds daily meetings and catches issues more quickly so they have more time to adapt. They don't *fully embrace* change yet, but they understand that it's a reality.

Acme Media can improve in this area by

- *Improving participation in the daily meetings*—Acme's project manager has to initiate many of the discussions, and the team eventually jumps in. In a perfect environment, the meetings will start quickly, with everyone discussing their personal status, goals for the day, and roadblocks they have encountered.
- *Learning which topics to discuss during the daily meetings*—Many times, roadblocks are worked in real time during the stand-up meeting, and the discussion pertains to only one or two people in the group. These discussions also extend the meetings beyond the 15 to 30 minutes allocated. As the Acme team matures, they will learn when a discussion is relevant for the majority of the team and when the troubleshooting discussion should be held by a smaller group after the meeting.

In the area of embracing change, we score Acme Media's team 20 percent before the pilot and 50 percent after the pilot. The team still has a long way to go toward embracing change, but they made good progress during the pilot.

23.2.2 *Customer involvement and feedback*

In the past Acme Media received feedback on the final product only as it went through a customer acceptance process. Acme allocated some time for customer requests that emerged from customer testing, but frequently serious shortcomings were identified and release dates were pushed out.

Acme Media's new iterative approach let Jay, the customer, provide feedback as the product was incrementally created and delivered. The team had time to identify and triage issues earlier in the release. Jay explained his ideas to the team and worked with the team to refine understanding of the requirements throughout development. This helped the team break down the features into more discrete functions and remove low-priority functions from the release. Jay's involvement and availability helped the team deliver the truly critical requirements and keep the delivery on schedule.

Jay's involvement also helped him identify requirements that he'd missed. As the team prototyped and iteratively developed the features, Jay occasionally noticed a feature he had overlooked. Some team members grumbled about scope creep, but many of the items identified were critical and would have prevented deployment if they hadn't been included.

The team can improve in this area by

- *Becoming more comfortable showing code to the customer before it's 100 percent complete*—The developers don't like to provide qualifications when they demo, to explain what is missing. They worry that the customer won't focus on the area being demonstrated and will instead be distracted by the missing functionality. As the Acme team matures, this will become less of an issue, and the developers will develop faith in demonstrating portions of a feature as opposed to all the functionality. The customers will get more used to seeing code that is still in development.

- *Improving their attitude toward customer change requests*—Because Jay worked with the team on a frequent basis, he often noticed requirements that he had missed earlier. Jay made discoveries throughout the project, as opposed to at the end. The team wasn't ready for these frequent findings and often complained about scope creep and not being able to lock down features. As we mentioned in chapter 7, you should do a thorough analysis in an agile environment so that obvious requirements aren't missed, but you must also understand that the customer may not entirely understand what they need until the solution starts forming. As the Acme Media team matures, this should become less of an issue. The team members will also get help from their coach and learn that customer discoveries are real and a normal part of the development process—not an exception.

- *Improving on getting internal feedback when they deliver internal features*—During the Auctionator project, the team created a support tool to help them measure system performance during high bidding periods. The team forgot that they were a customer and didn't take the feature through User Acceptance Testing (UAT). After the feature was live and in production, they identified several shortcomings with the utility. The team discussed this issue during the retrospective and agreed that in the future, internal features will be treated the same as paying customer features.

In this area, we score Acme Media's team 10 percent before the pilot and 50 percent after the pilot. The team has plenty of room for improvement, but the level of customer involvement increased significantly.

23.2.3 *Planning and delivering software frequently*

This is by far the area in which Acme Media improved the most. In the past, Acme delivered late and frequently delivered functionality that wasn't used by the customer.

With the new process, Acme became crisp on the features that were critical for the project and focused on delivering those features in the first iteration. Acme also did a good job of discussing priorities during the project's development period. If a team member identified a function that didn't appear to be critical, they discussed it with Jay to see if the function should be delayed or deferred. This helped the team focus on delivering the minimum, critical functionality.

Although Acme improved, the team has one area to work on to ensure frequent delivery: they must treat the end of an iteration as a milestone that must be adhered to. In their first iteration, the development work ran late, and the team wanted to extend the iteration. The team didn't view this as an issue because the work from the iteration was being queued but not deployed. They didn't think there would be an issue in pushing out the iteration by a day or two.

For a mature agile team, it isn't the end of the world to push out an iteration by a day or so (although they rarely do). Customers can be notified, and more than likely the schedule has enough slack to absorb the slip. But this is a terrible practice to get into as a new team. If you view the iteration deadline as optional, you'll start drifting from the agile principle of *just enough* and reduce the urgency around your work. The team needs to have discipline and support the iteration schedule.

Acme had an excuse for the first iteration in that the team's capacity planning was a guess, but the second iteration was scheduled based on how many story points they completed in the previous iteration. After the team gets a feel for their true capacity, there should be fewer requests to extend iterations.

In this area, we score Acme Media's team 0 percent before the pilot and 50 percent after the pilot. The team delivered usable software during the pilot, which was a major improvement over previous projects.

23.2.4 *Technical excellence*

Acme Media made slight improvements in its pursuit of technical excellence. The company's original practices weren't poor, but they lacked agility.

Acme made strides in building more frequently. In the past, the team built once a week. In the new agile model, the team attempted to do daily integrations, but they were able to perform a build only every 2 to 3 days. This was an improvement, but the delay in building complicated the ability to track down build issues.

The team also improved by embracing the use of prototyping, proof of concept (POC) work, and the use of other modeling tools. In the past, the team wanted to jump straight into development and avoid performing any work that might be thrown away. With the Auctionator, they found prototyping effective in demonstrating Jay's requirements back to him. They also pursued a POC test to verify their assumptions about system performance before coding the bidding functionality.

Acme's last area of improvement related to architecture. In the past, Acme wanted to create a perfect architecture for every project: an infrastructure that was flexible for any perceivable need and scalable for any performance requirements. This approach worked well on occasion, but many times the team spent so much time on the architecture that application delivery was delayed. During the Auctionator project, the team still focused on scalable architecture, but they time-boxed their work to be sure they could deliver the application on time. This was a struggle for the team, and they had many debates about when the architecture was good enough. The team will need time to accept and appreciate this approach.

To continue toward their goal of technical excellence, Acme Media will pursue testing automation so they can get closer to achieving a daily build. The team will also do a POC around test-driven development. Matt, the developer, has always wanted to try TDD, and he'll try to write his unit tests before coding on the next project. Matt will share his findings with all developers and hopes the team can move to this disciplined practice.

In this area, we score Acme Media's team 40 percent before the pilot and 50 percent after the pilot.

23.2.5 *Human-centric practices*

Let's start by looking at communication and collaboration. In the past, Acme Media did most of its communications formally during a project. If an issue was encountered, the project manager checked everyone's schedule and found a day to sit down and discuss it.

With the new model and daily stand-up meetings, small subsets of team members frequently gather immediately after the meeting and work out issues or design the same day. This works well because the attendees don't have to be refreshed about why they're at the meeting, and the resolution can be shared at the stand-up meeting the next day if needed. A few team members still looked to Wendy to get them together when a meeting is required, but 50 percent of the team like the new ownership and call and facilitate meetings on their own.

In support of the daily stand-up meetings, Wendy has created an intranet project-status site that displays status by feature. In the past, Acme team members gleaned Wendy's all-encompassing project plan to find status on the areas they cared about. The new web page lets the team easily see status by feature, and security is open so they can add their own comments related to status. Wendy uses a projector during the daily stand-up meetings to project the status of features and update them real time as team members provide status. Team members can also review and update the page at their workstations.

Acme Media started down the path to team ownership by creating the core team and involving team members in the move to agile. The company also ensured that a few core team members were on the pilot team to see how well the process worked and to record feedback from pilot team members.

Acme also had a few employees who had used agile before. These folks had a lot of input into the creation of Acme's agile process and served as evangelists for the need to move to a more agile methodology. Employees throughout Acme's web division also knew why the company was moving to agile. Everyone was aware that projects were usually delivered late and that advertisers were looking at competitors who could meet their needs in a timelier manner.

During the pilot, Jay and Wendy kept the team focused on the agile practices. The goal of the pilot was to create awareness of what agile was about. The pilot team wasn't forced to own the process, but they were encouraged to do so. Acme saw improvement in team participation, especially with the introduction of the daily stand-up meetings. In the past, only managers met, and then they brought the work back to their respective teams. The daily stand-up lets everyone ask questions and get a clear understanding about requirements and project status. Acme can also make quicker decisions because the customer is usually available for a discussion of scope, priorities, or issues. In the past, the team didn't communicate directly with the customer; they would spin for days, trying to reach agreement about what was critical.

Acme Media still has several items it can improve in this category:

- *Taking ownership of the process*—Although team participation improved during the pilot, the team still lacks overall ownership of the process. As mentioned, Wendy and Jay often have to initiate discussions or meetings around issues or design. Some team members are used to having a boss get them together to work out issues and designs. It doesn't yet seem natural for everyone to drive the project along with Wendy. This is expected during a pilot: the goal is to create awareness and head down the road to buy-in of the new process. After the team buys in, ownership will evolve over time, especially with good coaching from managers and mentors. The team also needs to see a few people go out on a limb and not get grilled for speaking their opinion or assuming leadership.

- *Addressing discipline issues*—A few team members come into the daily stand-up meeting late, which pushes out the meeting because everything has to be communicated again. Acme's managers will work with select team members and explain to them why the stand-up meeting is critical and the repercussions of their late arrival. The managers will also tie stand-up attendance into employee goals for the year.

- *Eliminating side discussions*—Although it's a minor issue, side meetings frequently take place within the stand-up meeting: two team members will begin whispering to each other as other people are discussing status. Again, the managers at Acme will coach these employees and encourage them to wait until after the meeting for their sidebar discussion.

- *Documenting design decisions*—In the past, Wendy always took meeting notes and emailed them to the team. With Wendy not involved, some team members don't document their decisions and assume that all they need to do is discuss the output during the stand-up meeting the next day. They're half right. It's good to discuss the output at the stand-up meeting, but numerous decisions are made during a project, and the team can become confused about agreements over time. Team members don't need to create formal notes every time they meet, but in projects as complex as the Auctionator, they must record critical decisions. Going forward, Acme will store these decisions on its intranet/project wiki site.

- *Participating in the daily meetings*—Some team members still needed to be prompted to give their status, leading Wendy to frequently go around the room and ask each team member for input. Certain team members may always be reclusive and reserved, but in the long term, Acme wants the team to own the process and speak up without being prompted.

Acme Media made good improvements with communication and collaboration. In this area, we score Acme Media's team 20 percent before the pilot and 50 percent after the pilot.

23.3 *Next steps*

After you finish the pilot project, where do you go next? Do you go for more pilot projects, or do you mandate agile for all the teams working in the organization? As you can see from the book so far, the pilot project usually brings out the benefits of agile and at the same time highlights some of the challenges of using agile in your environment. Your focus should be on taking advantage of the benefits that agile has brought about and spreading those around the organization. The million-dollar question is, how do you do that?

If you work for a small company, you may not need to have this discussion. You may have only enough people for one project at a time, and your pilot may be the start of using agile for all your projects. In addition, if your company never had a development process to start with, you may quickly move from a pilot to using agile on all of your projects.

But if you're a medium- to large-size company with a legacy development process, this chapter is for you. Continue reading to see the approach we suggest with larger companies.

23.3.1 *Spanning the chasm*

The approach we'll present in this chapter is based on Geoffrey Moore's book *Crossing the Chasm*. The book is based on the Technology Adoption Lifecycle, which is an interesting model for explaining the adoption of new ideas. Figure 23.1 shows the original bell-shaped lifecycle.

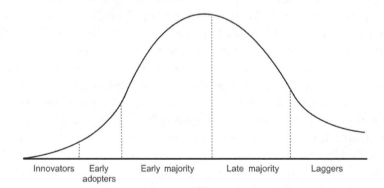

Figure 23.1   **The lifecycle for new-idea adoption**

In a nutshell, the model recognizes five categories of adopters:

- *Innovators*—Usually experimentalists who are interested in trying new things.
- *Early adopters*—Willing to take the risk and adopt a new technology because it either addresses a direct need they have or proposes a new strategic opportunity for them.
- *Early majority*—Pragmatists, conservative, but still open to new ideas if they're convinced. They usually prefer evolutionary change and are averse to taking risks.

- *Late majority*—Mainstream employees who are less comfortable with technology change and are usually skeptical.
- *Laggards*—May never adopt a new technology.

The Technology Adoption Lifecycle explains how a new idea gains acceptance by progressing through these five segments. Moore highlights in his book that cracks exist between each of the segments of the lifecycle, but what is of most interest to us is the chasm between the early adopters and the early majority (see figure 23.2).

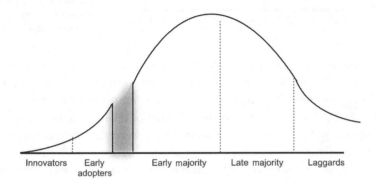

Figure 23.2 The chasm between early adopters and the early majority

Table 23.1 (adapted from Geoghegan, 1994) illustrates the difference in mindset between the early adopters and the early majority.

Table 23.1 The differences in the mentalities of early adopters and the early majority

Early adopters	Early majority
Proponents of revolutionary change	Proponents of evolutionary change
Visionary users	Pragmatic users
Project oriented	Process oriented
Willing to take risks	Averse to taking risks
Willing to experiment	Look for proven applications
Individually self-sufficient	May require support
Tend to communicate horizontally (focused across disciplines)	Tend to communicate vertically (focused within a discipline)

Similarly, your journey to enterprise-wide agile must progress through these segments: we believe that a gap exists in agile adoption between the early adopters and the early majority. Let's start by highlighting what we believe is the first stage of agile adoption.

Let's take a moment to look at each segment of the adoption curve and why it takes more than pilot projects to move the enterprise to an agile mentality.

INNOVATORS: THE FIRST PILOT PROJECT

A pilot project basically maps to the first stage (the innovators; see figure 23.3). The majority of this book has gone through the process of conducting a pilot project at Acme Media and at your organization. Let's quickly review.

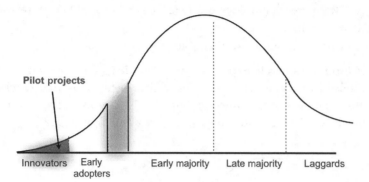

Figure 23.3   A pilot project initiates the move to a more agile process.

You start with an initial readiness assessment to determine which agile practices are suitable for your team. You begin injecting your current process with agile practices. Then you select a pilot project and assemble a team around the project to test your new agile process. The pilot project shows the benefits of using agile practices within your team. In Acme Media's case, the practices that were piloted succeeded and showed benefit. It may be the case in your organization that some of the practices you try during your pilot don't succeed. Nevertheless, the next stage according to the Technology Adoption Lifecycle is to move to the early adopters.

EARLY ADOPTERS: THE SECOND WAVE OF PILOT PROJECTS

In your journey to agile, the early adopters will map to a second wave of pilot projects. The pilot projects in this wave have a direct need for the benefits that the first agile pilot project exhibited (see figure 23.4).

Your practice during this phase is to look at the first pilot project, use the lessons learned to find out which practices worked, and then apply those practices to five or six more pilot projects within the organization. For example, in one of the organizations Ahmed coached, after finishing the first pilot project, the process-improvement director was impressed with the quick time-to-market and pointed out a number of projects in critical need of a shorter time-to-market. This new set of pilot projects acted as a second testing ground for the agile practices injected into the organizational software-development process.

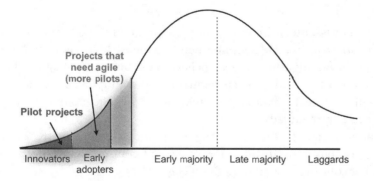

Figure 23.4   Pilots get you nearer to your goal, but it takes more than pilots to obtain enterprise-wide adoption in large companies.

EARLY MAJORITY: THE BIGGEST HURDLE

According to Geoffrey Moore, moving from the early adopters to the early majority isn't as simple as adding more projects. As we highlighted earlier, a chasm exists between the stages. This chasm maps to moving from a project-level agile adoption approach to an organizational-wide, enterprise-level agile adoption approach (see figure 23.5).

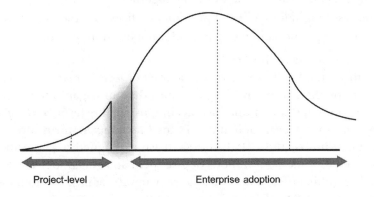

Project-level   Enterprise adoption

Figure 23.5 Spanning the chasm moves the company from using agile on projects to an agile mentality across the board.

We've seen some organizations take the *big-bang* approach. After they have evidence that the pilot project is successful, these companies mandate a company-wide agile transition. Although this approach may work with certain organizations, we aren't in favor of it because of the high risk of chaos and resistance to the transition. This is like applying the same methodology you used for pilot projects to the whole organization without respecting the different mindsets between the early majority and the early adopters.

Our approach to enterprise-level agile adoption is evolutionary change. This is more in line with the mindset of the early majority. Instead of introducing all the agile practices at once, you pick a small, coherent set of practices and introduce them to the organization one step at a time. You should choose practices based on the fact that they're proven to be effective during your pilot and the agile value they will introduce.

We suggest using a value-based roadmap to help you determine which set of practices to initially use across the enterprise. Ahmed has created his own roadmap called the Sidky Agile Measurement Index (SAMI). It highlights five agile values and guides organizations to focus on introducing the practices that satisfy each level first. The SAMI is discussed in detail in section 23.3.2.

THE LATE MAJORITY

These people need more time and will be skeptical until they see the majority of the company using a new process. Initially, they will resist even the smallest incremental changes; but after critical mass is reached, they will join in.

THE LAGGARDS

Some people will never adopt a new idea. You may have engineers who've been working for the past 20 years in a certain way on legacy code. For these people, change isn't an option. But if you can reach the point where the new process is being used for more than 90 percent of the portfolio, you should consider the move to agile successful.

23.3.2 *Using the SAMI*

The SAMI provides a framework for moving your enterprise to an agile mentality. Specifically, the SAMI helps with enterprise adoption by doing the following:

- Eliminating the random picking of practices
- Ensuring the practices you pursue work well together
- Focusing on instilling values, not just pushing practices into the organization
- Helping avoid the phenomenon of teams adopting random practices

Figure 23.6 shows an example of the SAMI.

In its simplest form, the SAMI can be viewed as a set of levels or steps, where each level represents one of the five essential agile values that an organization needs to embrace. Many in the agile community are against using the term *levels of agility* because it's too similar to the levels of maturity in the Capability Maturity Model Integration (CMMI). First, unlike the CMMI, the SAMI isn't designed as a certification framework or as a tool to rank organizations or give them an agile grade. The SAMI is designed as a tool to guide an organization's journey toward agility. Without delving into the pros or cons of CMMI, there is little doubt that a step-by-step approach to attaining any goal is beneficial. Partitioning the journey toward agility into steps, or

	Embrace change to deliver customer value	Plan and deliver software frequently	Human-centric	Technical excellence	Collaboration with business people
Level 5 Encompassing	Low-process ceremony	Agile project estimation	Ideal agile physical setup	Test-driven development Paired programming No/minimal number of Cockburn Level -1 or 1b people on team	Frequent face-to-face interaction between developers & users (collocated)
Level 4 Adaptive	Client driven iterations Customer satisfaction feedback	Smaller and more frequent releases (4-8 weeks) Adaptive planning		Daily progress tracking meetings Agile documentation (from Agile modeling) User stories	Collaborative, representative, authorized, committed and knowledgeable (CRACK) customer immediately accessible Customer contract revolves around commitment of collaboration, not features
Level 3: Integrated		Risk driven iterations Maintain a list of all remaining features (Backlog)	Self organizing teams Frequent face-to-face communication between the team	Continuous integration Continuous improvement (i.e. refactoring) Have around 30% of Cockburn Level 2 and Level 3 people on team Automated unit tests	
Level 2: Evolutionary	Evolutionary requirements	Continuous delivery (incremental-iterative development) Planning at different levels		Software configuration management Tracking iteration through working software No big design up front (BDUF)	Customer contract reflective of evolutionary development
Level 1: Collaborative	Reflect and tune process	Collaborative planning	Collaborative teams Empowered and motivated teams	Coding standards Knowledge sharing tools (*wikis, blogs*) Task volunteering not task assignment	Customer commitment to work with developing team

Figure 23.6 The SAMI can be used to lead an enterprise through an incremental process of increasing agility.

agile levels, is in tune with the agile philosophy of *early and continuous delivery and itera-tive development.* Instead of attempting to have an organization adopt agility in a single step, the SAMI breaks down the delivery into five *releases* or *levels,* with each release adding value to the organization. Another benefit of this step-based approach is that it helps decrease the amount of chaos and resistance caused by major change initiatives within organizations. Figure 23.7 shows the Virginia Satir change curve.

The curve illustrates how change initiatives cause organizations to go through an intense period of resistance and chaos. To reiterate from chapter 4, the Virginia Satir change curve indicates that if an organization can go through this period of chaos and resistance and embrace new transforming ideas, then the chaos will decrease and performance will increase to a new level higher than the previous status quo. The risk is that some organizations may not be able to handle these periods of chaos and intense drop in performance. Consequently, instead of moving forward, they may fall back to their old status quo.

In our experience, following the guidance provided by the SAMI approach to agile adoption can reduce the all-at-once chaos by introducing incremental, step-by-step change. More specifically, the SAMI breaks down the adoption of agile principles and practices into steps or levels, with each level delivering a new value to the organization and, subsequently, an increase in performance. By breaking down a major change ini-tiative into smaller, more manageable steps or levels, the resistance and chaos associ-ated with each step are smaller and shorter; hence, the consequent drop in performance becomes more tolerable, and the probability of embracing the new pro-cess of agility becomes much higher.

Let's take a few moments to review the sections of the SAMI.

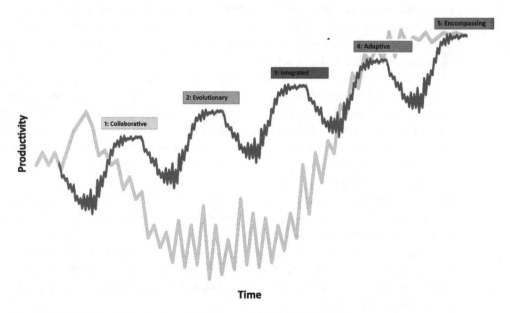

Figure 23.7   Virginia Satir change curve with an overlay of the SAMI change curve

AGILE LEVELS

The first component of the SAMI is the agile levels or steps toward agility. The agile levels are designed to represent the core values of agility as defined by the Agile Manifesto, rather than the values or practices related to any particular agile methodology like XP or Scrum.

The search for the most appropriate sequence of agile levels required us to review the Agile Manifesto and various other sources including books about agile development, articles, organizational change books, and even books about social change and its causes. One book in particular was beneficial: *The Tipping Point* by Malcolm Gladwell, which discusses the factors that cause new trends and social outbreaks to emerge and spread. The three factors Gladwell identifies provide the inspiration for the naming and ordering of values in the SAMI.

Gladwell's first factor relates to people and their importance in creating social outbreaks and trends. This factor maps easily to the agile value of *enhancing communication and collaboration*. This finding, along with the fact that collaboration is mentioned in the first and third statements of the Agile Manifesto, leads us to place this agile value at the first level of the SAMI.

The second factor Gladwell mentions concerns the content of the message being spread. From this factor, we evolve the next three agile levels (evolutionary, integrated, and adaptive) and their associated values. The ordering of the associated level/value pairs is determined by answering two questions: Which of these values will have the biggest impact on moving an organization toward agility? And, are the agile values dependent on each other, and if so, which one needs to be first?

The answers to these questions lead to the conclusion that agile level 2 must reflect an evolutionary approach to development and represent the agile value of *delivering software early and continuously*. This decision is based on the fact that most agile software practices depend on development being conducted in an evolutionary manner, rather than following the big-bang approach.

Agile level 3 is assigned the agile value of *developing high-quality, working software in an efficient and integrated manner*. It's important to realize that an organization must have an integrated development environment before it can realistically expect to be able to respond effectively to change. More specifically, for the development process to adapt to constant changes, the environment must be integrated and resilient to ensure that no changes will jeopardize the quality of the product.

Because these qualities must exist within an environment before you can hope to see the organization become adaptive, the *integrated* agile level has to precede the *adaptive* level. As a result, agile level 4, *adaptive*, is assigned the agile value of *responding to change through multiple levels of feedback*.

Gladwell's third factor, establishing a suitable environment for the trend to spread, inspires us to map the fifth level of agility to the agile value of *establishing a vibrant and all-encompassing environment to sustain agility*. Figure 23.8 illustrates the final sequence of the five levels of agility.

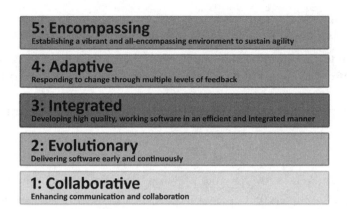

Figure 23.8
Levels of agile maturity

Each of these agile levels is composed of a set of synergistic and complementary agile practices that introduce and sustain the agile values touted at that level. Being organized into levels, the agile practices and concepts help an organization incorporate new agile values, which, in turn, leads to the realization of organizational goals and objectives.

The process of populating each level with practices is guided by the second component of the SAMI, the agile principles.

AGILE PRINCIPLES

As you may recall from chapter 1, the most common goal for all companies is to increase revenues and profits indefinitely. Most companies pursue the following five strategies to reach this goal:

- Retain customers
- Deliver products while the need still exists
- Motivate employees
- Deliver what the market asks for
- Pursue innovative products and processes

To take this approach one step further, what principles should a company adhere to? We believe a company should adhere to the agile principles.

Agile principles are the essential characteristics that must be reflected in a process before it's considered agile. For example, two key agile principles are *human-centric*, which refers to the reliance on people and the interaction between them, and *technical excellence*, which implies the use of procedures that produce and maintain the highest quality of code possible. The Agile Manifesto also outlines 12 principles that characterize agile development processes. After a careful grouping and summarization, we've identified 5 agile principles that capture the essence of the 12. These 5 principles guide the population of each of the 5 agile levels:

- Embrace change to deliver customer value.
- Plan and deliver software frequently.
- Human-centric.

- Technical excellence.
- Customer collaboration.

These principles guide the identification and incorporation of practices across all agile levels and ensure that each agile level embodies the essential characteristics of agility.

Now that we have principles, we can discuss the practices that bring the principles to life.

23.3.3 *Agile practices*

Agile practices are concrete activities and practical techniques that are used to develop and manage software projects in a manner consistent with their associated agile principles. For example, pair programming, user stories, and collaborative planning are all agile practices. Because the agile levels are composed of agile practices, they're considered the basic building block of the SAMI. You can attain an agile level only when you've fully adopted the agile practices associated with that level. After surveying the agile methodologies currently used in industry, we selected 40 distinct agile practices to populate the SAMI. These practices, arranged in a table with the agile levels and principles, are illustrated earlier, in figure 23.6.

That table is simply one instance of the SAMI. The SAMI doesn't dictate which practices should be placed at which level; this is up to the individual leading the adoption effort. Each agile coach or consultant will have their own preference about which practices are placed in each level. The kind of experiences gained from previous adoption efforts can and should serve as a basis for formulating a better arrangement of the practices within the agile levels. For example, Mike Cohn has suggested that user stories be introduced in the first level of agility because, in his experience, they enhance collaboration and communication between the stakeholders with regard to requirements. Others suggest that pair programming be in the first level because it helps to establish collaboration within teams. This diversity of opinions as to where to place agile practices emphasizes an important factor in providing guidance in an agile adoption effort: the adherence to agile values and principles when establishing the levels is paramount, not the positions of the actual practices.

The intention behind the SAMI is to guide the agile adoption process, not to dictate it. But that reorganization must be guided by (and adhere to) the intent and philosophies that underlie the levels of agility and the agile principles.

We contend that the SAMI provides an ideal basis from which to initiate value-driven agile adoption. But how is the SAMI perceived by members of the agile community? You can see a quantitative summary of feedback provided by the agile community in the index. But in summary, the agile community recognizes the utility and need for the SAMI and that it provides a value-based roadmap to agility.

23.4 *Key points*

The key points from this chapter are as follows:

- Almost every agile pilot has these issues: the process may be slower, the team struggles to normalize around the process, and agile cynics find reasons to stop using agile.

- Almost every agile pilot provides the benefit of letting the team experience agile and start understanding what the principles are all about.

- We've outlined what happened to Acme Media during its pilot, and the findings we entered weren't random. The benefits and issues that happened during the pilot actually happened to real companies we've worked with. You should expect to see similar issues and benefits with your pilot.

- If you work for a small company, the pilot may be your last test step before going live with agile across your company. Your goals will focus on maturing and on adding more agile practices as you mature. You can do this with the help of an agile coach.

- If you work for a medium- to large-size company, you'll need more than a pilot to move agile across your enterprise. We suggest using a tool such as the Sidky Agile Measurement Index (SAMI) to iteratively scale agile across large organizations.

- Similar to CMMI, the SAMI identifies levels of agility. But the purpose of the SAMI is to help you become more agile. The SAMI isn't meant to act as a scoring device.

- The SAMI focuses on helping you reach higher levels of agility by suggesting sets of complementary practices to use based on an assessment of your organization.

23.5 *Conclusion*

We've put the breadth of our experience into this book, and we hope that what we've learned will help you, too. We also hope that you use this book as a reference after reading it. We've made the chapters as granular as possible so you can use them as a quick reference.

We'd like to conclude with two of our key thoughts and beliefs.

First, we aren't agilists for the sake of being agile. We do embrace agile principles, and we believe a process focused around agile principles is the best way to develop software today. But what we mainly care about is developing software by the most effective means possible. Today, the most effective way is agile; tomorrow, 17 other individuals like the Agile Alliance may meet in Snowbird, Utah, and identify an even better process. If they do, we'll listen. We're dedicated to learning and improving every day.

Second, keep your eye on the big picture: making money. As we demonstrated in chapter 1, the agile principles tie directly to lowering costs and increasing revenues, but we rarely hear people mention this critical point. You should always be able to explain how your process ties to the bottom line.

appendix A:
Readiness assessment
tables by practice

We identified a set of 20 or so common agile practices. Then we created a readiness-assessment table for each of these practices. By creating a separate table for each practice, we've given people the flexibility to assess their team/organization for one particular practice without having to go through the assessment questions for all the other practices.

Table A.1   Adaptive planning

APN	Adaptive planning involves delaying the detail planning of the next iteration until immediately before the start of the iteration. By delaying the planning to the last minute, the plan can incorporate the latest feedback obtained about the product so far, including what was learned from the previous iteration. Adaptive planning helps teams embrace change because the focus shifts from adhering to a plan (which makes people less embracing of change) to continuously planning based on the latest feedback obtained (which inherently promotes the culture of welcoming change).

Various characteristics to be assessed to determine the team's readiness for this practice	Indicators
Management buy-in Whether the team's management is willing to base the planning for the next iteration on the client's feedback from the current (previous) iteration	APN_M1
Management buy-in Whether the team's management is willing to plan as late as possible for an iteration (immediately before the iteration)	APN_M2

Indicators (questions) to be answered by the manager(s)				

APN_M1	**The plan for upcoming iteration may change based on customer feedback from the previous or current iteration.**			
	Strongly Disagree	Tend to Disagree	Neither Agree nor Disagree	Tend to Agree	Strongly Agree

APN_M2	**You agree with developing the detailed plan for an iteration only after the conclusion of the previous iteration.**			
	Strongly Disagree	Tend to Disagree	Neither Agree nor Disagree	Tend to Agree	Strongly Agree

Table A.2   Backlog (maintaining a list of all remaining features)

BLG	A product backlog is a list of all the work that needs to be done to complete the system being built or enhanced based on the current knowledge of the system. This practice includes the tasks for creating the backlog and controlling it consistently during the process by adding, removing, specifying, updating, and prioritizing the backlog items.

Various characteristics to be assessed to determine the team's readiness for this practice	Indicators
Management buy-in Whether the team's management is willing to maintain an up-to-date list of all the remaining features for the project (backlog)	BLG_M1
Existence Whether it is a common practice for teams to create and maintain an up-to-date list of all the work that remains to be done for a project	BLG_M2 BLG_A1

Indicators (questions) to be answered by the manager(s)				

BLG_M1	**You are willing to keep an up-to-date list of all the work that remains to be done for the project.**			
	Strongly Disagree	Tend to Disagree	Neither Agree nor Disagree	Tend to Agree	Strongly Agree

Table A.2   Backlog (maintaining a list of all remaining features) *(continued)*

BLG_M2	When working on a project, you keep an up-to-date list of all the work that remains to be done.				
	Strongly Disagree	Tend to Disagree	Neither Agree nor Disagree	Tend to Agree	Strongly Agree

Indicators (questions) to be answered by the assessor(s)					
BLG_A1	After inspecting, the team has some mechanism by which all the remaining work in a project is known at any point in time.				
	Strongly Disagree	Tend to Disagree	Neither Agree nor Disagree	Tend to Agree	Strongly Agree

Table A.3   Continuous customer feedback

CCF	This refers to any mechanism to elicit continuous customer feedback about the product. This is important to ensure that the customer is satisfied with what is being developed and that it meets their business needs and expectations. This is contrary to the practice of gathering feedback after the product is completely developed.

Various characteristics to be assessed to determine the team's readiness for this practice	Indicators
Customer feedback existence Whether the team has a method by which they gather continuous feedback/criticism from the customer during the development process	CCF_M1, CCF_M2
Developer buy-in Whether the developers accept the fact that the customers are encouraged to continually rethink their requirements	CCF_D1, CCF_D2, CCF_D3
Management buy-in Whether the managers accept the fact that the customers are encouraged to continually rethink their requirements	CCF_M3, CCF_M4, CCF_M5

Indicators (questions) to be answered by the manager(s)					
CCF_M1	The customer should have the opportunity to give his/her feedback about the product throughout the development process by means of interacting with a working piece of software.				
	Strongly Disagree	Tend to Disagree	Neither Agree nor Disagree	Tend to Agree	Strongly Agree
CCF_M2	The team has a method by which it gathers continuous feedback/criticism from the customer during the development process.				
	Strongly Disagree	Tend to Disagree	Neither Agree nor Disagree	Tend to Agree	Strongly Agree
CCF_M3	Customers should be encouraged to regularly change their expectations for the product being developed to ensure that the product satisfies their business priorities.				
	Strongly Disagree	Tend to Disagree	Neither Agree nor Disagree	Tend to Agree	Strongly Agree

Table A.3   Continuous customer feedback *(continued)*

CCF_M4	As the perception of what they need changes, customers are expected to articulate those changes and so affect the product being built.				
	Strongly Disagree	Tend to Disagree	Neither Agree nor Disagree	Tend to Agree	Strongly Agree
CCF_M5	The customer should give his/her feedback throughout the development process even if it means that requirements must be changed.				
	Strongly Disagree	Tend to Disagree	Neither Agree nor Disagree	Tend to Agree	Strongly Agree

Indicators (questions) to be answered by the developers

CCF_D1	Customers should be encouraged to regularly change their expectations for the product being developed to ensure that the product satisfies their business priorities.				
	Strongly Disagree	Tend to Disagree	Neither Agree nor Disagree	Tend to Agree	Strongly Agree
CCF_D2	The team has a method by which it gathers continuous feedback/criticism from the customer during the development process.				
	Strongly Disagree	Tend to Disagree	Neither Agree nor Disagree	Tend to Agree	Strongly Agree
CCF_D3	The customer should give his/her feedback throughout the development process even if it means that requirements must be changed.				
	Strongly Disagree	Tend to Disagree	Neither Agree nor Disagree	Tend to Agree	Strongly Agree

Table A.4   Continuous delivery

CDL	This practice encourages dividing the development effort into releases and each release into iterations. Continuous delivery promotes delivering the product in small iterations at regular intervals.

Various characteristics to be assessed to determine the team's readiness for this practice	Indicators
Process definition existence Whether the team has any process in place for development and isn't relying on haphazard and ad-hoc approaches to software development	CDL_A1 CDL_D1, CDL_D2 CDL_M1, CDL_M2
Lifecycle experience Whether the team has previously used an incremental-iterative approach for developing systems	CDL_M3, CDL_M4 CDL_D3, CDL_D4
Management buy-in Whether management will be willing to use an iterative-incremental development approach	CDL_M5, CDL_M6

Table A.4 Continuous delivery *(continued)*

Management stress Whether managers can handle the additional stress of overseeing the delivery of workable iterations every 1–4 weeks	CDL_M7
Management competence Whether managers understand the principles of incremental-iterative development	CDL_M7, CDL_M9
Developer stress Whether developers can handle the stress of delivering a workable iteration every 1–4 weeks	CDL_D5
Developer buy-in Whether developers will be willing to use an iterative-incremental development approach	CDL_D6, CDL_D7
Developer competence Whether developers understand the principles of incremental-iterative development	CDL_D8, CDL_D9

Indicators (questions) to be answered by the manager(s)

CDL_M1	There is a clear and known software development process in place for this team; software development isn't ad hoc or haphazard.
	Strongly Disagree / Tend to Disagree / Neither Agree nor Disagree / Tend to Agree / Strongly Agree
CDL_M2	The software-development process consists of a clear set of activities. Each of these activities has clear, standardized deliverables.
	Strongly Disagree / Tend to Disagree / Neither Agree nor Disagree / Tend to Agree / Strongly Agree
CDL_M3	Indicate how often you develop a project using an incremental-iterative approach.
	Never / Seldom / Sometimes / Usually / Always
CDL_M4	It is a common practice for you to divide the system into mini-projects or phases. The system is seldom developed as one large project.
	Strongly Disagree / Tend to Disagree / Neither Agree nor Disagree / Tend to Agree / Strongly Agree
CDL_M5	The incremental-iterative approach has more benefits than the waterfall approach.
	Strongly Disagree / Tend to Disagree / Neither Agree nor Disagree / Tend to Agree / Strongly Agree
CDL_M6	You are willing to use the incremental-iterative approach to develop software.
	Strongly Disagree / Tend to Disagree / Neither Agree nor Disagree / Tend to Agree / Strongly Agree
CDL_M7	Delivering a working increment every 1–4 weeks will not cause you any additional stress.
	Strongly Disagree / Tend to Disagree / Neither Agree nor Disagree / Tend to Agree / Strongly Agree

Table A.4   Continuous delivery *(continued)*

CDL_M8	**No big up-front requirements-gathering and analysis should be conducted when using the incremental-iterative approach. In other words, you don't need to gather all the requirements before you start developing software in an incremental-iterative approach.**

Strongly Disagree	Tend to Disagree	Neither Agree nor Disagree	Tend to Agree	Strongly Agree

CDL_M9	**You fully understand the principles of the incremental-iterative development approach.**

Strongly Disagree	Tend to Disagree	Neither Agree nor Disagree	Tend to Agree	Strongly Agree

Indicators (questions) to be answered by the developers

CDL_D1	**Software development in this team isn't ad hoc or haphazard; there is a clear and known process in place.**

Strongly Disagree	Tend to Disagree	Neither Agree nor Disagree	Tend to Agree	Strongly Agree

CDL_D2	**Every project involves a clear set of activities. Each of these activities has clear, standardized deliverables.**

Strongly Disagree	Tend to Disagree	Neither Agree nor Disagree	Tend to Agree	Strongly Agree

CDL_D3	**Indicate how often you have worked on a project that was developed in an incremental-iterative approach.**

Never	Seldom	Sometimes	Usually	Always

CDL_D4	**It is a common practice for you to divide the system into mini-projects or phases. The system is seldom developed as one large project.**

Strongly Disagree	Tend to Disagree	Neither Agree nor Disagree	Tend to Agree	Strongly Agree

CDL_D5	**Delivering a working increment every 1–4 weeks will not cause you any additional stress.**

Strongly Disagree	Tend to Disagree	Neither Agree nor Disagree	Tend to Agree	Strongly Agree

CDL_D6	**The incremental-iterative approach has more benefits than the waterfall approach.**

Strongly Disagree	Tend to Disagree	Neither Agree nor Disagree	Tend to Agree	Strongly Agree

CDL_D7	**You are willing to do more integration (integrate after each iteration) in order to accommodate the incremental-iterative development approach.**

Strongly Disagree	Tend to Disagree	Neither Agree nor Disagree	Tend to Agree	Strongly Agree

Table A.4   Continuous delivery *(continued)*

CDL_D8	No big up-front requirements-gathering and analysis should be conducted when using the incremental-iterative approach. In other words, you don't need to gather all the requirements before you start developing software in an incremental-iterative approach.				
	Strongly Disagree	Tend to Disagree	Neither Agree nor Disagree	Tend to Agree	Strongly Agree
CDL_D9	You fully understand the principles of the incremental-iterative development approach.				
	Strongly Disagree	Tend to Disagree	Neither Agree nor Disagree	Tend to Agree	Strongly Agree

Indicators (questions) to be answered by the assessor(s)					
CDL_A1	After observation of the team, you affirm that the team has a process it uses to develop software. This process should include a set of activities with deliverables and standards.				
	Strongly Disagree	Tend to Disagree	Neither Agree nor Disagree	Tend to Agree	Strongly Agree

Table A.5   Client-driven iterations

CDI	The client determines the choice of the features for the next iteration. This makes the client in control and able to change the system based on whatever they perceive as the highest business value to them.

Various characteristics to be assessed to determine the team's readiness for this practice	Indicators
Management buy-in Whether managers are willing to give the customer the power to dictate the scope of the iterations	CDI_M1 , CDI_M2, CDI_M3

Indicators (questions) to be answered by the manager(s)					
CDI_M1	As the perception of what they need changes, customers are expected to articulate those changes by prioritizing the features they would like to see in the next iteration.				
	Strongly Disagree	Tend to Disagree	Neither Agree nor Disagree	Tend to Agree	Strongly Agree
CDI_M2	Customers should be encouraged to regularly change their expectations for the product being developed, to ensure that the product satisfies their business priorities.				
	Strongly Disagree	Tend to Disagree	Neither Agree nor Disagree	Tend to Agree	Strongly Agree
CDI_M3	The customer should be given the authority to determine which features need to be developed in the upcoming iteration.				
	Strongly Disagree	Tend to Disagree	Neither Agree nor Disagree	Tend to Agree	Strongly Agree

Table A.6 Continuous integration

CNI	The practice encourages members of the development team to integrate their work frequently. It is preferred that an automated build tool verify each integration in order to detect any integration errors as quickly as possible.

Various characteristics to be assessed to determine the team's readiness for this practice	Indicators
Developer buy-in Whether design is a continuous process or done once at the beginning of the development process	CNI_D1, CNI_D2, CNI_D3
Software tools experience Whether the developers are familiar with the tools that aid in continuous integration	CNI_D4, CNI_D5

Indicators (questions) to be answered by the developers				
CNI_D1	The usual time it takes to create a build of the system is			
	More than 1 hour	Under 1 hour	Under 15 minutes	Under 10 minutes	Under 5 minutes
CNI_D2	Instead of integrating the system at the end of the development effort, it is better to regularly integrate the system throughout the whole development process.			
	Strongly Disagree	Tend to Disagree	Neither Agree nor Disagree	Tend to Agree	Strongly Agree
CNI_D3	You are willing to integrate your software throughout the development process, even if it means more work for you.			
	Strongly Disagree	Tend to Disagree	Neither Agree nor Disagree	Tend to Agree	Strongly Agree
CNI_D4	You are comfortable and competent using a Software Configuration Management (SCM) tool.			
	Strongly Disagree	Tend to Disagree	Neither Agree nor Disagree	Tend to Agree	Strongly Agree
CNI_D5	You are comfortable and competent using a continuous-integration tool.			
	Strongly Disagree	Tend to Disagree	Neither Agree nor Disagree	Tend to Agree	Strongly Agree

Table A.7 Coding standards

CGS	This refers to a common language relative to the code syntax among all the developers. These coding standards include naming conventions, formatting issues, and other best practices.

Various characteristics to be assessed to determine the team's readiness for this practice	Indicators
Developer buy-in Whether the developers see the benefit and are willing to apply coding standards	CGS_D1, CGS_D2
Coding standards existence Whether any coding standards exist that are presently used	CGS_A1

Table A.7 Coding standards *(continued)*

	Indicators (questions) to be answered by the developers				
CGS_D1	There should be a coding standard for development.				
	Strongly Disagree	Tend to Disagree	Neither Agree nor Disagree	Tend to Agree	Strongly Agree
CGS_D2	If the team has a coding standard, then developers should use it when coding, even in crunch time.				
	Strongly Disagree	Tend to Disagree	Neither Agree nor Disagree	Tend to Agree	Strongly Agree
	Indicators (questions) to be answered by the assessor(s)				
CGS_A1	After observation or review of documents or other information, it is evident that the team has a coding standard that it adheres to.				
	Strongly Disagree	Tend to Disagree	Neither Agree nor Disagree	Tend to Agree	Strongly Agree

Table A.8 Daily progress tracking

DPT	The team has a means by which they can stay informed on a daily basis about the status of the iteration. During these meetings, team members discuss what they did the day before, what they will do today, and any factors that might affect their progress.

Various characteristics to be assessed to determine the team's readiness for this practice	Indicators
Management buy-in Whether management is willing to meet daily for progress updates	DPT_M1
Developer buy-in Whether the developers are willing to meet daily for progress updates	DPT_D1
Project management How often the team meets regularly to discuss the progress of a project	DPT_M2 DPT_D2

	Indicators (questions) to be answered by the manager(s)				
DPT_M1	You are willing to meet daily for the progress update of a project.				
	Strongly Disagree	Tend to Disagree	Neither Agree nor Disagree	Tend to Agree	Strongly Agree
DPT_M2	Indicate how often you meet with the rest of the team to discuss and update each other on the progress of the project.				
	Less than monthly	Monthly	Every couple of weeks	Weekly	Daily/ Hourly

Table A.8   Daily progress tracking *(continued)*

Indicators (questions) to be answered by the developers				
DPT_D1	**You are willing to meet daily to check in and synchronize efforts with your team members.**				
	Strongly Disagree	Tend to Disagree	Neither Agree nor Disagree	Tend to Agree	Strongly Agree
DPT_D2	**Indicate how often you meet with the rest of the team to discuss and update each other about the progress of the project.**				
	Less than monthly	Monthly	Every couple of weeks	Weekly	Daily/ Hourly

Table A.9   Evolutionary requirements

EVR	Not all requirements are gathered at the beginning of the project; they evolve and change over the lifecycle of the product. Requirements iteratively evolve instead of being fully developed in one major specifications effort at the beginning of the project.

Various characteristics to be assessed to determine the team's readiness for this practice	Indicators
Existence of requirements engineering Whether the team has an institutionalized procedure to gather requirements from its clients	EVR_A1 EVR_M1, EVR_M2
Experience with evolutionary requirements Whether the team has developed projects using the evolutionary requirements	EVR_D1, EVR_M3
Management uncertainty avoidance Whether management can handle the uncertainty involved at the beginning of the requirements-gathering phase and deciding on requirements and features as late as possible	EVR_M4, EVR_M5, EVR_M6
Management competence Whether the managers can recognize high-level (architecturally influential) requirements and differentiate them from detail requirements	EVR_M7, EVR_M8
Management buy-in Whether management is willing to accept changes from the customer and realize that all changes are reversible	EVR_M6, EVR_M9, EVR_M1
Management buy-in Whether management is willing to try evolutionary requirements instead of big up-front requirements gathering	EVR_M1, EVR_M2
Developer uncertainty avoidance Whether developers can handle the uncertainty involved at the beginning of the requirements-gathering phase and deciding on requirements and features as late as possible	EVR_D2, EVR_D3
Developer buy-in Whether the developers are willing to accept changes from the customer and realize that all changes are reversible	EVR_D4, EVR_D7, EVR_D8

Table A.9 Evolutionary requirements *(continued)*

Developer competence	EVR_D5, EVR_D6
Whether the developers can recognize high-level (architecturally influential) requirements and differentiate them from detail requirements	

Indicators (questions) to be answered by the manager(s)

	The team is familiar with the procedures to gather requirements from clients.				
EVR_M1	Strongly Disagree	Tend to Disagree	Neither Agree nor Disagree	Tend to Agree	Strongly Agree

	In any project, requirements are always gathered from the customer in a structured manner and not haphazardly.				
EVR_M2	Strongly Disagree	Tend to Disagree	Neither Agree nor Disagree	Tend to Agree	Strongly Agree

	Indicate how often you manage a project in which not all the requirements are known up front and an evolutionary requirements approach is used.				
EVR_M3	Never	Seldom	Sometimes	Usually	Always

	You can start development of a project without knowing the exact requirements of the whole project.				
EVR_M4	Strongly Disagree	Tend to Disagree	Neither Agree nor Disagree	Tend to Agree	Strongly Agree

	If circumstances dictate that not all the details are available before you start a project, you do not mind the uncertainty.				
EVR_M5	Strongly Disagree	Tend to Disagree	Neither Agree nor Disagree	Tend to Agree	Strongly Agree

	You do not mind starting a project knowing that its requirements will change in the future.				
EVR_M6	Strongly Disagree	Tend to Disagree	Neither Agree nor Disagree	Tend to Agree	Strongly Agree

	You can tell the difference between requirements that will influence the architecture and design of a project and requirements that will not influence it.				
EVR_M7	Strongly Disagree	Tend to Disagree	Neither Agree nor Disagree	Tend to Agree	Strongly Agree

	In a project, you can recognize the high-level features that most probably will not change versus detailed requirements that might change.				
EVR_M8	Strongly Disagree	Tend to Disagree	Neither Agree nor Disagree	Tend to Agree	Strongly Agree

	Throughout the project, the client has full right to change the requirements in order to meet his/her business needs.				
EVR_M9	Strongly Disagree	Tend to Disagree	Neither Agree nor Disagree	Tend to Agree	Strongly Agree

Table A.9   **Evolutionary requirements** *(continued)*

Indicators (questions) to be answered by the developers				
EVR_D1	**Indicate how often you are involved in a project in which not all the requirements are known up front and an evolutionary requirements approach is used.**			
	Never	Seldom	Sometimes	Usually	Always
EVR_D2	**You are willing start development of a project without knowing the exact requirements of the whole project.**			
	Strongly Disagree	Tend to Disagree	Neither Agree nor Disagree	Tend to Agree	Strongly Agree
EVR_D3	**If circumstances dictate that not all the details are available before you start a project, you do not mind the uncertainty.**			
	Strongly Disagree	Tend to Disagree	Neither Agree nor Disagree	Tend to Agree	Strongly Agree
EVR_D4	**You do not mind starting a project knowing that its requirements will evolve or change in the future.**			
	Strongly Disagree	Tend to Disagree	Neither Agree nor Disagree	Tend to Agree	Strongly Agree
EVR_D5	**You can tell the difference between requirements that will influence the architecture and design of a project and requirements that will not influence it.**			
	Strongly Disagree	Tend to Disagree	Neither Agree nor Disagree	Tend to Agree	Strongly Agree
EVR_D6	**In a project, you can recognize the high-level features that most probably will not change versus detailed requirements that might change.**			
	Strongly Disagree	Tend to Disagree	Neither Agree nor Disagree	Tend to Agree	Strongly Agree
EVR_D7	**Throughout the project, the client has full right to change the requirements in order to meet his/her business needs.**			
	Strongly Disagree	Tend to Disagree	Neither Agree nor Disagree	Tend to Agree	Strongly Agree
EVR_D8	**In order to deliver valuable software to clients, change should be welcomed and not constrained.**			
	Strongly Disagree	Tend to Disagree	Neither Agree nor Disagree	Tend to Agree	Strongly Agree
Indicators (questions) to be answered by the assessor(s)				
EVR_A1	**After observation or review of documents or other information, it is evident that the team has a process it uses to gather requirements from its clients.**			
	Strongly Disagree	Tend to Disagree	Neither Agree nor Disagree	Tend to Agree	Strongly Agree

Table A.10 Empowered and motivated teams

EMT	Managers empower and equip their teams with the authority to make decisions on their own. This authority helps motivate the team members, who believe that they can solve any problems the team faces.

Various characteristics to be assessed to determine the team's readiness for this practice	Indicators
Developer authority Whether management empowers teams with decision-making authority	EMT_M1, EMT_M2 EMT_D1, EMT_D2, EMT_D3
Developer motivation Whether people are treated in a way that motivates them	EMT_D4, EMT_D5, EMT_D6, EMT_D7
Management trust Whether managers trust and believe in the technical team in order to truly empower them	EMT_M2, EMT_M3, EMT_M4

Indicators (questions) to be answered by the project manager(s)

EMT_M1	You usually seek your subordinates' opinions before making a decision.				
	Strongly Disagree	Tend to Disagree	Neither Agree nor Disagree	Tend to Agree	Strongly Agree

EMT_M2	You frequently seek the input of your subordinates on technical issues.				
	Strongly Disagree	Tend to Disagree	Neither Agree nor Disagree	Tend to Agree	Strongly Agree

EMT_M3	If needed, you do not mind granting your subordinates unregulated access to the customer.				
	Strongly Disagree	Tend to Disagree	Neither Agree nor Disagree	Tend to Agree	Strongly Agree

EMT_M4	You allow your subordinates to choose their own tasks for a project.				
	Strongly Disagree	Tend to Disagree	Neither Agree nor Disagree	Tend to Agree	Strongly Agree

Indicators (questions) to be answered by the project manager(s)

EMT_D1	Your manager gives you the authority to make decisions without referring back to him/her.				
	Strongly Disagree	Tend to Disagree	Neither Agree nor Disagree	Tend to Agree	Strongly Agree

EMT_D2	Your manager seeks your input on technical issues.				
	Strongly Disagree	Tend to Disagree	Neither Agree nor Disagree	Tend to Agree	Strongly Agree

Table A.10   Empowered and motivated teams *(continued)*

	You usually participate in the planning process of the project you are working on.				
EMT_D3	Strongly Disagree	Tend to Disagree	Neither Agree nor Disagree	Tend to Agree	Strongly Agree
	When in a group, you feel that your participation is important.				
EMT_D4	Strongly Disagree	Tend to Disagree	Neither Agree nor Disagree	Tend to Agree	Strongly Agree
	The team values you and your expertise.				
EMT_D5	Strongly Disagree	Tend to Disagree	Neither Agree nor Disagree	Tend to Agree	Strongly Agree
	Your manager has high expectations of you.				
EMT_D6	Strongly Disagree	Tend to Disagree	Neither Agree nor Disagree	Tend to Agree	Strongly Agree
	You are motivated by your job.				
EMT_D7	Strongly Disagree	Tend to Disagree	Neither Agree nor Disagree	Tend to Agree	Strongly Agree

Table A.11   Pair programming

PPG	Pair programming is an agile practice that requires two software engineers to work in a combined development effort at one workstation. Each member performs the action the other isn't currently doing; for example, while one types in unit tests, the other thinks about the class that will satisfy the test.

Various characteristics to be assessed to determine the team's readiness for this practice	Indicators
Management buy-in Whether management can see the benefit of pair programming	PPG_M1, PPG_M2
Developer buy-in Whether developers are willing to try pair programming	PPG_D1, PPG_D2, PPG_D3
Measuring productivity What the team considers to be a measure of software productivity	PPG_M3
Team collaboration Whether an atmosphere of assistance exists within the team	PPG_D4, PPG_D5, PPG_M4

Indicators (questions) to be answered by the manager(s)					
PPG_M1	**Pair programming increases productivity, contrary to what others may say about pair programming (that it decreases productivity by half).**				
	Strongly Disagree	Tend to Disagree	Neither Agree nor Disagree	Tend to Agree	Strongly Agree

Table A.11   Pair programming *(continued)*

PPG_M2	You encourage your development team to use pair programming.				
	Strongly Disagree	Tend to Disagree	Neither Agree nor Disagree	Tend to Agree	Strongly Agree
PPG_M3	Productivity is about how much customer value you can create per dollar spent, not about how many lines of code or classes coded per dollar spent.				
	Strongly Disagree	Tend to Disagree	Neither Agree nor Disagree	Tend to Agree	Strongly Agree
PPG_M4	An atmosphere of assistance exists in the team.				
	Strongly Disagree	Tend to Disagree	Neither Agree nor Disagree	Tend to Agree	Strongly Agree
Indicators (questions) to be answered by the developers					
PPG_D1	Pair programming increases productivity, contrary to what others may say about pair programming (that it decreases productivity by half).				
	Strongly Disagree	Tend to Disagree	Neither Agree nor Disagree	Tend to Agree	Strongly Agree
PPG_D2	Indicate how often you program in pairs.				
	Never	Seldom	Sometimes	Usually	Always
PPG_D3	You are willing to program in pairs.				
	Strongly Disagree	Tend to Disagree	Neither Agree nor Disagree	Tend to Agree	Strongly Agree
PPG_D4	Helping other team members with their work is a waste of my time.				
	Strongly Disagree	Tend to Disagree	Neither Agree nor Disagree	Tend to Agree	Strongly Agree
PPG_D5	Whenever you need help, people are willing to help you.				
	Strongly Disagree	Tend to Disagree	Neither Agree nor Disagree	Tend to Agree	Strongly Agree

Table A.12   Reflect, and tune the process (retrospectives)

RTP	This practice relates to holding retrospectives at regular intervals within the development process to reflect and tune the process.	
Various characteristics to be assessed to determine the team's readiness for this practice		**Indicators**
Developer buy-in Whether developers are willing to commit to reflecting about and tuning the process after each iteration and release		RTP_D1
Management buy-in Whether management is willing to commit to reflecting about and tuning the process after each iteration and release		RTP_M1

Table A.12   Reflect, and tune the process (retrospectives) *(continued)*

Process improvement capability Whether the team can handle process change in the middle of the project	RTP_D2, RTP_D3, RTP_D4 RTP_M2, RTP_M3, RTP_M4

Indicators (questions) to be answered by the managers(s)

RTP_M1	You are willing to dedicate time after each iteration/release to review how the process could be improved.				
	Strongly Disagree	Tend to Disagree	Neither Agree nor Disagree	Tend to Agree	Strongly Agree

RTP_M2	You are willing to undergo a process change even if it requires some extra work from the team.				
	Strongly Disagree	Tend to Disagree	Neither Agree nor Disagree	Tend to Agree	Strongly Agree

RTP_M3	If there is a need for process change, that change should not be considered a burden on the team even if significant process changes have been made previously during the project.				
	Strongly Disagree	Tend to Disagree	Neither Agree nor Disagree	Tend to Agree	Strongly Agree

RTP_M4	Process change in the middle of the project isn't considered a disruption because the process change is worth the benefit it will bring.				
	Strongly Disagree	Tend to Disagree	Neither Agree nor Disagree	Tend to Agree	Strongly Agree

Indicators (questions) to be answered by the developers

RTP_D1	You are willing to dedicate time after each iteration/release to review how the process could be improved.				
	Strongly Disagree	Tend to Disagree	Neither Agree nor Disagree	Tend to Agree	Strongly Agree

RTP_D2	You are willing to undergo a process change even if it requires some extra work from the team.				
	Strongly Disagree	Tend to Disagree	Neither Agree nor Disagree	Tend to Agree	Strongly Agree

RTP_D3	If there is a need for process change, that change should not be considered a burden on the team even if significant process changes have been made previously during the project.				
	Strongly Disagree	Tend to Disagree	Neither Agree nor Disagree	Tend to Agree	Strongly Agree

RTP_D4	Process change in the middle of the project isn't considered a disruption because the process change is worth the benefit it will bring.				
	Strongly Disagree	Tend to Disagree	Neither Agree nor Disagree	Tend to Agree	Strongly Agree

Table A.13 Self-organized teams

SOT	Self-organized teams are empowered by management to make decisions on their own without waiting for management approval. When the team is given a task, it becomes the responsibility of the whole team, collectively, to finish it, not a specific person or a specific role. Management treats self-organizing teams as one entity without distinguishing between the individuals of the team.

Various characteristics to be assessed to determine the team's readiness for this practice	Indicators
Management buy-in Whether management agrees to have self-organizing teams	SOT_M1
Management competence Whether management is ready to treat the team as a true self-organizing team	SOT_M2, SOT_M3, SOT_M4, SOT_M5
Developer buy-in Whether the employees feel comfortable working as self-organizing teams	SOT_D1, SOT_D2, SOT_D3

Indicators (questions) to be answered by the manager(s)				
SOT_M1	**You agree that it is very important for the employees to work in teams where they can divide the team tasks among themselves.**			
	Strongly Disagree	Tend to Disagree	Neither Agree nor Disagree	Tend to Agree	Strongly Agree
SOT_M2	**You trust that your employees can determine the best way to accomplish tasks by themselves without your (management's) interference.**			
	Strongly Disagree	Tend to Disagree	Neither Agree nor Disagree	Tend to Agree	Strongly Agree
SOT_M3	**You are willing to allow a self-organizing team to grow and not micromanage it.**			
	Strongly Disagree	Tend to Disagree	Neither Agree nor Disagree	Tend to Agree	Strongly Agree
SOT_M4	**Employees are competent and disciplined enough to work in self-organizing teams.**			
	Strongly Disagree	Tend to Disagree	Neither Agree nor Disagree	Tend to Agree	Strongly Agree
SOT_M5	**The team is an entity that has its knowledge, perspective, motivation, and expertise and should be treated as a partner with management and the customer.**			
	Strongly Disagree	Tend to Disagree	Neither Agree nor Disagree	Tend to Agree	Strongly Agree

Indicators (questions) to be answered by the developers				
SOT_D1	**You like to work on a team that management regards as one entity: addressing not individual team members in rewards or tasks but one team.**			
	Strongly Disagree	Tend to Disagree	Neither Agree nor Disagree	Tend to Agree	Strongly Agree

Table A.13   Self-organized teams *(continued)*

SOT_D2	You do not mind working without direct managerial supervision as long as you are on a team that is treated as a partner with management.				
	Strongly Disagree	Tend to Disagree	Neither Agree nor Disagree	Tend to Agree	Strongly Agree
SOT_D3	You consider yourself competent and disciplined enough to work in a self-organizing team.				
	Strongly Disagree	Tend to Disagree	Neither Agree nor Disagree	Tend to Agree	Strongly Agree

Table A.14   Test Driven Development

TDD	TDD involves repeatedly writing a test first and then implementing only the code necessary to pass the test. The developers create one test to define some small aspect of the problem at hand. Then they create the simplest code that will make the test pass.

Various characteristics to be assessed to determine the team's readiness for this practice	Indicators
Developer competence Whether the developers are competent and experienced with writing unit tests	TDD_D1, TDD_D2, TDD_D3
Developer buy-in Whether the developers are motivated and willing to apply Test Driven Development	TDD_D4
Developer perception Whether the developers think that Test Driven Development is a hard task	TDD_D5
Management buy-in Whether management will encourage Test Driven Development and tolerate the learning curve	TDD_M1, TDD_M2
Test automation Whether the team has or can provide tools for creating and maintaining automated test suites	TDD_A1 TDD_M3

Indicators (questions) to be answered by the manager(s)					
TDD_M1	Test Driven Development will produce better software with fewer bugs.				
	Strongly Disagree	Tend to Disagree	Neither Agree nor Disagree	Tend to Agree	Strongly Agree
TDD_M2	You are willing to tolerate the learning curve of the development team while they transition to Test Driven Development.				
	Strongly Disagree	Tend to Disagree	Neither Agree nor Disagree	Tend to Agree	Strongly Agree
TDD_M3	The organization will be willing to provide software tools for creating and maintaining automated test suites.				
	Strongly Disagree	Tend to Disagree	Neither Agree nor Disagree	Tend to Agree	Strongly Agree

Table A.14 Test Driven Development *(continued)*

Indicators (questions) to be answered by the developers				
TDD_D1	**Indicate how often you write unit tests for every function/method/class.**			
	Never	Seldom	Sometimes	Usually	Always
TDD_D2	**You have no problems or challenges writing unit tests for functions/methods/classes.**			
	Strongly Disagree	Tend to Disagree	Neither Agree nor Disagree	Tend to Agree	Strongly Agree
TDD_D3	**The suite of unit tests that you write is comprehensive and usually encompasses all possible test scenarios.**			
	Strongly Disagree	Tend to Disagree	Neither Agree nor Disagree	Tend to Agree	Strongly Agree
TDD_D4	**You are willing to employ a test-driven approach to development.**			
	Strongly Disagree	Tend to Disagree	Neither Agree nor Disagree	Tend to Agree	Strongly Agree
TDD_D5	**You think Test Driven Development is easy.**			
	Strongly Disagree	Tend to Disagree	Neither Agree nor Disagree	Tend to Agree	Strongly Agree
Indicators (questions) to be answered by the assessor(s)				
TDD_A1	**After observation or review of the team's software tools, it is evident that the team has access to the tools for creating and maintaining automated test suites.**			
	Strongly Disagree	Tend to Disagree	Neither Agree nor Disagree	Tend to Agree	Strongly Agree

Table A.15 Task volunteering

TSV	After the list of tasks has been generated, the project manager encourages people to volunteer and commit to tasks that they choose rather than have the manager assign the tasks to them.

Various characteristics to be assessed to determine the team's readiness for this practice	Indicators
Management buy-in Whether management will be willing to buy into and can see benefits from employees volunteering for tasks instead of being assigned	TSV_M1, TSV_M2
Developer buy-in Whether developers are willing to see the benefits from volunteering for tasks	TSV_D1

Indicators (questions) to be answered by the project manager(s)				
TSV_M1	**You allow your subordinates to choose their own tasks for a project.**			
	Strongly Disagree	Tend to Disagree	Neither Agree nor Disagree	Tend to Agree	Strongly Agree

Table A.15   Task volunteering *(continued)*

TSV_M2	You believe that subordinates would perform better and be more effective if they were to choose their own tasks.				
	Strongly Disagree	Tend to Disagree	Neither Agree nor Disagree	Tend to Agree	Strongly Agree

Indicators (questions) to be answered by the developers					
TSV_D1	You would do a better job choosing your own task on a project instead of being assigned one by your manager.				
	Strongly Disagree	Tend to Disagree	Neither Agree nor Disagree	Tend to Agree	Strongly Agree

Table A.16   Unit tests

UNT	Unit tests are code procedures used to validate that individual units of source code are working properly. A unit of source code is the smallest testable part of an application. For example, in procedural programming, a unit may be a function or procedure, whereas in object-oriented programming, the smallest unit is usually a class.

Various characteristics to be assessed to determine the team's readiness for this practice	Indicators
Developer buy-in Whether developers are willing to write unit tests during the development process	UNT_D1, UNT_D2, UNT_D3
Developer competence Whether the developers have the required competence and previous experience writing unit tests	UNT_D4, UNT_D5 UNT_M1
Management buy-in Whether management accepts that developers will invest additional time to write unit tests while coding	UNT_M2 UNT_M3

Indicators (questions) to be answered by the manager(s)					
UT_M1	The developers are competent enough to write good unit tests for the methods and functions in the code.				
	Strongly Disagree	Tend to Disagree	Neither Agree nor Disagree	Tend to Agree	Strongly Agree
UT_M2	It is important for developers to write unit tests for their methods and functions while they code, even if that will take additional time from them.				
	Strongly Disagree	Tend to Disagree	Neither Agree nor Disagree	Tend to Agree	Strongly Agree
UT_M2	Writing unit tests for code is as important as writing new code for more functionality.				
	Strongly Disagree	Tend to Disagree	Neither Agree nor Disagree	Tend to Agree	Strongly Agree

Table A.16   Unit tests *(continued)*

Indicators (questions) to be answered by the developers				
UT_D1	It is important to write unit tests for methods and functions while coding them even if that will take additional time.			
	Never	Seldom	Sometimes	Usually	Always
UT_D2	Writing unit tests for code is as important as writing new code for more functionality.			
	Strongly Disagree	Tend to Disagree	Neither Agree nor Disagree	Tend to Agree	Strongly Agree
UT_D3	You are willing to commit to writing unit tests while you code for every method or function in your code.			
	Strongly Disagree	Tend to Disagree	Neither Agree nor Disagree	Tend to Agree	Strongly Agree
UT_D4	Indicate how often you write unit tests for every method or function in your code.			
	Never	Seldom	Sometimes	Usually	Always
UT_D5	You consider yourself competent enough to write good and comprehensive unit tests for the methods and functions in your code.			
	Strongly Disagree	Tend to Disagree	Neither Agree nor Disagree	Tend to Agree	Strongly Agree

appendix B:
Agile concepts from
a phase perspective

Many people learn software development from a phase perspective, performing each phase in a series. Common phases are analysis, requirements, design, development, testing, and delivery. Agile software development isn't performed in a series, but it can be modeled in a serial fashion to make it easier to envision the process.

B.1   Overview of the phases

Let's begin with a quick overview of the phases. Figure 1 shows all the phases and their relationship to each other.

At first glance, the diagram resembles a waterfall development process. In reality, it's a diagram of an agile process. The gates help define the phases and also act as circuit breakers for the project, supporting risk management in every phase.

The gates also reflect an approval process: a go/no-go decision can be made at each one. The approval process can be determined by your team and company. The approval could be from a management group, sponsor, or product manager. It could also be a project team decision.

It's important to note that the gateways are virtual. You won't complete all of your feasibility work before proceeding to planning, but you'll do the majority of it in the Feasibility phase. The Planning phase is similar: you'll do the bulk of the planning during the Planning phase, but you'll do a lot more during development. Feasibility and planning keep occurring until the moment the decision is made to deploy functionality into a Production environment.

As we continue our discussion, notice that each phase diagram lists tools that can be used during the phase. We don't discuss the tools in this overview; we discuss them in detail during the course of the case study in the book's chapters. Now let's examine the Feasibility phase.

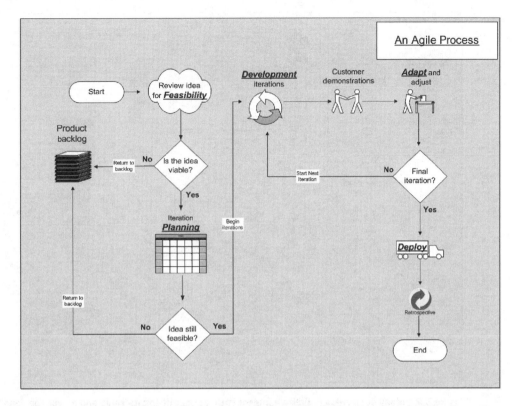

Figure B.1   A project begins when an idea is determined to be viable during the Feasibility phase. The Planning phase reviews the idea in detail to identify the features and priorities. The Development phase is used to refine designs, develop code, and iteratively surface working code for demonstrations. When development work is complete, the queued iterations are released to a Production environment during the Deployment phase. Although you do the majority of feasibility and planning work at the beginning of the project, you continue to evaluate value and re-plan until the project is delivered.

B.2   Feasibility: define and validate your vision

Phase objective: Determine if the idea has enough merit to justify going forward with more detailed requirements, planning, funding, and staffing.

Why are you here? Why are you doing this project? What is the value of this request? The Feasibility phase pursues the answers to these questions and more. The question that summarizes it all is, "Is there value in pursuing this request or idea?"

Look at figure 2 to get a better understanding.

The Feasibility phase begins with an idea or request. The idea can come from within the team, a customer, or practically any source. The person who collects or provides the idea bounces it off a supervisor or a management group that vets ideas. If the idea is given approval for further investigation of feasibility, it's assigned to a group or person for further research. It may be given back to the person who presented the idea.

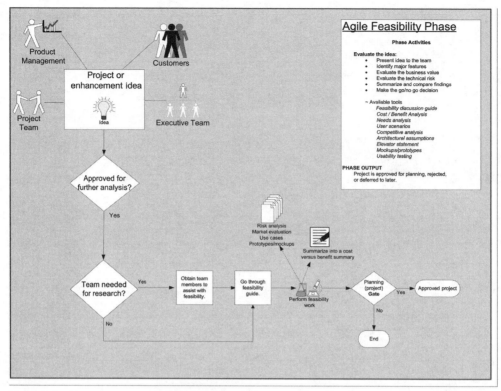

Figure B.2   **Many companies initialize a project without quantifying its value and goals. The Feasibility phase eliminates this issue by measuring the value before you make a major investment in the project. The team compares costs and benefits at the end of the phase and makes a go/no-go decision.**

The person assigned to the request then makes a decision about whether they can do the research on their own or if they need team members to help. To see it in practice, let's look at an idea within Acme Media.

Wes Hunter, a business analyst, suggests that Acme start providing news alerts to cell phones. He bounces the idea off the product manager for the news website and receives a green light to go further with feasibility and research. Wes can see the business value of the feature and explains the value from a perspective of audience share and competitive advantage, but he has no idea how wireless technology works or the architecture that will be required to support it. Wes requests the assistance of the lead architect to help him work through the high-level technical implications of pursuing the idea. In this instance, the feasibility team is Wes and the lead architect.

After the team or person has been identified, they continue the feasibility work. This additional work may include the following:

- Talking to customers
- Performing a cost/benefit analysis
- Looking at what competitors are doing in related areas
- Researching whitepapers on the subject from industry experts

- Checking compatibility with the current platform
- Researching technology needs
- Creating use cases to better understand the idea

The agile/lean concept of "just enough" applies here. You want just enough information to see if this idea is worth the effort required to create a plan for it.

When the work is complete, it's presented to the product manager or approving body for discussion. The feasibility investigator presents high-level requirements, a guess at project costs (funds and resources needed), risks identified during the research, a list of benefits, and a ballpark timeline. The meeting is concluded with a go/no-go decision.

This decision only provides approval to continue the investigation and planning for the idea—it isn't a blessing to take the idea all the way through to delivery. Showstoppers can still be identified during planning and development, so an idea can be cancelled at any time.

The last step in the Feasibility phase is the assignment of a planning team. If one person has been investigating an idea, they need a team to plan the idea after approval. Employees can be assigned informally or officially by a manager or management group. Team members can come from all areas of the organization, but you need representatives who have experience with the product. These team members will help estimate features at the end of the phase.

The team also needs the customer or a customer advocate to provide their input during the prioritization that occurs throughout the phase. It's desirable to have the planning team follow the idea all the way through to deployment.

B.3 *Planning: speculate and create a living plan*

Phase objective: Break the idea into discrete pieces of functionality called *features*. Prioritize the features, and assign them to iterations.

The first step in the Planning phase is to orient all the planning-team members to the idea. Frequently the planning team conducts an envisioning meeting to help everyone synchronize on the idea's benefits. The envisioning meeting can be viewed as a marketing meeting. The team pretends they're going to sell the idea to a customer. They identify the top three to five product highlights they would tell the customer about. In addition, they create a summary of key features that will be delivered. The idea becomes a project during this exercise.

Note that the Planning phase also continues the feasibility work. You've gathered enough information to justify planning during feasibility; now you must refine your financials based on the additional details gleaned during planning. See figure 3.

After features are identified, the team goes through the feature-card exercise. In this step, the features identified during envisioning are fleshed out just enough to prioritize them and sequence them into the order in which they would be developed. The team also uses the prioritization as another feasibility check: if a feature comes out of the feature-card exercise as a low priority, the team may choose to remove it from the project.

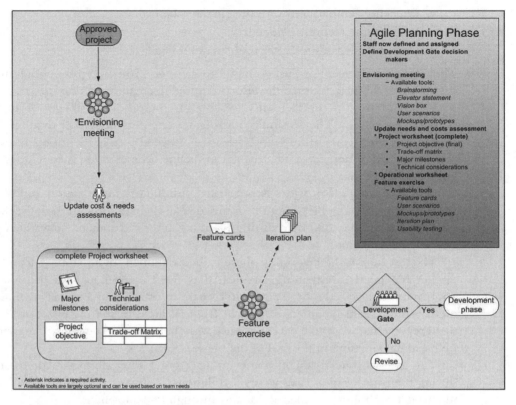

Figure B.3   The Planning phase brings together the project team to quickly convert the idea into features. Features are prioritized, sequenced, and estimated during this phase. The team creates an iteration plan to initialize development. Note that planning isn't a one-time event: it continues throughout the development cycle as you adapt to changes and discoveries.

The team estimates the remaining features at a high level, identifying the major tasks and resource types needed.

The last step of this phase is to assign features to iterations. The *iterations* are buckets of time in which the team develops features. A good timeframe for an iteration is 2 to 4 weeks. The team uses the previous estimates to determine which features will fit into the available iterations. Each iteration is structured so that it provides value on its own. This allows deployment even if something prevents all the iterations from being completed.

The main deliverable from this phase is the iteration plan.

B.4   *Development: exploration with a schedule*

Phase objective: Create, test, and demonstrate features. Queue iterations for deployment.

The Development phase begins with iteration 0. The iteration is so labeled because no features are delivered during it: it's used to put the necessary foundation pieces, both business and technical, in place to start development. Some typical activities are as follows:

- Finalizing contracts with vendors
- Initial architecture design
- Preparing the environments (operating system, database, development tools)
- Funding

Note that if you're building on an existing platform with dedicated employees, you may not need an iteration 0—you can begin development immediately after planning.

When the first development iteration begins, the team refines the tasks they identified during planning. This is common because the team provided only enough information to estimate the features during planning. After a project gets through the planning gateway, the team knows it's coming and begins doing detailed analysis of the required work.

The development done during an iteration doesn't use a waterfall approach. The process is one of collaborative development. The developers create code to the minimum specification and demonstrate it to the customer. At this time, the customer identifies requirements the developers missed or issues with the initial requirements. The developers may also identify technical issues. The developers and customer work through these issues during the iteration, evolving the code until it supports what is needed at the end of the iteration, not what was requested at the beginning. See figure 4.

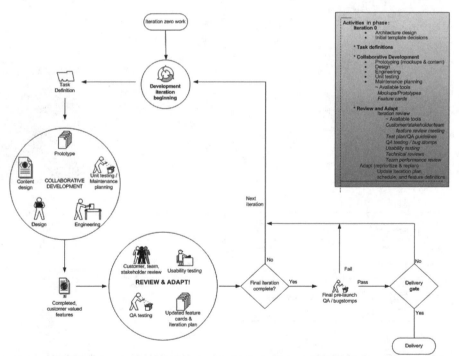

Figure B.4 Development starts by establishing a foundation in iteration 0. Iteration 0 includes items such as architectural design, environment preparation, and finalizing contracts. Development iterations follow, delivering working code in subsets every 2 to 4 weeks. The working code is surfaced for a demonstration and customer feedback. That feedback is incorporated during the planning cycle for the next iteration. When all iterations are completed, the code is delivered to a Production environment.

Testing occurs during an iteration and after. When an iteration is complete, the team holds a review meeting to adapt (see the following section).

Iterations are stored in Acceptance environments until all iterations are deemed complete. At that time, all the work is deployed into the Production environment.

B.5   *Adapt: react to new information*

Phase objective: Review the output of an iteration, and re-plan based on discoveries.

Adapting occurs informally throughout an agile project, but it happens formally during the Development phase. The team performs an iteration review at the end of each iteration for the following reasons:

- To demonstrate the state of the features assigned to the iteration
- To get feedback from the customers and stakeholders now that they can see the feature
- To refine feature definitions based on feedback and better understanding (priorities change; feature definition and requirements become clearer)
- To incorporate any changes and new information that has been discovered since the start of the iteration
- To evaluate the pace of feature development and adjust the next iteration accordingly

Adapting is illustrated in figure 5.

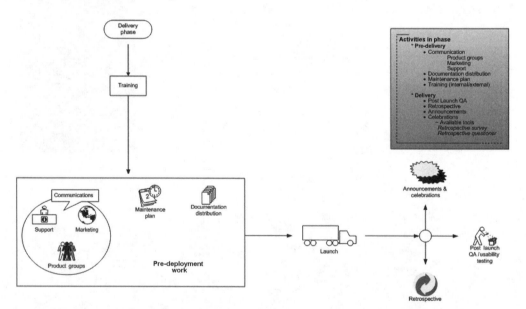

Figure B.5   The Adapt phase surfaces working code for demonstrations and feedback. You use this period to validate that you're on target with the customer's needs. You also use this timeframe to evaluate the previous iteration. How much work are you putting through, versus what you estimated? You plan the next iteration based on the velocity you recorded during the previous one.

When the review is complete, the project manager modifies the iteration plan based on the new information, and the team proceeds into the next iteration.

B.6 *Deployment: deliver, train, revisit, and close the project*

Phase objective: Deliver code to the Production environment with all support needs in place.

The Deployment phase begins after the last iteration is complete. Typical tasks for the Deployment phase are as follows:

- Train support and operations on the forthcoming release.
- Turn on your communication plan to employees and customers.
- When applicable, enable the marketing plan.
- Ensure that all pieces of the maintenance and support plans are in place.
- Release the code into production.
- Where applicable, perform post-release QA in the Production environment.
- Perform a project retrospective with the team within 2 weeks of the release.

Delivery is illustrated in figure 6.

In an agile methodology, you consider deployment needs throughout the previous phases. Optimally, the work done during deployment includes tweaking and finalizing the training, maintenance, marketing, and communication plans.

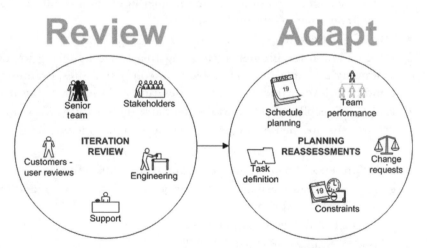

Figure B.6 When all iterations are complete, you kick into delivery mode. You train employees, customers, and support networks before putting the code into a Production environment. You also review the maintenance concerns you've recorded during the project and make sure a maintenance plan is in place. After delivery, you complete a project retrospective to review how effective the process is, and make adjustments as needed.

appendix C:
Agile process
overview in text

Our book is loaded with diagrams and flowcharts, but we recognize that some people are more verbal than visual. To support this need we have documented one example of an agile process from beginning to end in text format.

C.1 Feasibility phase

1 Project manager (PM) or any team member bounces idea off manager (may go up to member of executive team).
2 PM gets go-ahead to explore further.
3 PM does initial requirements gathering (may include talking to customers, examining available research, looking at competing sites, examining traffic trends. The level of documentation is determined by team and business needs.
4 PM holds feasibility meeting with potential team to explore idea more:
5 PM presents overview of project concept, which may include draft of features list.

   a PM presents initial requirements, and team helps refine.
   b Team discusses feasibility of the project, risks, and so on, and takes first pass at project worksheet.
   TOOL: Feasibility discussion guide
   TOOL: Project worksheet *REQUIRED
   c Team completes elevator statement.
   TOOL: Elevator statement
6 PM gets go-ahead from supervisor to move to Planning phase (may go up to senior team).

C.2 Planning phase

1 Project team holds envisioning meeting (PM may come in with initial drafts of following items):

    a Team refines elevator statement.

    b Team does envision activity and creates features list.

    c Team reviews and updates project worksheet.
      TOOL: User scenarios or use cases

    d Team completes operational worksheet.
      TOOL: Operational worksheet *REQUIRED

    e Team determines level of documentation according to team and business needs.

2 Team carries out feature-card activity:
  TOOL: Feature-card template

    a Write down features ("ability to" statements) on cards or separate pieces of paper. Include technical features.

    b Prioritize features into rough iterations according to value to customer.

    c For features in first few iterations, flesh out feature description and estimate story points (days). (May be assisted by flipchart drawings, flow charts, rough mockups, or listing major tasks associated with features. Drawings and notes get everyone on the same page and can be saved for reference.)

    d Refine iteration plan, considering details of features (risk, story points, and so on).

    e Create iteration plan:
      TOOL: Iteration-plan worksheet

      i Project may need iteration 0 for infrastructure, architecture design, or other non-customer-facing features.

      ii Use general guideline of 2 to 4 weeks per iteration.

      iii Associate dates with each iteration, including time between iterations for QA, for usability, and to review and adapt plan.

C.3 Development phase

1 Complete iteration 0 (if needed).

2 Work to complete iteration 1.

3 Perform daily stand-up meeting.

4 Perform QA and usability test if necessary.

5 Hold iteration-review meeting:

    a Consider feedback from team, users, and customers.

    b Incorporate any changes or new information that has arisen since start of iteration.

    c Consider number of features achieved in last iteration. Use information to target next iteration more realistically.

    d Adapt/re-plan: reorganize iteration plan, taking new information into consideration.

6 Work to complete next iteration.

C.4   *Delivery phase*

1 Training

2 Communication

3 Maintenance plan

4 Documentation distribution

5 Launch

6 Post-launch QA

7 Announcements and celebration

8 Retrospective
    TOOL: Retrospective survey and discussion guide *REQUIRED

appendix D: Example: determining process and document needs for a project

Throughout the book we have mentioned the need for the project team to determine the documentation and processes required for each project. In the example below we show an example from a real team. This team worked in a regulated environment and had to provide requirements traceability. Note that they revisited this matrix at the start of each project to reach agreement on what the deliverables would be. This matrix was originally one spreadsheet, but we have broken it into two pages to make it easier to view within the book.

Also note some unique terms used by this team: BRQs (Business Requirements), FRQs (Functional Requirements), FS (Functional Specification), and Ux (User Experience).

Document name	Details	When will the document be produced	Required for work package estimation	Required for PMLC/SDLC	Required before development begins	Required before testing begins
Feature cards/user stories	Context Scenarios - narrative describing the business needs	During Scoping	Y	Y	Y	Y
Business requirements catalog	Includes BRQs (references Context Scenarios for Rationale)	During Scoping	Y	Y	Y	Y
Functional requirements catalog	Includes FRQs and traceability to BRQs (May be same physical doc as Business Requirements Catalog)	During Design/Build Phase	N	Y	N	Y
Release functional specification	The official FS that will be passed along for Audit that will encompass the entire release	During Design/Build Phase	N	Y	N	N
Work package functional specification	These are the FSs that are created by the project team that go into more detail on specific work packages. These also link out to related documents.	During Design/Build Phase	N	N	Y	Y
Use cases	Includes both primary and alternative steps for actors and system, triggers, pre and post conditions	During Design/Build Phase	N	N	N	Y
Interaction flow diagram	Includes tables of supplementary information and is likely in Word format. Only for packages with a visual element.	During Design/Build Phase	N	N	N	N
Wireframe	Includes tables of supplementary information and is likely in Word format. Only for packages with a visual element.	During Design/Build Phase	N	N	N	N
Design specification		During Design/Build Phase	N	N	Y	Y
Release test plans	Describes the testing approach and what will be the scope of the testing for the entire release.	During Design/Build Phase	N	Y	N	N
Test cases	The specific steps and expected results for a specific work package. Very much related to the use cases.	During Design/Build Phase	N	N	N	Y
Technical test results report	Reports on the overall status of testing and risks.	During Test Phase	N	Y	N	N
Test coverage matrix	Percentage coverage of test cases	During Test Phase	N	Y	N	N

Document name	Details	Include in every package	Consumers of document	Responsible for creation	Customer signoff required
Feature cards/ user stories	Context Scenarios - narrative describing the business needs	Y	Project Team, Customer	Analysts	N
Business requirements catalog	Includes BRQs (references Context Scenarios for Rationale)	Y	Project Team, Customer	Analysts	Y
Functional requirements catalog	Includes FRQs and traceability to BRQs (May be same physical doc as Business Requirements Catalog)	Y	Project Team	Analysts	N
Release functional specification	The official FS that will be passed along for Audit that will encompass the entire release	Y	Auditors, Customer	Project Manager	Y
Work package functional specification	These are the FSs that are created by the project team that go into more detail on specific work packages. These also link out to related documents.	Y	Project Team	Analysts, Development, Implementation, Architecture	N
Use cases	Includes both primary and alternative steps for actors and system, triggers, pre and post conditions	Y	Development, Implementation, QA	Analysts	N
Interaction flow diagram	Includes tables of supplementary information and is likely in Word format. Only for packages with a visual element.	N	Development, Implementation, QA	Ux, Analysts	N
Wireframe	Includes tables of supplementary information and is likely in Word format. Only for packages with a visual element.	N	Development, Implementation, QA	Ux, Analysts	N
Design specification		Y	Project Team	Dev, Implementation, Architecture	N
Release test plans	Describes the testing approach and what will be the scope of the testing for the entire release.	Y	Project Team, Auditors	QA	N
Test cases	The specific steps and expected results for a specific work package. Very much related to the use cases.	Y	Analysts, Project Manager	QA	N
Technical test results report	Reports on the overall status of testing and risks.	Y	Auditors, Project Manager	QA	N
Test coverage matrix	Percentage coverage of test cases	Y	Auditors, Project Manager	QA	N

appendix E: Quantitative feedback on the SAMI

We gathered feedback about the Sidky Agile Measurement Index (SAMI) by presenting it to 28 members of the agile community and eliciting feedback about its objectives and its ability to achieve those objectives. We obtained this feedback during 90-minute personal visits with the participants (individually or in groups) that included a presentation of the SAMI, discussion, and a period of time to complete questionnaires. This appendix presents the results.

The questionnaire concerning the SAMI focuses on the index's comprehensiveness, practicality, and necessity, as well as whether the agile practices are placed at appropriate levels (labeled Relevance in the graphs).

Figure 1 indicates that more than 75 percent of the respondents either slightly or strongly agree that the SAMI is comprehensive, practical, and necessary. This indicates that there is indeed a need for structure and guidance about how to organize these fundamental agile practices and concepts—and that the SAMI addresses this need.

But the response to the question of the agile practices' relevance to the agile levels in which they're defined shows an agreement rate that drops below 50 percent, and the rate of disagreement rises to approximately 37 percent; the remaining respondents neither agree nor disagree. This result is anticipated because we know that each agile coach or consultant will prefer their own organization of the practices within the levels based on their personal preferences and professional experiences.

Figure 2 summarizes the feedback obtained from participants who have more than 6 years of experience in leading agile adoption efforts. The figure illustrates that 80 percent of these experts strongly agree with the comprehensiveness of the agile levels defined by SAMI; the remaining 20 percent neither agree nor disagree. There is 100 percent agreement with the practicality of the levels of agility,

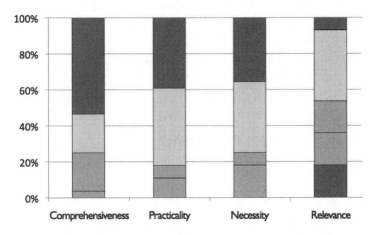

Figure E.1   Overall feedback about the SAMI

with 80 percent indicating strong support. Also, 80 percent agree with the necessity of the levels of agility; only 20 percent slightly disagree. Regarding the relevance of practices to levels, 60 percent agree that the practices are more or less in the right levels; 20 percent chose to remain neutral until they studied the five levels more thoroughly. The remaining 20 percent strongly disagree.

If you're looking for a more in-depth analysis of the SAMI and the results attained from this substantiation of the SAMI, we recommend that you read the Ph.D. dissertation in which the SAMI was presented. You can find the dissertation at http://scholar.lib.vt.edu/theses/available/etd-05252007-110748/.

In summary, the agile community recognizes the utility and need for the SAMI and that it provides a value-based roadmap to agility.

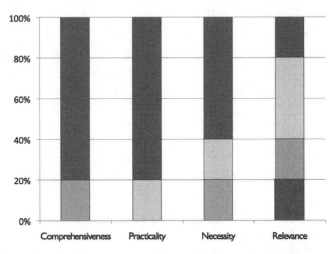

Figure E.2   Feedback about the SAMI from agile experts with more than six years of agile adoption experience

resources

All URLs listed here were valid at the time of publishing. A complete list of references is available from the publisher's website at www.manning.com/BecomingAgile.

Agile Alliance. http://www.agilealliance.org/.

Agile Manifesto. http://agilemanifesto.org/.

Anderson, Arthur, and Robert Hiebler. 1998. *Best Practices: Building Your Business with Customer Focused Solutions.* New York, NY: Simon & Schuster.

Christensen, Kurt. 2007. "Kent Beck on Agile Adoption & Values." Toronto: InfoQ.com. http://www.infoq.com/articles/kent-beck-interview-2006.

Cohn, Mike. 2004. *User Stories Applied: For Agile Software Development.* Boston: Addison-Wesley Professional.

————. 2005. *Agile Estimating and Planning.* Robert C. Martin Series. Upper Saddle River, NJ: Prentice Hall PTR.

Control Chaos. http://www.controlchaos.com/.

Deutschman, Alan. 2007. "Inside the Mind of Jeff Bezos." New York: Fast Company. http://www.fastcompany.com/magazine/85/bezos_2.html.

Doctor Agile. http://www.doctoragile.com/.

Ehlrich, Dianne. 2009. HRD 408: Glossary of Terms. Chicago: Northern Illinois University. http://www.neiu.edu/~dbehrlic/hrd408/glossary.htm.

Extreme Programming. A Gentle Introduction. http://www.extremeprogramming.org/.

Griffin, Em. 2009. *A First Look at Communication Theory.* Boston: McGraw-Hill Higher Education.

Highsmith, Jim. 1999. *Adaptive Software Development: A Collaborative Approach to Managing Complex Systems.* Boston: Addison-Wesley Professional.

————. 2004. *Agile Project Management: Creating Innovative Products.* Boston: Addison-Wesley Professional.

————. 2007. "No More Self-Organizing Teams." Arlington MA: Cutter Consortium. http://blog.cutter.com/2007/09/13/no-more-self-organizing-teams/.

Osherove, Roy. 2009. *The Art of Unit Testing.* Greenwich, CT: Manning Publications.

Poppendieck, Mary, and Tom Poppendieck. 2006. *Implementing Lean Software Development: From Concept to Cash.* Upper Saddle River, NJ: Addison-Wesley Professional.

Scanlan, Larry. 2005. *It's all in the planning.* San Francisco: BNET/CBS Interactive. http://findarticles.com/p/articles/mi_m3257/is_11_59/ai_n15863428.

Surowiecki, James. 2005. *The Wisdom of Crowds: Why the Many Are Smarter Than the Few and How Collective Wisdom Shapes Business, Economies, Societies, and Nations.* New York: Doubleday.

Twedt, Steve. 2007. "Quecreek Rescue Taught Some Valuable Lessons." Pittsburgh: *Pittsburgh Post-Gazette.* http://www.post-gazette.com/pg/07210/805297-357.stm.

United States Air Force. 2006. "Coming to Terms." National Security Personnel System. http://www.af.mil/library/nsps-af/nspscomingtoterms.asp.

index